WITHDRAWN

Theater and World

THEATER *AND* WORLD

The *Problematics of Shakespeare's History*

JONATHAN HART

Northeastern University Press
BOSTON

Northeastern University Press

Copyright 1992 by Jonathan Hart

Library of Congress Cataloging-in-Publication Data
Hart, Jonathan Locke, 1956–
Theater and world : the problematics of Shakespeare's history /
Jonathan Hart.
p.   cm.
Includes bibliographical references (p.   ) and index.
ISBN 1-55553-110-5 (alk. paper)
1. Shakespeare, William, 1564–1616—Histories.   2. Historical drama,
English—History and criticism.   3. Great Britain—History—1066–1687—
Historiography.   4. Literary form.   I. Title
PR2982.H37   1991
822.3′3—dc20   91-12903

Designed by Ann Twombly

Composed in Bembo by Coghill Composition, Richmond, Virginia. Printed and bound by Princeton University Press, Lawrenceville, New Jersey. The paper is Glatfelter Writer's Offset, an acid-free sheet.

MANUFACTURED IN THE UNITED STATES OF AMERICA
96   95   94   93   92   5   4   3   2   1

FOR HARRY LEVIN

Indolence, interruption, business, and pleasure, all take their turns of retardation; and every long work is lengthened by a thousand causes that can, and ten thousand that cannot, be recounted. Perhaps no extensive and multifarious performance was ever effected within the term originally fixed in the undertaker's mind. He that runs against Time, has an antagonist not subject to casualties.

Samuel Johnson, *Life of Pope*

Critics of Shakespeare are often supposed to be ridiculed by the assertion that if Shakespeare were to come back from the dead he would not be able to appreciate or even understand their criticism. This in itself is likely enough: we have little evidence of Shakespeare's interest in criticism, either of himself or anyone else. Even if there were such evidence, his own account of what he was trying to do in Hamlet would no more be a definitive criticism of that play, clearing all its puzzles up for good, than a performance of it under his direction would be a definitive performance.

Northrop Frye, *Anatomy of Criticism*

CONTENTS

ACKNOWLEDGMENTS

Writing often involves more debts than credit. Although, as the convention states repeatedly, the errors in the study are mine, the credit, however small it may be, that arises from the work should be given to many who helped me on the way. *Theater and World* began about 1980, but the preliminaries for a book often occur long before the specific research begins. To keep from reducing to absurdity the debt I owe, I shall avoid a search for origins and only mention those who have helped the study most directly. My parents, George and Jean Hart, have led me down the exciting but forked path of intellectual curiosity and have supported my efforts with great kindness and understanding. Mary Marshall has been unstinting in her support while working on many projects of her own. Julia and James, our twins, now hear me working at the computer on a study conceived long before they were and do not complain as much as they might. I have had too many good teachers to list here, but I thank them all for their vigorous discussions. The librarians at the University of Toronto, Harvard University, Dartmouth College, and the University of Alberta have been helpful and resourceful. My thanks to Lionel Gossman, who showed enough interest in the manuscript to get me moving again. At the University of Toronto, Brian Parker, Sheldon Zitner, and J. M. R. Margeson have all encouraged my work. Brian Parker showed good cheer and gave constructive criticism as he read early drafts of the study. Germaine Warkentin, the Director of the Centre for Reformation and Renaissance Studies at Victoria College when I was a Senior Fellow there, and the Fellows of the Centre provided a good place to work. I thank the Department of English and American Literature and Language at Harvard University for giving me the opportunity to be a visitor. Marjorie Garber kindly lent me her support before, during, and after my stay at Harvard and read parts of this research as well as some of my other projects. G. Blakemore Evans extended his hospitality to me, discussed textual matters when he was busy with many projects of his own, and read the manuscript (and other essays) with his characteristic thoroughness and good sense. Harry Levin's conversation is as learned and urbane as his criticism, and his hospitality, along with that of his wife, Elena, made my stay in Cambridge especially memorable. He has read my work with generosity, and I owe a particular debt to him. One of my friends at Harvard, Joanne Dempsey, with whom I had many discussions about Renaissance literature, recently died, so to thank her is also to remember someone who had done so much yet left us far too young. At the School of Criticism and Theory at Dartmouth College, I had the pleasure and privilege of taking seminars from Edward Said and Thomas Greene. My experience at the School, including those seminars, has helped me to think of new directions in which to work. At the University of Alberta, Linda Woodbridge had faith enough to want me as a colleague in her department. Robert Rawdon Wilson has been a wonderful example of how collegial and generous a colleague can be. The University of Alberta has given me research assistance and course relief and has provided me with a place where I can work happily and productively. My colleagues, especially in English and comparative literature, have contributed to that happy situation. Although I typed the manuscript myself, I want to thank Lynda Schultz, who put it on her hard drive, made corrections, and retyped the bibliography. The secretarial staff in the Department of English has typed and run off too much of my work to avoid a general thanks. Peter Meekison, the Vice President (Academic), and Patricia Clements, the Dean of Arts, have supported my scholarship in exemplary ways. I also thank the Social Sciences and Humanities Research Council of Canada for the fellowship it gave me for part of the time I worked on the early stages of this manuscript. The staff and editorial board of Northeastern University Press have been skillful, prompt, and humane. My particular thanks goes to Andrew Mandel and Deborah Kops, who thought the book worthwhile, and to Ann Twombly, who kept the production of the book going smoothly and who designed a beautiful book. And, finally, thanks to Simon Estok, Sharon Howe, and Benzi Zhang, who assisted me with the index, and to C. M. Hall and her staff at the British Library for tracking down the miniature on the dust jacket. Even still, much goes unacknowledged. With Chaucer, I realize that the craft takes so long to learn but send my little book into the world: even with its flaws, I hope this study is of some help.

I want to thank the editors of the following journals for giving me permission to reprint articles or brief sections of articles that have become a part of *Theater and World*. Chapter 2 contains a more recent version of "The Body Divided: Kingship in Shakespeare's Lancastrian Tetralogy," *CIEFL Bulletin* (New Series); Chapter 3 a revised version of "Temporality and Theatricality in Shakespeare's Lancastrian Tetralogy," *Studia Neophilologica;* Chapter 4 a later version of "*Henry V:* Towards the Problem Play," *Cahiers Elisabéthains*. Chapter 5 incorporates a brief section of "*Henry VIII*: The Play as History and Anti-History," *Aevum*. The Afterword includes short sections of "Alienation, Double Signs with a Difference: Conscious Knots in *Cymbeline* and *The Winter's Tale*," *CIEFL Bulletin* (New Series), "The New Historicism: Taking History into Account," *Ariel* (© 1991 the Board of Governors, the University of Calgary Press), and "Stephen Greenblatt's *Shakespearean Negotiations*," *Textual Practice*. (These articles all appear in the Selected Bibliography).

ONE

*Theater
and World*

HAKESPEARE HAS LONG PROVOKED CONTRO-versy. Since the seventeenth century, his works have been adapted, envied, and exalted, but critics seldom agree on important points of interpreta-tion. The history plays, especially the Second Te-tralogy (*Richard II*, *1 Henry IV*, *2 Henry IV*, and *Henry V*), have occasioned some of the most controversial debates in Shakespearean criticism. The rejection of Falstaff has caused the most notable and divided dispute. But other profound divisions have occurred in the theater and among critics: the poet-king versus the Machiavel, Richard versus Bolingbroke, and *Henry V* as heroic play or subversive war pamphlet. This book does not presume to solve these problems and dilemmas but only to make clearer their complex nature. The three central chapters will examine the problems that have been neglected (relatively speaking) or need new explanation—the fall into language, temporality: drama vs. history, and the relation of the history play and the problem play.

In chapter 2 I shall argue that the division among critics is like that among characters, for both use a language that cannot naïvely or directly correspond with the world they describe. This dilemma creates for the characters a fallen or secondary world in which they are blind to others and cannot readily institute a united and harmo-nious and lasting polity. Their conflicting actions are often founded in their use of images and words. For instance, the characters' use of the word "king" reveals that their notions of kingship are at odds, and they claim that God is on their side even when their goals oppose and conflict. Ultimately, consciously and unconsciously, the char-acters catch themselves in the ephemeral and temporal as they long for the eternal and pure. Language, especially, shows contradiction, limitation, and lack of communication in and among the characters in the fallen world of human history.

The third chapter pursues what the second raises: drama and its language make us particularly aware of the nature of time and the human predicament of infinite desire and finite performance. In the Second Tetralogy Shakespeare investigates the similarities and differ-ences between dramatic and historic time, looking, for example, at the relation of Falstaff and Hal. Shakespeare explores what drama and history can include and leave out, what is truth and what is

fiction. Telescoping, anachronism, invention, and self-conscious theatricality focus the contrast between drama and history. What happens when Shakespeare invents, or at least reinvents, Falstaff and
makes Hotspur younger? Many of these questions, like language
itself, hinge on temporality.

Chapter 4 analyzes the problems of representing history in plays.
How can a playwright shape and cut off time, write a history or
story about the past, when time or history continues? Shakespeare
shapes his plays using different genres, predominant though not
exclusive—tragedy in *Richard II*, comedy in *1 Henry IV*, satire in *2
Henry IV*, and the problem play in *Henry V*. The genres mix so
vigorously that by the end of *2 Henry IV* and the beginning of *Henry
V* there is so much generic friction that the Shakespearean history
play is questioning itself. Can the cockpit hold the vasty fields of
France? This self-reflexivity and self-critical language may contribute
to the problems that characters and critics have of deciding the
significance of history, the nature of kingship, and the relation of
public and private in these plays. The works question themselves and
lead to generic instability in the history play when it most needs
order. *Henry V* and the tetralogy it tries to end debate the possibility
of the history play and of history and lead toward the self-reflexive
debate of the problem plays.

One of the paradoxes of the Second Tetralogy is that through
dramatic irony and negative capability, or the ability to sympathize
with all sides until Shakespeare is apparently objective in representing
them, the playwright creates problems and dilemmas for the audience in theater or study, for it must contend with ambivalence or
even multivalence in its interpretations. The audience is invited to be
godlike, to be *katascopos* (an overviewer), but it is also being asked to
identify with the humanity of the characters. In the case of the
rejection of Falstaff, some critics choose the side of Henry the Fifth
or of Sir John, but it seems to me that the dilemma for many is that
Shakespeare presents us with the weaknesses and strengths of both
characters and allows us to see the complexity of the case. As the
characters and the audience are fallen into language—that is, as they
inhabit a world that does not correspond to word, where language
can be as much an impediment as a means to communication—only
a memory or a myth of a godlike or bird's-eye view coexists with

the realization of the fragility and fragmentation of human knowledge and judgment. The aspiration for peace, unity, and timelessness, the escape from temporality, is something that the characters and the audience cannot fulfill. Being as fallen as the characters, the audience is given an invitation to return to Eden, to judge from on high in a synchronic and simultaneous heaven, but in the course of attending a performance or reading the text the audience realizes that it also experiences diachronically and is more like the characters than at first appeared. Another dimension of temporality is the relation of history as narrative to history as drama. Shakespeare's characters consciously explore this relation or translation of time into another form. In seeking new shapes for the history play Shakespeare explores the problems of fashioning what is taken to be true into a fiction, of what is usually narrative into the dramatic, realizing as he goes along, it seems, that the boundaries between these opposites are open. Perhaps Shakespeare's most original contribution is his recasting and stretching of the history play. Even as we take sides in the Second Tetralogy, or even as we want to, Shakespeare's artistry shows us our problems and dilemmas. As we try to hover above the play and its characters, we are drawn to participate, and even as we take part, we seek higher ground. The movement of my book attempts to demonstrate this and other dilemmas.

We find ourselves caught between language and things, words and world, myth and truth, wanting to differentiate between them absolutely but realizing their interpenetration. In this sense we are fallen into language. The Fall remains a crucial myth in Western culture, the pattern of rise and fall occurring from Genesis through *A Mirror for Magistrates* to *After the Fall* and beyond. The argument of this book is that in the Second Tetralogy Shakespeare represents something akin to what in *The History of the World* Walter Ralegh calls the realm of secondary causes, a fallen world in which the search for meaning and the relation of cause and effect remain forever uncertain. Even though many characters seek divine authority for their ideas and actions, they cannot speak or act consistently, can only interpret something outside as if it were inside, in earth as in heaven, a kind of extended apostrophe or ventriloquy. But in the fallen world of human interpretation there is no proof of absolute authority, although it may exist and seems to be necessary as a justification of words and actions. In *Richard II*, *1* and *2 Henry IV*, and *Henry V*, Shakespeare explores the nature of language, showing through images and the characters' ambiguity, obfuscation, and misapprehension the lack of communication in this fallen world of history. These specific areas of language will occupy chapter 2, although other aspects of the fall of poetry and of nature deserve further exploration. The language reveals the limitations of the characters and complicates our notions of character and action and ensures that these plays do not make a caricature of history while using satire to qualify, not undercut, heroism. Shakespeare also gives to his characters self-conscious images of the Fall that call attention to this theological metaphor.

A large part of the Fall is the human predicament in time. In addition to the characters being caught in the temporal dilemma, Shakespeare and the audience have to cope with the tension between dramatic and historical time. Chapter 3 looks at some of the problems of writing history for the stage that Shakespeare, who has contributed to the history play more than any other playwright, confronts and creates for his characters, his audience, and himself. This problematic historical drama is enlivening and enabling as well as puzzling. Some of the problems that especially require attention are telescoping, anachronism, invention, fiction versus fact, and self-conscious theatricality. Our predicament in time will be at the center of our examination of Shakespeare's second group of history plays, as it is central to our experience of the theater and of reading, both of which contend and act intertextually in the drama. Some logicians balefully call a situation from which there is no escape a constructive dilemma. The person on the burning building either dies in the fire or jumps to his or her death. In colloquial speech this is called a no-win situation. By exploring the fall of language, the medium in which we try to communicate, and then the tension between drama and history in the temporality of the Shakespearean history play, we should become more aware of the complex ethical and aesthetic positions of the characters and, by analogy, of the playwright and us. The dilemmas of language and time have long perplexed us, and, rather than expect to solve them finally and irrefutably at once, we should try to understand the nature of the problems and to earn any suggestion for their resolution.

A specific application of these critical dilemmas is the way the individual plays and the tetralogy become increasingly like a problem play. The plays and the tetralogy show unity and disunity, assert and question their own structure. A generic tension also persists in the plays separately and as a unit. Each play questions itself, and this leads to generic instability in the history play where it most desires order. A problem play is one that interrogates its own genre. Although chapter 4 will examine all the plays, it will concentrate on *Henry V*, which demonstrates most intensely the attributes of the problem play, a name that critics have given to some of the plays Shakespeare wrote in the six or seven years after *Henry V*. This play and the tetralogy it ends debate the possibility of the history play and lead toward the self-reflexive discussion of the problem plays. Perhaps the problems ending history derive as much from the fall into language as from the difficulty of closing the flow of time in historical representation, especially in the brief compass of a play or even a series of plays.[1]

THE FALL OF LANGUAGE

The metaphor of the Fall calls attention to the temporality of language. As all texts are metonymic or synecdochic, they purport to represent the world fully. The world is the book, to use a medieval trope, and the Bible may be the Word, but the words of human interpretation contend with and contradict divine authority. From a Christian point of view, the one that predominated in the Renaissance, the Word is God but God's grace is necessary to fulfill the soul, to achieve atonement, to fill the gap—the fall into sin—between word and world. Fallenness extends the literal word of God to the metonymic and logical world of interpretation. As soon as the Word finds expression in human words, human interpretation has begun, and what is proclaimed as Truth is subject to fallible and fallen notions of truth. Like Shakespeare, Milton would have understood the importance of postlapsarian mythology to history. Not that the postlapsarian world of the Second Tetralogy is diminished by relating it to a common Renaissance context, for Shakespeare individualizes his representations of history, especially through generic experimentation.[2]

In many ways Ralegh's *History of the World* (1614) represents the epitome of a providential view of history among Renaissance historians, but his work is not as straightforward as it first appears, especially his view of fallen human nature. Apart from the direct participation of God in history, Ralegh's views, in the Preface, of the rise and fall of empires and the inevitable violence and miseries of kings resemble an important aspect of the Second Tetralogy. Ralegh asks: "For who hath not observed, what labour, practise, perill, bloudshed, and cruelty, the Kings and Princes of the world have undergone, exercised, taken on them, and committed; to make them-selves and their issues maisters if the world?"[3] Like Spenser in "The Mutability Cantos," Ralegh contrasts the eternity of God with the ruin of human time: we are born of the earth and inhabit it, while the heavens are "farr off, and unsearchable," so that we sense corporeal things directly but feel "eternall grace" only through revelation. "No mervaile then," Ralegh concludes, "that our thoughts are also earthlie." Making use of irony throughout the Preface, Ralegh comments on the vanity of the world, on how no man, high or low, is free from the vicissitudes of the earth (*History*, 45–53, 55). Ralegh's views of primary and secondary causes help illuminate Shakespeare's fall of language and representation of history in the Second Tetralogy. Whereas Ralegh thinks the sacred history recorded in the Bible to be a manifestation of primary causes, or direct participation of God in human events, he sees profane history in classical times, and in any period not described in the Bible, as a world of secondary causes. Ralegh divides *The History* into halves, the first showing God acting directly in biblical history and the second representing human actions apart from God. Because historians, and indeed all people, cannot see God's multiple shapes and ways in history, profane history is mostly a matter of conjecture, a flawed reconstruction in a ruined world using the faulty faculty of reason.[4] This world of secondary causes Shakespeare represents without direct commentary in the Second Tetralogy, so that, unlike *The History of the World*, these plays can only imply a providential frame, for God is not shown intervening directly in them. Sometimes in profane history, Ralegh must remind the reader of God behind the battles, something Shakespeare's characters may or may not do. Both writers show the influence of Augustine and Machiavelli and both represent complex views of history, but whereas Ralegh is torn between what should be and what is, Shakespeare focuses almost entirely on second nature. For Shakespeare as for Ralegh, historical truth is as flawed and inconstant as human reason itself, and as necessary. Shakespeare's irony is more dramatic than Ralegh's, so that although they both involve a split between the godlike knower and the human ignorant, they diverge over the amount of direct comment on the ironies of fallen nature, for, as we shall see, dramatic history has its own set of problems, and the ones that it shares with narrative history differ in degree.

Irony, which I shall use explicitly and implicitly in the discussion of the fall of language and in the chapters that follow from that treatment, also has much to do with the tension between overview and fallenness, between unity and division. If irony unites, it also divides, because dramatic irony consists of the audience sharing knowledge that a character lacks or of other characters knowing what the playwright and the audience do at the expense of the ignorant character. As the German romantics discovered, the artistic creator is able to sympathize with all his creations, so that he does not take sides and creates the illusion of objectivity or detachment.[5] This oxymoronic sympathetic detachment demonstrates the tension within irony between unity and division. Playwright and audience are caught between identifying with the human and the divine. According to William Empson, in life as well as in art the Elizabethans were able to sympathize with a criminal but could also detach him from his crime, so that the idea of sympathy to which Shakespeare was exposed and seems to have been inclined, nonetheless, is not merely one of pity but also one of understanding the wrong.[6] Like sympathy, irony, in my view, qualifies or modifies rather than simply undercuts. Each new contradiction about kingship contextualizes or qualifies the last, complicating the situation and views of the state but still challenging the audience to take sides between Richard and Bolingbroke, Hal and Falstaff, John of Lancaster and the Archbishop of York, Henry the Fifth and the French king or dauphin. Qualification, contradiction, and tension create dilemmas that may go to the very heart of the tetralogy and may culminate in the final play.

Irony itself is part of the philosophical dispute over subjectivity and objectivity. Does irony reside in the work or in the reader (or audience)? Which reader? At the extremes, an author can savor an irony without the reader's knowledge or a reader can discover an ironic attitude that the author may not have intended. For the most part, irony involves a relation between author and reader-viewer, although it would be optimistic to say the relation is always one of communication. By qualifying literal words or the surface of actions, irony complicates, thereby unsettling and exciting author and reader. While disciplining, irony undisciplines; it does and undoes. It multiplies but unifies, unifies but multiplies. Irony reinforces the godlike authority of the author by facilitating an overview, but it also qualifies that authority by destabilizing literal meaning and creating a tension between the author's intention and the reader's interpretation. Irony is paradoxical. And so our dilemma still goads us. Irony's self-conscious discovery of the rhetoric of temporality and the temporality of rhetoric—our fallenness in time and our wish to transcend it—does not allow for dissolution or totality, for it reveals sequence and consequence in their oppositions and interpenetration.[7] Irony represents the fallenness of language, theater, and structure, which is, roughly, the movement of this section of my study.

Before Shakespeare, the *de casibus* tragedies, chronicles, and poems like *A Mirror for Magistrates*, which often referred to providential history or to the wheel of fortune, all showed the appeal of the Fall as a narrative and representative shape in the popular mind, but Shakespeare not only looks at the Fall as a structural motif in his history plays but explores the fall into language by his use of verbal irony. This irony of words is a form of illusion or a disjunction between word and world, for it says something other or different from the literal meaning. It is true that literary language does this generally, but irony especially calls attention to the figurative nature of language. Litotes undervalues whereas hyperbole overvalues, neither hitting the mark. They are caught by the irony of their inaccuracy. The early uses of "eiron" or "eironeia" by such writers as Plato, Aristophanes, Theophrastus, Lucian, and Plutarch reveal a distrust of the deceit of the ironist and his irony, as if he were hiding his true intentions with acting and indirect words, as if the world has fallen out of honesty into sophistry. Beginning with Aristotle and culminating with the Schlegels, Tieck, Solger, Kierkegaard, and others, irony was raised up as something that could redeem art, and for many of the German romantics and their successors and critics Shakespeare was the ultimate redeemer, his sword of judgment being irony itself. Reader and audience find themselves today in a tradition that is split between suspecting and admiring irony, and they may realize that irony can divide or unify and lead them into fallenness or redeem their dissociated senses. In language we find our dilemma, wanting literal truth and correspondence on the one hand and literary fiction and divergence on the other. The moral and the aesthetic clash. In Renaissance England, Henry Peacham best summarized irony as "surprising incongruity," or antiphrasis. This rhetorical figure reprehends vice and folly by way of a "contrarie comparison," whereby an "offender" is forced to see the great difference between what he is and what he ought to be and what he has done and what he ought to do—a forerunner of Kierkegaard's view of irony as a disciplinarian.[8]

At the opening of *Richard II* we find the authority of Richard's language fallen, the breaking of sacred oaths, and the destabilization of the words "God" and "king." Later, we observe two kings, a Gardener who is a second Adam, and images of Cain and Abel and the violence and exile that their time brings. The audience balances Richard and Bolingbroke, fighting appearance and reality, to know who is falling and who is rising, to know who is right and who is wrong, taking a position and hovering above it. York supports Richard then Bolingbroke, and here the audience experiences a human decision as opposed to the divine "objectivity" that Shakespeare also encourages through his balanced and multiple irony.

In *1 Henry IV* Hal emphasizes his self-conscious tricking of the world in a soliloquy in which he unfolds his plan to the audience, giving it the benefit of dramatic irony, a greater knowledge than Falstaff, Hotspur, and Henry have, but also showing his deceit and dissembling, his use of language as a cloak. The rebel camp, court, tavern, and Wales all appeal to God. The contention over kingship and its divine sanction, as well as eschatological worries, especially those of Falstaff and Henry, reveal the disorganization of England and the further breakdown in the authority of language. The words of the dead king haunt the two parts of *Henry IV*, so that Richard, like God, becomes an authority to shore up the failure of language, the lack of correspondence between right and might, kingship and power.

In *2 Henry IV* the bonds of trust in oaths erodes further, characters hardly communicating with one another, while the worlds of the tavern, rebel camp, court, and Gloucestershire are isolated from one another. Deceit becomes a greater part of language. Falstaff deceives Shallow; John of Lancaster tricks the Archbishop of York by sticking to the letter of his own words; Hal rejects Falstaff. The rejection of Falstaff has created problems, for Hal had promised in act 1 of the first part his own conversion or later revelation of his true self from his role but had also seemed to enjoy the company of the fat knight. Falstaff himself is an ambivalent character who takes jibes at the prince and expects reward from their friendship but who appears to care for him. When Hal rejects Falstaff, his language echoes Christ, but the prince is also fallen, as well as aspiring to be God's representative on earth, so that he is ambivalent and creates a dilemma for the audience. It is as if Hal forgets the sin in himself and tries to assume the language of divine authority. The problem is that Hal must reject Falstaff to keep order and maintain the law, but in doing so he denies his private self and places himself above his former friends who are now subjects. A king is caught between being his highness and being a man: Richard, Henry the Fourth, and Henry the Fifth all explore this division and dilemma in their language.

Henry V represents the gap between theater and world, language and action, partly in the tension between the Chorus and the main action. It also shows us the questionable motives and rationalizations of Canterbury, Ely, and Henry in the invasion of France, something Henry the Fourth had recommended as a diversion from domestic problems and from the uncertain right of the House of Lancaster to the English crown. The young king's violent language—including threats of rape and murder—and his debate with common soldiers qualify but do not entirely undercut his claims to be a hero and a just king. Henry's courtship of Katharine represents another conquest and the humorous collision of the French and English languages. The translation and interpretation in the courtship scene demonstrate more gaps in language, different signs and views of the world. Nor do the problems end there. The Epilogue tells of the fall of the English forces in France and a return to civil war in England, thereby showing the momentary nature of the triumph of Henry the Fifth's kingship, which, the Epilogue reminds us, the Elizabethan audience had known because it had already seen the First Tetralogy. The Fall frames the Second Tetralogy.

TEMPORALITY: DRAMA VS. HISTORY

Dramatic time and historical time diverge at least as much as they converge. Shakespeare faced the problem of representing history on the stage, a task far less undertaken than the writing of historical narrative. He must have found a challenge in shaping the English history play, in condensing the flow of historical time into a play about the past with a beginning and end as well as a middle. Time and history are not identical. History is human action in time, its representation and interpretation. History is constantly in a state of crisis because no one can agree on the ultimate truth about this fallen world and because, in an etymological sense, crisis means "decision" or "cutting up," taking the Heraclitean river of time and cutting it up into sections to interpret, to translate or explain. The trouble is that the river shifts its course as rivers do over time: the landscape and banks change with the years and ages, and the difficulty is then to decide what is land and what is water. One of the large questions for history (historical writing) is where to begin and where to end, even if history (human time and events) does not always seem to have beginnings and endings. Historical writing is much like the Aristotelian plot, or *mythos*. The history play, as Coleridge noted, is complicated, and Dr. Johnson had mixed feelings about this mixed genre. Johnson noted one crucial difference between the history play and tragedy: the first ends more indeterminately than the second.[9] Censorship and other external pressures bore upon the development of the history play in Renaissance England. Skelton, Bale, Kirchmayer, Norton, Sackville, and others had all, more or less, written history plays, but they were not professional dramatists who had to endure antitheatrical prejudice; more particularly, Norton and Sack-ville, because they were of a higher social class, may have been more immune to royal displeasure than the playwrights of the public theater.

Whereas the Platonic Socrates had attacked the theater, Aristotle assumed its existence and importance in the state: both thought of tragedy and comedy as part of the domain of poetry, a view that Elizabethan critics often echoed. The controversial relation between theater and world had a long history before *The Book Named the Govenor* (1531), in which Thomas Elyot defends poetry against attack and defends drama on the moral ground that it leads people from vice toward virtue.[10] It is appropriate in Elizabethan England that the debates on history and theater should be related, for both flourished in the period. A former actor, Stephen Gosson, asserted in *Schoole of Abuse* (1579) that poetry and drama should be in the service of truth and virtue, thereby echoing Plato.[11] This attack on fable and poetry implied that factual and ethical writing was superior to them. Although, for Elizabethans, history was partly literary, it also claimed truth and accuracy, buttressed by Cicero's high praise for historical narrative.[12]

Although Gosson dedicated his work to Philip Sidney, Sidney apparently wrote *An Apology for Poetry* (ca. 1580, pub. 1595) in reply. Sidney prefers to argue the differences between poets and historians, mainly on the grounds by which Aristotle distinguished them in his *Poetics*.[13] Perhaps having predeceased the golden age of English drama, including the development of the English history play, Sidney could not envision a meeting of history and dramatic poetry as readily as could Aristotle, who lived at a time when great tragedies about history were being staged. Like Aristotle, Sidney values the truth of poetic fiction above the truth of historical fact. He follows Aristotle in showing the inferiority of the historian to the poet, whom historians emulated when they invented long orations for their kings and captains. Great poetry, according to Sidney, tries to mend fallen nature by creating heroes, demigods, cyclopes, furies, and other beasts not found in the fallen world, so that a great poet creates a golden world. The broken world of the Second Tetralogy would not seem to meet this criterion. For Sidney, historical or philosophical poetry (and he inverts Aristotle's ranking of philosophy above poetry) lacks invention and does not lift up the soul (*Apology*, 5–12, 40). At some point, Sidney says, the historian must go beyond the solidity of example or fact to interpretation. He will find events that will "yield no cause" and then he must imitate the poet, to whom he is, therefore, subject. The poet can "beautify" with imitation the historian's causes and descriptions and can teach and delight more than the historian. According to Sidney, the poet can teach more about virtue and vice than the historian because he can use *poetic justice*, a term that was not used to describe the phenomenon until the Restoration, whereas the historian cannot because life does not necessarily punish the wicked and reward the good (*Apology*, 13–21). By Sidney's measure, Shakespeare from *Richard II* to *Henry V* would be a poet when he invents speeches that never occurred for his characters, provided that these speeches were appropriate to the given situation that the poet explores, but would also be a historian in his failure to enact poetic justice and create a golden world that repairs rather than imitates the ruins of a fallen world. Whereas, for Sidney, the poet "nothing affirmeth, and therefore never lieth," the historian "affirming many things, can, in the cloudy knowledge of mankind, hardly escape from many lies."[14] Sidney, who has mocked Cicero's notion of the historian as the light of truth and the life of memory, repeats the idea that a poet tells us what should and what should not be rather than what is and what is not. He also criticizes the stage and the ruinous state of poetry in England, yielding a little to critics like Gosson. Perhaps Sidney's warning against "mingling kings and clowns" solely for the sake of entertainment and "not because the matter so carrieth it" is an imputation that Sidney would have reconsidered had he lived to see how successfully the Second Tetralogy mixed the serious and the comic in entertaining and instructive ways.[15]

The status of English drama was in doubt in the Renaissance. This doubt occurs in Sidney's *Apology*. Sidney seems to prefer epic to drama, though he defends Euripides' power to save lives, and classical drama to English drama, though he likens *Gorboduc* to Seneca while criticizing it for lacking the unities of time and place. Under the influence of Whetstone, Sidney says that other English plays are worse because they have absurd plots whose writers fail to realize that tragedy is governed by the laws of poetry and not of history.

Like epic poetry, a tragedy "has liberty either to feign a quite new matter, or to frame the history to the most tragical conveniency," and Sidney says that much that cannot be shown can be told. To begin a story, he asserts, the playwrights must start, as Euripides does, in medias res and not ab ovo. Sidney theorizes at length about the contrary and complementary relation of laughter and delight to pain and scorn (*Apology*, 40–44). He catches himself in a topos that has expressed what it should not have but does because its author so wished, for Sidney has not shied away from the stage:

> But I have lavished out too many words of this play-matter. I do it, because, as they [plays] are excelling parts of poesy, so is there none so much used as in England, and none can be more pitifully abused; which, like an unmannerly daughter, showing a bad education, causeth her mother Poesy's honesty to be called in question. (*Apology*, 44)

In Sidney's interpretation, by applying to poetry a commonplace of male poets gendering their muse that reflects a stereotypical labeling of women in the culture, he leaves poetry to the "unmannerly" interpretation of "honesty" in the sense used in relation to the Hostess and Doll Tearsheet. Even in the defense, this apology for drama in England admits much that occurs in the attacks on the theaters. The positions for and against the theater in Elizabethan England often interpenetrated, for whereas Sidney defended the theater while criticizing it, Gosson admitted good uses for it while vilifying it. Representing history on stage was controversial in that it was caught in the ancient battle between poetry and philosophy, in the rift between poetry and history, and in the class and religious strife in England during the Renaissance.

George Puttenham and Spenser also discussed the relation between history and poetry in a way that has implications for the Shakespearean history play. *The Arte of English Poesie* (1589) gives poets priority over historians but still praises history for making memory more active and states that "poesie historical" is most worthy, thereby enhancing history the more and breaking down the division between the two. Like Sidney, Puttenham asserts that the poet historical has more freedom than the historian in representing history, for he does not have to stick to fact. Like the historian, he teaches through example.[16] Puttenham discusses a wide array of subjects relating to drama—various genres, classical drama, and English drama. He criticizes native drama, especially its rhymes, but also considers its music, costume, and character types. He refers to individual plays, but does not allude to Marlowe and seems more familiar with the works of contemporary poets like Ralegh, Sidney, and Spenser.[17] Spenser's letter to Ralegh (1589) makes it clear that Spenser is following the epic poets, whom he calls the "Poets historicall," and does not find the phrase "historicall fiction" contradictory because history can be rearranged as a story by the poet though not by the historian. Whereas, according to Spenser, the historiographer represents affairs as they were done, attending to "the times as the actions," a poet "thrusteth in the middest," where he has recourse to past and future events and makes "a pleasing Analysis of all." And Spenser adds: "The beginning therefore of my history, if it were told by an Historiographer, should be the twelfth booke, which is the last."[18] Like Sidney and Puttenham, Spenser thinks that the historical poet, or epic poet, differs from the historian in method, especially in the freedom that he may take with chronology and with which he may enter into his narrative in medias res. Shakespeare begins *Richard II* in the midst of things, causing his characters to refer ambiguously to the past, presenting Richard's reign in crisis. For Spenser, a historian would not dare select so radically.

By 1612, Thomas Heywood's *Apology for Actors* still defended the virtue of the stage and its actors, but, by 1642, not all the arguments of Sidney, Puttenham, Heywood, and others could prevent the closing down of the professional public theater. Heywood reiterates the central defense of drama: it teaches moral values through example. To this he adds that all things have their abuses, that London has a greater variety of entertainment than any other city in Christendom, and that plays improve the English tongue through the competing art of writers and can stir the conscience to confess crimes. These are the main reasons for representing human temporality in dramatic time. Heywood, in his *King Edward IV, Parts One and Two* (1600), presents, in theory at least, an example of the history play that is compatible with the Elizabethan world picture and would not raise the wrath of the Lord Chamberlain. In the *Apology*, he says:

Plays have made the ignorant more apprehensive, taught the unlearned the knowledge of many famous histories, instructed such as cannot read in the discovery of all our English chronicles, and what man have you now of that weak capacity that cannot discourse of any notable thing recorded even from William the Conqueror, nay from the landing of Brute, until this day? being possessed of their true use; for or because plays are written with this aim and carried with this method: to teach subjects obedience to their king, to show the people the untimely ends of such as have moved tumults, commotions, and insurrections; to present them with the flourishing estate of such as live in obedience, exhorting them from allegiance, dehorting them from all traitorous and felonious stratagems.[19]

James the First could not have done better in promoting order and obedience to the king, and he sought to bring the professional companies under royal patronage. Heywood's description, unlike Shakespeare's execution in the Second Tetralogy, is the history play with poetic justice, with the delight and freedom that Sidney would have liked. This kind of history play supplements rather than reflects nature, filling in the gap between humanity and its fall into sin, death, and moral complexity. Although some of Shakespeare's characters speak as Heywood does, and although Shakespeare, the person, may or may not have shared some of these views, the Second Tetralogy is more varied and difficult than Heywood's idea of historical drama. Nonetheless, Heywood reminds us of one aspect of English history plays, including Shakespeare's contributions to the genre: that they served as public education, to spread the nation's history, as well as public entertainment. For the most part, Shakespeare's histories seemed to have pleased all levels of society, and even though they may have drum and trumpets in them, they are too complex to stop there. The Second Tetralogy explores the untidy relation between history and drama in the history play, a genre that by necessity yokes them.

In *The History of the World* (1614) Ralegh's theatrical language and history share much with Shakespeare's representation from *Richard II* to *Henry V*. Although many of Ralegh's views and practices relate to Shakespeare's idea of history, we shall concentrate on his metaphor of world as stage. Ralegh observes part of the irony that we

find in the Second Tetralogy: "Wee are all (in effect) become Comae-
dians in religion: and while we act in gesture and voice, divine
vertues, in all the course of our lives wee renounce our Persons, and
the parts wee play" (*History*, 46). People, according to Ralegh, put
on appearances, which God pierces through with his truth and that
history tries to uncover. Apparently, Ralegh not only opposes
theater and world as well as earth and heaven but also represents
acting as a perversion of sincerity and criticizes the difference between person and role. Unlike Shakespeare's second group of history
plays, Ralegh's "drama" directly involves Providence: "For seeing
God, who is the author of all our tragedies, hath written out for us,
and appointed us all parts we are to play: and hath not, in their
distribution, beene partiall to the most mighty Princes of the world,"
why should common men complain of wrongs? (*History*, 56). Here,
Ralegh calls into doubt his own division between person and roles
(on the grounds that we abuse our religion by becoming actors who
try to fool others) because he says that God, the author, determines
and assigns our parts in our tragedies. Ralegh does not seem to
adhere to the Tudor notion of the divine right of kings. A fool to the
sorrow of fate and fortune, each man, beneath his clothing, opulent
or simple, wears "but his own skin" and must face death in this
theater of the world. Shakespeare, too, takes a positive and a negative
view of the relation between theater and world. In addition to
speaking about the world as a play on the *de casibus* pattern, Ralegh
expresses a view like William Baldwin's address in *A Mirror for
Magistrates* (1559 ed.)—that in Ralegh's history men will see virtue
and vice according to the capacity of their own souls.[20] Shakespeare's
method is more representational than Baldwin's or Ralegh's, and
poetic justice does not qualify his dramatic irony.

An important aspect of Shakespeare's historical representation is
irony of theater. In the Renaissance, writers never tired of likening
theater and world. This trope extended to the writing of history, so
that the ironic relation of acting and action is vital to our discussion
of problems and dilemmas in the Second Tetralogy. The development of the irony of theater is almost indistinguishable from the
growth of the irony of words. The irony of theater is the ironic
relation between theater and world. Self-conscious role playing,
dramatic irony, use of theatrical terms, references to the theater and

acting, disguise and deception, all contribute to this irony. The dramatic poet must be godlike in his creation and regulation of his characters but must also have human sympathy for them, so that the playwright himself is caught in a dilemma from the start. The audience also experiences this division.[21] Without sympathy or detachment, the audience cannot understand the characters and their actions in historical drama, but it is the nature of temporal sequence to require choice and hierarchy as opposed to a simultaneous suspension or balance of involvement and indifference. Playwright, characters, and audience may want to escape time, but, ironically, when they think they have most transcended time, they are trapped in it. Shakespeare calls attention to the characters' temporal dilemma, which is at the core of history and of which they may or may not be conscious.

Rather than restate commonplaces about Shakespeare's ability to condense historical time into a concentrated dramatic action—for example, by representing years in the reigns of Richard the Second, Henry the Fourth, and Henry the Fifth (thereby fracturing the so-called classical unity of time that restricts the action to a single revolution of the sun); by making Hotspur Hal's contemporary; by half-inventing Falstaff to complicate actual time with ritual, fictional, or mythical time; by ending the story of Henry the Fifth before it was done—I should like to focus on characteristics of temporality that have not been widely examined and that pertain more closely to my argument. The relation between the Fall, the temporality into which we are fallen, and the human problems of genre and representation that have artistic implications especially for Shakespeare's representation of history should be uppermost in our minds throughout the book. The opposition and collision of drama and history in time manifests itself most when Shakespeare calls attention through language to time or to the theater and how it copes with representing history, with the passage of time in the world. The two sections of chapter 3 will concern the characters' use of terms referring to time and their self-conscious theatricality and other theatrical ways they call attention to the relation of drama to history. Instead of drawing examples from throughout the plays, I shall concentrate on certain important scenes for this discussion. In *Rich-*

ard II the opening scene, the Aumerle conspiracy, and Richard's end in Pomfret Castle require the most attention, as they emphasize the fall of time, the self-reflexive nature of the play, and the groping to come to terms with time. The opening scene of *1 Henry IV*, Hal's "I know you all" speech, Falstaff's sense of time (I.ii; II.iv; III.iii; V.iii, iv), and the tavern playlet (though in less detail, for this scene has been much debated) will provide further instances of the relation of historical to dramatic time, the theater trying to remake time. By beginning *2 Henry IV* with Rumor, Shakespeare throws into doubt the nature of communication, of human words and action in time. The art of acting in Part Two is still alive in the tavern (II.iv). Another important illustration of the challenge of time is the difference in interpretation of time between Henry and Warwick (III.i). Shallow's misrepresentation of the past sets up a conflict with Falstaff, who does not realize that he misreads Hal in the same way that Shallow misinterprets him (III.ii, esp. 295f.). Pistol's allusions to the theater and to his role as a messenger of new times help us explore the temporal nature both in this play and in *Henry V*. Ultimately, the rejection of Falstaff (V.v) fulfills Hal's promise to control time in his "I know you all" speech. This rejection is crucial in challenging the Shakespearean history play to continue because it complicates the reaction of the audience and creates tension between the private and the public side of history, straining generically the relation of the tragic to the comic aspects of historical drama and threatening to push it toward satire or what we have come to call a problem play. The Epilogue of Part Two displays this disjunction, as well as textual corruption. Although in passing we shall look at other aspects of temporality in *Henry V*, we shall concentrate on the Chorus, Henry's idea of time (particularly his Saint Crispian's speech), and the Epilogue, which crams a vast time into the constraints of a sonnet. Of all these examples in the four plays, the Chorus in *Henry V* will be discussed most extensively, for it most characterizes the temporal crisis in the relation between drama and history, which pushes the history play toward the problem play, the subject of chapter 4.

TOWARD THE PROBLEM PLAY

History plays concentrate more on the relation between private and public time than any other dramatic genre. The metaphor of theater and world reveals ironic complexity and the seeping of opposites, so that the audience finds itself in a situation that is both/and as well as either/or because the theater is part of the world and represents or supplements it and because the world contains the theater and borrows expressions like "upstaging" and "histrionic." Many of the theatrical terms that the world adopts belie an uneasiness and even a hostility toward the theater, as if it is of the world but, at least for some of our ancestors, should not be. A similar open boundary exists between history and fiction, which we observe perhaps most clearly in legal fictions and historical fiction. [22]

One of my principal arguments is the importance of shape to the Shakespearean history play, both individually and in interrelation. Genre is important and need not be a deadening formalism. The narrative and representational choice should be appropriate to the subject or period depicted. A generous and changing decorum should guide author and reader alike. It would be naïve, however, to think that we, who are time's subjects, will select a form for the representation of the world that is atemporal and objective, however much we might attempt to make it so. Genre depends on an author selecting from past genres and changing the genre by his or her contribution and on the reader or audience deciding over time (and perhaps changing their minds) to what genre the work is most affiliated. [23] Even though the Elizabethan playwrights, except perhaps Jonson, were a little lackadaisical about using the words "comedy," "tragedy," and "history," and might have laughed at Polonius, they also experimented and radically reshaped the genres in which they worked. Shakespeare was particularly radical in this regard, so much so that he contributed most to making the history play a popular form in England and to such a degree that modern critics have called some of his works problem comedies or problem plays.

Shakespeare did not avoid representing the world in the theater but faced his national history squarely in the 1590s. He experimented, bringing different genres into collision with the history play, and thereby shaped and destabilized individual plays and groups of plays. Even though the public theater and the history plays were only beginning to gain social and literary status, Shakespeare earned his living by them and seems to have taken them at least as seriously as his efforts in the more aristocratic forms of epyllion and love poetry. Perhaps the newness and the relative lack of fixed rules and expectations provided as much freedom as anxiety. The idea that the Second Tetralogy is an ironic form can perhaps throw light on the vexed question of what in the Shakespearean canon constitutes a history play. Irony, as I have been using the term, qualifies and does not simply undercut, represents sympathy and detachment, and creates situations for an audience that is godlike in its knowledge but also, being human, wants to judge or take sides or recognize its own limitations in those of the characters. The history play is an unstable genre, tending toward and including other genres. Each play contains various generic traces, but *Richard II* is a tragic history with incipient comedy, *1 Henry IV* a comic history with elements of satire, *2 Henry IV* a satiric history with a crisis that compounds existing problems, and *Henry V* history as a problem play in which generic friction probably reaches its greatest heat between the comic wooing of Henry and Katharine and the tragic implications of the Epilogue, although the satiric remarks of Bates and Williams to the heroic king are also crucial. Such imprecision and instability may be seen in the controversy over the term "history play" as it relates to Shakespeare, which begins in the difference between the designation of genre in the quartos and the First Folio and continues to the present. Irony, I shall argue, is the primary tool that Shakespeare uses in stretching the bounds of the history play, but first we should look at what people thought a history play was in Elizabethan England.

The problem of the relation between tragedy and history was observed at least as long ago as Aristotle and comprises part of the debate between history and poetry.[24] Puttenham praises both history and poetry but discusses drama more extensively than Sidney, but whereas he discusses a variety of plays—comedies, interludes, satyr plays, and tragedies—he does not examine history plays.[25] In 1598 Francis Meres listed both *Richard II* and the *Henry IV* plays as tragedies. The term "history," not having a classical antecedent, may have seemed less serious and has been controversial since the Renaissance. The printers of the quartos called *Richard II* a tragedy, but the editors of the First Folio placed *The life and death of King Richard the Second* among the history plays.[26] In 1612, like Polonius (II.ii.395f.), Heywood could proclaim without prejudice against any genre: "Briefly there is neither tragedy, history, comedy, moral or pastoral from which an infinite use cannot be gathered."[27] The case of *Troilus and Cressida* is instructive. As Anne Barton points out, the seventeenth-century "editors" of the play are of little help in determining its genre. Both the first and corrected title page of the quarto of 1609 call *Troilus and Cressida* a history, whereas the preface to the quarto claims that it is comic and the First Folio (1623) designed a place for it amid the tragedies but transferred it to a position between the histories and the tragedies in what appears to have been an emergency at the time of publication. The audience, Heywood implies, can learn by moral example from the new genre of the history play. Behind this controversy of genre lies the Elizabethan meaning of the word "history," which then meant a story told in the past tense (built on what Aristotle called *mythos,* or plot), and not necessarily history as we think of it. The printers of the quartos provided the following titles—*The Tragedie of King Richard the second, The History of Henrie the Fourth* (the title of Part Two sounds more like an advertisement of the life and death of characters, with appearances by favorite humor figures like Falstaff and Pistol, as does the Folio title of Part One), and *The Cronicle History of Henry the fift*—and called a play we consider a tragedy *M. William Shakspeare: His True Chronicle Historie of the life and death of King Lear and his three Daughters.* In these instances I give the short titles. Unlike the printers of the quartos, the editors of the First Folio collected as histories only stories about the English (not Scottish or British) past. As early as 1765, Thomas Percy asserts that the mystery plays gave rise to the history plays—which "though now confounded with Tragedy or Comedy, were by our first dramatic writers considered as quite distinct from them both"—and suggests that histories should be judged only according to the principles under or by which they were composed.[28]

Controversy over the definition of the history play has not died. I am able to offer only a few suggestions, not a strict definition. Owing to the magnitude of the problem, it is best to examine the history play as it is represented in the Second Tetralogy, as opposed to analyzing plays as diverse in time and temperament, scope and emphasis as *Gorboduc* and *Perkin Warbeck*. In this second group of histories Shakespeare makes the genre diverse, unstable, accommodating, and ironic. The tetralogy contains a mixture of genres: each play is predominantly one genre while moving toward the genre of the next play. Just as the ironies of words, theater, and structure—the constituents of the larger irony of which I speak—represent a complex world full of limited points of view, the structure of the whole tetralogy causes the audience to look at history from many points of view and to understand the dilemma they experience between synchronic and diachronic positions. The characters and their relations are often complicated, so that the plays do not simply set up straw heroes and villains to enable Shakespeare to trumpet a naïve patriotism, a simple Providence, or a set of detachable moral *exempla* for statesmen to use in the present. That does not mean that some members of the audience will not bristle at Exton, laugh at the relation between Hotspur and Glendower, find Shallow amusing, think John of Lancaster's motives for tricking the Archbishop of York odious, and consider the Dauphin a fool, but Shakespeare uses language and structure to complicate character, and, by avoiding the sharp contrast of good and evil, he keeps his plays from becoming melodramas. Even though the Second Tetralogy "houses" tragedy, comedy, satire, and problem play, it differs from these genres in their "pure" forms in that the history continues from one play to another. Shakespearean tragedy only suggests a future taken up by the second rank of characters; Shakespearean comedy points to a new world beyond comic dance or marriage; Shakespearean satire stops when the lovers marry, or Troy or the rebels have fallen; and the problem play leaves some unsatisfactory resolution to nag the mind of the audience but is a more self-contained play, with little dramatic past or future. Those genres effect closure more than the histories, so that in the second group of histories, which combines history with other kinds, there is a tension or disjunction between the drive for completion and the drive for continuation. The history play demands succession, a sequel. The historical dramatist must almost arbitrarily cut the ribbon of time to end his historical pattern. Tragedy and comedy do not. The end of a Shakespearean tragedy tends to center on the tragic figure or figures more than does a Shakespearean history play, which broadens its focus to include the public realm. Shakespearean comedy moves toward the communal but not necessarily toward the public. Shakespeare's history play is versatile, for it contains both satire's sense of the individual's isolation in the crowd and the use of parody, as well as the instability and uneasy questioning of the problem play.

Irony of structure is closely related to the ironic shape of the tetralogy, the tendency toward unity through sharing genres and toward diversity through a movement in the direction of a new genre and the questioning of the very genre of the history play. Role playing and the irony of words work together with the irony of structure, which is the ironic comparison, contrast, or juxtaposition of different parts of a play and can include an ironic reversal (or peripeteia)—a movement in the action that is opposite to or different from the expected outcome of a play. Irony can unify the various plot lines of a play and by doing so can make the representation of history more multiple than a single plot can. The ironic arrangement of scenes and of incidents can also make a seemingly univocal play polyphonic. The classical notion of the *katascopos*, or overviewer, a commonplace of the Renaissance, also applies to irony of structure. The godlike audience may itself be a victim if the artist acts as *eiron*, a descendent of Socrates, by trying to trap the audience in its own ignorance. Whereas some would say that irony either unites *or* divides writer and reader, I would say that it does both, often at once.[29] The irony of structure also involves an interplay of the general and particular aspects of form, most notably the arrangement of scenes and the overall shape of the play. Thus, structural irony helps create dilemmas for the audience, challenges it to examine its own knowledge and ignorance, and helps it explore the nature of the history play and tetralogy as well as of history itself.

The problem play questions genre: in this case *Henry V* presses at the bounds of the history play and examines the possibility of the persistence, if not the existence, of the history play. Although *Henry V* is the problem history in the Second Tetralogy that will be the principal subject for discussion in chapter 4, there are problem elements or generic frictions in the earlier plays. In *Richard II* the existence of two kings destabilizes the authority of kingship, the garden scene steers the play from mimesis to allegory, and the Aumerle conspiracy qualifies the tragedy with comedy. The satiric qualification of comedy in *1 Henry IV* occurs in the use of parody by Hotspur, Hal, and Falstaff and in the broader critical spirit of other characters—such as the rebels' critique of Henry and the king's criticism of his son. The existence of Mortimer, the memory of Richard, and the counterfeits of Henry on the battlefield also keep open the debate on the right to the crown. Part Two of *Henry IV* emphasizes the critical and parodic spirit of satire. Rumor calls the possibility of truth—an objective of history—into doubt. Falstaff and Hal are, among other things, satirists, and Pistol is a butt of satire. The characters in Part Two are increasingly isolated and lack communication: the prince and Sir John meet less often. The ultimate breakdown in communication in this play is the rejection of Falstaff. Just as John of Lancaster's lie to the Archbishop and as Henry the Fourth's counsel to his son to invade France in order to divert attention from his questionable right to the crown throw kingship into a crisis, so the rejection of Falstaff makes the audience query the private side of Henry the Fifth just when the play asserts its order most with the victory over the rebels and the ascension of the new king. In *Henry V* the Chorus's self-conscious remarks on the relation of drama and history, Henry's violent threats, the debate of Bates and Williams with Henry, and the friction between the comic wooing of Henry and Katharine and the tragic reports of the Epilogue all help create problems in the history play and have it question itself. To avoid repetition, the fourth chapter will concentrate on the aspects of the problem play that were not discussed in chapters 2 and 3 and will only note these problem elements to demonstrate the close relation among the three parts of my argument.

The fall into language creates problems for characters in the Second Tetralogy and for their claims to the authority of words in representing the world, kingship, and God as they flounder in contradiction and self-trapping images. This metaphoric fall questions the effectiveness of metaphor and language in general in presenting truth. By observing the characters in these plays, the audience learns more about its dilemma between godlike knowledge and human ignorance. A principal way of understanding this dilemma is dramatic irony. The overarching irony I have discussed and its three constituents are related to dramatic irony and help make our notions of history and drama, truth and fiction more complex. Irony makes us more conscious of our situation in temporality, our yearning for overview and synchrony, even as we realize that we are subject to participation and diachrony. The Shakespearean history play, especially in the Second Tetralogy, provides us with an occasion to comprehend better the complexity of our fallenness into history. With irony, Shakespeare complicates the history play and so the relation between history and drama. Of all human studies, history is the only one that devotes itself exclusively to human time. The history play is, therefore, a good place to study temporality in art and drama. In examining the relation of drama and history in these plays, Shakespeare and his audience are able to discover the subtleties of the problems of language and time in life and art until they may even question the use or existence of history and the history play. Shakespeare was not the first to help raise these questions about history, but the power of his art widens the discussion of the nature of history and furthers debate over the nature of art and, perhaps uniquely, the constitution, aesthetics, and utility of the history play. Nor is it by chance that Shakespeare promotes the debate over politics and authority, which affects us today whether we experience democracy or tyranny. The world is not the book, and the stage is not all the world, but still the relation is as pressing as it is intricate. It is to these matters of fallen language, the temporality of drama and history, and the relation of the problem play and the history play, as well as the implications these subjects have for theater and world, that we shall now turn.

TWO

*The Fall of
Language*

HE METAPHOR OF THE FALL, THE DISOBEDI-
ence against the Word in words, to use a Christian
view, conveys humanity caught in the temporality
of its own language. In the Second Tetralogy the
characters speak a fallen language and have difficulty communicating: they are fallen in the gap
between word and world, language and nature. As soon as the Word
finds expression in human words, human interpretation has begun,
and what is proclaimed as Truth is subject to fallible and fallen
notions of truth. Throughout these four plays, many opposing
characters claim that God is on their side. In this view, language is
both revered as descending from God and reviled because it is bound
by human desire and reason. We are fallen into our rhetoric, but
history goads us to discover a relation between language and the
world. Texts are metonymic and can only be symbolic representations of the world or a response to it. In a kind of dramatic irony the
audience is limited like the characters and, to some extent, the
playwright. The limited point of view of reading and of the interpretation of live theater puts us in a similar dilemma, but at one remove.
If the early meanings of "interpretation" have to do with explanation
and translation, in a sense all writing, reading, and observation
involve translation, a reconstitution of perception. Like the author
and characters, we attempt to interpret the world through a fallen
language that cannot be identical to the world. Language tries to fill
the gap between what ought to be and what is, but, because we lack
direct and universally accepted evidence about our origin, meaning,
and end, our words inhabit a Babel. The characters in these four
history plays may share many assumptions, but they disagree on
such important matters as authority and rebellion. Disagreements
over the origins, meaning, and end of kingship pervade the Second
Tetralogy.

Paradoxically, we need reason to define the potential and limitations of reason. To qualify patterns of images, we must agree on the
existence of patterns. To speak about the hell of incommunication,
we must have some idea of communication. Here, once more, we
experience dilemmas and problems. It is as if pragmatism and
rhetorical persuasion provide the measures of the effectiveness of
language in the interpretation that the characters perform in deci-

phering the complexities of war, peace, and kingship. It is as if we, if our fall is in part fortunate, must observe the unreason in reason and the reason in unreason to grasp language and history as a whole, momentarily, before it dissolves and we qualify our search further. Reason is the ability to think, to observe and to challenge patterns, to view problems, texts, and nature logically, to discern meaning and to justify it with evidence to other inquiring minds. Reason permits us to communicate and to examine the nature and difficulty of communication. The trouble with metaphor, as well as its power, is that it is unlogical, alogical, or even antilogical, for it identifies through words two objects that are not identical, and so is like writing itself because texts represent the part as the whole and often try to identify word and world. The etymology of the term "logic" proclaims our dilemma: reason was first expressed in the *logos*. Traditionally, criticism has attempted to argue logically about metaphor, which challenges or defies logic. Language expresses and creates problems for reason. Shakespeare's characters discover the trouble of making sense of the historical world that they inhabit. Often these characters take their circumscribed points of view and attempt to apply them to the world around them and to its inhabitants as if one vantage could be generalized into the laws of nature and politics. The exploration of language provides ways of speaking about character and action in the world that seeks to prove the partisanship and limitation of kings and rebels in the incidents in which they participate. Like others before them, the Elizabethans found the metaphor of fallenness important for making sense of their world and their art, and, even if individuals differed in their beliefs and there was not a monolithic Elizabethan worldview, Shakespeare and his contemporaries probably felt the theological immediacy of the trope. Even if some of them privately doubted or rejected the fallenness of humanity, publicly they explored the metaphor in relation to the soul struggle of the individual and the tension between order and chaos in the state. Why does the Fall matter to us, to a culture that is still largely wedded to progress and whose religious orthodoxy is probably more tenuous than that of Renaissance Europe? The question raises at least as many questions as it answers.

The metaphor of the Fall involves myth (*mythos*, or story), and the bringing together of two opposite or disparate objects or notions, and its symbolic or representative nature helps us better to understand literature and its relation to people and the world. Shakespeare consciously uses the Fall to set his characters and their actions in the history that they inhabit. The self-consciousness and blindness that the playwright gives to his historical characters helps reveal, rather than merely assert, the complexity of these history plays and shows that the lack of precise and literal communication does more than enrich the individual and the polity: it also creates conflict and misery. Even the language we use to criticize or affirm ideas in theology, philosophy, literature, and criticism is fallen or fallible, for it is rhetorical and figurative with or without metaphor or myth because it is symbolic and representative. This exploration should mean as much to readers as to writers, to us as to the Elizabethans. Shakespeare's vital and entertaining representation of the Fall, and the problems and dilemmas that accompany it, can provide the best kind of instruction. The fall into language enables dramatic poetry but also calls attention to the problems of representation and life, to which it bears an intricate relation. Without language, dramatic action and character could not exist. By examining aspects of language in the four plays, we will also touch necessarily on character and the structure of events. In this chapter we shall concentrate on the self-conscious use of the image of the Fall, the problematic and contradictory use of important images, and the breakdown of communication.[1]

RISE AND FALL

The self-conscious reference to images of the Fall represents the characters' awareness in language of their predicament. There are, of course, other unconscious uses of the images that show the limitation of the character when, unlike the author or audience, he or she is not aware of that limitation. As with any polar opposition, each qualifies the other, so that a fall involves rising and rising a fall. In a world of broken images, it is difficult for the characters (and even for the audience) to know which is which. In the ambiguous world of Shakespeare's history, the characters and *mythos* are too complex to yield a literal view of fallenness. This kind of imagery demands imagination to fill it out, but, in the terms of the play itself, our very fallenness prevents us from transcending it or comprehending it fully. Imagery of rise and fall can be self-conscious or unconscious and occurs throughout the tetralogy, especially in the first and last plays.

Richard II reflects the basic *de casibus* tragic pattern of a central and illustrious character falling from power because of pride, but Shakespeare broadens the Fall from Richard to Bolingbroke and England, and this shared limitation complicates the relation between good and evil as well as the nature of character. The ruins of time govern *Richard II*. Bolingbroke's first words to Richard display verbal ambiguity and dramatic irony: "Many years of happy days befall / My gracious sovereign, my most loving liege!" (I.i.20–21). By the end of the play, Bolingbroke has cut Richard's days short and has felled the king. The word "befall" becomes increasingly ironic as the play unfolds, especially in light of the imagery of Bolingbroke's rise and Richard's fall. In the opening scene Richard is "your Highness," but Bolingbroke and Mowbray are "High-stomach'd" (I.i.14, 18). Whereas Mowbray would mount his horse to defend his honor, Bolingbroke aspires to the flight of a falcon (I.i.82, 109). This kind of incrementally repeated imagery is not missed in the theater. Shakespeare puns on rise and fall when he has Bolingbroke ask: "Shall I seem crest-fallen in my father's sight? / Or with pale beggar-fear impeach my height / Before this out-dar'd dastard?" (I.i.188–90). Bolingbroke describes himself "As confident as is the falcon's flight" and once more is the hunting bird ready for his prey (I.iii.61).

Clearly, the imagery of rise and fall reaches beyond simple correspondence with the myth of the Fall or the vicissitudes of fortune and takes on predation and aspiration. So far, while using images of fallenness, the characters do not consciously refer to the Fall, and Shakespeare's repetition of this motif recalls not only the Edenic Fall but also the wheel of fortune. Bolingbroke is more subtle and restrained in his overreaching than Tamburlaine. In a line that is pregnant with dramatic irony, Bolingbroke appeals to Gaunt's spirit to "lift me up / To reach at victory above my head"—words that will affect Richard as much as they do Mowbray because Bolingbroke will raise himself to kingship (I.iii.71–72). If Bolingbroke likens himself to a strong tower, another image of aspiration, Richard stops the combat at the height of suspense and says that he and his council deplore "the eagle-winged pride / Of sky-aspiring and ambitious thoughts" (I.iii.102, 129–30). In plotting rebellion Northumberland describes England as "this declining land" (II.i.240). For the most part, the early images of the play have stressed the decline of the king and kingdom, while associating Bolingbroke with the ascending sun and soaring birds. According to Northumberland, England's broken wing must be mended, "imp" meaning to graft new feathers in the wing to improve flight (II.i.291–98).[2] In this passage, at least for the scholar who has the inclination to look into the matter, "broking" emphasizes the king as renter, dealer, and pawn, through a pun and a half-rhyme ("broken"–"breaking," "crown"–"pawn"), and the crown as cracked and traded. Here, Northumberland says, the country sags, kingship is sick and disfigured, and the dust of death lies on the scepter, so that he proposes that the conspirators "make high majesty look like itself." These images not only foreshadow the fall of the king but also become ironic in light of Richard's prophecies concerning Northumberland's fall into disfavor and his rebellion in the *Henry IV* plays.

How conscious the characters are of their use of the imagery of rise and fall partly depends on how much they are acting. When Bolingbroke returns to England, York does not believe his humility: "Show me thy humble heart, and not thy knee, / Whose duty is deceivable and false" (II.iii.83–84). This accusation of outward obeisance, as opposed to inner arrogance, makes the audience wary of Bolingbroke and encourages it to question whether the public imagery and action show Bolingbroke rising in the world while his soul is becoming baser. It is Richard's fall, however, that receives the most emphasis at this time in the play. Salisbury compares Richard to a shooting star falling to the base earth, but soon, as Scroope reports, the swelling rage of Bolingbroke gathers force (II.iv.18–24; III.ii.106–10). As in *King Lear,* a powerful storm over power is brewing. When Richard and Bolingbroke meet for the first time since the banishment, Richard stands high in Flint Castle while Bolingbroke stands below until the king descends to give himself up to his cousin's power.[3] The imagery implies that Richard's tower will topple, for the castle where Bolingbroke corners him possesses "tottered battlements," meaning both unsure and tattered, something of a Humpty Dumpty wall, unable to give the king stability or refuge (III.iii.52). Richard worries about debasing himself and likens himself to a falling and "glist'ring" Phaeton and says: "Down, court! down, king!" (III.iii.121–30, 176–83). Richard self-consciously dramatizes his fall and, by associating the word "king" with fallenness, questions its power. There will be two kings alive at once in this play, so that the authority of the word and the office becomes problematic. As York had, Richard uncovers Bolingbroke's role playing in similar images of rise and fall: "Up, cousin, up; your heart is up, I know, / Thus high at least, although your knee be low" (III.iii.190–95). Bolingbroke's answer is that "I come but for mine own," a dramatic irony that echoes throughout the play.

The most obvious self-conscious allusion to the Fall is the garden scene. In describing Bolingbroke's triumph, the Gardener says that Richard's crown was "quite thrown down" because he wasted "idle hours" (III.iv.57–66), a premonition of Richard's view of himself in prison. When the Man asks the Gardener whether Richard will be deposed, the latter answers in the same foreboding images: "Depress'd he is already, depos'd / 'Tis doubt he will be" (III.iv.67–69). The next scene will show the deposition of Richard, in which the verbal images find another objectification on the stage. The garden scene represents a second Eden, for the queen calls the Gardener "old Adam's likeness" and asks him: "What Eve, what serpent, hath suggested thee / To make a second fall" (III.iv.73–76).[4] By speaking of Fall, deposition, and downfall, Isabel emphasizes a moral and biblical allusion and implies debate on free will and determinism, pride and "knowledge," heaven and hell. In many ways Richard and England have already fallen before the action of *Richard II*: it is as if the murder of Gloucester were an echo of original sin. From different points of view, the characters speak of England as a garden. Gaunt described England as this "other Eden" suffering a second Fall (II.i.42, 59–60), and the Garden scene (III.iv) is a stage image that develops this idea. As an overt allegory, the garden is also England in little and, in the opinion of Bolingbroke and the Gardener, needs pruning and weeding, especially of the "caterpillars of the commonwealth" (II.iii.161–66; III.iv.1–55). "Pale" becomes a central word in the Garden scene. More than just a fenced-in area, "pale" also means a boundary or limit or, more importantly, an "English pale," which represents "the confines or dominion of England, the pale of English law."⁵ York later sounds like the Gardener in his images of cutting off sick people like festered branches (V.ii.50–51, iii.83–84). This garden itself demonstrates the fall of language as it is not simply Eden or a second Eden but has taken on more meanings and cannot be identical to the original garden.

The playwright also complicates the garden imagery, which relates to the Fall, with other religious images. Shakespeare associates bloodguilt with the story of Cain and Abel: the sins of the parents are visited on the children. Bolingbroke is aware of the fallen state, for he accuses Mowbray of murdering Gloucester, sluicing out his "innocent soul," "Which blood, like sacrificing Abel's, cries / Even from the tongueless caverns of the earth / To me for justice and rough chastisement" (I.i.104–6). In the final scene Bolingbroke, however, identifies himself closely with Exton, his agent, who reminds him of his own guilt and whom he then exiles "With Cain" (V.vi.43–44). On the other hand, Richard compares himself to Christ and his betrayers to Judas. Without knowing the true situation, Richard calls Bagot, Bushy, and Wiltshire "Three Judases, each one thrice worse than Judas!" (III.ii.132). Not only does the hyperbole heighten our sense of Richard's emotional and wavering nature but it also qualifies his character, for he jumps to conclusions and, implicitly, makes his betrayal three or nine times as great as that of Christ—a vain boast even in sorrow. As the cause for Richard's grief increases, so too does his exaggeration, deepening the pathos but exposing his limitations at the same time. In the deposition scene Richard, surveying the men at court, remembering his favors to them, says that they had cried "All hail!" to him as Judas did to Christ, "But he, in twelve, / Found truth in all but one; I, in twelve thousand, none" (IV.i.167–71). As Richard makes the comparison more explicit, the hyperbole grows from three to ten thousand, becoming almost as ludicrous as Falstaff's numbering of his foes at Gad's Hill, only sadder. To be fair to Richard, he is not the only one to think of his likeness to Christ, for, implicitly, Carlisle (in the king's absence) also compares him to Jesus when he prophesies that men shall call England the "field of Golgotha and dead men's skulls" (IV.i.143–44). Death, suffering, and disorder will make a world where none can answer the devastation of sin and incommunication. The words "voyage" and "pilgrimage" also strengthen the representation of bloodguilt, resonating as metaphors or images of the soul's quest, and become associated with Christ. Bolingbroke uses these images, which come back to haunt him. He says that he and Mowbray "vow a long and weary pilgrimage," but whereas Mowbray dies, as Carlisle describes it, "For Jesu Christ in glorious Christian field, / . . . [rendering] his pure soul unto his captain Christ," Bolingbroke lives, driven by his guilt to promise a pilgrimage to Jerusalem, one on which, as the *Henry IV* plays show, he can never go (I.iii.48–49; IV.i.91–100; V.vi.45f.). Having called his exile "an inforced pilgrimage," Bolingbroke, after Richard's murder, vows to go on "a voyage to the Holy Land, / To wash this blood off from my guilty hand" (I.iii.264; V.vi.49–50). Death, suffering, and shame—a fallen nature and polity—occur throughout *Richard II*.

Shakespeare links the tragedy of Richard inextricably to Bolingbroke through the image of the balance, which unites the imagery of heaviness and lightness with that of rising and falling. The Gardener notes that Richard's scale is light in comparison to Bolingbroke's, in whose "mighty hold" the king lies and who weighs him down (III.iv.83–89). Ironically, the scales are those of power rather than of justice. According to Richard's imagery, unlike the Gardener's, the crown is Fortune's scale, a well in which two buckets cannot balance, Richard's down and full, Bolingbroke's empty and mounting (IV.i.181–89). Richard's bucket is full of tears. Even if the theatricality of the image of the buckets may represent one of Richard's weaknesses, insofar as the longstanding cultural attitude of antitheatricality reduces everything "dramatic" to foible or sin, what he says is true enough: a man is king of his griefs, and a king is a man who grieves.[6] The tragedy of kingship becomes a public matter. The fall from equity into "baseness" also affects the men in or near the court. If Richard had called Bolingbroke "base," so too does Aumerle call Bagot, whose accusations against Aumerle the would-be king takes seriously, a "base man" (IV.i.20). The images of balance and of rise and fall most often center on the struggle for the crown. Whereas Bolingbroke was a soaring bird, Richard is "plume-pluck'd." York tells Bolingbroke that Richard yields his "high sceptre" to him and says: "Ascend his throne, descending now from him," and Bolingbroke, as Carlisle protests in God's name, vows to ascend (IV.i.107–14). Both kings are subject to the fall into interpretation and cannot prove their claims to divine sanction. Like the image of the scales before it and that of the two buckets after it, there are two sides to the balance of the crown. Here, on either side of Bolingbroke's eagerness, lie York's approval and Carlisle's repudiation.

In the deposition scene Richard finds himself "a traitor with the rest" because he has made "glory base" by consenting to abdicate (IV.i.244–52). Richard addresses the chief means for the ascent of the new king, "Northumberland, thou ladder," and predicts that he will find Bolingbroke ungrateful because the king will fear his ladder (V.i.55). A "true king's fall" are Richard's last words before being led away. The world of the *Henry IV* plays, a political snakes and ladders, bears out Richard's prophecy. The difference between moral and physical rising and falling becomes more explicit in the final scenes. Exton strikes down the fallen king, who, as he dies, curses his murderer to hell, exhorting his own soul to "mount" while his "gross flesh sinks downward" (V.v.106–12). Kingship and humanity are caught between body and soul, between two mutual and contending entities in identity.

Images of the Fall also occur in the remaining three plays of the tetralogy, although less often. The religious imagery reveals the dark side of *1 Henry IV*. It represents murder, crime, and exile, and yokes money and God. Trying to extricate himself from another predicament in which Hal wants to expose and shame him, Sir John says to the prince: "Thou knowest in the state of innocency Adam fell, and what should poor Jack Falstaff do in the days of villainy? Thou seest I have more flesh than another man, and therefore more frailty" (III.iii.164–68). In jest or not, Falstaff worries insistently about punishment and subsequent suffering for his sins, so that the comic mood and subversive energy that he creates cannot achieve a sense of wholeness and harmony, even at the end of the play when the court celebrates its victory. Even though Eden is lost and the Fall, to which Falstaff refers, is mentioned only once, religious images play a substantial role and limit the characters. If Edmond Malone is right, Shakespeare derives Henry's image of the earth swilling the blood of its children from the description in Genesis of the earth receiving Abel's blood on Cain's banishment.[7] The gloss, which is more likely to occur to someone immersed in the text than to someone coming to it for the first time, proves especially effective in light of the images of Cain and Abel in *Richard II*, particularly in Bolingbroke's banishment of Exton, his murderous agent and his Cain (*RII*, V.vi.43–44). This violence and conflict are the result of a fallen world. Although the images of Christ are not as central as in *Richard II*, in 1 *Henry IV* such imagery still reveals irony. For Henry, the crucifix is both the "blessed cross" and the "bitter cross." Rather than visiting the sepulchre of Christ to chase pagans from "those holy fields," Henry will fight a civil war at Shrewsbury, and, as Richard had appealed to Christ, the new king's Christian service seems ironically abrogated. As if the king himself can read the will of God, Henry upbraids Hal for his wantonness, explaining it as a scourge that Providence has sent to punish him, although he claims not to know the cause of God's displeasure (III.ii.4–11). Henry misses the irony, which the audience shares with Hal, that the prince will not be heaven's avenger against the king. Later, Hal actually saves his father's life in battle (V.iv.42). Although Henry is related to Cain at the end of *Richard II*, he still censures Worcester for his dishonesty and says that many men would have been alive "If like a Christian thou hadst truly borne / Betwixt our armies true intelligence" (V.v.9–10). It is debatable whether Henry's plan for a crusade was to enable him to repent or to divert attention from Richard's death. Hell, punishment, and factional division among friends qualify the celebratory nature of the comedy and of laughter in 1 *Henry IV*.

The sin of Adam and Eve is the biblical representation of how sin brought death into the world, and the consequence of this fallenness occurs in both parts of *Henry IV*. When in the second and more satirical part Feeble refuses to bear a base mind and wants to serve his prince because death relieves him of all the debts of the next year and because "we owe God a death," or "debt" as the pun would have it, he recalls for us Hal's words to Falstaff before Shrewsbury and Sir John's corrupt recruiting practices in Gloucestershire, where a debt is a bribe to prevent death. Owing God a death also recalls Doll's question to Falstaff: When will you "begin to patch up thine old body for heaven?" Sir John's reply calls to mind another ironic relation to Part One. If he commands, "Peace, good Doll, do not speak like a death's-head, do not bid me remember mine end," he had also seen in Bardolph's face a *memento mori*, full of hell-fire where the glutton Dives is "burning, burning." As in Part One, Sir John fears damnation and death when others remind him of his spiritual and financial debts (II.iv.227f.; cf. *1HIV*, III.iii.27f.). Shakespeare modifies the suffering of the king with the pain and humor of a Lord of Misrule and a doting country justice. For Henry, the tavern companions are like carrion from which little sweetness and nourishment can arise (IV.iv.79–80). The king's slumber may fool the audience into thinking Henry dead, as Hal does (IV.iv.125f., v.20f.). After waking, the king chides Hal, saying that this son will mock his father at his funeral, but to show filial love Hal offers to kill himself if he is not telling the truth: he thought that the sleeping king was dead (IV.v.104–19, 152–59). Richard had died violently in a prison cell, "scrap'd from Pomfret stones," instead of dying quietly in a monastery as he had wished; Henry dies in the Jerusalem chamber instead of in the Holy Land as he had dreamt (IV.v.234–40). Even kings have little control over their fates: human desire is subject to grim ironies.

Satire represents human vice and folly and isolated characters in a crowded tapestry.[8] Shakespeare creates a satire that represents a fallen personal and political world, the isolation that sin and vice cause in the ruins of England. Like tragedy but unlike comedy, satire concentrates on the problems and dilemmas of an individual in society, though satiric focus is more communal than that of tragedy. In *2 Henry IV* the limitations of human knowledge and greed for power often isolate the characters, making an almost tragic mockery of a fragmenting community, set against the memory or fiction of some prelapsarian unity. Nothing is permanent in Part Two: oaths, friendships, alliances, the configuration of the characters and their social worlds, all are unreliable. The most noticeable separation occurs between Hal and Falstaff, who do not have nearly as close a relation as they do in Part One, for their meetings are shorter than before and they part permanently in the rejection scene. Characters in the play do not communicate, as we shall later see, and the rejection cannot mask the continued fragmentation of the comic community of *1 Henry IV*. Part Two transforms the comic imagery of jolly fat, which at least occupied the surface of Part One, into images of disease and decay that are often associated with satire. Falstaff's sweat is growing rancid; the sexual jokes are becoming drier, sadder, and more obscene; death is nearer at hand for the comic characters; the rebels are cheated into execution; and the old king dies.[9]

The use of disease imagery distinguishes *2 Henry IV* almost as much as the image of the unweeded and cankered garden does *Richard II*. Rumor first mentions disease, telling the audience about Northumberland's crafty sickness, which helped precipitate Hotspur's death and which qualifies Northumberland's mourning for his son in the opening scene (IN. 36–37; I.i. 137–39). The Archbishop says that the disease is more general, for the common people have been fickle toward Richard and Henry (I.iii.87–90). The tavern is also sick. Through a structural use of imagery, Shakespeare compares the sickness of Northumberland and Falstaff ironically (I.ii. 1–5). Sir John discusses the king's apoplexy and pretends to be deaf to deflect the Chief Justice, who says: "I think you are fallen into the disease, for you hear not what I say to you," and Falstaff admits that he is only troubled with "the disease of not listening" (I.ii. 55–132). Here is a consequence of the fall of language, the lack of reception as well as the imprecision and deception of words. Later, when Falstaff is alone, he worries about the "consumption of the purse," laments his gout and pox, and resolves that his wit will "turn diseases to commodity" (as Northumberland has) (I.ii.237–50). With irony, Shakespeare associates Northumberland, Falstaff, and Henry. As Scroop says, all England is sick. Pox, gluttony, and general disease characterize the inhabitants of the Boar's Head (II.iv.36–46). The sick can know their medicine but ignore their own cure. Unable to repent or to cure his physical ailment, Falstaff realizes the relation of the bad corrupting the good to the illness gnawing at people: "It is certain that either wise bearing or ignorant carriage is caught, as men take diseases, one of another; therefore let men take heed of their company" (V.i.72–75; cf. *1HIV*, III.iii.9–10). In Gloucestershire, Bullcalf has a "whoreson cold" that he caught ringing the bells on the anniversary of the coronation of Henry the Fourth, an ironic comment on Henry's ascension and government (III.ii.175–82). At court, whereas Henry thinks "the body of our kingdom" is diseased to its very heart, Warwick considers it a distempered body that may be restored to health "With good advice and little medicine" (III.i.38–44). The body politic—kingdom and king—is sick. Rebellion is not the only disease, for treachery occurs in all camps: Northumberland deserts Hotspur, Glendower and Mortimer never show up to battle, Hal uses Falstaff (who uses Shallow), and Lancaster tricks the Archbishop. Language has become a fallen tool for deception.

As especially in *Richard II*, so in *2 Henry IV* the imagery of rise and fall and of balance also shows the limits of human language and action. Rumor spreads the false story that Hal and the king fell to their deaths, but Morton tells Northumberland the truth: the prince beat Hotspur down so that he could never rise again (IN.28–32; I.i.109–11). Mowbray describes the time after Bolingbroke and his father had mounted, when Richard threw his warder down, thus casting "down himself and all their lives / That by indictment and by dint of sword / Have since miscarried under Bolingbroke" (IV.i.117–29). The image recalls the fall at the opening of *Richard II*, of which Mowbray the younger presents yet another interpretation. After Henry discovers that the prince has taken the crown, he confronts him: "Pluck down my officers; . . . / Harry the fifth is crown'd! Up, vanity! / Down, royal state!" (IV.v.117–20). The imagery of rise and fall in this "deposition scene" ironically echoes similar images when Bolingbroke deposed Richard, so that Henry fears the "noble image of my youth" (IV.iv.54). The son reconciles himself to the father, who hopes that the crown will descend (be passed on) with peace from a king with whom the crown may have descended (become more base) because his descent did not make him heir to the throne (IV.v.187). For Hal's sake, Henry also hopes that "what in me was purchas'd / Falls upon thee in a more fairer sort" and says that his friends, "By whose fell working I was first advanc'd," fell out of favor because Henry feared that they might dislodge him with the same power that made him king (IV.v.199–206). Breaking the rules, Bolingbroke tries to impose similar authoritative regulations on the country, but his difficulties partly arise from the realization that the old order has fallen and that kingship is arbitrary and relies on power alone.

Generic friction, which will be discussed in chapter 4, intensifies in *Henry V* and includes the conflicts of language. Violence informs Henry the Fifth's language as well as the threats of Pistol and the French. For the moment, the most pertinent aspect of the Fall in this play is images of broken peace, especially Burgundy's description of France as a ruined garden. Characters evoke Eden and deadly sin. According to Canterbury, when Henry died "Consideration like an angel came, / And whipp'd th'offending Adam out of him, / Leaving his body as a Paradise, / T'envelop and contain celestial spirits" (I.i.28–31). Consideration, a spiritual self-examination, scorned Adam—"Old Adam," or innate wickedness—or, in other words, restored the lost paradise or achieved heaven itself. Nevertheless, Canterbury will help push Henry into the fallen world of war. Ely, who will "tempt" the king to invade France, likens the young Hal to a strawberry that grows beneath a nettle, the best of which "thrive and ripen best / Neighbour'd by fruit of baser quality," for the prince hid his "contemplation / Under the veil of wildness" where it grew unseen and unhindered (I.i.60–66). Ely uses the gardening image to explain Hal's earlier actions and "sudden conversion," a shift and calling into question of identity. This is not the only interpretation of the acting and action of the king.

Henry is an ambivalent garden, perfection to some, fallen to others. Repudiating the Dauphin, the Constable uses garden images to describe the hidden virtue of the English king. The Constable's garden is as classical as it is biblical, for he compares Henry to Lucius Brutus, who concealed his wisdom under "a coat of folly; / As gardeners do with ordure hide those roots / That shall first spring and be the most delicate" (II.iv.38–40). These images of Henry's hidden virtue contrast it to the nettles and ordure of the world and emphasize the close relation between acting and action, theater and politics.

Even though Henry realizes the virtue of humility in peace, he believes that men must "act" brutally in war. This idea may be the admission of his own fall, even if it occurs amid talk of disguise and pretense (III.i.4–6ff.). During Henry's debate with Williams and Bates, the king argues that men who have "gored the gentle bosom of peace" with violence and robbery find their divine punishment in the ill fate they meet in war, and afterward he says that common men who enjoy the fruits of peace do not enjoy the labors of the king to keep the peace (IV.i.169–79, 287–90). If the end of *2 Henry IV* and the beginning of *Henry V* are any indication, Henry, like his father, may be accused of stealing a crown and of purposefully disrupting the peace. The Chorus, however, extols Henry, who is about to return to France to negotiate peace (V.CH.38–39).

This peace is not without qualification. In Burgundy's speech on Peace, to describe negotiations for an armistice, he uses the images of men exchanging greetings "face to face, and royal eye to eye," which is reminiscent of Richard's order for the entrance of Mowbray and Bolingbroke, "face to face / And frowning brow to brow," in the opening scene of *Richard II* (V.ii.30–31). It seems that the breach that began in England is being mended in France: Henry has won peace, glory, and unity for England. Later, however, the Epilogue tells of England's fall into civil war and its loss of France after the death of Henry.

Burgundy says that "fertile France," "this best garden of the world," a phrase that the Epilogue echoes, lies overgrown, corrupting in "her" own fertility, unpruned, and like a prisoner with long, unkempt hair. France, according to Burgundy, is a garden grown savage "as soldiers will / That nothing do but meditate on blood . . . / And every thing that seems unnatural," one needing "gentle Peace," which will be transformed from "naked, poor, and mangled Peace." Burgundy sounds like Gaunt lamenting that unweeded garden Richard has made of England, which, among other things, Gaunt calls "This other Eden, demi-paradise." England has exported strife and ruin, and Burgundy assumes a role similar to the Gardener's in *Richard II*. The unruly garden becomes a metaphor for the ruined state of politics as it had in earlier plays in the tetralogy. Part of the reason for this breakdown and strife is the faltering of language. The Fall in the Epilogue of *Henry V* is not simply a representation of *de casibus* patterns or a more sophisticated recasting of *A Mirror for Magistrates*.

Other matters reveal the fall of language in the tetralogy: self-trapping images, appeals to God and ideas of kingship, and lying and incommunication. The rest of the chapter will explore these manifestations of the fall into language, which reveal a tension between conscious and unconscious uses of words, for sometimes the characters consciously manipulate language to deceive others, whereas at other times they limit themselves unawares or only later become aware of the traps they are setting for others and for themselves.

SELF-TRAPPING IMAGES

Characters reveal their limitations by getting tangled in their language, especially their images. Self-trapping images include all kinds of imagery, but it is the way in which they are used that distinguishes them. Often unconsciously a character finds himself caught in an extended image, as if the playwright has set a trap for him. This entrapment sometimes puts the audience off guard—it is caught, as it does not know whether the author intended the linguistic trap, whether the character involved is a bad actor found out in his or her incompetency, or whether the observer is situated in a dilemma between motive and representation, intention and reception. This dilemma creates an ironic relation between author, character, and audience. Usually, the self-trapping images uncover the limitation of the character, but obliquely this delimiting blurs the boundaries between character, author, and audience, for, paradoxically, dramatic irony emphasizes limitation as much as omniscience. In other words, the author and audience empathize with the human faults of the character as well as sharing a godlike knowledge. Like the author and the characters, we fall into history as we interpret and participate in it.

One image cluster—the elements—will illustrate this limitation in *Richard II*. The sun is an emblem of kingship. Hearing of his own banishment, Bolingbroke says:

> Your will be done; this must my comfort be,
> That sun that warms you here, shall shine on me,
> And those his golden beams to you here lent
> Shall point on me and gild my banishment.
>
> (I.iii.144–47)

This ambiguous passage may have three different meanings: Bolingbroke is flattering Richard by saying "I shall find sustenance by being under the same sun as you"; or, as in the proverbial "the sun shines upon all alike," he is expressing the equality of the two men and his ability to weather exile; or (considering the present tense of "warms" and the future tense of "shall shine") he means "the sun that shines on Richard now will later shine on me" (Tilley, *Proverbs*, S985). Dramatic irony complicates the meaning and thereby the relation between Richard and Bolingbroke as well as the idea of kingship. In repudiating imagination Bolingbroke asks who can "wallow naked in the December snow / By thinking on fantastic summer's heat?" and in the deposition scene he makes Richard wish: "O that I were a mockery king of snow, / Standing before the sun of Bolingbroke, / To melt myself away in water-drops!" (I.iii.298–99; IV.i.260–62). The situation has ironically reversed itself. Rather than contending with the heat of the sun, Bolingbroke is now that heat. Richard's imagination teems with consolations that Bolingbroke rejects in his conversation with Gaunt in favor of imagination as an intensification of sorrow. From a sun king, Richard is reduced to a weeping king of snow melted by Bolingbroke. Even though by the end of the play these two monarchs will have shared similar problems of kingship, Shakespeare also uses the irony to distinguish their personalities and some of their shortcomings.

Richard later likens himself to the sun, although he says that his followers can go "From Richard's night, to Bolingbroke's fair day" (II.iv.18–24; III.ii.36–53, 215–18). But it is Bolingbroke who drives himself most into a corner:

> See, see, King Richard doth himself appear,
> As doth the blushing discontented sun
> From out the fiery portal of the East,
> When he perceives the envious clouds are bent
> To dim his glory and to stain the track
> Of his bright passage to the occident.
> (III.iii.62–67)

Whereas a pale Richard has just appeared, he is now blushing, a deathly fear yielding to a living rage. Shortly before, Bolingbroke had been red with anger and had thought that Richard and he should meet like fire and water, tearing "the cloudy cheeks of heaven"

(III.iii.54–61). It seems that, through his own metaphor, Bolingbroke has made himself one of the envious clouds that would eclipse the sun and "stain" King Richard's path. As in *Venus and Adonis* (ca. 1593), Shakespeare employs the conventional image of the red morning as a sign of discontent, foreshadowing a stormy day, a chaotic future for the kingdom.[10] York echoes Bolingbroke's "stain," fearing "That any harm should stain so fair a show [Richard]!" (III.iii.68–71; see Sonnet 33:14). Shakespeare underscores the irony when York is surprised that Richard without power should look like a king still and when York dreads, prophetically, that violence and bloodshed will overtake the reign of Bolingbroke, for, deserting Richard, York has joined the man who will "stain" the king (III.iii.68–71).

Bolingbroke and Richard use similar images differently. Richard warns the rebels that although they have "torn" their souls by turning from their souls, they will find a worse fate: God is mustering in his "clouds" pestilence to curse their progeny for generations. He also predicts blood for the pastures of Bolingbroke's England, as his cousin had for Richard's kingdom (III.iii.85–100, cf. 31–50). The imagery of sun and weather appears to betray Bolingbroke, for it is warlike, stormy, sudden—all indicating sad consequences for Richard. When trapping himself with his own images, Bolingbroke anticipates the fall of Richard :

> Methinks King Richard and myself should meet
> With no less terror than the elements
> Of fire and water, when their thund'ring shock
> At meeting tears the cloudy cheeks of heaven.
> Be he the fire, I'll be the yielding water;
> The rage be his, whilst on the earth I rain
> My waters—on the earth, and not on him.
>
> (III.iii.54–60)

The images backfire. Water usually puts out fire. Bolingbroke will "rain" on Richard, will take his "rein" and his "reign," a pun that supports the dramatic irony that alludes to images of weather, horses, and kingship, all of which are important in the play. Downward like Phaeton will Richard fall, unable to hold the reins of his horse, his life, and his state.[11] In what may be a Freudian slip, Bolingbroke catches himself when he says "on the earth, and not on him." Characters are not conscious of their desires or consciously repress them. When Bolingbroke landed, he had said that he wanted only to reclaim his lands from Richard and not to take the crown, but his language reveals the conflict within him. The sun imagery also represents Bolingbroke's moral decline, as well as Richard's fall, eclipse, or loss of control. Bolingbroke, the new Apollo, now takes up the sun, but by the end of the play he puts on black, his guilt wandering with Exton, like Cain, "thorough shades of night," never showing his head "by day nor light" (V.vi.38–52).

In *1 Henry IV* the festive and comic images of food and drink relate to the satiric image of gluttony and to the tragic imagery of England drinking its own blood in civil war. The link between the comic and serious aspects of this imagery arises at the beginning of the play, when Henry remarks that even the earth has been thirsty for the blood of her children, and when, in Hal's first words to Falstaff, who has been quenching his thirst, the prince says: "Thou art so fat-witted with drinking of old sack" (I.i.5–6, ii.2). Shakespeare uses irony to represent the blindness of the king. Henry likens the success of his state to a banquet, which, like his presence, "Seldom, but sumptuous, show'd like a feast." On the other hand, Richard, says Henry, let common men swallow him daily like honey until they were surfeited (III.ii.56–59, 70–73). In their sickness they were to Richard's "sun-like majesty . . . / As cloudy men use to their adversaries, / Being with his presence glutted, gorg'd, and full" (III.ii.76–84). In *Richard II* Bolingbroke was such a cloudy man. He remains blind or tries to forget his murder of Richard, his spiritual sickness, and his lack of repentance. Henry uses the same images to describe Hal, whom he compares disdainfully and wrongly with Richard—sweetness being devoured by the commonality. Later, however, the king is satisfied with Hal's promise of redemption and says that they must hasten to meet the rebels, for "Advantage feeds him fat while men delay" (III.ii.180).[12]

England is predatory, the feeders often being unwittingly fed upon. Falstaff feeds and drinks in festive and predatory ways, unaware, however, of the possibility that he is unconsciously celebrating his own fall from grace—that by preying on others he is preying on himself. Although still fat, Sir John thinks he is dwindling—a fretting that, Bardolph warns, will cause death if he continues (III.iii.1–11). Subsequently, Falstaff admits that he has "more flesh than another man" and therefore more frailty, but he will not stop draining the prince, the taverners, and the country. The soldiers he presses into service are starvelings but, in Sir John's words, "food for powder, food for powder." Hotspur later dies with the phrase "And food for" on his lips, which Hal completes with "For worms," a variant of Falstaff's phrase (V.iv.85–86). Hal sees the so-called corpse of Falstaff, at first feeling sadness, then criticizing the fat deer and saying that he should be disemboweled, prompting Sir John to complicate this oxymoronic moment: "If thou embowel me today, I'll give you leave to powder me and eat me too tomorrow" (V.iv.108–11). In jest, Sir John has become powdered food, but he has no intention of being buried. His resurrection on this earth enjoys the prerogative of fiction and contrasts with the apparent finality of death in history. Shakespeare represents the ironic limits and potentialities of the comic resurrection, for although the audience may wonder at the probability of Falstaff's ruse for self-preservation, it also looks forward to the continuation of his riot. The last use of the feeding image limits Sir John: "If I do grow great, I'll grow less, for I'll purge, and leave sack, and live cleanly as a nobleman should do" (V.iv.162–64). Falstaff finds himself between sin and guilt, celebration and lamentation. Another example of characters being caught in their own images, in their own devices, is the feeding of the king and Worcester. Falstaff and Henry are accused of stealing and preying on others. Henry had told Hal that Richard had mixed too much with the multitude and so had been "swallowed." Whereas the king had spoken about the rebels having their advantage fattened, Worcester reminds Henry that he has devoured king, friends, and country. In the next scene Worcester describes to Vernon a similar image of feeding, except the ones who eat are devoured: "And we shall feed like oxen at a stall, / The better cherish'd still the nearer death" (V.ii.14–15). If Henry, according to Worcester, will feed on the rebels, Worcester devours Hotspur in self-interest. Like the king and Falstaff, Worcester consumes others only to devour himself in death. The limited fields of speech and action represent the circumscribed position of the individual in history, although, for the moment, a character like Hal can seem to be triumphant, directorial, and almost omniscient ("I know you all").

The emphasis in *2 Henry IV* is more satiric than in *1 Henry IV*, so that the imagery of death, disease, and feeding is more prominent. As characters become more isolated in this satirical world, even and often subject to isolation in a crowd, they trap themselves increasingly in their own words. Although all parts of England are sick, I want to concentrate on the tavern, especially Falstaff, who with his language traps himself as he traps others. Sir John's habit is to reverse the actual situation, to deflect inquiries into his own health by discussing the king's apoplexy. While pretending to be deaf, Sir John diagnoses Henry's ailment as being caused by grief and study and says it "is a kind of deafness." The Chief Justice makes this irony explicit when he says Falstaff has a hearing problem and Sir John admits it (I.ii.55–132). Later, Falstaff is alone and worries about his sickness but, like Northumberland, swears to make the best use of it (I.ii.237–50). Throughout scene 2, Sir John has tried to find refuge from the law by means of his wit and his "sickness," but it appears that he has as many real as imaginary maladies. With some irony, Falstaff asserts that wisdom and ignorance, like diseases, are caught in company (V.i.72–75). In the next breath he talks about entertaining Hal with Shallow's inanity but does not perceive, as the audience does, that the prince thinks of Falstaff too as a base contagion that must be purged (*1HIV*, I.ii.193). Hearing the news of Henry's death, Sir John knows that the "young king is sick for me," whereas in fact he sickens *of* Sir John (V.iii.131). Falstaff is aware of his self-dramatization and can impugn his tavern company to the point of saying that he will reject them, but he can never actually conceive of Hal's thinking of him in the same way or of the rejection. The character who thought he could escape all traps through entrapment, all tricks through trickery, cannot escape. Henry the Fifth, who is also a trickster, later finds that he, who has been so successful in fooling the world, is fooled. Besides the debate with Bates and Williams, in which he achieves a Pyrrhic victory through false logic and the glove trick, Henry the Fifth's imagery drives him into a corner.

Henry's language is heroic and brutal. He is a good soldier who listens to his men (even if he does not always like what he hears) and who behaves bravely in crisis, but his language harbors a menace that seems to show an enjoyment of power, violation, and carnage. The central speech that qualifies Henry's gentleness, in war at least, is his threat against Harfleur. Siege is an important verbal and stage image in *Henry V*: this imagery is sexual, the sack of the city being its rape—Shakespeare equates the city with virgins, as Marlowe had in *Tamburlaine* and Homer had in the *Iliad* when he identified Helen with Troy.[13] For example, Henry threatens: "If I begin the battery once again, / I will not leave the half-achieved Harfleur / Till in her ashes she lie buried" (III.iii.7–9). If the people of the city refuse to surrender, they will find no mercy, and hard-hearted soldiers "in liberty of bloody hand shall range / With conscience wide as hell, mowing like grass / Your fresh-fair virgins and your flowering infants" (III.iii.10–14). Besides telling these citizens that they will witness "impious war," dressed in fire like Satan, wreaking "waste and desolation," the king emphasizes the rape of their young daughters:

> What is't to me, when you yourselves are cause,
> If your pure maidens fall into the hand
> Of hot and forcing violation?
> What rein can hold licentious wickedness
> When down the hill he holds his fierce career?
> (III.iii.19–23)

Like Phaeton, Richard had fallen, unable to control his horses, but Henry the Fifth is supposed to have learned from Richard's mistakes and to have disproven his father's comparison of him to Richard. It appears that Henry has lost control of his language as he disclaims control over his men. Despite J. H. Walter's claim that contemporary writers often wrote about the sack of a city and its horrors, that Henry's procedure accords with contemporary military law, and that this violent language may have prevented actual violence, the king continues his penchant for making others responsible for his actions and his tendency to relish the thought of sexual violation. Does he have more options than to use a rhetoric of terror to achieve a gentle peace?[14] As for the uncontrollable horse of licentiousness, Henry can control his men if he chooses, for he rigorously keeps discipline when he sanctions the hanging of Nym and Bardolph and when he orders that no Englishman brag about the victory over the French (see IV.viii.115–18).

Ironically, Henry still associates himself with purity and heavenly grace, as if these violent images have pushed up from his unconscious or as if he has consciously hidden his true intent from others. In the "I know you all" speech in *1 Henry IV*, Hal thought of himself as the sun to "contagious clouds"—Falstaff and the taverners—and here he sees himself as the "wind of grace" blowing over the "contagious clouds" of his soldiers' marauding (III.iii.24–32). Although Henry describes the slaying of daughters, old men, and infants while mad mothers wail as the women of Judaea did "At Herod's bloody-hunting slaughtermen," he begins, significantly, with the rape of daughters and uses such vivid images that his threats suggest a relish of the idea of violence, if not of massacre itself. Not only does Henry liken his men to the army of a tyrant who tried to kill the infant Christ and was a renowned butcher but he also, by implication, compares himself to Herod. If the men of Harfleur do not capitulate, they will watch "The blind and bloody soldier with foul hand / Defile the locks of your shrill-shrieking daughters" (III.iii.34–35, cf. 36–43). The dashed heads of old men, the spitted heads of naked (innocent) infants, and mothers whose confused keening breaks the clouds (Henry saw himself as the sun breaking through the clouds in the "I know you all" speech) also characterize the king's threat to the citizens, whom three times he makes responsible for such violence if they do not surrender (III.iii.4, 27–28, 42–43). This is the kind of clever politics that is used to go to war and then to justify it. The civilian victims become responsible for the war waged on them. Nor does Henry refrain from threatening more deserving victims like Montjoy, envoy of the haughty French army: "if we be hinder'd, / We shall your tawny ground with your red blood / Discolour" (III.vi.165–67). This violence against the French may be justified, if invasion that is not the self-defense of counterattack is ever justifiable, only if Henry has a proper right to the English and French crowns. In a fallen world it is doubtful that anyone—including the French—has a proper right, and a person can only claim priority.

The king's responsibility is precisely the theme Bates and Williams broach with Henry. Rather than discuss their view that an unjust

king must answer for the deaths of his men, Henry prefers to remark
that the spotless king always leads a few spotted soldiers into battle.
These men, Henry says, have committed premeditated murder,
beguiled "virgins with the broken seals of perjury" (a variation on
Henry's theme of rape and seduction as we saw before Harfleur), and
"gored the gentle bosom of peace" with theft and robbery. According to the king, God punishes with death in war men who have
escaped the king's law in peace, and, besides, if each man prepares
his own conscience before death, dying is an advantage. The king
held the men of Harfleur responsible for the virtue and lives of their
wives and daughters, but now, playing another role, he wants to
have it both ways: "Every subject's duty is the king's; but every
subject's soul is his own" (IV.i.182–84, see 163–92). Perhaps the
bishops should have applied this kind of logic to Henry when he
wanted them to be accountable for the war in France, but then it is
not entirely clear how much responsibility they want to assume, and
their motives are self-serving and their agenda hidden—they want to
busy the king's mind with foreign wars and bribe him, so that he
will not implement heavy taxes on the church (see I.ii.13–32). In a
fallen world words can become masks, and contradictions can hide
another grammar of motives.

Neither in love nor in war can Henry refrain from violent imagery.
He is not adverse to cutting throats; he orders his men to kill their
French prisoners (IV.vi.35–37, vii.5–11, 57–67). Even in the love
scene, Henry joins Burgundy in likening maidens to flies that men
must catch (like flies to wanton boys!), but he admits that one French
maid, Katharine, saves many a French city from his conquering
hand. With his own daughter present, the French king joins in this
repartee of witty double entendre that makes Katharine a sexual
object and renders explicit the image of the besieged city as a sexually
assaulted woman. To Henry, he says: "Yes, my lord, you see them
perspectively, the cities turned into a maid; for they are all girdled
with maiden walls that war hath never entered," and Henry confirms
the image of the "maiden cities" (V.ii.338–47, cf. 309–37). The
defeated French share with their conqueror this image of military
assault and intercourse, although they do so in the context of
marriage whereas Henry has also talked about rape, unless they are
equating the two. Other characters, such as Canterbury, Pistol, and

the Dauphin, also use images of violence, blood, and death, but the hopes of killing and spoils turn against them ironically. I am not arguing that Henry is alone in his violence, but that his threatening images of war and rape qualify the hero whom the Chorus proclaims and whose promised marriage at first appears entirely comic in Frye's structural sense. Possibly, violence and the male treatment of women as love objects was at the heart of traditional military heroism, but I find it difficult to believe that Shakespeare did not modify and question this notion as much as he did other contemporary views, forms, sources, conventions, and language. It is disturbing to find desires of rape and violence identified with the virtues of marriage and peace. These violent images are perplexing, making the play and the culmination of this historical tetralogy problematic. In some ways, Henry's trap is our own and shows the limitations of the Second Tetralogy, as well as the Shakespearean history play. In this limitation or dilemma, paradoxically, we seem to find the complexity and power of language in which readers, audiences, and critics have seen their own contradictions and perhaps even their own negative capability. At the same time, we seem to share the limits of the characters, as well as the katascopic omniscience of Shakespeare.

APPEALS TO GOD AND IDEAS OF KINGSHIP

Like self-trapping images, claims of divine sanction reveal the desire to legitimate and sanctify one's actions and words. From the point of view of each of these players in history, God is particularly on his side, but from the point of view of the author and audience (which includes playgoers, readers, and critics) God is claimed by all sides. As the characters make godlike claims, they become more human, as the inevitabilities of time will limit them. In a fallen world the desire for a union of word and world, humankind and the divine only emphasizes the ironic gap between the ideal and the actual, the godlike and the human. The author and the audience, who also share an omniscience, learn by analogy that they, too, cannot be godlike in their history, in their representations and misrepresentations. Intention and reception are as human as they are godlike, as diachronic as they are synchronic.

In these plays Shakespeare relates kingship to God through the divine right of kings and the challenges to it. Before proceeding to the plays, I want to provide some medieval and Renaissance legal and political ideas that lie behind the key words "God" and "king," which characters reiterate from *Richard II* to *Henry V*.

As long ago as the middle ages, if not before, as Ernst Kantorowicz has noted, people conceived of the division between the king's two bodies: the divine and the human.[15] Such a division has important implications for the mature history plays of Shakespeare's Second, or Lancastrian Tetralogy. The significance of these plays lies partly in the dynamic representation of the tension in the king as a representative of human nature and the body politic. Those who witness the play are like the author and characters because they struggle to make sense of history, of human and divine authority, and they contend with the problem of interpretation. They grapple with such issues as where fact ends and interpretation begins and the relation between word and world, language and power. Language, as Foucault, Barthes, Eco, and others have noted, expresses power, so that ideology, or attitudes to power, takes shape in rhetoric, which orders and systematizes language.[16] In the Second Tetralogy the king himself cannot control his own power or his language about kingship no matter how much he tries. The society and the king create a fiction of the king's two bodies to accommodate their mutual power and vulnerability. The words "God" and "king" provide a locus for questions of power, truth, and interpretation, but they can be understood better through some of the political, theological, and legal contexts for Shakespeare's dramatic representation of kingship. By examining some of the uses of the word "king" and other signs of rule and authority in these plays, I hope to demonstrate that once the sanctity of the king's natural or mortal body is challenged then that of his political or divine body is soon called into question.

The word "God," to which the characters make frequent and diverse appeals, is highly contested. If, according to the doctrine of the king's two bodies, one aspect of kingship is divine, then there must be similar contestable appeals to kingship. The attempts to co-opt the word "king" and its cognates relate closely to the arguments over the word "God." In the Second Tetralogy, then, Shakespeare represents the conflict over the king's authority and how—when rules are contested in politics, which is closely allied to theology and the law—the pattern of history appears controversial if not arbitrary and the participants attempt to use verbal, military, and other power to occupy the throne and make an official history. As much as the characters in the Second Tetralogy claim that the authority of the king is godlike, in the blindness and confusion of a fallen world they cannot prove the king's divine right and place in a providential plan but, instead, constitute opposing sides with conflicting and confusing claims. God and kingship are political, and because Shakespeare subverts or qualifies the authority of the king's party and of the rebels no position can claim historical truth plain and simple. Shakespeare's tetralogy neither confirms nor disclaims that the king has the right to authority or has none. It represents both sides, if not many sides, of the debate on kingship and authority and shows their strengths and weaknesses.

As the doctrine of the king's two bodies contains within it disjunctions and paradoxes that complicate the idea of kingship, it is necessary to discuss briefly that doctrine before proceeding to an examination of appeals to God, and their implications for kingship, in the plays themselves. Even though there are many sources that elaborate the king's two bodies, I shall use illustrations that will be familiar to readers of Ernst Kantorowicz's indispensable work and of Marie Axton's complementary study, *The Queen's Two Bodies,* which takes on great importance, as Elizabeth was the English prince in the 1590s.[17] Edmund Plowden's *Commentaries or Reports*, which was written and collected during the reign of Elizabeth the First, outlines the difference between the king's "Body mortal" and "Body politic," the first "subject to all Infirmities" of nature, the second, which "cannot be seen or handled," not subject to nature. Plowden concludes, "what the King does in his Body politic, cannot be invalidated or frustrated by any Disability in his natural Body."[18] Kantorowicz notes the usefulness of this idea while implying its absurdity for twentieth-century readers because, like other concepts, it has been stripped of its historical context, although it is perhaps no more outlandish than the fictions that we use in an age familiar with Orwellian doublethink. The medieval idea of the king's *character angelus*, which likens the king's body politic to sprites and angels because they all represent the immutable in time, is, for Kantorowicz, a precursor to the ideas of Elizabethan jurists like Plowden, whose concepts also resemble those of medieval jurists. Theology, law, and politics are bound up in the middle ages and the Renaissance. If in Elizabethan juridical theory the two bodies cannot be distinguished, in practice the natural body and the political body are distinguishable but indivisible. The latter is superior to the former and can dignify the mortal part of the king and so give him godlike legal power as a man (*deus absconditus*). This fiction or paradox finds a crisis in death when the two bodies separate, for the mortal man ceases but the political man continues: "The king is dead; long live the king!"

Christian tradition provides a linguistic and theoretical background to the doctrine of the king's two bodies. Kantorowicz's analysis of *Richard II* reveals, as Axton also notes, Shakespeare's acquaintance with the jurists' royal Christology. Axton is perceptive in noting the complex relation between language, theology, and law that surrounded the doctrine as Shakespeare found it:

> An elaborate tradition of ritual and belief justified the Church's share in Christ's immortality. But there were no tenets in either law or theology stating plainly that Christ guaranteed immortality to England. There was only an analogy. Only by metaphor could the king impart immortality to the state and the state reciprocate the gift. Lacking an acknowledged tradition which would make their theory acceptable law, the lawyers attempted to cross the irrational abyss with a bridge of legal logic. (14)

This use of language to rationalize one's view is akin to the strategy that Bolingbroke and his son use in calling themselves king. They appropriate Richard's divine right, in which he represents Christ the king through the word "king," but by doing so oppose the possibility of making the term "king" correspond to the person of the monarch. Perhaps the conflict between those who see the king as God's deputy and those who see him as anyone who has the power and prowess to call himself king (even if the new king appeals to the old view of divine right as a means of keeping others from taking his crown) resembles what Richard Waswo calls the "semantic shift" in the Renaissance. Waswo argues that during the Renaissance a shift occurred from "referential to relational semantics," from "the cosmetic view" to "the constitutive view," from meaning as clothing to meaning as articulation. Waswo aptly states: "The word, of man and of God, is one of the primary energies of the period that is liberated. Free, it causes problems so tremendous that they must finally be evaded."[19] In the Second Tetralogy the problem becomes the following: is the word "king" a container for the man who is king, or is it a word that can be associated with anyone if it is articulated enough? In other words, does the term "king" signify one person that God authorizes to represent him in nature, or does the word rely on human power to maintain the relation between word and world? The doctrine of the king's (or the queen's) two bodies reveals a tension between the monarch as an immortal representative of God and the monarch as a mortal, changeable, and even expendable agent.

The doctrine was not, then, simply an arcane discussion in the Elizabethan Inns of Court but had its foundations in medieval law and theology. The succession of Elizabeth preoccupied lawyers, theologians, and dramatists throughout her reign. The *Duchy of Lancaster Case* (1561), first printed in Plowden's *Reports* (1571), and *Calvin's Case* (1608), first printed in Edward Coke's *Reports*, focus the debate of the king's two bodies. In the former case Elizabeth wanted to invalidate a grant of land that Edward the Sixth gave as a minor so that she could give the land to someone else. The judges ruled that Edward contained the body politic and so his body was never underage and, therefore, Elizabeth's claim was unwarranted, a ruling that the queen could never have overturned as hard as she tried (see Axton, 16–17). The latter case decided whether Robert Calvin, a Scot, was an alien in England. It was crucial in determining whether James the First's body could rule over Scotland and England as if they were one kingdom, but the case also reopened the debate on whether James was an alien who had no right to rule England or was a legitimate heir to Elizabeth. In the minds of the jurists the doctrine of the king's two bodies was crucial in deciding the power of the monarch and the right to succession. This historical, political, and legal context surrounded the drama, so that the Shakespearean history play could only express a controversy that reached a crisis in the reigns of Elizabeth the First, James the First, and Charles the

First. In act 2, scene 4 of *1 Henry VI* Shakespeare himself could set the succession debate and the beginnings of the War of the Roses in a fictional quarrel among aristocratic students at the Inns of Court.

Plowden helped to popularize this mystical doctrine until playwrights shared with lawyers like Bacon and Coke an interest in the subject. In this view the dead king and the living king become incarnated immortally in the King. According to Coke in *Calvin's Case*, the natural body is subject to death, but the "politique body . . . is framed by the policy of man" (also known as the "mystical body") and is "immortal, invisible, not subject to death." Allegiance, Coke concludes, is due to the king's natural body, which is always accompanied by the political body. This raises problems, however, because the natural body gains in authority from its immortal and invisible counterpart (1–2). To pledge allegiance to the natural body is to make the pledge changeable. The conflation of policy and mysticism, humanity and divinity reveals a tension between the two regal bodies, if not a will to believe or an ambivalence in the theorists and subjects themselves. Shakespeare's Richard the Second likens himself to Christ at a critical moment of betrayal, a comparison that seems monomaniacal to some modern audiences but that makes sense in the traditions of *imitatio Christi* (behaving like a fool in Christ) and the king's two bodies, in which he is like Christ, mortal and immortal (IV.i.168–76). The Elizabethan concept of the king's two bodies raises questions similar to those that arise from the medieval idea of the two natures of Christ. The Christian images that Henry the Fourth and Henry the Fifth use also make more sense in the context of these two ideas, although a modern audience may experience some alienation in which the historical context has fallen away and made the doctrine of the king's two bodies seem ridiculous, as F. W. Maitland suggested at the turn of our century.[20] In both medieval canon law and theology the church and its society was considered a *corpus mysterium* in which Christ is the head. Like Christ, the king is temporal and sempiternal, material and immaterial. In the complex world of the Second Tetralogy the characters and the audience will probably agree with Coke that "a king's crown was a hieroglyphic of the laws" (7). An ironic gap exists between the human and the divine, so that the characters inhabit a fallen world of interpretation. Like the king and author, the audience has two bodies—the godlike and the human, the omniscient and the ignorant. Through dramatic irony, Shakespeare explores the power and limitations of king and subject and, by implication, of author and audience.

The conflicting and dramatic nature of the doctrine of the king's two bodies was not lost on the playwrights of the English Renaissance. Anne Barton discusses, as a separate genre, history plays between 1561 and 1642 that represent the "king as common man."[21] Axton traces the relation between law, political theology, and drama in representations of advice on succession or apparent challenges to authority, which occur in the revels of the Inns of Court during the middle ages and the Renaissance and in the Senecan plays of the 1560s. *Gorboduc* becomes an obvious focus for her analysis and illustrates her view that theatrical conventions protected the dramatist and left him less vulnerable to censure or punishment than the jurist was. The queen does not seem to have punished an author of an Inns of Court play (3, 38–54). Axton also reminds us that Plowden, who did not publish his succession treatise for fear of reprisal, said that the monarch's two bodies existed in Trojan times and followed its manifestations from Greek to English rulers. She also notes that Plowden uses Ovid's tale of the sacrifice of Iphigenia as an example of the king's two bodies (18, 26–27). Other fictions persisted in the court entertainments between 1575 and 1590. To match the queen's immortal political body, Leicester's poets, like George Ferrer and George Gascoigne, created in the Kenilworth entertainments a double mythical immortality when they gave him Olympian and Arthurian pedigrees (62–66). As Axton notes, contrary to Irving Ribner's view, historical romances, like Robert Greene's *Friar Bacon*, may by the very improbability of their magical or theatrical solutions be showing skepticism and political awareness (74).[22] The imprisonment of Peter Wentworth, who was questioned by Thomas Sackville (one of the authors of *Gorboduc*), implies that the playhouses seemed safer than Parliament for a discussion of succession. Characters in Elizabethan history plays, Axton says, rarely express uncontradicted a contractual view of kingship, although *Woodstock* represents such an idea: the king should govern well or lose the right to reign (89–90, 97). The notion of the king's two bodies was not, from about 1561 onward, a rarefied idea. It may have received its greatest public exposure on the stage.

The doctrine of the king's two bodies had political as well as theological and dramatic significance for the Elizabethans. Tillyard aptly notes the *Homily of Obedience* (1547), which attempts to assert regal control: "In earth God hath assigned kings princes with other governors under them, all in good and necessary order."[23] Shakespeare's Second Tetralogy may have produced a historical situation in which critics fight over Shakespeare's two bodies just as lawyers, theologians, and characters in the drama fought over the king's natural and political bodies in Elizabethan days. Just as the jurists mined precedents from the past to make their case in the present, so too do we make cases out of the Elizabethans for our own ends. This tetralogy emphasizes the complexity and difficulty of truth in history for us as well as for Shakespeare and his characters.

It is not surprising that in the view of the characters if the king has two bodies, one divine and one human, the persons in the play would appeal to God for kingly authority.[24] The contentious issue is whether the Word must legitimate words, whether God must support his representative on earth. Such appeals uncover the desire to legitimate and sanctify one's actions and words. If the fallible interpretation of original and divine authority throws into question human authority, history, as past event and as writing about the past to and for the present, threatens to become chaotic and senseless. Even though the audience has come to recognize the limited nature of its human hermeneutic, it also has to keep in mind the possibility of evaluating with rigor the evidence and attempting to find out the precarious and evasive historical truth. From *Richard II* to *Henry V*, Shakespeare represents many-sided and conflicting appeals to God that appear to suggest that humans operate in a fallen history in which truth is elusive. The human agents appeal to divine authority as a means of enabling their power, so that the king represents himself as God's substitute on earth. The usurper, on the other hand, legitimizes his power and appeals to himself as God's substitute, but his fellow rebels remind him that he cannot appeal to the mystical divine right that he demystified.

The otherworldliness in these plays is very much of the world. *Richard II* begins with the mystery of the murder of Gloucester. For the audience, it seems that only God knows who has done what. In a reversal of dramatic irony, Shakespeare reminds the audience of its limitations, as the characters seem to know more than it does. Although in the opening scenes Richard, Mowbray, and Bolingbroke all speak about England with great devotion and all appeal to God to witness their truth, none wins our unqualified sympathy (I.i.114, 187). Shakespeare avoids siding with any character. For instance, against the Duchess of Gloucester's desire for revenge against Richard for Gloucester's death, Shakespeare balances Gaunt's answer: "God's is the quarrel" if "God's substitute" has wrongfully caused Gloucester's death (I.ii.30–41). Both want vengeance, but, whereas the Duchess tends toward retribution, Gaunt shows a Christian duty by deferring judgment to God. The sound of "God" also echoes in the self-righteous but contradictory pronouncements of the second confrontation between Bolingbroke and Mowbray (I.iii.20, 37, 78, 85, 180, 183, 204). Other contradictory claims on God persist. Richard even prays to God to help him to acquire the Lancastrian lands by causing Gaunt's death (I.iv.59). York protests in God's name against this unjust seizure of the Lancastrian lands, but Richard ignores the criticism and makes York lord protector (II.i.200). Northumberland and the other rebels swear before God their resistance to this errant policy (II.i.238, 251). The Queen invokes God in her fear of Bolingbroke's landing, while York in his frustration swears by God (II.ii.51, 76, 98–100). Nor will Bolingbroke leave events up to God, for Richard's appropriation of his land appears more important than the life of his uncle Gloucester. Richard identifies with Christ but also vacillates between seeing himself as God's deputy on the one hand and wanting to be a private man on the other (III.ii.60, 98–101, 115, iii.77, 85; IV.i.169–76, 214–15). Opposed to this authority is Bolingbroke's rebellion, which entails coming for his own as much as avenging Richard for contravening divine laws. In a situation that is almost an ironic reversal of the opening of the play, Carlisle prophesies that the deposition of Richard will bring God's pestilence on Bolingbroke (IV.i.114–49), just as Gaunt had prophesied a similar fate for Richard. A character like York changes sides when Richard is no longer the legal, or at least potent, king and Bolingbroke is. York says that during the coronation people cried "God save" for Bolingbroke but not for

Richard and attributes this preference to God's purpose (V.ii.10–40). Bolingbroke says in response to Aumerle's conspiracy "I pardon him, as God shall pardon me" (V.iii.4, 129). Although Bolingbroke appears to be confident in his ability to be subject to divine forgiveness, he speaks in a more doubtful and tenuous context, for he cannot let Richard live and understands how horrible is the deed he will have Exton do. He would also banish his henchman and promise a pilgrimage in guilt although really unable to do penance. The last reference to God especially destabilizes self-righteousness and all certainty in the invocation of God and in Bolingbroke's claim to the throne and leads to the idea of right political action sanctioned by heaven and theology. This network of shifting meanings of God's relation to kingship and the polity represents the multiplicitous relation between religion and politics, the governor and the governed.

In the *Henry IV* plays, as in *Richard II*, the characters contradict themselves in their invocations of God. They find themselves in a dilemma. Those who want the power of kingship must discredit it and then reinstate it when they become king. A corollory of this dilemma is that to challenge the king one must separate the king's two bodies and question his divine function while concentrating on his human foibles. In *1 Henry IV* Henry calls Hal God's scourge against his father but says he does not know God's displeasure (*1HIV*, III.ii.4–11). Punning veers from the literal often by the arbitrary means of yoking identical sound with disparate meaning; so to modify the word "God" in multiple human contexts. This verbal play shapes new fictions that counterbalance the fiction of the divine in the doctrine of the king's two bodies.[25] To yoke God with money is and is not arbitrary, for the author seems to stress redemption and the mercenary use of God for human power. Most of the characters' jests about God and the spirit relate to money, so that Shakespeare joins the sacred and the profane. Falstaff mentions God while punning on "grace" and plays the pious Puritan, calling smugly on God while addressing Hal as a sinner. Twisting the scriptures himself, he accuses the prince of this perversion (I.ii.80–90, 147–49). This hypocritical stance resembles Henry's attitude to his son. Hotspur also displays his limitations through this imagery, proclaiming in his anger over Henry's treatment of the Percies and

Mortimer, "By the God he shall not have a Scot of them, / No, if a Scot would save his soul he shall not," quibbling on "scot," a small payment, and "soul" or "sol," the alchemical word for gold or a French coin (II.iv.132, 385f., 464–68).[26] Once again, Hal stands between his two rivals, for he too subjects God to coinage. The prince expresses his plan for reformation in a monetary metaphor, promising to "pay the debt I never promised" (I.ii.204). Pecuniary language is part of the Christian tradition. To redeem is to buy back. But the characters make their sacred trust in such extended puns that they seem in part to parody the Christianity that they profess or adapt. In a scene dominated by the theme of debt, Hal says that he is the good angel for Falstaff, who then asks the prince to rob the exchequer again, for Hal has paid back the stolen money (III.iii.176f.). Punning on "angel" and yoking once more the sacred and the secular, Hal would be both a heavenly guardian and a gold coin.[27] Amid the preparations for the battle, the prince has time to pun on "death" as "debt," telling Falstaff that he owes God a death (V.i.126).[28] Although Hal has paid Sir John's financial debts, he may be acting as self-righteously as his father, for, rejecting Falstaff later, he seems to lose both a generous and self-critical side of his personality, though it is difficult to imagine him as king with Sir John at his side. Characters from court, rebel camp, Wales, and tavern all show their limitations by swearing by God, claiming him for their own, or making him witness to their oaths (V.ii.35, iii.34, 51, iv.10–16, 50, 68, 162). Part Two and *Henry V* qualify the notion that God seems to bless Hal at the end of Part One. The religious punning helps destabilize the idea of God and heaven by modifying transcendental authority with play and multiple meanings, but, as the characters increasingly reveal their blindness and shortcomings, their modification of divine authority calls itself into question. To question the Word with words is to make it harder for others, like Falstaff and the taverners, to believe that the ruler is not himself in part a rebel against kingly authority and the divine right and makes it more difficult for him to rule. The mortal body of the monarch reminds the audience of his fallibility and his reliance on his subjects.

Part Two of *Henry IV* provides particularly good examples of the verbal war over God. Characters on all sides continue to claim God for their own, whether they think he is condoning their free will or exonerating them through his will. Part Two represents in the rejection of Falstaff a crisis between the private and public roles of kingship and continues to show the chaotic consequences of questioned and questionable authority. In oaths, curses, expressions, exhortations, and justifications, the characters all use the name of God. While the house of Lancaster believes that God is on its side, the men of the tavern and Gloucestershire curse and salute in God's name, and the rebels claim God for their own. Ironic contradictions abound in the claim of God's blessing for the ruling house. When Henry says that "God knows" that he had no intent to seize the crown, the expression takes on more weight than it usually does, for throughout the play the king worries about what God thinks of his actions (III.i.72–74). This disavowal is ironic because, if "necessity" alone made Henry assume the throne, then it is incongruous that he is so haunted by Richard's prophecy that he later claims to have come to power by "crook'd ways" and that he asks God's forgiveness for his assumption of the throne and for his reign. Henry's self-exoneration occurs as a parenthesis in his fearful speech about the prophet, Richard. Just before the disavowal, Henry had lamented his own blindness to the pattern of life and time: "O God, that one might read the book of fate, / And see the revolution of the times" (III.i.45–46ff.). The audience is reminded of a similar frustration that it thinks of in reading or hearing Henry's words. Later, Henry maintains that "if God doth give successful end / To this debate that bleedeth at our doors," then the king will lead the youth of England on a crusade (IV.iv.1–4). The king, God knows, will not or cannot keep his promise. Henry praises God because he will die in the Jerusalem chamber (IV.v.234–40). There seems to be an irony in the relation between Henry and his God and between all the characters and their Maker (God) as well as their maker (playwright). The audience or reader is not necessarily exempt from this ironic anxiety.

It is also ironic that in the midst of what will soon be revealed as treachery, Westmoreland interjects, amid his hope for peace, the phrase "which God so frame!" (IV.i.180). Seemingly, the peace that Westmoreland and John of Lancaster achieve will be founded on the deception of human policy and not on the design of God. It is these two characters who "frame" the rebels. In condemning the Archbishop, Lancaster interprets the ways of God to men. According to

Lancaster, Scroop was reputed to be learned in the "books of God," to be "th'imagined voice of God himself, / The very opener and intelligencer / Between the grace . . . of heaven, / And our dull workings." John displaces the Archbishop as the interpreter of God by condemning him and his interpretation. Counterfeiting himself, he says that Scroop erred in persuading the subjects of God's "substitute" on earth, "Under the counterfeited zeal of God," to rebel against the king and his heavenly peace (IV.ii.16–30). Lancaster is using an argument equally applicable to his father's rebellion against Richard. After this upbraiding, he lies to Scroop and then claims righteousness: "Strike up the drums, pursue the scatter'd stray: / God, and not we, hath safely fought today" (IV.ii.120–21). Even if this couplet did not sound false, and even if Lancaster's cause was just, he has broken a rule of ethics, has breached his "Christian care," for the end does not justify the means, and he may have contravened the honesty demanded by a soldier's honor. On the other hand, John thinks that he has not lied but has told the truth with precision and that he will sacrifice the lives of a few to save the lives of many.[29] Perhaps he also thinks that whatever happens is the working of Providence and that God would not have let him achieve victory if he were not right. Appeals to God are as complex as the myth of the Fall and the relation of free will to determinism, so that it is our awareness of this complexity, and not its resolution, that ironizes the claim that this and other plays in the Second Tetralogy are strictly providential and the absolutely opposite view.

Shakespeare links Hal and Henry by showing the closeness of their views about the will of God. Although Hal can joke with Bardolph about the grace of God, as Falstaff does in Part One, he becomes more like his father as the play progresses (II.ii.69–70; *1HIV*, I.ii.16–21, cf. I.i.49, II.i.70). Hal's grace and mercy will not necessarily be as close to God's as he thinks. Like Henry, Hal considers that God will be good to him, guarding the crown—which his father will soon reclaim—from intruders. Unintentionally, Hal has usurped his father's crown and now swears by God how he grew cold considering the death of his father. After the reconciliation, Henry claims that he knows the divine will: God made Hal take the crown to increase his father's love through an eloquent defense (IV.v.177–80, cf. 149–51). Shakespeare makes the king's view of God and of his own kingship complicated, for Henry understands the convolutions of power, saying that "God knows" the "by-paths and the indirect crook'd ways" by which he attained the crown and that as king he knows "How troublesome it sat upon my head" (IV.v.183–86). Just when Henry seems to admit wrongdoing, he cannot tell explicitly about his assumption of power: "How I came by the crown, O God forgive, / And grant it may with thee in true peace live!" (IV.v.218–19). With the phrase "O God forgive," the king only implies his wrongs, but his recommendation to Hal that he fight foreign wars shows that Henry still schemes. Apparently, the prince endorses such Machiavellian piety, though Hal makes his hopes for successful rule conditional upon God's benevolence (IV.v.202–24; V.ii.143–45). No matter how many "God saves" Sir John utters, Henry the Fifth banishes him, warning him not to treat his king as the friend he was, "For God doth know, so shall the world perceive, / That I have turn'd away my former self" (V.v.57–58). Hal has literally converted, having turned about as well as turning away his former self, as if all sacrilege could now cease and a new self could be made ex nihilo, discontinuous from its former existence before God without divine grace. The new king appears to believe even more firmly than his father that his own actions are divinely sanctioned. This conversion was, however, partly planned by the prince if we can believe Hal in the second scene of *1 Henry IV*, where he speaks as if he were a god unto himself.

The rebels and taverners refer to God as much as the kings and court do. The Archbishop revolts in God's name, but, while the rebels hold up the example of the wronged Richard, the dissidents do not often call directly on God to justify their cause. Tavern and Gloucestershire modify the Lancastrian view of God. The tavern takes God more lightly, except for Sir John's fear of hell, and a little less self-righteously than the court. Falstaff's jokes have serious ironic consequences, for what he says in jest the new king will say in earnest. When the Chief Justice exclaims, "Well, God send the Prince a better companion!" Sir John replies, "God send the companion a better prince!" (I.ii.199–200). As a public man, Falstaff ignores his vices as much as Henry tries to deny his, though he sometimes admits his sins in private. Of Shallow, Sir John says: "Lord, Lord, how this world is given to lying!" echoing his self-righteous and mock-puritanical words to Hal, to whom he had lied about killing Hotspur, in Part One: "Lord, Lord, how this world is given to lying!" (*2HIV*, III.ii.296–98; *1HIV*, V.iv.144–45). Not only does Falstaff take the Lord's name in vain but he also parodies two biblical passages on judgment and hypocrisy. In addition to emphasizing the theatrical nature of selfhood as Hal's conversion did, this parody may reveal the deceptive ways of some of the Puritans (a convenient label for many different and complex "Calvinist" or "fundamentalist" groups, which history has rightly or wrongly made stick), but it also exposes Falstaff through irony. Christ says: "Not euery one that sayeth unto me, Lorde, Lorde, shall enter into the kingdome of heaven, but he that doeth my Fathers will which is heaven." Jesus then talks about those who in the Day of Judgment will cry "Lord, Lord" and claim to have prophesied and done wonderful works in his name, but swears he will reject them, saying: "I neuer knew you: depart from me, yee that work iniquitie" (Matthew 7:21–23). Whereas Falstaff is obsessed with damnation and cries "Lord, Lord" for amusement, Henry the Fifth will speak words like those of Christ, "I know thee not, old man," to begin the rejection speech. In parodying hypocrites, Sir John becomes one, pledging redemption but never redeeming himself, so that the words of Jesus become ironic: "But why call ye mee Master, master, & do not the things yet I speake?" (Luke 6:46). Even though Shakespeare identifies Hal with Christ and Falstaff with the "wicked," the wider context, the contradictory claim and behavior of the members of the house of Lancaster, calling on God to justify their questionable actions, qualifies their justness. If Falstaff is a hypocrite, someone who pretends to be something he is not—if questions of self are so black and white—then Henry the Fifth and his family can also be hypocrites. The audience must decide whether Hal is invested with the authority of Christ or is unconsciously parodying him. The nagging critical questions about the rejection, about the status and nature of Henry the Fifth and Falstaff, demonstrate the ironic instability of these characters. Even if Sir John and Shallow lace their drinking songs with God, this "divine comedy" qualifies the self-righteous calls on God by the royal house (V.iii.5, 18). When the Hostess, who is being arrested by the king's officers, inverts the proverb "O God, that right should thus overcome might!" her words may be inverting the respective positions of court and tavern. In the references to God in this and the other plays of the tetralogy we discover inscrutability, so that we are fallen into language even though we partake of the more omniscient view that the playwight's dramatic irony gives us. The four plays all reveal this contradictory and limiting appeal to the word "God" and related terms.

In *Henry V* the appeal to God occurs throughout, from the clergy's debating the reasons for war in France, to the punishment of the traitors who recommend the punishment of others, to Henry's asking God forgiveness for the murder of Richard and his celebration of God's hand in the great English victory at Agincourt, and beyond. The most striking manifestations of the ambivalent use of God in the play are, first, the ambiguity over whether the clerics' motivation for explicating for Henry his right to succession in France is self-serving and financial, or religious and patriotic, and, second, the disjunction between Henry's public confidence in God's will being done through him and in his own divine body on the one hand and his private doubts over his right to rule, his relation to God, and his family's treatment of Richard on the other. The king triumphs, but, as the Epilogue and the First Tetralogy remind us, the house of Lancaster soon suffers another fall.

The equivocation over God complicates notions of kingship in *Henry V*. The private and public contexts for Henry's view of God neither make the king just nor unjust but rather render him divided and complex. Even though Scroop and Henry agree that God has uncovered the conspiracy of Scroop and his confederates against God, and even though Cambridge, a coconspirator, and Henry associate God and king, these interpretations are not so straightforward (II.ii.151, 158–60, 166, 179–91). In the next scene Shakespeare presents the Hostess's report of Falstaff's death, which qualifies Henry's confident talk about God: " 'How now, Sir John?' quoth I: 'what, man! be o' good cheer.' So a' cried out 'God, God, God!' three or four times: now I, to comfort him, bid him a' should not think of God, I hop'd there was no need to trouble himself with any such thoughts yet" (II.iii.18–23). Falstaff's anguish about his relation to God contrasts with Henry's present certainty about his own relation with heaven and foreshadows the king's coming uncertainty. Canterbury and Ely think of Henry as a reformed Adam and worry

about the heavy taxes that the king might levy against the church
(I.ii). Although Henry himself repeatedly calls on God to help him
with his right in France, he later shows doubt in his role as God's
deputy (I.ii.23, 222, 262, 289–310; IV.i.171–92, 295–311). Henry
uses the name of God to justify his actions, either himself or through
his surrogates, but Bates and Williams shake his confidence in his
identification with God (II.iv.77; III.i.34). Even the comic invocations of God by Pistol, Fluellen, and Macmorris modify Henry's
unique and solemn relation with God (III.ii.8, 80–116, vi.10, 23).
Bardolph hangs, even if the king is also a thief. Henry asks God's
forgiveness for bragging before Montjoy and says with more pride
than humility, "We are in God's hand" and not in the clutch of the
French (III.vii.155, 174). Henry's brash imputation of evil to the
French soon turns to an examination of the darkness within him
(IV.i.3–5, 298–300). Shakespeare repeats the interspersion of Henry's
invocations of God with the comical appeals that Pistol, the French,
and Fluellen make to God (IV.iii.78, 120, iv.1–11, v.1–6, vii.35–36,
89, 146, 168, viii.66; V.i.69). The encounter with Bates and Williams
and the admission before God of the Lancastrians' mishandling of
Richard do not create a chastened public image, for Henry continues
to thank God for his victory and sees divine sanction in his wooing
of Katharine (IV.viii.108–25, ii.145–56). The friction between the
private and public uses of the word "God," as well as the disjunction
between solemn and comic uses, qualify the reference and appeal to
the transcendental. These contending significations underscore the
fallenness of human language in the most important matter, in the
ultimate appeal to authority for human action.

The contradictions and dilemmas in the relation between "God's
substitute" and God leads to the related issue of kingship. The king,
a man and a ruler, God's substitute to some and he who holds power
to others, occupies the center of these plays.[30] No matter what
Plowden, Coke, and other supporters of the doctrine of the king's
two bodies maintained, it was not an uncontested view. The trouble
is that kingship has fallen and that others challenge the authority of
the king and the idea of single united rule in all four plays. The more
the assertion of authority, the more the challenge to it. Rather than
take sides in the debate on succession, as Ernest Talbert and Henry

Kelly have argued, Shakespeare represents the conflicting and intricate assertions of the various claimants.[31]

At the beginning of *Richard II,* Shakespeare represents the Lancastrian opposition to Richard as a tyrant, not as a ruler to be obeyed for his divine right, and makes it resound throughout the tetralogy. Bolingbroke challenges Mowbray for the murder of Woodstock and so the king. When Richard attempts to assert his power, he turns it into tyranny, for he expropriates Bolingbroke's lands not out of a sense of justice but out of a need of money for wars and perhaps of revenge against the house of Lancaster. Richard's dilemma is that if he does not assert his authority, someone else will assume it, but, if he does too much, then someone will claim it nonetheless. As soon as the king is not seen as the agent of God with no questions asked, he is subject to human interpretation, and the word "king" loses its absolute authority. Just as the Word in the Bible becomes words with interpretation, so too does kingship in a fallen political world. Gaunt would let God punish his substitute, but Bolingbroke will substitute himself for Richard. Soon England finds itself with two kings—Richard and Bolingbroke—and we find ourselves in York's situation, having to choose between kings who both wrong and are wronged. York chastens Northumberland for dropping the "King" before Richard but later chooses the king who has the most power: Bolingbroke. The word "king"—and related words like "liege," "sovereign," and "highness"—becomes as displaced as the people who occupy the throne. The deposition scene uses stage symbolism to illustrate this political and linguistic struggle, for Richard and Bolingbroke grip the crown from either side. For Bolingbroke the embarrassment and for Richard the pain derive from two kings coexisting. No one can shout with certainty "The king is dead, long live the king!"

Richard's authority as king is called into question from the beginning of the play. By the middle of the action, the ambivalence of Richard's claim to kingship appears in his language. After Richard returns to England from Ireland, Carlisle reminds the king that he is God's representative: "That Power that made you king / Hath power to keep you king in spite of all" (III.ii.27–28). Aumerle, however, appeals to pragmatic and earthly means of exacting God's work.

This is the last moment when Richard is certain of his immortal or political body:

> Not all the water in the rough rude sea
> Can wash the balm off from an anointed king;
> The breath of worldly men cannot depose
> The deputy elected by the Lord;
> For every man that Bolingbroke hath press'd
> To lift shrewd steel against our golden crown,
> God for his Richard hath in heavenly pay
> A glorious angel: then, if angels fight,
> Weak men must fall, for heaven still guards the right.
>
> (III.ii.54–62)

Shakespeare qualifies Richard's proud proclamation of the divine power that God has invested in him, for Salisbury enters and announces that the Welshmen have fled to Bolingbroke.

Richard tries to recuperate: "I had forgot myself, am I not king? / Awake, thou coward majesty! thou sleepest. / Is not the king's name twenty thousand names? / Arm, Arm, my name! a puny subject strikes / At thy great glory" (III.ii.83–87). But he cannot overpower events with rhetoric, lend his nominal apostrophe the force of ritual magic, and ignore the terrible news of Bolingbroke's successful rebellion: "All goes worse than I have power to tell" (III.ii.120). Minutes later, Richard dwells on death and his mortal body: "Let's talk of graves, of worms, and epigraphs, / Make dust our paper, . . . / For God's sake let us sit upon the ground / And tell sad stories of the death of kings" (III.ii.145–46, 155–56). Richard's views on his two bodies shift over the course of this scene. In the first instance Richard says that his "name" is worth twenty thousand names and apostrophizes—"Arm, arm, my name!" as if the term "king" has power enough to assert authority. Soon, however, Richard learns the disjunction between the power and name of king and, in the second instance, he tells how kings have been deposed, slain, and poisoned for their crown, where an allegorical death keeps his court, allows the king "a little scene," infuses him "with self and vain conceit," and, the pomp allowed to swell, deflates the king. In this view the king is a player king and not the king himself, an on-stage reference that calls attention to the impotence of the theater before the world. Richard now asks his subjects to throw away reverence and ceremony because he considers himself a mere man with ordinary needs and wants, and adds: "subjected thus, / How can you say to me, I am a king?" To have authority over his subjects the king must be subjected to their protection in the name of God, for once they think that God no longer sanctifies him, they leave him unprotected and the king is only a name and his power and authority are unfounded.[32] Shakespeare has Richard repeat plays on "king," its cognates, and related words: "Go to Flint Castle, there I'll pine away— / A king, woe's slave, shall kingly woe obey" (III.ii.209–10). In addition to disregarding Carlisle's advice to be wise and not to bewail his woes, Richard emphasizes his sadness over the rift between the king as person and as ruler.

The beginning of the next scene also stresses the word "king" when Northumberland says "Richard" and York chastens him for not saying "King Richard." The third scene of act 3 concentrates on the title of "king," so that York's correction of Northumberland leads Percy to call the king "King Richard" and Bolingbroke to do so five times in one speech. York, who is so censorious on Richard's behalf, sounds surprised when he sees his monarch: "Yet looks he like a king." Richard describes himself as Northumberland's "lawful king," wonders where the evidence is that God has dismissed him from his stewardship, and prophesies that God, his own master, will revenge himself against the rebels. Northumberland is afraid to breach openly this patriarchal status quo: "The King of Heaven forbid our lord the king / Should so with civil and uncivil arms / Be rush'd upon!" The chain of authority from God to monarch appears to make Northumberland uncomfortable with the challenge to the king's power. Richard invokes God and speaks about himself as "the king" in the third person and reiterates his nominal or titular concerns: "Must he lose / The name of king? a God's name, let it go." Richard would like to give up the public side of kingship for privacy and obscurity, until he is willing to descend into the base court, "where kings grow base, / To come at traitors' calls, and do them grace!" (III.iii.180–81). This king dramatizes what the word "king" means to him by contrasting public humiliation with private obscurity. He reveals his feeling of vulnerability when he imagines himself buried beneath "the king's highway, . . . where subjects' feet / May hourly trample on their sovereign's head" (155–57). Here, Richard becomes more aware of his mortal or natural body, although he speaks as if he is surprised that the king has a dual nature and is not revered as only divine. The Gardener, unlike Northumberland, calls his monarch "King Richard," but the name cannot save Richard, who is reduced to a private man, although the specter of his divinity haunts the subsequent three plays (III. v. 77, 83, 89).

Richard II is a series of crises over the meaning of kingship. In the next scene, an allegory of the kingdom as a second Eden, the Gardener reports that "Bolingbroke / Hath seiz'd the wasteful king." When the audience next sees Richard, he shifts the signifier "king" to Bolingbroke: "Alack, why am I sent for to a king / Before I have shook off the regal thoughts / Wherewith I reign'd?" (IV. i. 162–64). York is now being legalistic, telling Richard that he resigned his crown of his own free will, but Richard calls into doubt his willingness to resign and Bolingbroke's right to kingship, for he invites him to "seize" the crown. Richard wants, with Bolingbroke, to hold the crown, which would be a stage symbol of the predicament of the country, one symbol and two kings, an impossible situation if the king is God's deputy, trying to represent his Word on earth. Once there is no exact identification between the word "king" and the man who holds the office, kingship loses its authority. Although in *Calvin's Case* Edward Coke is discussing the significance of the crown and coronation for the kingship of James the First, he is writing in the tradition of Plowden and the Elizabethan succession debates of the 1590s and generalizes with the cases of other English monarchs, so that his observations pertain to the views of the crown that Shakespeare might have brought to the instance of Richard and Bolingbroke:

> In the first year of his Majesties [James the First's] reign, before his Majesties coronation, *Watson* and *Clerke*, Seminary priests, and others, were of the opinion, that his Majesty was no compleate and absolute King before his coronation, but that coronation did add a confirmation and perfection to the descent; and therefore (observe their damnable damned consequent) that they by strength and power might before his coronation take him and his royal issue into their possession, keep him

prisoner in the Tower, remove such Counsellors and great officers as pleased them, and constitute others in their places, & c. And that these and others of like nature could not be Treason against his Majesty, before he were a crowned King. But it was clearly resolved by all the Judges of *England*, that presently by the descent his Majesty was completely and absolutely King, without any essential ceremony or act to be done *ex post facto*, and that coronation was but an royal ornament, and outward solemnization of the descent.[33]

Coke, who was attorney general under Elizabeth the First, admits his opponents' arguments and so the existence of dissent and proceeds to oppose them by precedents and cases, such as Henry the Sixth being "absolute and compleate a King" before his coronation, which occurred eight years into his reign. There cannot be, in Coke's view, an interregnum. Perhaps, as Bolingbroke shares a similar view with Coke's opponents, in order to legitimize his own power he wants to take Richard's crown away and be crowned himself. Coke's discussion reveals that in Renaissance England there was anxiety over coronation, and this concern must have been especially acute in the deposition of a king—when two kings coexisted. Using Coke's kind of legal logic, Bolingbroke could never become king through coronation if the crown did not properly descend to him.

Carlisle opposes York and Bolingbroke in this exchange of kings. York, who once supported Richard as his king, now proclaims that Richard has adopted Bolingbroke as heir, forgetting how much force and duress that Bolingbroke has used to obtain this bill of succession. When York declares, "Ascend his throne, descending now from him, / And long live Henry, fourth of that name!" and Bolingbroke replies, "In God's name, I'll ascend the regal throne," Carlisle protests, "marry, God forbid!" and chides the whole company that no one there is worthy to judge Richard, for they are mere subjects:

> And shall the figure of God's majesty,
> His captain, steward, deputy elect,
> Anointed, crowned, planted many years,
> Be judg'd by subject and inferior breath,
> And he himself not present?
>
> (IV.i.125–29)

Repeating the word "king," Carlisle appeals to God and specifies his complaint against Herford, or Bolingbroke: "My Lord of Herford here, whom you call king, / Is a foul traitor to proud Herford's king, / And if you crown him, let me prophesy—" (134–36). After completing the list of pestilences that Carlisle foresees for England if it deposes Richard, which Carlisle frames in Christian language with threats from heaven and with the view that England will be like Golgotha and Richard like Christ crucified, he finds himself under arrest by Northumberland for treason. It seems that those with power define treason and that secular power, as much as it seeks religious justification for its actions, will use force against religious leaders to achieve political ends. Coke and Carlisle have a different view of treason from that of Bolingbroke and Northumberland. Thomas Egerton displays the ambivalence among Elizabethan jurists over kingship, which also occurred in the society at large, for in discussing authority he cites Saint Augustine on God's ordaining kings and authorizing them to govern their subjects but also Saint Cyprian of Carthage on the necessity of the ruler gaining popular consent. Egerton, or Ellesmere, wrote about the history of kingship in the *Post-Nati* and in 1608 had to rule on the relation between king and subjects in *Calvin's Case*. The debate on royal prerogative in the sixteenth and seventeenth centuries was founded on the medieval idea of the king's two bodies. If, as we have seen, the political body was the incorporation of the monarch and his subjects and the natural body was the part of him that was mysterious and never died, Egerton, who owed much to Jean Bodin and other Continental jurists, believed that the king had a single, natural body, although this jurist's views of kingship changed over his legal career. Many common lawyers, as Louis Nafla has observed, located sovereignty in the common law, which they placed above the king. In the *Discourse concerning the Prerogative of the Crown* William Camden and in *A breefe Proiect* John Dodderidge argued that the king had obligations that accompanied his prerogatives.[34] Like the French Calvinist jurist Lambert Daneau, Egerton thought of the state as a system of social groups joined by contracts and unified and led by the monarch. Some subjects believed in contract law, in which the rule of a king and the obedience of his subjects depended on an agreement between the two sides, so that when one party violated the terms the contract was broken. Thus the division in Shakespeare between Richard and the house of Lancaster is related to a pervasive legal, religious, and political rift in Renaissance England. It is no wonder that the interpretation of kingship and, more specifically, the word "king" is contradictory and charged and remains so throughout the tetralogy.

In the deposition scene Richard himself wavers, wanting and not wanting to resign, understanding that to keep up the illusion or fallen nature of the power and unity of kingship there can be only one king. He recognizes that he must die: "Long may'st thou live in Richard's seat to sit, / And soon lie Richard in an earthy pit. / God save King Henry, unking'd Richard says, / And send him many years of sunshine days!" (IV.i.218–21). To justify Bolingbroke's claim to the crown, Northumberland wants Richard to admit his crimes, but Richard emphasizes the greatest of political transgressions: deposition. Richard continues to show his instability and to destabilize kingship as he wishes he were "a mockery king of snow" to melt before the sun of Bolingbroke's kingship, characterizing the usurper as "Good king, great king, and yet not greatly good," and so attacking the ethical basis of rule. Holding the mirror he has asked for, he questions as much the mimesis of art as the representation of kingship, shattering it into slivers, but Bolingbroke is literal-minded and tries to protect his claim to the crown by saying that the mirror is the illusion and not the reality. Even in sarcasm Richard addresses Bolingbroke as king and speaks about himself as king only in the past tense: "I am greater than a king; / For when I was a king, my flatterers / Were then but subjects; being now a subject, / I have a king here to my flatterer" (IV.i.305–8). Richard uses the term "king" as a means of questioning kingship itself. He destabilizes the difference between king and subject, king and flatterer. When Bolingbroke will not grant Richard his last wish, the deposed king calls his situation "a true king's fall" and implies that Bolingbroke is neither a king nor true. The frequent repetition of the word "king" in the deposition scene, especially in Richard's mouth, is incremental, as the verbal exchange between the kings becomes as dramatic as the change of kings.

The deposition scene does not resolve the crisis in kingship because kingship continues in its various representations. The Queen still calls her husband "the king," "King Richard," and "king of beasts," but he can only play on her words and imagine her telling a tale of those who will mourn "For the deposing of a rightful king" (V.i.1–50). York describes the popularity of the newly crowned king and the unpopularity of the deposed king, so that two kings still occupy the play. He also depicts the two kings in theatrical terms, as if to show the staginess of politics, but justifies Bolingbroke's ascension through God's purpose (V.ii). York, the Duchess, and Aumerle call Bolingbroke "king," whereas Exton calls Bolingbroke and Richard king (V.ii–iv). Richard cannot give up the name of king, playing his own play of "Beggar and King," which Bolingbroke had participated in and witnessed (V.v.32–38, cf. iii). For Richard, he is a king or nothing. He cannot help playing with the word "king," saying that he is sometimes a beggar and sometimes a king—another opposition that Richard dissolves. In prison he imagines roles in which he is kinged and unkinged in an unhappy play about his past and present, but this temporal drama is not strictly fictional (V.v.31–41). Whereas the Groom calls Richard "king," Exton addresses Bolingbroke as "king," so that the juxtaposition of the two kings occurs to the very end of the play and continues after Richard's death (V.v, vi). That juxtaposition will persist into subsequent plays. Even when the king is dead, it is difficult to say "Long live the king!" because one king has expedited the death of the other, and there have been two kings for about half of the play.

The challenge to "kingship" continues in *1 Henry IV*, the memory of Richard haunting the office and the word. Henry the Fourth opens the play with an unsettled royal we, "So shaken as we are, so wan with care," so that kingship is troubled and faces opposition (I.i.1). In the first speech the king admits that he has to give up his crusade, which would deflect attention to foreign and religious matters, in order to address divisions over the legitimacy of his rule. The rebels defy Henry and his title, and Hotspur would raise Mortimer and depose the king; he then finds out from Worcester that Richard proclaimed Mortimer heir before leaving on the Irish expedition (I.iii). Hotspur now rails against Henry as "this subtle King," "this proud King," and the rebels, who helped raise Bolingbroke to the throne, would now topple him. King and rebels do not trust the grounds of the relation between monarch and subjects because it is merely one of power and convenience. For Hotspur, the king is "this vile politician Bolingbroke," "this king of smiles." He shows sympathy to Richard, whose side his family had opposed, and tries to rewrite history in order to undermine the legitimacy of the king. Worcester makes explicit the basis for kingship—power: "The King will always think him in our debt, / And think we think ourselves unsatisfy'd, / Till he hath found a time to pay us home" (I.iii.280–81). The tavern also qualifies the authority of the "king." On the prince's suggestion, Falstaff assumes the role of Hal's father, the king, and becomes another usurper (II.iv.370f.). Hal does not like the image of this player-king and decides to play the king himself while Falstaff takes the role of the prince and heir. The characters do not agree on how the king and prince should behave. Kings and heirs multiply. They all act and practice illusion in politics and in the play extempore. The king himself admits to his son his acting in Richard's reign:

> And then I stole all courtesy from heaven,
> And dress'd myself in such humility
> That I did pluck allegiance from men's hearts,
> Loud shouts and salutations from their mouths,
> Even in the presence of the crowned King.
>
> (III.ii.50–54)

This is a variation on York's account of Bolingbroke and Richard in the streets in *Richard II*. Henry admits his Promethean achievement and deceptive acting when he challenged the king but now wants to assert his own authority against those who would usurp his power. The king also criticizes the acting style of Richard, the "skipping King," for he, among other things, "Mingled his royalty with cap'ring fools," and Henry fears that Hal is like Richard. Comparing Hotspur now to himself in Richard's England, Henry destabilizes succession and misreads Hal's acting.

In addition to deception, force, not right, seems to make kings. Hal swears his revenge on Hotspur "in the name of God" and will contend for the king's confidence and, ultimately, for the title of "king." Douglas calls Hotspur "the king of honour," and Falstaff, as well as Hal, redefines honor (IV.i.10). Hotspur himself has little respect for Henry; "The King is kind, and well we know the King / Knows at what time to promise, when to pay" (IV.iii.52–53). He reiterates the rebels' reinterpretation of history, exposing Henry's deceit, his vow to God that he came to be but the Duke of Lancaster, and he reminds Blunt, the king's envoy, that Henry deposed the monarch and that Mortimer now is really Henry's king, claiming that Henry broke his oaths. This last claim questions the king's sincerity about words. Worcester also recalls "Richard's time," identifies Henry with the dukedom of Lancaster, calls Richard "the King," and accuses Henry of violating "all faith and troth"—this time to Henry's face (V.i.30–72). Henry dresses counterfeits on the battlefield and so himself multiplies substitute kings and calls into question his own bravery. Here are many kings, pretending like actors, illusions on the actual field of battle. In order to survive, the king will replicate and cheapen his image with the representations of himself. This strategy redefines kingship and may be good politics in neglecting traditional military honor (V.iii, iv). As Douglas says, "Another king! They grow like Hydra heads," and he asks Henry: "What art thou / That counterfeit'st the person of a king?" The question displays dramatic irony because the audience, unlike Douglas, knows that this man is the king. The audience, however, has observed that some think Henry the true king while others do not, so that it experiences ambivalence over Henry's claim, somewhere between Douglas's view and his. Henry gives us the substance and the shadow of the matter when he replies: "The King himself, who, Douglas, grieves at heart / So many of his shadows thou hast met, / And not the very King" (V.iv.24–30). When Hal meets Hotspur on the battlefield, he wants only one king of honor and one heir: "Two stars keep not their motion in one sphere, / Nor can one England brook a double reign / Of Harry Percy and the Prince of Wales" (V.iv.64–66). Kingship contains within it succession and so focuses as much on the future king as on the present and past kings, thereby subjecting kingship to another kind of multiplication. In the last scene the king must still contend with more rebels, who challenge his right to rule. This is a king who himself questions the meaning of the word "king" and his own right to be so called. Deceit and force seem to be displacing appeals to divine right.

Part Two of Henry IV also contains multiple images of kingship and the rebellion against Henry's rule. It provides new contexts for the word "king" and for the enactment of the regal role. Rumor, in the Induction in Part Two, spreads false stories about the fall and death of king and heir. The king is and is not the king. Appeals to the past qualify Henry's authority. Morton explains that the Archbishop of York "doth enlarge his rising with the blood / Of fair King Richard, scrap'd from Pomfret stones" and says that the Archbishop derives his quarrel from heaven, calling the king Bolingbroke, a reversion to his earlier and less authoritative name (I.i.204–5). The Archbishop describes the populace, which like a common dog had vomited "royal Richard" and then howled to find him dead, recasts York's speech in *Richard II* and Henry's variation on it, and addresses the absent commoners:

> Thou that threw'st dust upon his goodly head,
> When through proud London he came sighing on
> After th'admired heels of Bolingbroke,
> Cry'st now, "O earth, yield us that King again,
> And take thou this!" O thoughts of men accurs'd!
> Past and to come seems best; things present, worst.
>
> (I.iii.103–8)

This historical review encourages a glance back at the reign of Richard and emphasizes, from the Archbishop's point of view, the error of the populace and, by implication, of York. If the Archbishop's sense of time is accepted, Henry's reign is worse than Richard's, and Henry's successor's, and kingship may be seen as a continuum rather than a frozen point. The Archbishop may also share a bias against the common people that the kings display in private moments in the tetralogy.

Henry himself laments the travails of kingship. He apostrophizes sleep and says it gives repose to the sea boy but not to the king (III.i.1–31). In a traditional trope Henry contrasts the heavy burden that the king experiences with the restful and carefree existence of his subjects. This attitude ignores contract theory—which implies that the king is, in part, a subject to the will of other subjects—or the doctrine of the king's two bodies, which reveals his divine powers as well as his mortality. Henry ignores his vulnerability before his poorest subjects and his privileges (III.i.4). Apostrophizing God, Henry interprets history and kingship, reiterating the Archbishop's view of the people's fickleness, but this time in describing the nobility. Henry speaks about Richard and recalls his prophecy "Northumberland, thou ladder," which the audience might remember from *Richard II*. Seeing, perhaps, that Henry is questioning his own authority, Warwick asserts that "King Richard" may have made a "perfect guess" about the future by reading past events, but he cannot escape the memory that Richard was a king rebelled against and so, too, is Henry (III.i.80–92). The king, once again suffering guilt, promises a pilgrimage to the Holy Land. As if the ghost of Richard is not invoked enough, the Archbishop speaks of the disease—the ailing realm—they all have suffered and of which King Richard died, and even Bullcalf has been sick celebrating Henry's coronation (IV.i.53–58; cf. III.ii.175–80). Westmoreland thinks that it is the necessities of time and not the king that have injured the rebels, but Mowbray reiterates Henry Bolingbroke's wrongs, even reinterpreting the events at the opening of *Richard II*. Predictably, Westmoreland, Henry's subordinate, interprets the king and history more positively for his master. When Westmoreland leaves, Mowbray restates the mistrust between king and subjects that Worcester had expressed in Part One, but the Archbishop is more optimistic about the king's ability to forgive and forget, and Hastings concurs. The various views of word and action demonstrate the fallen nature of interpretation, something that affects both audience and critics.

The tangle of opposing claims of truth worsens. John of Lancaster will vow and break his oaths as his father had. Hal apostrophizes the crown, then takes it up, and when the king awakens he thinks that the prince has usurped it. The prince's apostrophe treats the crown as if it were alive, as if it represents the king's immortal and mortal bodies. If Hal reiterates his father's apostrophe to sleep, in which he laments the weary, responsible life of kings, the prince mistakes his father's sleep for death, which has divorced English kings from the crown, and concludes that while he shows love to the mortal man, his father, he will take up the crown of immortal kingship. He is determined, with God's help, to defend his right "and put the whole world's strength / Into one giant arm, it shall not force / This lineal honour from me" (IV.v.19–46; cf. III.i.1–31). Just before this apostrophe and seizure of the crown, Hal refers to his father as "the King," which emphasizes the impersonal and public office (10, 18). Once again, the playwright uses dramatic irony to fracture kingship, not just between the king's two bodies but between the king, whom the audience knows is alive, and the son, who does not know this and thinks he is king. Shakespeare repeats the critical issues of coronation and deposition. Symbols, like words, are not the world, so why do characters like Richard, Bolingbroke, York, Northumberland, Henry, Falstaff, and others, and Renaissance commentators on the law like Watson and Coke, take these symbols so seriously? It is as if the symbol has ritual power to become the thing it represents, which is a form of magical thinking. When Coke opposes Watson by maintaining that the king is, and does not need coronation to make him a king, he is trying to fight this translation of metonymy, synecdoche, and metaphor into the thing itself. Shakespeare's characters will not ignore the word "king" because words are too powerful in their incitement to action, if not their participation in, or constitution of, action and power. Hal's father dramatizes his self-pity and his chastisement of his own son, saying that Hal will celebrate his coronation rather than Henry's death, that Hal will break his father's degrees and "mock at form" (IV.v.110–19). Henry also judges Hal by appearances and makes false prophecies about the reign of Henry the Fifth.

Here, the incommunication between generations continues and makes the succession uneasy. Hal displaces his father's anger onto the crown, which, he admits, he personified and blamed for killing his mortal parent (IV.v.138f.). A tension exists between the two mortal kings, father and son, and between the inherited and familial bond of continuation at death that makes kingship immortal. When father and son are making up, Henry tells Hal that "God knows, . . . / By what by-paths and indirect crook'd ways / I met this crown," and he seems to think that the culpability and strife will disappear with his own death (IV.v.183–85). The king admits that he wanted to cut off those who helped him to power, that he wanted to go on a pilgrimage to the Holy Land "Lest rest and lying still might make them look / Too near unto my state." He recommends that Hal fight foreign wars to "waste the memory of my former days" and asks God to forgive the way he became king. Hal justifies his father's reign with a view akin to might is right: "You won it, wore it, kept it, gave it me" (IV.v.221). This stance is a long way from the divine right of kings. When Henry dies, Hal becomes king, but Falstaff does not know that the old king is dead.

The exchange between Shallow, Pistol, and Falstaff, in which there is confusion about who is king, Henry the Fourth or Henry the Fifth, represents the comic muddle over the crown (V.iii.105–34). Although we have just seen Henry the Fifth reappoint the Chief Justice, Falstaff expects the new king to let him have his way: "I know the young King is sick for me. . . . The laws of England are at my commandment." The king is sick of Falstaff, not sick for him. The Lord of Misrule must not rule. Henry the Fifth rejects Falstaff, a rejection that is necessary but that suppresses the private side of the king (V.v.47). Here, kings are public selves. The new king may "have turn'd from my former self," may have been converted, but the controversy over the rejection illustrates that he has lost as well as gained something. As treacherous a character as John of Lancaster ends the play with rumors that Henry the Fifth is planning an invasion of France, an exercise in realpolitik. Henry punishes Falstaff for his misrule, but he himself has inherited a usurped crown. The world is fallen in this play. The next play represents the invasion that Henry the Fourth recommended to shore up the authority of the king.

From the beginning of *Henry V*, it is not certain what right Henry has to the French crown, and the motives of the English church and state in the invasion are suspect. Canterbury and Ely hope that Henry's claim to the French crown will keep his mind from crippling the church financially (I.i). Although to modern audiences this debate on succession and Salic Law may seem boring or extraneous because it is not as immediate as similar debates today, the lengthy disquisition makes great sense in relation to the long debate in the tetralogy on the nature of kingship, which, of course, includes royal succession, power, and prerogatives. (Olivier's film may have parodied the opening legal arguments because the modern audience is estranged from them.) The king himself warns the clergy in God's name not to "fashion, wrest, or bow your reading" of laws because many shall die as a result of their interpretation if they say that Henry has a right to France (I.ii.8–32). Canterbury's involved reply, which may sound outlandish to modern ears, is no more detailed or ingenious than the arguments in Plowden, Browne, Leslie, Coke, Craig, Harrington, Hayward, or Egerton, or the various claims to the crown made in favor of the Suffolk line or those made by Peter Wentworth in the 1590s for the Stuarts. The arguments have at least as much to do with power as with logic: for instance, by the so-called Salic Law, the French nobles elected Philip of Valois to prevent the French throne from being occupied by a woman and, ostensibly, denied Edward the Third the French crown because his claim was through his mother (Walter ed., 15). Here, Canterbury uses the Salic Law for the opposite purpose—so that an English king can claim the French crown. The use of a body of examples to argue for contrary ends is typical of the law, and the Elizabethan and Jacobean law was no different in this regard. Henry claims the right to the French crown, but there already is a French king. The word "king" is once again divided. There are two claimants to the French crown. The entire debate on the Salic Law questions the way one becomes a king and so renders the authority of kingship equivocal (I.ii). Henry's reference to the Scots invading England makes one think of the English invasion of France. Perhaps, even in the 1590s, as Axton argues, an irony resides in the comparison: James the First has as much right to be heir as Henry the Fifth had to be king of France— for some, that means every right; for others, none (I.ii.11, 21–22, 90f.). The appeals to history, to past kings, once again bear on the definition of the king in the present.

Other characters present points of view that question the king. Bardolph and Nym recall his rejection of Falstaff, who is now sick of heart (II.i). Henry is a qualified hero, and he, the son of a rebel, asserts his authority against Scroop and the other insurgents (II.ii). Bates and Williams debate with Henry over the responsibilities of the king at war, over what constitutes a king. In this scene the king is and is not the king, being disguised as an ordinary soldier to Bates and Williams but, through dramatic irony, being still the king to the audience (e.g., IV.i.119–35). After Bates and Williams speak about the responsibility of the king for an unjust war, Henry gives a soliloquy on how all men lay their sins on the king and how the king is full of cares whereas his subjects are not. This speech recalls others on the cares of kingship—Richard's on "the death of kings," Henry the Fourth's apostrophe to sleep, and Hal's apostrophe to the crown (*RII*, III.ii.144–77; *2HIV*, III.i.4–31, IV.v.21–31). These speeches lean toward self-pity and tend to underestimate what it is like to be subjected to someone else's rule, as well as the sometimes attendant problems of poverty and powerlessness. Henry the Fifth laments:

> Twin-born with greatness, subject to the breath
> Of every fool, whose sense no more can feel
> But his own wringing. What infinite heart's ease
> Must kings neglect that private men enjoy!
>
> (IV.i.240–43)

This is a partisan view of the burdens of the king's two bodies. The only difference between private men and the king, Henry argues, is "ceremony." Like Falstaff's honor, it cannot mend the mortal body of the king, but this catechism—which catalogues the role playing, the "proud dream," the accoutrements of kingship— makes light of the ease of the lives of the private man, "the wretched slave, / Who with body fill'd and vacant mind, / Gets him to rest, cramm'd with distressful bread" (274–76). Except for ceremony, Henry says, this man has "the fore-hand and vantage of a king," although Henry cannot resist insulting the peasant's brain (284–90). If the king is no different from the subject but for ceremony, then the king is also a fool. If kingship were entirely unbearable, Richard, Bolingbroke, and Hal would not have gone to such extents to hold onto or attain the office. Even these speeches on the cares of kingship are conventional, expanding on the royal view of the problem of the gulf between king and subject, a vantage that differs considerably from that of subjects like Pistol, Bates, and Williams.[35]

If Henry doubts the worth of kingship, he also questions his own right to the throne. He recollects the specter of the dead king— Richard—and how the house of Lancaster had abused him. Although Henry repents, the penitence itself reminds us of the unsteady grounds of his kingship and of the split between the private man who admits his doubts and wrongs and the public king who is ruthless and heroic. When the king reasserts his authority through the glove trick, Williams submits to him but with qualification and with an eye to the power of the king: "Your majesty came not like yourself: you appeared to me but as a common man" (IV.viii). The king is mortal and godlike. Henry wins France, is to marry Katharine, but is only made heir, so that in another sense he is and is not king (V.ii.350–60). The Epilogue points out that, contrary to Henry's hopes, his son will lose France, and the wars over kingship will continue, as Shakespeare's audience had seen in the First Tetralogy. The word "king" contains divisions.

It is also difficult for other characters to take the king's word literally, for kings lie, counterfeit, and act. The word "king" generates divisions between the mortal and immortal aspects of kingship. Neither Richard, Henry the Fourth, nor Henry the Fifth is without role playing, deception, and figurative language that divide them between their public and private, conscious and unconscious selves. Whatever right the king has to the crown, he is not consistent and transparent to himself and to others, even to the author who made him and to the audience who so often shares with the playwright a godlike knowledge. A king's acting and action is complex and oblique, just as an author's representation and an audience's reconstitution are. Fiction, as Shakespeare knew and Wilde said, is a lie, so that the difficulty with historical fiction such as the history play is that it is a true lie or the lying truth. This is similar to the kind of fiction that so puzzled Hamlet when watching the First Player cry and has placed critics and the audience in a quandary, for Hamlet is a fictional character and Shakespeare a maker of fictions.[36] Similarly, in the Second Tetralogy, Shakespeare calls attention to limits of fiction and his authority as well as the fictions of truth: he questions the relations between God and humanity, king and subjects, playwright and audience. However playful or solemn, we are, like Plato, caught between the power of fiction and the power of truth, the supplement to nature and nature itself. Shakespeare's historical fiction translates into a new medium the legal, theological, and political fiction of the king's two bodies.

LYING AND INCOMMUNICATION

Deceit and misunderstanding also reveal a fallen state of word and world. Just as multiple stage images of kings, puns, and contrary claims to regal power fracture a unified idea of kingship, mendacity, deception, and isolation represent a strain between the ideal and actual rule of a king. A division persists between right and power and leaves an opening for the possibility of doing without kings, something Shakespeare does not pursue here, although he had done so earlier in *The Rape of Lucrece* and would return to the topic later in the Roman plays. A few examples will suffice to illustrate this point.

The opening of *Richard II* raises the dilemma of who is lying about the death of Gloucester, and Richard himself says that either Bolingbroke or Mowbray flatters the king by accusing the other of treason (I.i.25–29). When Richard is in prison, he uses extended metaphors to try to understand the world (V.v.1f.). First, he compares his prison to the world, but he cannot make his solitude a populous world, though he continues in his attempt. According to Richard, the better sort of thoughts, like divine ones, are mixed with scruples "and do set the word itself / Against the word," and he cites two biblical passages that discuss conscience and illustrate the way interpretation is set against itself, how proud and ambitious thoughts die in their pride in the prison of the self even as that self attempts to break through to a larger and more populous world. Human interpretation is like the fall of pride, a second revolt of Lucifer. Thoughts that tend to happiness flatter themselves like those who suffer shame and confinement and gladden themselves with the thought that others have suffered thus. Richard is fractured into many theatrical selves: "Thus play I in one person many people, / And none contented" (V.v.31–32). In metaphors Richard wavers between being kinged and unkinged, being something and nothing, and compares music and time. The music he hears is oxymoronic, broken and without proportion but capable of concord. He was deaf, wasted time, and was wasted by time, and he continues his metaphor by likening his own face to a clock. But the metaphor does not stop Richard's vacillation or identify his words with the world, for the music he weighs in his metaphor is a "sign of love" in "this all-hating world." When others visit Richard in prison, we observe more ambivalence, for the Groom is loyal and loving to him, but Exton is murderous and hateful. Richard's last speeches are hopeful but fallen. Answering the Groom's description of Bolingbroke riding Richard's horse Barbary, Richard asks about the animal as if it had human volition—"would he not fall down, / Since pride must have a fall, and break the neck / Of that proud man that did usurp his back?"—and then catches himself in the act of personification (V.v.87–94). The fallen king's words become violent action when he strikes the Keeper and fights the murderers. His last words contain images of hell, kingship, and rise and fall, for Richard curses Exton to hell for killing his king and now hopes that his own soul will mount while his body sinks to earth. Death (which Richard has once more personified), the consequence of the fall of Adam and Eve, makes him long for transcendence of the division of self and nature, I and others, body and soul, humankind and God. He dies with the word "die," as if the very utterance of the sign for death would unite him with death itself. Richard would untime time.

But Bolingbroke lives despite Richard's wish for his fall. Nonetheless, so does the memory of Richard haunt the following three plays. Henry the Fourth cannot, as he says, lead a crusade to the Holy Land but must fight division at home (I.i). In *1 Henry IV* characters lie or create myth and fancy. Hotspur would teach Glendower to "tell truth, and shame the devil," but Hotspur likes to pun and speak the metaphors of poetry even if he complains to the Welshman:

> I had rather hear a brazen canstick turn'd,
> Or a dry wheel grate on the axle-tree,
> And that would set my teeth nothing on edge,
> Nothing so much as mincing poetry —
> 'Tis like the forc'd gait of a shuffling nag.
>
> (III.i.125–29)

Even those who would break away from language are its prisoners or subjects. Hotspur can long for immortality and divinity as much as Glendower, but, whether he is conscious of it or not, he is like Hal, who cannot brook rivals and wants to be the only one to rule with God's grace. If Henry has lied, so too has Falstaff, whose language is as expansive as his belly, who lies about his ring and about killing Percy, who, in short, likes to tell tall tales and contend with the audience on and around the stage for their interpretation (III.iii.50–205; V.iv.120–64).

Rumor, in the Induction, influences our view of the whole of *2 Henry IV*, emphasizes the slanders, surmises, conjectures, discords, and lies that language comprises. The audience is still unsure of truth. Northumberland "Lies crafty-sick," but amid his obfuscation and the incommunication of the larger community he can still exhort Morton "to speak truth" (I.i.210). Act 2, scene 3, is a discussion between Northumberland and Lady Percy about Northumberland's lying and breaking of oaths, especially to his son, Hotspur, whose memory arises like Richard's. Falstaff will not listen to the Chief Justice, who comments on such unwillingness to listen and hears Sir John's admission of his disease, a sickness that enables him to hear but not to listen. The Chief Justice asks Falstaff to do the impossible—to be honest (I.ii.113–30, 222). Falstaff, himself an old man given to lying, laments, especially after hearing Shallow's falsifications of the past: "Lord, Lord, how subject we old men are to this vice of lying" (III.ii.296–98). Besides amplifying the vices of the lying Shallow, Falstaff has stung himself, the satirist, with his own barbs, for he has lied with great wit, for instance to Doll about marriage. As we have seen, a lack of trust exists between rebels and king, and the sickness and lack of communication extend to the relation between Hal and his father (III.i). John of Lancaster accuses the Archbishop of York of lying in the name of God, of claiming to be ordained to interpret the divine will but misinterpreting it willfully and "Under the counterfeited zeal of God." Lancaster himself comes from a deceitful family and lies to the Archbishop by staying to the literal meaning of what he promised him and the other rebels. John of Lancaster's father used actual counterfeits in battle to protect himself and deceitful theatrics to usurp a crown. John abuses the truth by sticking cleverly to its letter rather than its spirit, by dividing the rebels from the rebellion, the grievers from the grievances (IV.ii.110–23). He keeps this deceit to himself, so that his family praises his deeds by their outcome. Language is a weapon as much as a means of seeking communication and truth.

The truthfulness and motives of Canterbury and Ely are questionable and have as much to do with invention as the Prologue's theatrical exhortations. With Henry the Fifth, they use long, elaborate arguments to justify the self-serving decisions that they have already made (I.i, ii). Henry himself has learned from his father the benefits of foreign wars in deflecting interest at home from the crooked ways in which his father ascended the throne. The king wants the church to take full responsibility for the decision to invade. Language is a way to justify action, rationalizing arguments for the status quo, aggression, hypocrisy, and the maintenance of power in the name of God. Henry is a confident hero in public and a doubtful king in private, haunted by the debate with Bates and Williams so much that he admits guilt and attempts to appease God and the ghost of Richard (IV.i). The French and English also speak different languages, literally and politically, and it is a union of the two countries and cultures that Henry imposes on them by the end of the play until the Epilogue speaks of the dissolution of that unity. The so-called low-life characters also lie. The Boy sees through them all, particularly through Pistol. According to the Boy, Pistol "breaks words" but keeps his weapon whole; he sees that Pistol is a full voice from an empty vessel, more a character from an old play that speaks in tags—like the roaring devil of morality plays—than a person (III.ii.28–57; IV.iv.69–80). Beaten but not defeated, Pistol himself admits that he will play the liar, the old soldier who will make his scars into stories of heroism in France (V.i.84–93). Language is given as much to fictions and myths as to facts, for words are subject to human interpretation.

The fall of language represents the gap between the word and the world. Rather than trying to fill that gap in the Second Tetralogy, Shakespeare explores it by having his characters, consciously and unconsciously, use images of rise and fall, images of gardens and Eden, self-trapping images, appeals to God, ideas of kingship, and lying and incommunication. Language is a means of action and a block to action. From the beginning of *Richard II*, lies and obfuscation call into question the authority or divine right of kingship, and in the following plays the positions of the rebels become equally uncertain. Second nature, which occurs after the Fall, has implications for all human action, for it reveals that people judge or interpret with a large degree of blindness, so that, even as they appeal to God or nature or causes, they qualify their own ability to judge, to interpret. The characters experience a kind of interpretative measure for measure. As language appears to be diachronic as well as synchronic, there is a conflict between the view from on high, or the katascopic perspective, and the one from below in the human crowd. The temporality of rhetoric depends on the rhetoric of temporality. Limitations of time and space create problems and dilemmas in these history plays, so that their achievement is as uncertain as it is great. Through dramatic irony, the audience may be given greater knowledge than the characters, but it also lacks the information that the narrative historian gives to his readers. The audience shares the playwright's knowledge but can also be as victimized as the characters. If Worcester relates interpretation and misinterpretation, it is perhaps because it is difficult to maintain an authoritative reading through an appeal to an absolute standard: "Look how we can, or sad or merrily, / Interpretation will misquote our looks, / And we shall feed like oxen at a stall, / The better cherish'd still the nearer death" (*1HIV*, V.ii.12–15). Even when we share the playwright's overview, we come to the play with a point of view and continue to want to take a stand. Similarly, as Worcester says, Henry brings his needs and wishes to his view of the rebels. We shall now examine these and other dilemmas.

THREE

Temporality
Drama vs. History

RAMA, AND ESPECIALLY HISTORICAL DRAMA, emphasizes the temporal nature of writing, reading, or viewing. Historical drama makes the past present or it represents, for the player embodies the dead king. The presence of representation is gone even as we say the word. This literal and literary emptying out of the present is one of the primary difficulties that we face in literary criticism and historical writing. Shakespeare's history plays represent the problems of joining world and word, life and art, showing us their relation but distinguishing between them. As the actor plays, the audience identifies actor and role, present and past but at the same time differentiates them. It is as if the audience experiences both the lure of Aristotelian representation and the distance of the Brechtian alienation effect. Dramatic time, the three hours' traffic on the stage, contrasts, if not collides, with the more diffuse historical time. Owing to the telescoping of the vast flow of history, historical drama makes us conscious of the possibilities and limitations of time and mimesis.

In each of the plays of the Second Tetralogy the characters call attention to time. A reference to time occurs in the first line of *Richard II*, and *Henry V* begins and ends with concerns over the relation of dramatic and historical time. The concern with temporality is not identical with a sense of history, although both are closely related as history is preoccupied with time and anyone who is aware of time is likely to have considered history. A playwright and an audience focus on dramatic time, the few hours it takes to play out the play, but within historical drama there are numerous references to past and future as well as the present, and the present of a history play is past for the audience. The awareness of the complexity of time becomes a central preoccupation as dramatic or existential time enables and opposes historical time. When we think about the Second Tetralogy, we observe that important characters like Richard the Second, Bolingbroke, Hal, Falstaff, and the Chorus are taken up with temporality either consciously or not. In examining the problem of temporality, we shall find that, if anything, the difficulties increase as the tetralogy progresses and that these temporal anxieties contribute to an atmosphere of fallenness and pushes the Shakespearean history play toward the problem play. It is its tentative and necessarily incomplete solutions to the dilemmas of temporality that help to make the Second Tetralogy exciting, provocative, and dramatic.

Historical writing tries to make sense of the apparently ineluctable or daunting movement of time. A history play emphasizes its own metonymic and synecdochic nature in representing the world because it is more condensed than many historical poems and most historical novels. That the part represents a larger whole than the tragic individual or the comic society makes us more aware of the dilemmas of representation and even the difficulties of the claims of truth. Perhaps the ultimate convention or fiction of the history play is that it is showing the world as it was, that the representation corresponds to past events. The Second Tetralogy explores the truth of fiction and the fiction of truth, the theater of the world and the world of theater. These oppositions both interpenetrate and demand a stance. The theater is more and less the world. Because Shakespeare particularly uses the Chorus in *Henry V* to play with this paradox and to explore the difficulty of representing history, we shall concentrate more on the Chorus here than on any other aspect of the tetralogy. The two sections of this chapter examine the references by the characters to time in its various manifestations and their allusions to the theater and their actions that are especially theatrical.

Drama does not seal life from art but enables the audience to witness the interpermeability of this opposition and others. Historical drama declares its likeness to the world, so that the very issue of mimesis is raised in the representation of people impersonating characters impersonating people who once lived outside the theater. Shakespeare's second group of history plays is often self-reflexive. Through theatrical irony, these plays examine their own limitations and potentialities. The playwright invites us to measure Richard's histrionics against Bolingbroke's dissembling, Falstaff's demand for mimetic theater or a willing suspension of disbelief against Hal's estrangement or alienation effect, and Henry the Fifth's private thoughts against his public deportment. In history, acting and action are inseparable. By sheer weight of theatrical allusion, Shakespeare makes the audience conscious of the relation between acting and action, histrionics and history. For instance, York contrasts the entrances of Bolingbroke and Richard into London in terms of the theater. Actors are playing these political roles in a theater as in a theater. That the rebels asked the Lord Chamberlain's Men to perform *Richard II* as part of the Essex Rebellion of 1601 affirms the theatricality of politics. In the wake of the rebellion, as is well known, Elizabeth is reported to have likened herself to Richard the Second.[1] The open sky of the Theatre and the Curtain (and later the Globe), and even the possible *ad quatratum* construction of these theaters, placing man at the center, are metaphors that both play and display seepage between art and life and proclaim personified or humanized nature.[2] Possibly, the very building was a stage symbol that underscored the ironic relation between theater and world that York and others discuss so freely in the Second Tetralogy. This background or general irony lies behind the specific irony of speeches like York's "As in a theater" in *Richard II*. In a much-reprinted preface on the benefits of history, Simon Grineus, a humanist, asks: "What can be thought more pleasaunt or profitable then sytting as it were in the Theatre or Stage of man's life (the whiche an Historye hath most exquisitely furnished in all points . . .) to be made ware and wyse at the perilles of other men, without any daunger on his own behalfe?"[3] This commonplace alerts us to the interpenetration of theater and world, though its common occurrence does not detract from Shakespeare's subtle elaboration and exploration of this trope.

In *An Apology for Actors* (1612) Thomas Heywood dreams his own version of a katascopic theater. This view also contains obvious parallels with Jaques's "All the world's a stage," written about the time of the Second Tetralogy:

> then our play's begun,
> When we are borne, and to the world first enter,
> And all finde exits when their parts are done.
> If then the world a Theater present,
> As by the roundnesse it appears most fit,
> Built with starre-galleries of hye ascent,
> In which *Jehove* doth as as spectator sit,
> And chiefe determiner to applaud the best,
> And their indeavours crowne with more then merit.
> And their evill actions doomes the rest,

To end discrac't, whilst others praise inherit.
He that denyes the Theater should be,
He may as well deny a world to me.[4]

Heywood's God on high has a penchant for poetic justice that Shakespeare does not give us. It is not certain that Heywood believes what he says or that, writing under his own name in a document that does not purport to be a fiction, he writes a more official line to make the theater appear respectable and to keep the censor at bay. Heywood is more overt than Shakespeare in challenging the world to accept the theater and in making drama moral but less interested in exploring the limitations of theatrical representation. Shakespeare used an ancient comparison between the theater and the world, but it is interesting what he did with this widespread trope, particularly in the self-consciously mimetic sphere of the history plays. The two major parts of this chapter are concerned with temporality and theatricality, the first with time as it occurs in the world, the second with time as it happens in the theater, assuming that world and theater overlap.

TEMPORALITY

The conscious and unconscious references that the characters make to time do not always refer specifically to the problems of the history play. This temporality I call worldly time. It is Richard's musical and clock time, Hal's time to redeem, Falstaff's hours as cups of sack and the hour of his death. This worldly time can also be references to the relation among past, present, and future, as well as to more immediate time. How does it differ from theatrical time? It does not call attention overtly to history in the theater, though it may be theatrical. Falstaff's image of hours as cups of sack is theatrical but not self-consciously so because he neglects to discuss openly the dramatic representation of history, whereas the Chorus's references to time draw direct notice to the history play as such. The distinction allows us to understand better where, at the extremes, history and drama do not meet. It also reminds us that the relation between drama and history is more often one of convergence rather than divergence. One of the most important aspects of worldly time in these plays is whether a character thinks that he controls time or is controlled by it, and each chararacter, most notably the kings—Richard, Henry the Fourth, and Henry the Fifth—struggles with this dilemma. From this problem arises dramatic irony in which the audience decides whether the character is in or out of control as much as he thinks he is. In a dramatic sense a player king like Falstaff is caught in the same dilemma. This section will compare briefly instances of the fall of time, especially in the openings; allusions to history and prophecy; and the different views of time among the kings, which includes Hal's promise to redeem time and culminates in his rejection of Falstaff, a lord of misrule.

The Fall of Time

The first line of *Richard II* emphasizes time twice in its appeal to age and the honor time pays it. Richard says: "Old John of Gaunt, time-honoured Lancaster," but the king does little to honor Gaunt and his son, Bolingbroke: he welcomes the death of the first and banishes the second for six years. There is little correspondence between Richard's professed love of the house of Lancaster and respect for time and age and his subsequent actions. Gloucester's death in the past affects the present, and Bolingbroke, who accuses Mowbray and perhaps indirectly Richard of the murder, compares his dead uncle to Abel. By the end of the play, however, he is associating himself obliquely with Cain (I.i.104; V.vi.43). This fall from Eden is in the very imagery and contains within it an ironic reversal. Like Henry and Worcester in *1 Henry IV*, Bolingbroke and Mowbray differ vehemently in their interpretation of the past. In each case the present cannot be free from the past and a grievance, like original sin, separates the parties.

The beginning of *Richard II* is also a dispute over honor. It widens to a contest between the rebels and Henry, Glendower and Hotspur, Hal and Hotspur, to Falstaff's satiric commentary on honor, to a contest between French and English, the Dauphin and Henry the Fifth. In this fallen world the conflict over honor multiplies over time. At the beginning of the first scene of act 4, Bolingbroke has to contend with more contestants in the game of honor than Richard did. The situation becomes more complex until, in *Henry V*, the problem of time and honor questions the authority of kingship and of the history play to represent those issues. Nor is there any doubt that honor is bound to time. Mowbray says to Richard: "My dear dear lord, / The purest treasure mortal times afford / Is spotless reputation—that away, / Men are but gilded loam, or painted clay" (*RII*, I.i.176–80). If Mowbray says that to take honor from him is to take away his life, Bolingbroke also defends his honor. Hotspur, too, relates honor and life, preferring death to a loss of honor. The loss of his "proud titles" to Hal wounds his thoughts, "But thoughts, the slaves of life, and life, time's fool, / And time, that takes survey of all the world, / Must have a stop" (*1HIV*, V.iv.80–82). Hotspur has been blind to Hal's honor and prowess. Like Richard in prison, Hotspur explores the relations among thought, pride, slavery, and death. To figure out time or overcome it is the goal of the honorable man. In the interim, however, Falstaff has satirized and qualified honor in his catechism. For Sir John, honor is simply a word, can do nothing positive and practical in the world, is insensible to the dead who lived by it, and is nothing more than the basest ensign hung in churches during funerals (*1HIV*, V.i.127–41). Falstaff later adds his contempt for deadening honor that ends a life, or individual time: "I like not such grinning honour as Sir Walter hath. Give me life, which if I can save, so: if not, honour comes unlooked for, and there's an end" (*1HIV*, V.iv.58–61). In fact, Falstaff steals Hal's honor by claiming to have killed Hotspur. Henry chides Hal's apparent impatience for the throne, as if youth cannot wait for honor: "Dost thou so hunger for mine empty chair / That thou wilt needs invest thee with mine honours / Before thy hour be ripe?" (*2HIV*, IV.v.94–96). The dramatic irony here is that Hal thought his father dead, so that when he thinks he is grieving the king's death with honor, the elder Lancaster impugns him for lacking honor and for hurrying time. Soon Henry and Hal are reconciled, but the king's notion of honor and history makes us wonder why he was so outraged and sanctimonious over his son's affronts to honor and time. He speaks of his friends' "fell working" in deposing Richard and raising up Henry, admits to cutting them off from power because they might displace him, says he wanted to divert attention from his claim to the crown by leading his friends to the Holy Land, and recommends that Hal "busy giddy minds / With foreign quarrels, that action hence borne out / May waste the memory of the former days" (*2HIV*, IV.v.213–15). This king's contradictory and obfuscating positions, his acting, keeps the audience guessing from *Richard II* to *2 Henry IV*, as well as catching him in his own hypocrisy: this double exposure reminds us of the temporality of the characters, as well as our own. The Constable of France brags that French peasants should have been enough to defeat the English while the French nobility stood on high in "idle speculation," but now the nobles must come down into the valley of battle (*HV*, IV.ii.25–32). The French are caught in their overconfidence, so that their katascopic view is a false one. If Henry the Fifth says that with so few soldiers his army will be able to gain a greater share of honor than if there were many English combatants, he also focuses this honor on a specific day, as a local time with which to remember their glorious deeds in stories when all else is forgotten: "And Crispin Crispian shall ne'er go by, / From this day to the ending of the world, / But we in it shall be remembered" (*HV*, IV.iii.57–59, see esp. 22, 28, 30, 56). Ironically, many have forgotten Crispin Crispian but now remember it in Shakespeare's play. Stories beget stories. Irony qualifies the relation between time and honor and points to the relation between acting and fiction and the world.

The fall of time leads us to the connection between truth and fiction, order and chaos. If the beginning of *Richard II* shows that the king is out of control and that his immediate preoccupation with time is duplicitous, it is not surprising that the other plays represent a concern with the fallenness of time from the opening lines. At the beginning of *1 Henry IV*, the king speaks about "a time for frighted peace to pant," so that he can divert attention from his shaky hold on power with righteous wars in the Holy Land, but time, like Henry's image of the hastening horse, will not give the king such an opportunity because a post has brought news of rebellion in Wales (*1HIV*, I.i.1–48, esp. 2, 34). Henry is caught in his own hope and scheme by events that are outside even a king's control. His son, whose honor he would exchange for Hotspur's, will try to manipulate and redeem time (*1HIV*, I.i.80). Rumor begins Part Two by manipulating news of past events, misinterpreting history willfully, words becoming more misleading than ever. Northumberland continues the horse imagery that Henry and Rumor have used: "The times are wild; contention, like a horse / Full of high feeding, madly hath broke loose, / And bears down all before him" (*2HIV*, I.i.9–11). The rumors that ensue make it particularly difficult to re-create the truth of the times and reflect the fallenness, the deafness, of the characters and the audience. Northumberland has deceived his son and withdrawn from battle, so that when he finds out that Hotspur is actually dead, he is not an impartial historian but a power whose aloofness has changed the events themselves. In the rage of Northumberland, which divorces him, as Morton says, from his honor, there is a gap between word and action, for the father would have saved the son only after Hotspur is dead and not when such action was dangerous (*2HIV*, I.i.162, see 157). After the crucial time, Northumberland can raise a rebellion, but it seems a little late and selfish and for all the wrong reasons. When Hotspur fell, rebellion did not end, and, as Morton says, the Archbishop of York now makes men who before feared the word "rebellion" think that God is behind their insurrection (*2HIV*, I.i.194–209). The times in each of these plays are given to revolt and war. The Prologue to *Henry V*, as we shall later see, compares theatrical and historical time, theater and world, by continuing the use of the horse as a temporal trope. Canterbury begins the main action with a discussion of a bill against the church, except "that the scambling and unquiet time / Did push it out of farther question" (*HV*, I.i.4–5). For the church, the chaos of civil war protected its "temporal lands," so that it is in self-interest that Canterbury and Ely plan away to divert the king from his father's bill. Even in these machinations, Canterbury can say that an angel "whipp'd th'offending Adam out of him, / Leaving his body as a Paradise" (*HV*, I.i.29–30). Canterbury praises the king's conversion, his learning, but, amid considerations that are hardly Edenic, he then talks about the church's offer of a gift to the king for wars in France, "a greater sum / Than ever at one time the clergy yet / Did to his predecessors part withal." Although the king liked the idea, "there was not time enough to hear, / As I perceiv'd his grace would fain have done" the various titles he has to the French crown (*HV*, I.i.75–89). At four o'clock, Canterbury says that he will meet with Henry because the French ambassador had interrupted their earlier meeting. The awareness of immediate time and the appearance of deals and self-interest reinforce the contradictions and pieties of postlapsarian time.

From beginning to end of the Second Tetralogy, the fallen nature of time appears in a language that is often trying to impute to itself a divine or ideal authority, God and truth, but seems to fall short. The opening of the plays raises the problem of the gap between heaven and earth, now and eternity, as well as the gap between professions of honor and honor itself, if not, indeed, the questioning of the possibility of human honor and truth. The rhetoric of temporality and the temporality of rhetoric qualify each other.

Prophecy

In attempting to control the state, the characters attempt to manipulate time, especially through curse and prophecy. The appeal to the future particularly complicates the views of history that the characters and the audience hold. Prophecy collides with the present and often relates to the past: the future for the characters is the past for Shakespeare and his original audience, so that the prophecies can be measured against what may be called the future past, future for the characters, past for Shakespeare. A historian, unless writing contemporary history, is often in the position of knowing the outcome of events, of looking back at the past from its future. In a sense the historian is a prophet who comments on the past and present with the benefit of a future, although each of these tenses shifts a little, for the historian's past, present, and future are not precisely the same as for the participants in the events of history. Shakespeare gives to Gaunt, for instance, a view of the future that benefits from his own view of the past.

An important device in Shakespeare's irony of structure is the use of prophecies, which modify our view of temporality, for although some of the characters may not be able to control their own fates, it seems they can predict the collective course of England. This split reveals a limitation in interpreting the private role of the speaker and an almost katascopic or divine view of the implications of events. In the first half of *Richard II* most predictions emphasize the fall of Richard, but in the second half others diffuse that tragedy by foreshadowing Bolingbroke's troubles and the difficulties England will face in matters of war and government. All the prophecies in *Richard II* come to pass either in that drama or in *1* and *2 Henry IV*. As the play progresses, the audience senses increasingly that Gaunt's prophecy of Richard's fall will probably be fulfilled (*RII*, II.i.93f.). More concise, less noticeable, but also important is Mowbray's earlier two-line prediction that Richard will live to regret Boling-broke's actual motives (I.iii.204–5). The warnings that Richard, Bolingbroke, and Northumberland ignore show their limitations before a more omniscient audience, which observes ignorance and wisdom side by side. Self-knowledge often comes too late, and characters will not learn from one another: Richard ignores the prophecies of others, but later others are equally deaf to his. York also warns Richard as Gaunt had done, even saying that the king's actions will lead him to rebellion, but, although this speech is treasonous, Richard ignores the warning and calls York an honorable man (II.i.205–8). In the next scene the queen's prophecy also helps create a cumulative effect that foreshadows Richard's misfortune. Her prophecy remains indefinite, "Some unborn sorrow" and "some thing" that Bushy's philosophy cannot dispel and that Greene's news can only specify: Bolingbroke has landed (II.ii.10–15ff., 49). With each prophecy, there is a structural momentum that contrasts with the blindness and deafness of characters like Richard and Bushy. As in the case of the Welsh captain and his soldiers, superstition and fancy also interpret prophecy. Because the bay leaves have withered, the moon is bloody, and "lean-look'd prophets whisper fearful change," the Welsh believe Richard dead and, by fleeing, actually help to bring about his death. Salisbury prophesies that Richard's glory will fall like a shooting star and setting sun and fears that a storm of ill fortune is about to break (II.iv.7–24). The images of fall and storm reinforce the structural movement toward Richard's downfall.

Not all the prophecy goes against Richard. In the deposition scene, Carlisle tells Bolingbroke's supporters that their leader is a traitor (IV.i.136–47). Like Gaunt, Carlisle thinks that civil war can be avoided if the offender will heed his counsel, but Bolingbroke is as deaf as Richard said Mowbray and Bolingbroke were at the begin-ning of the play or as much as Richard himself was before his fall. A further example of limitation is Northumberland, another dissenter who becomes the butt of Richard's newfound wisdom. The fallen king predicts that for England the years ahead look bleak and broken (V.i. 58–68). The scene has reversed itself from the beginning of the play: once deaf to prophecy and jealous of power, Richard exposes similar faults in Bolingbroke and Northumberland, who brush off Richard's comments. Like Carlisle's prediction, this one looks ahead to the *Henry IV* plays. The ironic use of prophecy uncovers the complexity of time and represents the struggle people have in coping with their blindness and ignorance in history while emphasizing the possibility of intelligible historical patterns, of reading the future through the past.

Although prophecy is less prominent in the next three plays, it still serves similar temporal functions. In *1 Henry IV* the king hopes for peace and for a war to fight in the Holy Land, but after forty seven lines of the play he gives these plans up. He cannot control the future. His son has better directorial ability as he shapes time through *1* and *2 Henry IV*. Hal immediately questions Falstaff's relation to time at the beginning of act 1, scene 2. The prince promises to play a role that hides his true self under apparent faults, "Redeeming time when men think least I will" (*1HIV*, I.ii.190–212). The rejection of Falstaff is part of the reformation, though the controversy over the rejection makes the prince's control over the future less successful than it first appears (*2HIV*, V.v.47–72). Sir John's repeated expectations of profiting from Hal's ascension to the throne, "when thou art king," are deflated fully with the rejection (*1HIV*, I.ii.16). Even though Falstaff thinks that he can shape time, as he says in regard to controlling Shallow, clearly he cannot, except that the sympathy that he has received from at least a good portion of the audience shows that his temporal direction extends beyond the characters (*2HIV*, III.ii.325–27). Northumberland, as Richard prophesied, has turned against Henry as he had against Richard, and he even has the nerve to invoke the spirit of the dead king to justify his rebellious thoughts (*1HIV*, I.iii.145–50). Hotspur's predictions backfire and the death he says will overtake the king's party in battle overcomes him (*1HIV*, IV.i.111–24). When Northumberland, who has betrayed his son, hears about Hotspur's death, he dramatizes himself hollowly: "Now bind my brows with iron, and approach / The ragged'st hour that time and spite dare bring / To frown upon th' enrag'd Northumberland" (*2HIV*, I.i.150–52). But his spite and anger turn against him, and his betrayal and rebellion fail. Despite John of Lancaster's tricking of the Archbishop of York, he is right about the future invasion of France, so that knowledge and humaneness are not necessarily related (*2HIV*, V.v.105–9). Shakespeare makes John's representation ambiguous. In *Henry V* Pistol is wrong, saying that his tavern friends and he will live: some of the horse leeches—Nym and Bardolph—will die, as Falstaff does, because of the king's judgment (*HV*, ii.125–28, iv.55–58). Henry the Fifth and the French king have great hopes for the accomplishment of the future son of Katharine and Henry, but instead of taking the Turk by the beard and unifying France and England, Henry the Sixth, as the Epilogue says, loses France, experiences another civil war in England, and falls (V.ii.215–31, 366–73; EP.). Even the hero king, who redeemed time, cannot escape his human predicament in time. He dies young and his son loses what he gained. The playwright shows the blindness and insight of interpreting the future just as he has the interpretation of the past.[5]

Different Views of Time among the Kings

Rather than look at the views of time extensively, we shall concentrate on moments of particular importance, occasionally relating them to other parts of the play and to the other plays in the Second Tetralogy. The kings grapple with time but often experience ironic reversals. For the kings, especially, time involves a tension between private and public selves. Self-knowledge and the ability to manipulate time to build power and control other people lies at the center of the conflict. Another division arises between words and actions, between the interpretation of time and the participation in time. No one can control time for long, but to shape it, to mythologize it in order to justify one's past and power, seems necessary to these kings. Temporality traps them as it does Falstaff and Hotspur, rivals of Hal just as Bolingbroke was of Richard. When relevant to Hal's view, we will look at their conceptions of time. When pertinent, other views of temporality will be mentioned briefly. The kings sometimes admit their predicament privately but seldom publicly, though Sir John, for instance, seems to be deluded personally. Their views of time, however, possess more dimensions than this outline suggests.

Richard, who thought he controlled his kingdom by imposing order and the terms of banishment, languishes in prison and considers his predicament (*RII*, V.v). The jailer is jailed (cf. I.iii.160–69). Richard has trouble hammering out his metaphor of the prison because of his isolation. Until now he has been accustomed to a social and political world full of action, so that he must populate his world with thoughts, which, like people, are not contented. This king will create his time and space through language. It is precisely this aloneness in which Richard engenders his world with feminine brain and masculine soul, creating thought through language, that provides a new perspective on the political struggle that he has lost. Richard begins to achieve humility and self-knowledge, to recognize his ironic limitation as a person. Like people, the best thoughts, according to Richard, are a mixture of doubt and the divine, setting one scripture against the other, ignorant of divine judgment. He quotes Jesus about admitting "children" freely into the kingdom of heaven—the disciples being baffled by the mystery of salvation—and about how difficult it is for a rich man to enter heaven.[6] Richard broadens the conception of time to eschatology and teleology. Having failed in meting out human justice and in judging human character, he begins to recognize human ignorance and contradiction and the inscrutability of God. By implication, Richard is also commenting on the deficiencies of the other judges in and of the play, such as Bolingbroke and the audience. Still using thoughts as a metaphor to describe his situation and the condition of humanity, Richard deflates his ambition and laments his own weakness, his nails unable to gouge a hole in the "ribs / Of this hard world, my ragged prison walls," his thoughts dying in their prime, personified to the end. Like Bolingbroke, who refused to assent to Gaunt's stoic optimism, Richard does not let "Thoughts tending to content flatter themselves" that they are either the first or the last to be the slaves of fortune, just as he had shattered the flattering glass in the deposition scene.

In prison Richard struggles with many roles, making thought action, the inner self and the outer world, attempting to sort out the

difference between appearance and actuality. His is the Fall into a
broken world:

> Music do I hear?
> Ha, ha! keep time—how sour sweet music is
> When time is broke and no proportion kept!
> So is it in the music of men's lives.
>
> (V.v.41–44)

This scene demonstrates the intricacy of time, especially through
Richard's musical metaphor. He generalizes his lot to the existence
of all men, taking his observations about the prison of temporal
limitation into the public and existential realms. With this trope of
musical time, he interprets his role in history, lamenting that he can
hear the discord now but could not during his reign, when his state
fell into ruin and when he wasted time until it wasted him. If
Richard will be considering minutes in prison, it is partly because he
did not listen to Gaunt's lesson on the limitations of men and kings
in time: a king can take away life (and, therefore, time), but he
cannot add a single second to a man's life. Richard suffers the slow
hours that he described to Mowbray, whose reputation as a crusader
appears to be more fortunate than the ends that await either Richard
or Bolingbroke. Once Richard thought that he would control the
length of Bolingbroke's banishment, telling Aumerle that he would
make it indefinite. Nor would he listen to York, who predicted that
by expropriating the Lancastrian lands the king would bring chaos
to and in time (I.iv.16, 20–22; II.i.177–223, ii.84–121). Kings should
consider their limitations as men when they are dealing with temporal matters (V.v.41–49).

But time is out of joint. Richard and Bolingbroke are fools of
time. Speaking with Isabel, the Gardener came to the conclusion
that later occurs to Richard in prison—the "waste of idle hours" lost
him his crown (III.iv.66–67). Although Richard admits to Isabel that
his "profane hours" have thrown the world down and that he must
take up a holy life, he also predicts the future correctly, casting into
doubt York's view of Bolingbroke's reign as "this new spring of
time" (V.i.25–26, 57f., ii.50–117). In prison Richard apprehends that
time measures human grief, from seconds to a lifetime, and, still

theatrical in his images, he views himself as a clock whose finger wipes away tears from a dial, a strong metaphor describing fallen humanity. The clocklike Richard, who does not make harmonious sounds but "clamorous groans," would control his experience, moralize the world through words, but finds that nature resists its transformation into a fable or myth. Richard tries to define space and time, to identify the inside and outside of the prison. The playwright and the audience experience problems similar to Richard's and, through his exploration of inside and outside, come to terms with the dilemmas of living in a political and symbolic world and of understanding the relation of the present to representation. Richard attempts to comprehend a vanishing past as a historian might but cannot control the world with his metaphors.

With some irony, Shakespeare has the fallen king associate time, music, and horsemanship. When Richard relates horses to time, he harkens back to Gaunt's use of horsemanship to signify the sudden violence that preys on itself: "He tires betimes that spurs too fast betimes" (II.i.33–39). In prison, Richard realizes that his own time "Runs posting on" into the proud time of Bolingbroke. Bolingbroke's pride should teach Richard calm, but he lacks sufficient self-knowledge to renounce politics and to understand the full irony of Bolingbroke's victory. According to Richard, the world is upside down: music that usually helps make madmen sane drives "wise men" to madness. Richard continues to waver, blessing the "heart" who gives him the music as a sign of love, a gift in "this all-hating world." Self-pity tempers self-knowledge—Richard still cannot take a stand and still experiences a conflict between the inner world of mind and spirit ("heart") and the outer world of politics and society. Shakespeare makes a stage image of horse imagery as the Groom, the last man loyal to the fallen king, enters; his presence makes Richard joke about his own worth, now a prisoner and not a prince. The Groom, who in his humility shows that goodness does not need high social station and emphasizes the king's humiliation, adds to York's story details of another of Bolingbroke's proud processional rides (cf. V.ii.7–11). The story concentrates on an important time: Bolingbroke's coronation day. On that day Richard's horse carried Bolingbroke, so that the deposed king wishes that the horse were almost human and would fall and break proud Bolingbroke's neck,

"Since pride must have a fall." Richard, who fell because of his pride, catches himself for personifying his horse, though he wonders why proud Bolingbroke still "reigns." Richard attempts to supplement his words with action and to identify action and word, for he dies with the word "die." Here, he would repair the fall into time and language at the end of his life, but others remain to contend with the gaps.[7]

Bolingbroke is curiously reticent about time in the opening scenes of *Richard II*. His temporal sense is only aroused when the king stops the combat with Mowbray: "How long a time lies in one little word! / Four lagging winters and four wanton springs / End in a word: such is the breath of kings" (*RII*, I.iii.212–15, cf. 194). Ambitious Bolingbroke is most concerned about his fall into time, which he associates with the language and power of the king. It is, however, Gaunt who reacts most to the shortening of his son's banishment, happy for Bolingbroke but sad that he will not live to see his return from exile. When Richard says to Gaunt that he has many years to live, Gaunt replies bluntly on the relation between time and power, remarking particularly on the limits of a king's power: "But not a minute, king, that thou canst give: / Shorten my days thou canst with sullen sorrow, / And pluck nights from me, but not lend a morrow" (I.iii.226–28, see 216–25, 229–48). Gaunt elaborates the idea that a king is only a man and cannot repair the ruins of nature and time. He also blames himself for being unfair to his son by trying to be too fair, but the banishment holds and Bolingbroke and Gaunt debate its meaning in the context of time. Bolingbroke contradicts his father, calling present what Gaunt says is absent and absent, present, their views of time and space contending. Gaunt cannot talk Bolingbroke out of his grief: the son ignores his father's unconsciously prophetic "Think not the king did banish thee, / But thou the king" (I.iii.279–80). The imagination that Gaunt recommends to Bolingbroke will not change his view of time and space, for according to Bolingbroke thoughts of pleasure will, if anything, only make grief seem longer and harder and the distance further (I.iii.158–309). For Bolingbroke, his exile is sad and literal, the pilgrimage he so often speaks of is about to begin. Bolingbroke does return to exile Richard from an Edenic England fallen into temporality and, appropriately, confronts him in the ruins of Flint

Castle (III.iii). When in the deposition scene Bolingbroke says "In God's name, I'll ascend the regal throne," he is no longer talking about the nature of time, perhaps because he now controls it, his kingly breath being time itself (IV.i.113). Bolingbroke returns to the taciturnity that his father mentions in the third scene of act 1; his measure of time is silence, as opposed to Richard's loquaciousness. The only time that concerns him is "Wednesday next," the day of his coronation (IV.i.319). But time is not so easy to control, even for kings, as Gaunt had observed, and this dilemma catches Bolingbroke in its irony. There are two kings and two royal times. After Bolingbroke is crowned, he comes to worry about Richard, his own life, and his son. The new king cannot control his son: " 'Tis full three months since I did see him last. / If any plague hang over us, 'tis he" (V.iii.2–3). Now and later, Bolingbroke will differ with his son over the nature of time, just as Gaunt and he had done. Bolingbroke is also thrown into the dramatic time of "The Beggar and the King," as the new king calls it, the unexpected drama that Aumerle, York, and the Duchess of York play before him (V.iii). Rebellion returns to the rebel: the times are out of joint. The exiled Bolingbroke ensures the last alienation for Richard—death—and exiles Carlisle and Exton, whom he likens to Cain. If the play begins with Richard addressing Gaunt, "time-honoured Lancaster," it ends with Gaunt's son caught in a violent contradiction, admitting that he wanted Richard dead but saying, in the last lines of the play, over the dead king's coffin: "grace my mournings here / In weeping after this untimely bier" (V.vi.51–52). In time, a reversal occurs: Bolingbroke's pilgrimage changes from grief over an involuntary exile to hope for a voluntary one. The former was to avenge the murder of Gloucester, his uncle, and this exile is to atone for his murder of Richard, his king, who, he believed, was supposed to be behind the earlier murder. Time is alienated from itself and manifests itself in violence and exile.

If Bolingbroke begins to lose control over time in *Richard II*, he does so even more in the *Henry IV* plays. During the first few lines of *1 Henry IV*, the king thinks that he has found "a time for frighted peace to pant," so that he could lead a pilgrimage to the Holy Land. He also dwarfs his frustration—"But this our purpose now is twelve month old"—when he compares it unwittingly to Christ's suffering on the bitter cross "fourteen hundred years ago" (*1HIV*, I.i.18–30). His plans are foiled because of new civil strife, and he wishes he could exchange his riotous son for Hotspur (I.i.47–48f.). Henry the Fourth is absent much of the play, taken from the center of dramatic time and space. The king misreads his son and the times: "The hope and expectation of thy time / Is ruin'd, and the soul of every man / Prophetically do forethink thy fall" (III.ii.36–38). Henry contrasts his effective acting style with Hal's and Richard's, but he is unaware of Hal's plan to redeem time through his very acting. Content with appearances to interpret past, present, and future, Henry tells Hal: "For all the world / As thou art to this hour was Richard then / When I from France set foot at Ravenspurgh, / And even as I was then is Percy now" (III.ii.93–96). But the king is willing to accept Hal's version and can still maintain a tough, practical view of time, for he organizes his forces over the next dozen days and proclaims, "Advantage feeds him fat while men delay" (III.ii.179–80). Henry now thinks of himself as old and his times as those in which insurrection creates confusion (IV.i.13, 79–82). Not only is Henry often absent but he also counterfeits himself on the battlefield, so that he multiplies and qualifies the authority of kingship and uses illusion as a means of maintaining his power. He seems to be in many places at one time and admits that Hal has redeemed himself (e.g., V.iv.24–56). At the end of Part One, Henry sends Worcester and Vernon to their deaths and organizes the immediate measures against the surviving rebels (V.v).

In *2 Henry IV*, Henry and others are subject to Rumor, but it is the rebels who are most prone. They, not Henry, begin the main action. As Northumberland says, "The times are wild, " and in the confused aftermath of the battle he listens to conflicting interpretations of the outcome (*2 HIV*, I.i.9). Not until the middle of the play (act 3, scene 1) do we see the king, when he apostrophizes sleep, wanting to rest at an hour when the sea boy can sleep. He personifies his troubled conscience and makes his cares external so he can blame them. The burdens of kingship make a shambles of time and keep Henry from controlling it. Henry has lost track of time, and Warwick sets him straight. They discuss the king's sickness and the disease of the body politic, but, most of all, Henry apostrophizes God and considers the nature of time: "O God, that one might read

the book of fate, / And see the revolution of the times" (III.i.45–
46f). For Henry, interpretation and time are inseparable, "one,"
generalizing his desire for power to humankind, but it is his own
dilemma that brings him to a consideration of temporality. According to Henry, time levels and melts everything in nature or restores
the earth and adds to it, like a sea of change, so that change is time's
most noticeable attribute (cf. Ovid's *Metamorphoses XV*). If youth
saw this change and the dangers of the past and the adversities of the
future, it would die, shutting the book of fate like some text whose
meaning is too bleak to bear. This view of time reminds Henry of
Richard's prophecies of Northumberland's betrayal of the new king.
Henry tries to reconstruct his intentions, of which he gives many
views in the first three plays of this tetralogy, and thereby revises his
view of his role in history. Warwick reads history a little differently.
He argues that by figuring out the past one can read the general
probability of the future, as if past events ab ovo "become the hatch
and brood of time." Whereas Henry imputes to Richard the power
of a prophet, Warwick tries to qualify his prediction by calling it a
"perfect guess." Henry and Warwick attempt to read the times, and
Warwick seeks to dissuade the king from heeding rumor. Time also
presses in on Henry, who is gravely sick, and he still speaks about
the pilgrimage to the Holy Land like some symbol of unattainable
desire that kings possess. The next time we see Henry he still wants
to go on a crusade but he is weak and sick (IV.iv.1f.). When he now
considers the future it is with frailty and death in mind, his grief
stretching "itself beyond the hour of death." Speaking to Clarence
and others, Henry personifies his heart, making it weep blood "when
I do shape / In forms imaginary th'unguided days / And rotten times
that you shall look upon / When I am sleeping with my ancestors"
(IV.iv.58–61). Once again, Henry misreads the future, and Warwick
is more sound in his interpretation of Hal's actions, past, present,
and future. Warwick says that Hal studies his tavern companions like
a strange tongue in which the most immodest word needs to be
learned, though known and hated more than used. Continuing the
analogy, which likens life to translation and which relates to the
interchange between the French and English—especially between
Katharine and Henry the Fifth in the next play—Warwick says:

So, like gross terms,
The Prince will, in the perfectness of time,
Cast off his followers, and their memory
Shall as a pattern or measure live
By which his Grace must mete the lives of other,
Turning past evils to advantages.

(IV.iv.73–78)

But Henry wrongly doubts this interpretation of time, perhaps knowing the motives of his own youth and suspecting Hal as a result. Warwick's speech coincides with Hal's view of himself as the redeemer of time at the beginning of *1 Henry IV*. Possibly, however, Hal's place in time is located somewhere between the views of Warwick and the ailing king. Henry has learned to ask: "Will Fortune never come with both hands full, / But write her fair words still in foulest letters?" (IV.iv.103–4). Even after hearing about the defeat of the rebels, Henry feels sick. After Gloucester and Clarence discuss signs, omens, and the chronicles, as if portents of their father's death were occurring, Henry would measure his time with music, soothing the sickness and discord within him. When Henry awakes and finds that Hal has taken his crown, he likens himself to a bee that has worked to find wax to feed the hive and is murdered for his troubles by those he would nourish. Time brings the father a bitter taste when his son would kill him for his gold. He chides the prince with what he himself considers to be a rhetorical question: "Dost thou so hunger for mine empty chair / That thou wilt needs invest thee with my honours / Before thy hour be ripe?" (IV.iv.94–96, see 101, 108). Repeatedly, he accuses his son of not waiting a few hours or less to let his father die with dignity. According to Henry, time now mocks with bad form or decorum, and the old king describes his son's state as a carnival, a vast misrule, a country divided by civil war. (He has little faith in his son, who once saved his life.) The woes of succession bear on Henry's mind, which now judges by appearances without first asking an explanation. He interprets Hal's stealing away with the crown as God's way of increasing the king's love for his son (IV.v.177f.). As was evident in the discussion of the fall of language, Henry interprets his relation to Richard and the past in varying ways. Here, he says that he got the crown via "by-paths and indirect crook'd ways," alluding to his usurpation but not elaborating on it, except to say that he tried to make powerless those who raised him and that, when Hal is king, he should busy their minds with foreign wars to "waste the memory of the former days."

Henry dies, his mind obsessed with the interpretation of history as a way to maintain his family's hold on power. Understanding time is a means to power. With some irony, which Henry himself sees, for he vainly thought that he would die in Jerusalem as the prophecy said, he asks to die in the Jerusalem chamber. He makes the prophecy true in one sense but also illustrates the vanity of human wishes. In Christian typology time and space are telescoped in the body of Christ, with the fall, incarnation, and redemption all focused on Jesus. At the end of his life, Henry sees the double image of the chamber and the Holy Land as Jerusalem after he has offered Hal political advice based on realpolitik and has chastened himself for vainglorious interpretations of time. Henry wavers between the private and public selves that constitute a king, caught in a dilemma. The circumscription of the king's dreams of the Holy Land into a single room reveals the limits of power, as Henry has said that the crusade was only a political ploy, but one that may, for his troubled Christian conscience, also be a lesson in necessary humility. Time is elusive, perhaps most for those who would use it to will themselves to power.[8]

It is Hal who passes the time with his subjects in order to control it. When we first see the prince, however, we have no such notions, for he merely replies to the first words we hear of Falstaff's—"Now, Hal, what time of day is it, lad?"—by saying that the fat knight has drunk, eaten, and slept too much to know the time of day (*1HIV*, I.ii.1f.). The prince also uses time as a measure of his wit and as a litany for Falstaff's sins or fallenness:

> What a devil hast thou to do with the time of day? Unless hours were cups of sack, and minutes capons, and clocks the tongues of bawds, and dials the signs of leaping-houses, and the blessed sun himself a fair hot wench in flame-coloured taffeta, I see no reason why thou shouldst be so superfluous to demand the time of the day. (I.ii.6–12)

Rather than taking offense, Falstaff admits that Hal understands him and then measures his time by his theft of the moon and seven stars and the future by his expectations of misrule and sanctioned theft when Hal is king. Sir John expounds at length about the "when" of Hal's kingship. Although the prince agrees with Falstaff's view of the future as a thief's carnival, he qualifies it with imagery of the tides that forebode the decline of Sir John and his cohorts, especially the hanging of Bardolph and Nym, for he says that the fortune of "Diana's foresters," as Falstaff calls them, of "the moon's men," is, like the tides, to be subject to the moon, to ebb and flow. According to Hal, such lunatic thieves are "now in as low an ebb as the foot of the ladder, and by and by in as high a flow as the ridge of the gallows" (I.ii.36–38). The prince's jests about time contain within them the threat of punishment. Falstaff concurs with Hal's witty view of time and observes his quibbles. Hal promises that Falstaff will have the office of hangman when the prince is king, and they continue in their repartee, acting all the while, so that Falstaff, for instance, takes up the kind of ironic stance that Cicero recommends in *De Oratore:* his bearing and his words are apparently at odds. Sir John uses this strategy to hide vice behind virtue and so obviously that Hal will delight in this role that turns "Puritan" hypocrisy on its ear. Falstaff acts as if Hal is corrupting him and not he, Hal. The prince revels in the role playing and commends him for amending his life from praying to purse snatching.

When Poins enters, the talk turns more to Satan and to teleology and eschatology, to end and judgment in more eternal Christian terms. There is, nonetheless, also jest in this deadly serious subject, for Poins would have them rob pilgrims on their way to Canterbury to honor saints who honored Christ. This transhistorical or synchronic time reminds Christians of the tree of knowledge, the crucifix, and the throne in the new Jerusalem; the fall, incarnation, and redemption; the beginning, middle, and end—all subsumed in the body of Christ. The jests among Hal, Falstaff, and Poins are much like the profane jokes in which Mak participates in *The Second Shepherd's Play* (ca. 1425) and that Mankind experiences in the eponymous morality play (ca. 1465). Time extends from drunken jokes about drunken hours to the jests of the inebriated about eternal matters. Like a drunk, Falstaff repeats himself, obsessed with the time when "thou art king," but he has his wits about him enough to parody Puritan cant, hoping in this sanctimony that Poins may move Hal, "that the true prince may (for recreation sake) prove a false thief, for the poor abuses of the time want countenance" (I.ii.150–53). The prince bids Falstaff farewell in seasonal images, calling him "the latter spring" and "All-hallown summer," or age with youth and Indian summer, both of which can be construed as compliments, for Falstaff behaves like a young man; but the images may also contain a hint of someone past his prime or nearly in the decline of winter and so imply insult. This double edge occurs almost always when Hal and Falstaff meet. Poins wants Hal to help enact a small drama, which entails dramatic irony: they will rob those who rob the pilgrims—Falstaff, Bardolph, Peto, and Gadshill. He tells the prince that Falstaff's lies will make the whole trick worthwhile and even predicts how Sir John will exaggerate the number of his assailants. In good directorial fashion, the prince agrees and then proceeds to speak a soliloquy mainly on his manipulation of time, one that helps to feed dramatic irony until the rejection of Falstaff and even into *Henry V*. Even as we attempt to divide dramatic from historical or, more broadly, nondramatic time, the division is tenuous and the temporalities interpenetrate. Similarly, it is difficult to separate Hal's views of time from those of other characters, especially of Falstaff and Hotspur, his rivals, and the king, his father.

Hal's soliloquy begins with a direct address that can make the "you" both his tavern companions and the audience, for although he may seem to be referring only to Falstaff and company, he is speaking a soliloquy and is also speaking to the "you" in the theater (I.ii.190–212). As in the last chapter, where we examined the similarities between Hal's imagery of sun and cloud and that of Richard and Bolingbroke, we should now look briefly at his conception of time. The prince will imitate the sun, hiding his beauty from the world, breaking through the foul vapors and mists to be more wondered at: Falstaff and the others, as it happens, are those contagious clouds who may seem to strangle him. He justifies this metaphor with another comparison, this time more strictly of time than of space. He reasons that if all the year were holidays when people played, holidays would become tedious, so that he will be like a rare accident, and, to mix metaphors, will "pay the debt I never promised," a little translation of his self and of the idea of redemption. He continues his series of metaphors, saying that he will be better than his word, thereby throwing into doubt the virtue of language because action and the world can improve on it, likening himself to a jewel that is brighter because of the foil, more attractive because it has faults to set it off, images that are like those that Worcester and, later, Canterbury use to describe the prince's reformation.

Hal uses words as a foil. He is so skilled at language that other characters cannot often guess his motives, but he denies the word, as it falls short of his goal of redemption, of integrating his self. For Hal, the word is not the Word, and he, not Christ, will be his redeemer. He needs free will to want to overcome sin and seek atonement, but it seems the heavenly grace is either implicit or missing. Hal will make apparent sin or offense offend, to create a grand illusion, "Redeeming time when men think least I will," his final line and one that amplifies his idea of himself as his own redeemer. Later, as king, Hal will doubt this supreme confidence, seeing perhaps that instead of being the imitator of Christ he was the son of a usurper, one who had deposed God's deputy, as Richard had called himself.

The play extempore in the tavern, which will be discussed further in the next section, is important for Hal's view of time because it is not only dramatic but also echoes his vow to redeem time and foreshadows the actual rejection. In the play within the play, the prince vows to banish Falstaff, whom he likens to Satan, and so continues to view their acting and actions through a Christian temporality and worldview (II.iv.456–57, 475). In the tavern scene Hal and Falstaff also parody Hotspur, a different kind of rival the prince cannot abide. Shakespeare has juxtaposed Henry's historical sense of time, his one-year truancy from his crusade, and the fourteen hundred years since the crucifixion with Falstaff's comic suspension of time. History represents temporal limits, while comedy attempts atemporal patterns and character types. Hal observes that Sir John's clock is made up of sack, capons, bawds, and the like. Not only does Falstaff's sense of time invert Henry's urgency and sense of history but it also provokes a comic contradiction to the tearful and metaphorical clock that Richard imagines in prison (*1HIV*, I.ii.6–12; cf. *RII*, V.v.50–61). Perhaps no other passage better illustrates the contrast between the comic aspect of *1 Henry IV* and the tragic perspective of *Richard II*. Both Hal and Richard speak about minutes, hours, clocks, and dials, but the prince learns about the death of time in the tavern rather than the time of death in a prison. The lesson Hal learns throughout this play is one that Richard learns too late: time will waste youth if youth will waste time. Whereas the tricksters and robbers never learn, concerning themselves only with the "minutiae" of time, Hal yokes all time with the immediate time of thieves: "I am now of all humours that have showed themselves humours since the old days of goodman Adam to the pupil age of this present twelve o'clock at midnight" (II.iv.90–93). Hal thinks about the temporality of the fall and the fall into temporality. By way of irony, Shakespeare also raises the truth about time. Falstaff lies about killing Hotspur in battle in a way that resembles Percy's description of the fight between Mortimer and Glendower, both lasting an hour: "we rose both at an instant, and fought a long hour by Shrewsbury clock" (V.iv.146–47; cf. I.iii.98–100). Falstaff fictionalizes time, but even the "true" man, Hotspur, in Henry's view is fabricating a myth with and in time.

The word "time" also reveals the ironic gap between desire and execution among the characters, as well as the limited views of time that the characters hold. Because Henry is dealing in appearances, he says to Hal "The hope and expectation of thy time is ruin'd," but, instead, Hal is right in his prediction, for Hotspur will yield "even the slightest worship of his time" (III.ii.36–37, 144–51). Through the word "time," the audience experiences the most uncompromising aspect of the prince's character, for he would control it and compete with all those around him. Hotspur has the most heroic conception of time, but even he falls short, unable to conceive of his human predicament—which military heroism by definition tries to ignore. Hotspur thinks naïvely that his father and uncle will atone for their abetment of Bolingbroke in Richard's time (I.iii.178–80, 239). Rather than redemption, Worcester views time as bringing revenge and ripening opportunity. After hearing these words, Hotspur's wishes are full of irony: "O let the hours be short, / Till fields, and blows, and groans applaud our sport!" (I.iii.295–96, cf. 282–88). Hal, not Hotspur, will redeem time, at least in part. Impatience helps shorten Percy's hours. Neither Richard's teary dial nor Hal's description of Falstaff's "sackclock" resembles Hotspur's urgent timepiece: "O gentlemen, the time of life is short! / To spend that shortness basely were too long / If life did ride upon a dial's point, / Still ending at the arrival of an hour" (V.ii.81–84). As Percy lies dying, his heroic time almost over, he begins to experience the ironic tension between loss of youth and reputation and loss of life. The "proud titles" that Hotspur loses to Hal wound his thoughts worse than any sword could flesh, "But thoughts, the slaves of life, and life time's fool, / And time, that takes survey of all the world, / Must have a stop" (V.iv.76–82). This breathless comparison is like that in Hal's "sackclock." In these words we may observe a notion common to Shakespeare's tragedies, that the characters are fools of time. The oxymoron of the temporal *katascopos* also seems to be functioning here. While dying, Percy, like Richard, relates thoughts to time in a chain of association (cf. *RII*, V.i.5f.). Both Richard and Hotspur try to make sense of their life and times, to order their misfortune by metaphorical thought, but discover foremost their moral limitation and, both poetic and flawed, they evoke in their audience ambiguous and mixed feelings.

Hal stands between Hotspur and Falstaff, where he learns not to be impatient like Percy and not to waste time like Sir John. If Hal will redeem time partly by rejecting Falstaff, Sir John would have cast off Poins "hourly any time this two and twenty years" but could not because he was "bewitched with the rogue's company" (II.ii.15–17). Lacking discipline, Falstaff could probably neither reform nor reject Poins nor show more humanity than Hal. Time fulfills while it limits. Falstaff is not always a true friend in word—he is most often a loyal friend in deed. Although he has seen hell in Bardolph's face for "two and thirty years," he does not dispose of him (III.iii.13–47). At the end of *1 Henry IV*, Percy dies, while Falstaff lives, for rather than to stand and die, for Sir John "'twas time to counterfeit" and live. The audience will observe that Henry did almost the same thing to survive. Through this comic perspective, Shakespeare complicates Hal's view of time, as well as Hotspur's death and idea of time.

Shakespeare's irony also qualifies Hal's comic triumph. Even though the prince seems to enjoy tavern life, he confides to the audience about his redemption of time, so that how much of his biding of time is prudent wisdom, harmless celebration, or callous deception remains uncertain (I.ii.212). The prince seems to display these attributes simultaneously. For all Hal's mock-serious preaching to Sir John on wasting time—an important theme in *Richard II*—he drinks himself to the point where he proposes to Ned small tricks "to drive away the time till Falstaff come" and asks Francis ironic questions about time (II.iv.28–29, 41f.). With as much determination and grimness as Hotspur shows when he swears he will kill the prince, Hal will redeem time on Percy's head (III.ii.36–37, 144–46). In another mood Hal asks Sir John, who even jokes on the battlefield: "What, is it time to jest and dally now?" (V.iii.55). In Percy's death Hal has had his wish, for although he praised Percy as gracing more than anyone else "this latter age with noble deeds," he seems to have wanted more than anything to displace his rival (V.i.92, iv). Even if Hal is at the center of the comic resolution of *1 Henry IV*, he will in *2 Henry IV* fall again into the king's disapproval and have to redeem himself once more, and at the end of *Henry V* time will play similar grim tricks with his triumph.

The conflict in time in *2 Henry IV* is between king and rebels, king and son, and prince and Falstaff. The last of these relations deserves more attention. Ideas of time consist of remembrance of things past, formal views of the past, daily concerns, and thoughts for the future, the present age, and, more generally, time itself. Rumor governs time in the play but so, too, does Hal. Unlike the king, Warwick understands that Hal will cast off his followers and perfect himself in time (IV.iv. 68–78). Warwick's speech echoes the "mete" and "measure" of Mark 4.24 in which Christ says: "Take heede what ye heare. With what measure ye mete, it shall bee measured unto you: and unto you that heare, shall more bee giuen." Hal's judgment will be judged, if not by his God, then by his fellow characters, so that he must not look for a speck in the eye of another if a beam lodges in his own eye. As Falstaff, playing Henry, said to Hal: "But to say I know more harm in him than in myself were to say more than I know" (*1HIV*, II.iv.460–61). According to Warwick, the prince will also make the lives of others more esteemed by knowing the worthlessness of his former companions.[9] The old crux remains: does Hal learn from his experiences, turning "past evils to advantages," or does he reject his companions out of political expedience? In other words, does the prince use history or does history use him? We experience a tension between Hal's need to reject his companions and the costs of proud judgment. Hal is in a "constructive dilemma": he cannot win either way. The characters continue to be caught between the time of day and the historical times. Northumberland has challenged personified time, but his actions are less heroic than his words, and Henry's time is an ironic reversal: once he eclipsed Richard but now fears that Hal will overshadow him (*2HIV*, I.i.150–52; IV.v.96–100; *RII*, III.iii.54–67). The prince finds himself in times that his fellow characters think out of joint: Northumberland calls them wild and troublesome; the Chief Justice, "th'unquiet time" (as do Hall and Holinshed); Hastings, brawling; Scroop, misordered; but Falstaff recommends that Hal "Repent at idle times as thou mayst," speaking truer than he knows. While members of court and rebel camp realize the frantic danger of the time, Sir John represents the idleness of the tavern. Whereas the rebels personify time— Northumberland considering it spiteful yet something to resist but capable of conferring advantage on the patient man, Hastings thinking that time rules men and thus its dictates must be followed, the Archbishop seeing time as a flowing stream that forces the rebels from their quiet with "the rough torrent of occasion" until time will show the king their grievances—Hal blames himself for so idly profaning "the precious time" in the tavern (I.i.150, iii.110; II.iii.67–68, iv.358–62; IV.i.69–76). Already the prince is renouncing in public the wasting of time at the Boar's Head. By way of dramatic irony, the audience observes how seriously Hal follows Falstaff's advice at repenting "at idle times" (II.ii.122). The irony is both prospective and retrospective, for early in Part One Hal promised to redeem time, and, when the rejection occurs in Part Two (act 5, scene 5), the audience knows how earnest he is about atonement in time. Sad and laughable is Falstaff's concern that he did not have time enough to order new liveries for Hal's coronation, for the new king is about to redeem time by banishing Falstaff until he repents. Shakespeare yokes ironically the idle and redeemed times, showing Hal taking Sir John's mock advice and sweeping aside his low companions. Nor does Falstaff even promise to repent as he did in *1 Henry IV*. Time reflects the movement of an ironic reversal from the beginning of the first part to the end of the second. Only Hal seems to survive the reversal, but, considering the critical uproar over the rejection, even he controls time with qualified success. Henry and Falstaff misunderstand Hal's idea of time; dirty tricks help make the rebels victims of time; and, through an ambivalent rejection, the taverners also fall. Whether or not Hal himself is more a victim of time than he now appears will be a question raised in *Henry V.*

Falstaff's rejection is a kind of last judgment that is not final: history continues and the measure is not measured out in a way that is satisfactory to everyone. About half the critics, and the taverners themselves, do not seem to have accepted the rejection: Falstaff is stunned by it. But there is also the question of history that is raised for Hal. Henry's last advice to his son is to fight a foreign war that "May waste the memory of former days" (*2HIV*, IV.v.215). This "forgetfulness"—the obliteration of the past by the present—differs from Sir John's and has more to do with policy than with forgiveness. The present can try to use the past to manipulate the future, but these machinations and expectations are as imperfect and finite as the people who implement them. The remembrance of the "impartial spirit" of justice also appears to concern Hal (V.ii.116). It is with some irony that Falstaff, sweating to see the prince, chose "not to remember," "putting all affairs else in oblivion," because the new monarch will forget Sir John, only remembering him when turning past evil to advantage (V.v.21–26). History is partial to each character, though more partial to some. Hal does not use the word "history," but Warwick, as we have observed, does, saying that Richard could foretell events in the lives of men by examining past examples to elucidate them, a commonplace doctrine of history in the Renaissance.[10] Clarence refers to the chronicles and echoes Holinshed, but this transformation of a source is not a systematic view of history and is the character's and not explicitly Shakespeare's.[11] The self-reflexive reference to history is scant, and it is Hal's manipulation of time that calls attention most to temporality in the play. In the second part of this chapter, we shall see that Shakespeare is more particularly interested in the history play than in nondramatic forms of history.[12]

Henry V reveals that Falstaff's rejection does not solve the problem of time for Hal. The Chorus tells us a great deal about the nature of time in the play, but its concerns are mostly with the nature of the history play. Henry the Fifth's views of time should reveal how continuous or discontinuous they are from the character of Hal in the *Henry IV* plays. Henry's views of time do not occur without a context. Although in *Henry V* there are many references to the past, present, and future and to time in general, the word "history" occurs only twice, once in the Chorus and once in Henry's speech, both near the beginning of the play. He says to Canterbury and others who have spoken for the war with France: "Either our history shall with full mouth / Speak freely of our acts, or else our grave" shall be mute without even an epitaph of war (I.ii.230–33). History, for Henry, is a record of victories, famous and glorious. Anticipating the king, Canterbury views the chronicles of England as writings laden with "sumless treasures" that have served subsequent generations as the memory of the glory that Edward the Third, whom he thinks Henry should emulate, won in the French wars (I.ii.155–65).[13] This is the official and heroic view of history, the one the Boy supplements at scene 2 of act 3. Speaking to the king, Fluellen makes the second and last mention of the chronicles: "Your grandfather of famous memory [John of Gaunt] . . . and your great-uncle Edward the Plack Prince of Wales, as I have read in the chronicles, fought a most prave pattle here in France." Henry agrees with the Welsh captain, and both think famous victories serve as exempla for the great (IV.vii.94–98). In life, as J. H. Walters reminds us, Gaunt was six years old at the time of Cressy. Either the chronicles that Canterbury and Fluellen read were wrong or these readers forgot or Shakespeare lapsed or decided to telescope history for greater dramatic effect. For whatever cause, the playwright changes the "facts" and chronicles. Once again, a character associates formal history with the perpetuation of past glory and displays a more limited view of history than the author.

The tavern still represents the unofficial view of history, although without the eloquence of Falstaff. The Boy remembers when Falstaff, who has just died, saw a flea on Bardolph's nose and said it was a damned soul burning in hell, which reminds Bardolph that he will no longer drink Sir John's liquor (*HV*, II.iii.41–45). This personal remembrance recollects Falstaff, his references to Bardolph's face and damnation, the rejection, and, more generally, the events of

1 and *2 Henry IV*. The rejection of Falstaff relates to Richard's deposition, for both are falls, of crucial importance for the Second Tetralogy, that recollect the fall of England if not the Fall itself. The allusion also refers to the eschatology that Hal and Falstaff used as their temporal framework. The rejection marks the meeting of two fictional characters: Henry is mostly "historical" whereas Falstaff is mostly "unhistorical," although fact, myth, and legend interpenetrate in their constitutions. Myth and legend are part of history and blur the demarcations between history and fiction. In recalling Sir John, Shakespeare is reminding the audience of the importance of fiction in his history as well as history in his fiction, the Oldcastle in Falstaff, the prodigal son in Hal. The similar root meanings of "history" and "myth"—story and plot—may signal their long-potent conflation, and we ignore this coexistence and collision at our peril.

Henry's view of time is still a matter of his control over others as it was in *1* and *2 Henry IV*. For the king, individual soldiers should prepare their souls for death. If they die, death in Christ is an advantage (as time becomes eternal blessedness); if they do not, the preparation was a blessed time. Bates and Williams contest Henry's views of time and responsibility vigorously and make them problematic. Henry uses a favorite distinction of his—the relation of outward and inward—in defying the French, saying that although time has worn the appearance of his men to slovenry, their hearts remain firm and brave (IV.iii.114). This is a king who sees time as adversarial, as he did when he was a prince. When peace comes, Henry and Burgundy indulge in temporal metaphors and sexual jokes at the expense of Katharine (V.ii.54–62, 309–37). For a modern audience, Henry's sexual perspective of the women he would like to be his wife qualifies his heroism and raises questions about his intentions. Henry has not escaped the issue of Falstaff entirely, and his time of triumph is modified by his violent and sexual images and by the fall that the Epilogue describes. Later, these qualifications and problems will lead us to a discussion of the movement of the Second Tetralogy toward a problem play and to a discussion of the critical nature of the Shakespearean history play.

Each king—Richard, Bolingbroke, and Hal—attempts to control time, something that is impossible in a fallen world. Hal, or Henry the Fifth, is more successful at achieving this control than his two predecessors, but even he is caught in the human dilemma of being in time and hovering above it, being of time and trying to shape it. Even if Henry the Fifth is the most successful, his victory over time is temporary, for the rejection of Falstaff lingers, and his view of kingship and death calls into question his own responsibility and authority in controlling time and governing England, let alone France. Through the kings particularly, Shakespeare explores the nature of time and history, using the fall of Richard and the broken succession as a point of departure, raising questions about the nature of authority, including his own. Playwright and audience write and hear (or read) in time and, especially through dramatic irony, share a katascopic view of the characters and their world, but both are caught in time and have also to identify and empathize with the human limitations of the characters. Neither author nor audience can have control over time (and thus over interpretation), so that, although they draw together through the paradoxes and dilemmas that irony emphasizes, they are, at the same moment, also divided. As the history plays devote particular attention to time and try to shape time, the very accomplishment or even possibility of the history play is called into question. We shall now examine the relation, if not collision, of historical and dramatic time by looking at irony of theater, the self-conscious or self-reflexive allusions to the theater or use of acting and directing.

THEATER

Dramatic time occupies a crucial place in the Second Tetralogy. Shakespeare's characters explore the methods of representing history in the theater in several primary ways—by referring self-consciously to the theater, by knowing they are acting or behaving with the godlike control of the playwright, and by being choruses and other overtly theatrical devices.[14] These methods remind the audience that this history is dramatic. Not only does this theatrical self-reflexivity emphasize the fall of language and the fall of time but it also elaborates the problems of trying to represent history on the stage. The rest of this chapter will look at irony of theater generally. It will end with an examination of choric scenes and choruses, concentrating on the Chorus to *Henry V*, the history play that most manifests itself as a problem play. Although the problems in these plays were not usually raised until this century, Elizabeth is reported to have found problematic her relation to Shakespeare's Richard the Second, and the whole tetralogy represents an Elizabethan anxiety over succession and order. Unfortunately, but perhaps inevitably under a more absolutist government, the Elizabethans had no systematic dramatic criticism that might indicate views some members of the audience held without fear of reprisal. When dramatic criticism develops in English, some early critics also challenge the accepted view of the plays. For instance, in the 1770s Maurice Morgann thinks that there is a secret or ironic meaning to Falstaff's character, and in the early 1800s William Hazlitt does not think that Henry the Fifth is heroic. When in the 1890s Frederick Boas borrows his term "problem play" from modern plays about social issues like those of Bernard Shaw and the French *pièce à thèse*, he observes that some of Shakespeare's comedies are problematic. Each age is probably aware in different forms of the simultaneous existence of patriotism and the questioning of it. In this century we have two films of *Henry V*, Olivier's patriotic and epic version and Kenneth Branagh's opposite view. Both positions can exist in the same person. *Henry V* and the earlier plays of the tetralogy represent these views at the same time.

The Theater and Its Ironies

Shakespeare probes the relation between acting and action, actuality and appearance. Irony of theater emphasizes the difference between the appearance of human pretense (or expectation) and what is taken for reality, between theater and world, acting and action, character and actor. Generally speaking, the ironic gap between the public actor and the private man precipitates the tragic fall of Richard, the torment of Bolingbroke, and the dilemmas Hal faces in his relation to Falstaff and the world and in maintaining power in England while conducting a war in France. Shakespeare represents the possibility that theatricality makes the world seem more and less real, that playing defines human nature and politics but falls short of life, that drama is a great celebration and an act of treason against the central self. Identity and integrity lose themselves and disintegrate as they search for character and unity. They do not, however, fall apart into a discontinuity of shattered selves. Through the truths of fictions and the fictions of truth, characters and the people for whom they are analogues—as well as the playwright and the audience—shape themselves, create a central self around whom the debris of orbiting moons fly in warped paths. Each personality, like the history play itself, plays between centripetal and centrifugal forces. In this section we shall discuss the role of the irony of theater in defining the individuality of each play, as well as their common pursuit of representing history.

The person playing Richard is actor and character, a presence representing the past while moving into the future, integrating and alienating in time. Richard is the glory of the theater and a pretext for antitheatrical attitudes. His bent for histrionics and deception prevents self-knowledge and knowledge of the world, but he is a character in the theater, the world of illusion whose truths bear on life in strange and important ways. In prison, when Richard has learned much more than he knew before, his conscious reaching after metaphor keeps him from stripping down to the bare, essential man that Lear tries to become. Shakespeare's theater criticizes itself as much as it tries self-promotion. Richard cannot throw off all his roles, for he continues to judge others at the beginning of the play and to act uncontented and woeful roles, consciously, in his fallen world, though he is a more substantial man and a less ceremonial king than he was before (*RII*, V.v). He was a stately upstager to a king of mirrors to a king of metaphors, all the while trying to discover something about the king and the man. Richard's acting, failed him at the opening of the play, for he could control Mowbray and Bolingbroke, and Gaunt saw through his roles (I.iii, iv; II.i). By evoking an awareness of the theatricality or the fiction of the theater, Shakespeare calls attention to deceit, illusion, and acting in life. In ceremony Richard has an actor's sense of timing, stopping the lists at Coventry at the most dramatic moment, turning the deposition scene into a sad but subtle occasion in which he unmasks Bolingbroke's generous and unambitious pose by asking him pointed questions, making him seize the crown and so stressing the usurpation as much as Richard's defeat, and forcing him to break the promise of granting Richard freedom. Richard's acting has also broken his identity (or the shadow of himself, as Bolingbroke so subtly puts it) into a thousand pieces, like the mirror in the deposition scene. Politically, Richard fails to see the difference between substance and shadow as much as Bolingbroke, and he has underestimated his rival. Richard has realized earlier, as York later confirms, that Bolingbroke, with his "craft of smiles," plays to the common people in a kind of political theater, but Richard realizes too late how crafty Bolingbroke really is (I.iv.23–34; V.ii.7–40). Whereas Bolingbroke controls his acting, Richard gets carried away with histrionics. When Richard spoke about "the death of kings," he worked out his woe in an "epic" metaphor until Carlisle reminded him that he had to take practical action (II.ii.144–79). The theatrical image of the coronation stays with Richard in prison, where he comes closest to resolving his (and humanity's) ironic, fallen nature, the gap between public and private selves.

The theatrical metaphor becomes even more open and explicit. Even York will criticize Richard's theatricality in the face of Bolingbroke's public, political acting, his dissembling, his profession of and play at humility to gain popularity. York's simile "As in a theater" compares the acting styles of Bolingbroke and Richard, the two kings who destabilize regal authority (V.ii.23–28). Within the likeness of this worldly theater, York differentiates Richard and Bolingbroke. The world to which York refers is within a literal theater, a self-consciously complex irony beyond York's scope that Shakespeare shares with his audience. For York, Bolingbroke is the "well-grac'd actor." The theatrical Richard cannot play to win the hearts of the commoners but may be more successful with the hearts of the audience. The supposition, "As in a theater," demands this comparison between the two reactions. The audience comes to realize the complexity of roles in the play. Bolingbroke acts many parts—the upholder of justice, the loyal son, the humble subject, the ruthless king, the forgiving monarch, and the penitent murderer. Richard also plays many roles, as he himself recognizes, for he is more public about his consciousness of role playing than Bolingbroke is—the proud king, the tyrant, the wavering man beneath the trappings of divine right, the broken man, the separated husband, and the courageous king in death. By the end of the play, Bolingbroke, like Richard, also finds that he is trapped in the shadowy prison of himself and, in the ways of the world, that his success limits him as Richard limited himself through failure. Like Bolingbroke, the audience discovers that faces and mirrors, light and shadows blend but are not identical in the theater of the world and the world of the theater. The mirror held up to human nature is not simply reflective and reflexive. Kingship does not correspond directly with divine right. There are two different kings playing different roles, and so they question their representation and the word "king" itself. This disjunction between signifier and signified questions the authority of the ruler in the theater and outside, an opposition that interpenetrates. By analogy, we should also scrutinize the integrity and authority of author and audience. We are to wonder who, if anyone, has authority to interpret history.

Shakespeare also experiments with the relation between narrative and representation in the theater. A peculiar situation occurs in plays in which characters tell stories within the context of dramatic representation. People—actors—play roles in which they relate tales. Effectively, we observe presentation and representation, the teller and the tale, narrative made flesh. The teller is always part of the tale, conflating the supposed opposition between fiction and truth, story and world, collapsing all into the antilogic of metaphor. The ontology and epistemology—his attempt (and ours) to know what exists and what does not, to understand what we know or, perhaps, how we know—becomes especially difficult in the theater because the teller is telling and listening to the tale while being part of it while being represented in the theater in the world. The person is an actor who impersonates a character who represents a person who once existed in the world or who could have existed or could exist in the world, depending on whether he or she is a historical character. The audience is present before this representation and must also play with the multiplicitous elusiveness of selves in the play and in itself. These tales in a theater emphasize that we are caught between the integration and disintegration of selves. In *Richard II* the theater is one of sorrowful tales and other fictions: Gaunt's "death's sad tale" (II.i.16), Richard's "sad stories of the death of kings" and the winter tales of old folks recounting "woeful ages long ago" (III.ii.156; V.i.40–42), York's broken story of Bolingbroke and Richard (including "As in a theater") (V.ii. 1f.), and the Groom's story of Bolingbroke on roan Barbary (V.v.76f.). By making these characters view analogies between fiction and life, Shakespeare invites the audience to see similar likenesses and, caught themselves, to witness characters caught in a broken tale about a broken world. He makes the audience more aware of the ironic gap between theatergoer and the person with many functions apart from attending plays. Shakespeare teaches the audience the self-knowledge that Richard moves toward and a broader knowledge of identity and the various limitations of the characters and, by analogy, of people. Irony of theater shows that the self is complex and knowledge is not easily attainable. The trouble is that the theater is part of the world, makes history as it represents it, so that the opposition between inside and outside interpenetrates. The irony of theater makes the audience aware of the difficulty of defining world and theater, of what exists and what does not, of the difficulty of knowing.[15]

The first thing that comes to mind when considering the irony of theater in *1 Henry IV* is the tavern acting as a theater, as a dramatic school that Hal turns into a training ground for his political acting. Because this play within a play has been discussed well on many occasions, we shall examine it briefly, and only where it most matters for our argument. Theatrical irony in Part One serves both its comic and historical aspects. The comic value of acting, unlike the more tragic acting in *Richard II*, draws characters together in a community, although Hal's and Falstaff's parodying of Hotspur can be divisive in *1 Henry IV*. Shakespeare shows Hotspur to be closest to Kate when they enjoy his gift for parody (II.iii; III.i). Parody reveals tragic political sidecurrents as well as the comic community of actors. Hotspur parodies Glendower and later loses his support. The poetic Percy chastens the Welshman for his poetry; and, as in other instances, Hotspur's blindness to his own nature, to his own acting, helps lead to his demise. Nor does Falstaff fathom the depths of Hal's acting, not realizing the difference between histrionics and political dissembling. Many characters are blind to the difference between the roles of power and those of comic celebration.

Acting reveals the dilemma of the characters between unity and division. The inhabitants of the Boar's Head include the audience in their festive scene, and the parodies that Hotspur, Hal, and Falstaff perform invite playgoers to laugh at the foibles of men and to see that characters from the rebel camp (including Wales), court, and tavern can all enjoy such sport and are humanly much alike despite their professed differences. Hotspur, Glendower, Henry, Hal, and Falstaff all express their rivalries and disagreements in the same way—they assume roles. The relation between acting and action, theater and politics destabilizes the notion of central self while reinforcing it, for to play a role is to be other than one is, but to be entirely other, especially in a physical sense, is impossible. The confusion and conflation of true and false self among person, actor, and character complicates any drama, but this is especially so for a history play, which foregrounds the relation between theater and world, fiction and fact. Hal was a person, a player in history, and while Shakespeare looks to the chronicles for information about him, he also transmutes the Hal of legend who plays the role of prodigal son, as well as inventing lines for the prince and transforming the historical and fictional traditions that represent him. Hal participates but remains aloof, giving a conscious political purpose to his acting more than Hotspur and Falstaff could ever do. In Hal's victory, on one level, Shakespeare uses the antitheatrical, proessentialist, and antirepresentational view of much of his culture to represent the cool triumph of political acting and action over mere theatrics and histrionics; but, on another level, he qualifies Hal's triumph with the loss of friendship, sincerity, and warmth, qualities the culture idealized. In the theater north of the walled city, Shakespeare may have been preaching to the converted, but then playwright and audience also participated in a larger society, some of whose members were deeply suspicious of the theater and the representations of art generally. Author and audience play various roles, and their central selves are the governance of those roles. Shakespeare does not dismiss the antitheatrical view but interrogates it by yoking it with its protheatrical counterpart.

Hal is the consummate actor in *1 Henry IV*. His roles are masterful, his ultimate disguise deeper than the one he wears to Gad's Hill, for he shares with the audience the political design of his acting early in the play (I.ii). Henry, Hotspur, and Falstaff misread the man for the role, but Worcester and, later, Canterbury interpret Hal's acting the way he does. Henry the Fourth plays a tawdry game of counterfeits at Shrewsbury, but his son will have nothing to do with such an obvious multiplication of the self. Even though in this play Hal rewards Falstaff, his acting dupes the fat knight, so that the audience is aware that despite Sir John's comic resurrection his future is far from secure. One of the old cruxes in Part One is how much Hal plans the rejection and stands aloof and how much he loses himself in his roles in the tavern, an uncertainty from the opening of this play through the rejection to Falstaff's death. This unsureness emphasizes the relation between author and actor, synchrony and diachrony. Hal is simultaneously the true self he reveals and the roles he plays, creating confusion for other characters and for the audience. The prince is drawn to Falstaff and repulsed by him, is sympathetic and alienated. Through the dramatic irony of the "I know you all" soliloquy, Shakespeare draws together character and audience, but through the revelation of Hal's design he makes the audience aware of Hal's alienation from Falstaff and others. Political dissembling becomes the mark of the house of Lancaster. Neither Henry, Hal, nor Prince John can be trusted as plain men who show their motives to the world. Acting is as divisive as it is celebratory. The indirection of role playing, that of metaphor, is rhetorical and strictly antilogical. It attempts to communicate between author and audience, which is the first aim of rhetoric, but also uses or abuses or teaches and amuses the audience with manipulation, another ancillary part of rhetoric and acting. The audience learns from the stage, a place for *Homo ludens*, the importance of role playing in the world. In the prince the theatergoer observes, perhaps, the subtlest challenge and danger political acting can represent. Even Hal, the coolest and most self-controlled actor in the play, cannot see that by giving his role playing a political purpose he may be changing play to design and making dissembling a part of his nature, so that he has no true self to reveal to others and to himself when he reforms. How true and how fictive the self is becomes a problem as much in life as in literature and history. In a fallen world illusion and actuality mix. Paradoxically, in this community after the Fall, the very bonds between actor and audience, theater and world will cause division among people.

The tavern playlet concentrates the various components of irony of theater (II.iv). One is parody. Waiting for Sir John, Hal parodies

Percy's honor—which consists in a love of killing that permeates his domestic life—plays both Hotspur and Lady Percy, and uses hyperbole to reduce their way of life to absurdity by having Percy pay attention to his wife only when he wants her to feed his horse or to answer her (after an hour) that he has killed fourteen men (adding "a trifle, a trifle") (II.iv.99–106). Shakespeare also juxtaposes Hal's parody with the conversation of Hotspur and Lady Percy in the previous scene, providing a qualifying perspective on Percy's nobility. Hal's festive wit has a political edge. As Hotspur declaims in a Marlovian style, Hal calls Sir John his "sweet creature of bombast," a stuffed man, perhaps, given to verbal inflation (I.iii.199–205; II.iv.323).[16] Intertextuality, which produces many effects, is another part of parody. Falstaff asks for a cup of sack to make his eyes red and weepy, for he will speak passionately in the old-fashioned rant of Thomas Preston's *Cambises*, a parody that may also ridicule some of Shakespeare's contemporaries as being out of date: "Weep not, sweet queen, for trickling tears are vain" (II.iv.380–82, 386).[17] Sir John's mock bombast is history made present, both as a general parody of high, astounding terms and as a more topical parody. The intertextuality and oblique relation among fiction, life, and history challenges notions of essence and essential character. In Sir John, Shakespeare represents the riotous and skeptical elements of England that official history often neglects on purpose but without which historical narrative remains incomplete. A history play—which combines the traditional attributes of poetry and philosophy, that is, imagination and reason—can also present a fuller view of human experience and history by looking at the whole from the vantages of the various groups that make up society.

Another component is dramatic irony. Much of the first part of act 2, scene 4, consists in the enjoyment by Hal, Poins, and the audience of Falstaff's performance. Sir John lies, and in his comic exaggeration the question of truth creeps in. Still another component, which is closely related to dramatic irony, is the gap between actuality and illusion. The "play extempore," which only gives the illusion of spontaneous acting, begins when the prince and Sir John agree to rehearse Hal's appearance before the king. The theater will be a school for life, but the two players do not agree on what kind of rules their theater will use. Falstaff makes the theater mimetic and asks that its illusion be accepted through imagination: "This chair shall be my state, this dagger my sceptre, and this cushion my crown." Hal refuses Falstaff's assumptions and names the nature of the "outside world" as he sees it: "Thy state is taken for a joint-stool, thy golden sceptre for a leaden dagger, and thy precious rich crown for a pitiful bald crown"(II.iv.373–77). The prince inverts theatrical illusion or reduces it to props without the imaginative transformation of author, actor, and audience. He divides the theater from the world; he separates himself from Falstaff. It is as if Sir John has read Aristotle and Hal, Brecht. One assumes representation, the other alienation. Through Hal's view of the theater in this context, Shakespeare may be showing how precarious are the illusion and imagination that bind the community of audience and stage. Shakespeare is possibly exploring the idea that the theater requires both representation and alienation just as history does, for to interpret drama and history one must identify with them enough to empathize, to be interested enough in the characters and events to want to interpret, but estrange oneself enough to realize there is a gap between past and present, author and audience. Audience and readers must recognize that they are fallen into the text or performance; only through imagination and reason can the gap be mended or made fortunate with great difficulty and humility or tentativeness. Just as the prince strips down Falstaff's illusion to theatrical properties, so too by analogy does he remind the audience that he is an actor playing Hal who is considering acting in a play within a play and that his actions and the part of the history they depict, which are represented through the illusion of the play, are multileveled and oblique. Here, the irony of theater is like a Chinese box.

If Hal sees himself as a foil when speaking about his reformation, he is not using the modern theatrical term, however tempting it might be for a twentieth-century interpreter, but he is using "foil" as the setting of a jewel that makes it look more brilliant, a meaning found in Gaunt's words to Bolingbroke on the occasion of his exile: "The sullen passage of thy weary steps / Esteem as foil wherein thou art to set / The precious jewel of thy home return" (*RII*, I.iii.265–67; cf. *1HIV*, I.ii.207–10). Bolingbroke differs in interpretation, for he says that he wanders from the jewels at home he loves, but Shakespeare has given to the house of Lancaster a preoccupation with the image of the foil and with the crown. The *Oxford English Dictionary* suggests that the word "foil" depends on the substance of the stone (and, to use the Lancastrian metaphor, the mettle of the person), for the term means: "A thin leaf of some metal placed under a precious stone to increase its brilliancy or under some transparent substance to give it the appearance of a precious stone." England, as Gaunt says in his famous speech in *Richard II*, is a "precious stone set in a silver sea." Whereas Hal sees himself as a precious stone, the audience may not do so readily as it must contend with his roles and his rejection of Falstaff. Like a jewel, the prince has many facets and it is difficult to see his center. In *2 Henry IV* the irony of theater complicates our view of Hal as well as our idea of the nature of the history play and of the theater.

In Part Two, Falstaff and the prince do not act much together, and this separation reflects the increasing satiric distance between these major characters and among the characters in general. Nor is the acting as inventive and as celebrative as the comedy of Part One. Time limits the play of wit in the tavern, so that in *2 Henry IV* there is no play extempore. The acting becomes darker, more political and predatory in the second part. To a certain extent, the characters are actors in a community that is dissolving partly because it has grown unaware of the similarities among people and their common play, their theater of the world as well as their world of the theater. Even though role playing in Part One occurs more frequently and is more complex, Part Two is not without its acting parts. More importantly, as we shall see in the next section, an induction and an epilogue envelop the action of the second part.

Theatrical terms remind the audience of being in a theater. Henry speaks about his troublesome rule, in which he has answered with peril men who thought him a usurper, and he concludes in dramatic terms: "For all my reign hath been but as a scene / Acting that argument" (*2HIV*, IV.v.197–98; cf. V.ii.23–24). The king is not sure whether he is playing a role with a supporting or not so supportive cast about him. If all the world's a stage, Henry is not certain how happy that state is. This instance particularly blurs the distinction between theater and world, and, even if a player king dignifies drama with his authority, it is also the power of the historical figure who was a king that gives the world as theater some weight. But then

Henry, like many of the characters, does not always speak a simple, direct truth—if truth can be so plain. These self-reflexive references to the theater are small reminders and play only a supporting role in the irony of theater.

On the whole, *2 Henry IV* displays less theatrical irony than *1 Henry IV*, for it does not contain great, self-conscious acting scenes such as those in which Hal and Falstaff play prince and king and Falstaff plays dead. A good way to see the dissolution of playacting is to compare act 2, scene 4, of both parts. Here, however, we shall only look at the role of Pistol, who was so popular, it seems, that he joined Falstaff as a humor on the title page of the quarto. As opposed to the characters of the earlier scene, in act 2, scene 4, of the second part Pistol loses himself in his role: he becomes so much the swaggerer that there is nothing behind or beside that part that is Pistol (*2HIV*, II.iv.108–211). His identity comprises tags from old plays, his soul being an intertextual creation about which the ancient himself seems naïve. He inflates lines from old plays, making Tamburlaine's horses go thirty instead of twenty miles a day and raising the three-headed dog of the underworld to kingship, which may be appropriate in a world where the term "king" has been called into question. Shakespeare creates a theatrical irony that relies heavily on dramatic irony when the Hostess takes these lines to be "very bitter words," although the audience knows them to be bombast from earlier plays and realizes that there is some Pistol in Tamburlaine but little Tamburlaine in Pistol. Part of the irony derives from the impossibility of the Hostess ever watching a performance of *Tamburlaine*, because of anachronism, although the actor playing her and the audience could have seen it. Shakespeare may be paying more than a parodic debt to Marlowe and, to a lesser extent, his predecessors and contemporaries, thereby separating himself from the community of playwrights in London while bonding with its "members" or their memory through a shared joke that is also shared with the audience. He makes Pistol as ludicrous as possible, for he causes the ancient to echo Muly Mahamet in Peele's *Battle of Alcazar*, in which Muly offers the lion's meat to Calypolis, his mother, who is starving, so that together they may meet the foe.[18]

Pistol has gone to many plays, like most members of the Elizabethan audience. Through the Pistolic blustering, "our humble author" parodies the dramatic rant of the late 1580s and early 1590s, creating amusement for the audience by sharing a joke that the actors can understand but the characters cannot, and reminding it of the contrast between these plays and his own. This parody is a kind of imitation that involves identity and an alienation that requires author and audience to distinguish the old from the new. In addition to Pistolian "interpretations" of Tamburlaine and Muly, the audience may be witnessing burlesques of some other of George Peele's plays and apparent echoes of Elyot's *Ortho-epia Gallica* (1593).[19] Shakespeare may have wanted the parody to be general, and, except perhaps for Marlowe, probably did not suffer the anxiety of influence through Pistol. The ancient speaks like a character from an old play, and, later, the only way that Falstaff thinks that he can get the news from this messenger is to join Pistol's "play." When Sir John asks his ancient to "deliver them like a man of this world," Pistol replies, "A foutre for the world and worldlings base! / I speak of Africa and golden joys." In the best Pistolian rhetoric, Falstaff answers: "O base Assyrian knight, what is thy news? / Let King Cophetua know the truth thereof" (V.iii.94–99). For Pistol, the world of the theater is world enough. Sir John tries to reach his ancient with his own language, but Pistol will not be rushed in his performance. His many theatrical tags and his ranting style, which is reminiscent of earlier plays, remind the audience that he is an embodiment of drama, a comic retrospective to the fledgling public theater.[20] The world is too mundane for Pistol. Shakespeare is a little like Pistol, for the tags of old poems and plays float through his mind. We cannot know the difference between conscious and unconscious echoes unless they make explicit their source. For instance, the playwright gives to the ranting Pistol fragmentary echoes of a poem by Anne Boleyn or her brother George on death, written as they awaited execution.[21] Unknown to Pistol, behind the bombast and the jokes lies a sad foreshadowing of death and punishment. Here is a strange interface between life and art, history and historical representation.

The characters play roles, even if their performances are increasingly transparent, lack conviction, or reflect a political meanness. Sir John plays the young, deaf man for the Chief Justice, acts and lies his way out of repaying his debts to the Hostess, delivers soliloquies in which he plays to the audience, and dupes Shallow while not perceiving Hal's role of the reformer. The Chief Justice sees through Falstaff's acting, and perhaps the fat knight wants him to as part of the performance. Sir John's soliloquies give the audience knowledge about other characters and himself that will enrich its enjoyment of future instances of dramatic irony—sometimes at Falstaff's expense. Deception seems to occupy Northumberland, Lancaster, Westmoreland, and Henry, so that acting becomes more and more an aspect of Machiavellian politics. Northumberland musters his rage against others when he himself appears a primary cause of his son's death and the defeat of the rebels, perhaps at least as much to diffuse the blame of his family and friends than out of sorrow for his son. There are other crafty actors. Westmoreland and Lancaster deceive the Archbishop, who appears open and direct, by pretending to be happy friends with him rather than the entrapping foes they really are. Henry, who seems to have fooled even the audience about his motives for leading a crusade, professes to Hal that the holy war was to serve as a diversion on another political stage. Irony of theater can play on the audience's knowledge or ignorance, unite or divide it from the author and characters. Ultimately, Hal deceives most of the other characters before he becomes king, so that he is the most effective actor in the play, although he may have strayed from his plan from time to time and may have sacrificed too much compassion in the process, and although Falstaff's great acting may have won the audience too much to his side to leave Hal's acting crown undisputed. Although playacting is less evident in *2 Henry IV*, it does yield an important irony. For the prince, the world, including the tavern, is a stage where men act out their lives to the scorn of the dead: "thus we play the fools with the time, and the spirits of the wise sit in the clouds and mock us" (II.ii.134–35). This is a mixture of the human and the godlike, the fallen and katascopic views that reveal the ironic wisdom of Hal. This may be an admission on the prince's part that his overview and control is not the ultimate one, and this understanding of temporality and his ultimate limitation qualifies the qualification of his triumph. By implication, we should comprehend the limits of our interpretations.

The Chorus is the main part of the irony of theater in *Henry V*, although other ironies complicate the reign of Henry the Fifth. Through a character's use of theatrical terms, Shakespeare conveys that character's awareness of acting to an audience watching an actor playing a part. A subsidiary element of the problem play is this self-referential role playing, so that the irony of theater shows the close relation of *Henry V* to that kind of drama (the other histories, however, also show this attribute). Many characters employ cognates of the word "play." According to Canterbury, the Black Prince "play'd a tragedy" for the French in battle; the Scots, Ely says, often "play" the mouse when the English cat is bruised with foreign wars; the Boy comments on Pistol's full voice and empty heart and says that Nym and Bardolph were much more valorous than "this roaring devil i' the old play"; the ancient wonders whether Fortune "plays" the hussy with him (*HV*, I.ii.105–6, 172; IV.iv.69–74; V.i.84). Most importantly, through the Boy, Shakespeare reminds the audience of morality plays in which the devil wielded the "dagger of lath." Here, however, Shakespeare inverts the tradition because Pistol (not just any old player) is a vice figure whom Fluellen beats with a leek rather than a wooden dagger. Even if the characters refer to role playing and to early English drama, they cannot understand the application of these references to *Henry V* as much as the actors playing the characters or, even more so, the audience, which weighs the views of each character. Irony sometimes limits the self-conscious acting for the character but enriches the theatrical experience of the audience. Dramatic irony reminds us that history is dramatic.

Henry is himself a major source of dramatic irony in the play. Perhaps the most effective type of dramatic irony, which is an integral part of the theater, occurs when the playwright has a character share with the audience information about a situation of which other characters are ignorant. Henry's distinction between the outward and the inward provides an example of this type. Possibly, however, the irony behind this irony is that inner and outer interpenetrate, and Henry's repression of his private side cannot help but influence his public side. The differentiation is closely related to the king's awareness of acting. He contrasts the private man with the public monarch, calls the pomp of *ceremony* a "proud dream," *playing* "so subtly with a king's repose," and criticizes the symbols, accoutrements, and "farced title" of kingship for not preventing him from staring into hell during sleepless nights while the common man sleeps without *ceremony* (IV.i.245–90).[22] Ironically, Henry finds himself in a similar predicament to that of his father, who lost sleep over kingship while the ship boy slept through the storm (*2HIV*, III.i.4–31). Still, Henry shows his men a brave face. Even though the king is an actor, he does not like the processions and appearances of kingship: the private man is apparently at odds with the public self. Whereas in *1* and *2 Henry IV* Hal shared his idea of inward and outward only with the audience, in this play he sometimes shows his generals his disdain for gold, dependents, or garments, for "Such outward things dwell not in my desires," saying that he covets "inward" values like honor (IV.iii.24–29).[23] When Henry invades France, the audience may wonder whether he came for honor or for titles and lands. Whereas Hal was anything but plain and rough and open, as king he claims to Katharine and to Burgundy to be such. Instead, in the wooing scene, Henry takes on some of the manner and tone of Hotspur. It is, however, this same apparently shy and awkward man who insists that "nice customs curtsy to great kings" and kisses a seemimgly reluctant Kate and then proceeds to match his wit with Burgundy while claiming to be a barbarian with a rude tongue (V.ii.231–337). Irony of theater makes character more complex and harder to read. Henry is much like an *eiron*, being too slippery for the audience to make him or his opinions marble.

The irony of theater manifests itself more or less in the different plays of the tetralogy by means of self-conscious references to the theater, intertextualities, and plays within plays—including self-reflexive speeches and dramatic irony. The most overt self-referentiality of theatrical irony is the use of choric scenes and choruses. These devices often question the history play and move it toward the problem play.

The Choric and the Chorus

Choric scenes, like those in *Richard II*, are less noticeable and, therefore, less self-reflexive than the Induction and Epilogue in *2 Henry IV* and the choruses in *Henry V*. The choric is a dramatic strategy not available in the same form to narrative historians. The chorus is the closest a playwright can come, except perhaps by including a character by his or her own name, to revealing an authorial voice. Like Chaucer in "Sir Thopas," an author can also satirize or hide ironically behind the author as character. Shakespeare varies his use of the choric, from the structural purpose in *Richard II*, to the emblematic in *2 Henry IV*, and to the narrative in *Henry V*, all of which raise problems about the relation of theater to world as well as representation in the history play.

The ironic representation of the choric scene of the garden broadens the tragedy from Richard's private life to England and the Fall. It is a commonplace that the garden of act 3, scene 4, represents a microcosm of England, but the garden also shows another conflict over Richard's rule. The irony reveals the flaws of England and the world as much as those of Richard. The scene, which has been called an allegory, attempts to objectify the situation of the characters, crystallizes much of the play's important imagery, and upholds themes integral to the rest of the play. England is a fallen garden gone to weeds; its gardener is like Adam after the Fall, trying to repair the ruins. When Isabel irrationally associates the sad news with the speaker, the Gardener replies: "Pardon me, madam, little joy have I / To breathe this news, yet what I say is true" (*RII*, III.iv.81–82). Even though the Gardener pities Richard, he realizes that the king should have weeded his kingdom sooner (III.iv.55f.). Shakespeare balances this opinion with those of the Servant and the queen. Except for showing Richard's encounter with the Groom and the Keeper, this is the only time he lets us hear the opinions of the commons. This scene allows another point of view, generalizes and symbolizes his conflict through allegory, and permits the audience to take a moment away from the rush of the main action to consider its significance. From the scene, the audience gains the necessary intimations of Bolingbroke's plan to dethrone Richard, and it reveals, through dramatic irony, the powerlessness of the Gardener before the queen (of whose presence he is ignorant until she approaches him), and, in spite of high position, her lack of control of events.

Another choric "scene"—the Aumerle conspiracy—is comic or tragicomic and plays the fool to the tragedy, providing a perspective on Bolingbroke's succession and government as much as on Richard's fall and misgovernment (V.ii., iii).[24] These scenes treat a conflict between duty to the family and loyalty to the state and represent the wavering allegiances of York and Aumerle. Ending comically with Bolingbroke's mercy, they also lead to reports of the ruthless executions that result from the discovery of Aumerle's plot (V.iv). Although York balances his theatrical description of the reaction of the people to Richard and to Bolingbroke, he rejects sympathy for the fallen king because "heaven hath a hand in these events" (V.ii.7–40). The audience experiences dramatic irony when York urges his son to be loyal to Bolingbroke, for it has already seen that Aumerle has joined a conspiracy against the new king (V.ii.50–51; see IV.i.321f.). York's house is like the theater, if not England itself: he has been caught between Richard and Bolingbroke, just as the audience finds itself caught between the family and the nation. This father seems to obey power and exercises power for its own sake. As the conflict in York's family progresses, it almost turns to comic opera or a tragicomedy. The Duchess urges her husband to be loyal to his family, creating dramatic irony, for while York disowns his son, she sees their likeness, that Aumerle "is like thee as a man may be, / Not like to me, or of any of my kin, / And yet I love him" (V.ii.108–10). But York runs out to accuse the son who is so like himself. Polonius might have called this the beginning of a "tragical-comical-historical" scene.

By causing Bolingbroke to mention his own son, Shakespeare links scene 3 with the previous one. He compares this relation between father and son with that between York and Aumerle. Like York, Bolingbroke has a son whom he is too ready to condemn (V.iii.1–4). Aumerle, then York, then the Duchess begs Bolingbroke, who sees the serious scene turn farcical. Richard, the suppliant, had repeated the word "beg" in asking mercy of the new king, but Bolingbroke will pardon Aumerle and not Richard, who was more of a rival and a threat. Of this conspiracy and begging, the new king observes that "Our scene is alt'red from a serious thing, / And now chang'd to 'The Beggar and the King.' / My dangerous cousin, let your mother in; / I know she's come to pray for your foul sin" (V.iii.77–80). Shakespeare juxtaposes light rhyme with heavy content. The sadness of Bolingbroke's denial of Richard remains in the background. In examining the comic or "serious" nature of the scene, York's arrival is a fulcrum because from here on the characters speak in clumsy rhymed couplets rather than in blank verse

(V.iii.68f.). Besides seeing the comedy, Bolingbroke says that Aumerle's fellow conspirators will be executed (IV.i.181–319; V.iii.135f.). Bolingbroke combines theater and world. Hal will later act out with Falstaff another scene of the beggar and the king, another variation on the popular ballad "A Beggar and A King," or "King Cophetua and the Beggar-Maid," as well as Sir John's nomination of himself as Cophetua in his fustian drama with Pistol (see *2HIV*, V.iii.99).[25] The choric scenes, tragic and comic, in *Richard II* emphasize the dramatic nature of history and to the characters' realization of this theatricality.

In *2 Henry IV* both the Induction and the Epilogue call attention to the theatricality of the play, serve as intermediaries between the audience and the characters of the main action, and involve the spectators more directly in the body of the drama. The highly theatrical figure of Rumor begins *2 Henry IV* with a command to the audience: "Open your ears" (IN.1). Rumor demands that the people in the theater participate and emphasizes that their experience with hearsay is much the same as that the characters exhibit. The audience, too, must wrestle with illusion, ambiguity, and incomplete knowledge, except that Rumor does give the audience information that will allow it to enjoy dramatic irony in the first scene and throughout as it observes the gullibility of many of the characters. The world, as well as the theater, involves appearances. In Rumor's speech the audience will also notice images that the playwright develops ironically in the main action—horses, discord, and fall. This emblematic figure painted with tongues characterizes itself in the first and third person (as "I" and "Rumour"), as if a narrator and a character, and tells of the confusion that will occur in this satiric history. Rumor, he says, is a pipe with many stops that "the blunt monster with uncounted heads," the multitude, can play. The Induction makes the audience immediately aware of theatricality, so that when the characters appear it will wonder how reliable Rumor, the playwright, and the characters are and will consider the ironic similarities and differences among actors, characters, author, and itself. Rumor calls attention to itself, a painted, verbal, and interpretive babel that can occur in history and in the theater, to the satiric isolation of characters who cannot communicate.

In addition to Rumor, the Presenter, who unfolds the action of

Part Two, the Epilogue draws attention to the theatricality of this history (IN.4–5).[26] The Epilogue is difficult to interpret because its different parts may have been performed on different occasions.[27] Besides the general irony that each theatrical performance changes in time and so mimics life outside the theater, Shakespeare may have built this constant change into the Epilogue as if to end the play with various and varying perspectives. Whatever the presentation, the entire Epilogue speaks directly to the audience (as epilogues commonly do), continues from the main action themes of debt and human judgment (asking pardon), and, amid dancing, outlines the events of a sequel. The Epilogue engages the audience in the ironic topos of modesty, for, although the audience must judge favorably for a play to survive, the playwright has led it where he wanted, and it is he who will win the applause by the way of his politeness, humility, and ingenuity. For instance, the Epilogue tells the audience that as far as he knows "Falstaff shall die of a sweat, unless already a be killed with your hard opinions" (EP. 30–31). Here, Shakespeare seems to be playing with the disjunction between author and character, thereby exploring dramatic irony and intention. The second part of *Henry IV* begins with rumor and conjecture and ends there, except the Epilogue assures the audience that it is a direct participant in the play. Playgoing is not simply the watching of an imitation of an action but becomes part of the play. In this subtle text there are probably remnants of an earlier version of *2 Henry IV*, as in the references to Oldcastle. Phrases like "for anything I know" and "for Oldcastle died a martyr, and this is not the man" show the subtle irony with which the author ends the play, for if the actor playing the part of the Epilogue (who might have been Shakespeare) does not know the fate of Sir John, the author has at least some idea and "plays" with the Oldcastle question.[28] In a way that leaves us unsure (the gap of history separating present and past), this question may be history and the outside world entering the performance of this history play. At one point, the Epilogue promises that "our humble author will continue the story," the first reference in the text suggesting that Shakespeare is considering these history plays as a single story and an indication that this part of the Epilogue was probably spoken by an actor and not by Shakespeare himself (EP. 27–28). A. R. Humphreys thinks that Shakespeare spoke the first paragraph but, on another occasion, that a dancer spoke the second and third paragraphs. The changing nature of the Epilogue, the oxymoronic nature of the author as powerful in his modesty and modest in his power (which includes the assumption of the participation of the audience), and the question of closeness and distance between author and the Epilogue—these three invite the theatergoers into the community of the theater but also show their separation from it. The audience sometimes wrestles with different problems from the characters and the playwright. The representation of these various concerns anticipates the Chorus in *Henry V*.

If two different choruses envelop the main action of *2 Henry IV*, the choruses in *Henry V* do that and more, punctuating nearly all the acts into which editors have divided the play (although the divisions are absent from Quarto 1). The Chorus, as I shall call the choruses in *Henry V*, reveals a generic tension in the play itself between narrative and representation, comment and action, and heroism and antiheroism. Challenging the imagination of the audience directly, the Chorus asks it to consider the problems of the theater. Imagination and the relation of the theater to the "world outside" and to the historical world represent the foundation of the speeches of the Chorus.[29] Through choric agency, the audience becomes involved with interpreting experience, history, and self-conscious theatricality. Paradoxically, the Chorus, while being represented, is a narrative mediary between the audience and the representation of the main action. At first, the Chorus appears to be what Kernan calls "the image of the poet" in the theater, but such is not entirely the case.[30] While the Chorus exalts Henry's heroism, the action shows him to be both a great soldier and a schemer and qualifies but does not undercut the speeches of the Chorus. Actually, the choruses and the main action modify each other as the action follows the action, and so on. Once again, context is important. Even the choric envelope, the glory the Prologue declares and the disaster the choric Epilogue proclaims, has a context, the First Tetralogy, but also a time period, afterward, when the Second Tetralogy was written. Shakespeare did not come to history chronologically. Rather, he approached it forward then backward then forward then backward and forward, *1 Henry VI* to *Richard III* to *Richard II* to *Henry V*, whose Epilogue points to *1 Henry VI* again. He soon turned to the

Roman plays and the British tragedies, thereby going further back in history (although he had done so briefly in *Titus Andronicus* [1593] and *The Rape of Lucrece* [1593]). The Essex Rebellion and its use of *Richard II* represents another backward and forward movement of history that the Chorus to *Henry V* unintentionally helps to point out for a postrebellion audience.

Invoking a muse (as classical writers did), through which Sidney says the poet finds inspiration for "good invention," the Prologue begins the play and conveys the theme of poetic inspiration to the audience. His muse of fire and his invention, or, in other words, his imagination, and the rhetorical term for the discovery of topics inhabit the "brightest heaven."[31] The problem is whether poetry can capture history. With ambivalent language, the Prologue represents the art of the playwright: "A kingdom for a stage, princes to act / And monarchs to behold the swelling scene!" The Prologue wishes for a kingdom in exchange for a theater but implies that princes are actors and that monarchs look at the world as a play divided into magnificent roles. In some ways a stage is a kingdom and a kingdom is a stage. By punning on "port," which, according to Gary Taylor, means both bearing and part, the Prologue, when saying "Then should the warlike Harry, like himself, / Assume the port of Mars" means that the king, in his own "historical" person, could act the role of the god of war.[32] "Like" may also mean someone worthy to play Henry. On behalf of the playwright and the actors—those "flat unraised spirits" who have too much presumed—the Prologue asks the audience to pardon lowly illusion for not being able to measure up to the heights of actuality.

Using irony, Shakespeare further complicates this stance. Besides using the topos of modesty (or is it "false modesty"?), the Prologue, through repetition, amplifies the idea of the beggarly stage and the kingly world. The playwright had earlier represented the beggar-and-king motif ironically in the Aumerle conspiracy between Falstaff and Pistol and Hal and Falstaff. The Prologue contrasts the "unworthy scaffold," a small number of planks, with "So great an object," a "cockpit" with "the vasty field of France," wonders whether this "wooden O" can contain the military gear from the Battle of Agincourt, and asks whether the theater can hold the world. Shakespeare is calling attention to the theater but also to the machinery of the history play itself, a self-referentiality that is characteristic of the problem play. He is also having some fun here, for as in the sonnets he boasts that poetry "shall" outlast "the gilded monuments / Of Princes," so the poetry of the plays (although the medium was more mutable in Elizabethan times) would perpetuate the memory of Henry and his age.[33] Past events need historical writings. The playwright causes the Prologue to pun on "O," "cipher," and "accompt." The Prologue's punning, like its ("his" or "her"? I settle on "his" as a rhetorical convention) uses of apostrophe, destabilizes the authority of language but in a different way. Whereas apostrophe attempts to call the outside inside, thereby breaking down the opposition between world and self—outside and inside—punning plays with simultaneous meanings of the same word, thereby multiplying the relation between word and world. The pun informs the audience that the term does not have a singular authority. The theater where this play was performed, which was most likely the Theater or the Curtain, was shaped like a "wooden O," like the mathematical figure zero or nought, being something and nothing at once, containing author, actors, and audience, who are both nothing and a great deal, as a circle also represents perfection. If the Prologue addresses the audience as nothings, "O pardon!" he also reminds it that a crooked figure (in other words, a curved number, zero) added on the right of a hundred thousand makes a million.[34] The use of apostrophe is playful and involves the audience in a game, more like direct address that is not direct address. Apostrophe is not embarrassing in the sense that Jonathan Culler, who is discussing the lyric, considers it. However, as George Puttenham says about this figure, the more supernatural or unverifiable it is, the "greater wit and sharper invention" the poet needs in using it.[35] Conscious or not of this challenge, Shakespeare gives his Chorus ample wit to explore the relation among apostrophe, invention, theater, and world. Apostrophe is vocative: it calls forth something. Often, it summons poetic power, inspiration, God, the gods, nature, or something absent or dead as if it were alive or something outside as if it could be made inside, as if the very apostrophe could transform inside and outside, as if they already did not interpenetrate. Deriving from the Greek, "apostrophe" means to turn away, and it resembles invocation and prosopopoeia, which may be loosely called personification. Not

surprisingly, Puttenham has a vivid English term for apostrophe—
"the turnaway or turnetale"—and it is quite possible that Shakespeare
knew his views on this scheme or figure. The Chorus is invoking
the heavens and the power of representation to identify the words
and action of the play with the world itself and so bridge the almost
impossible gap between language and nature—making history and
the past, historical writing and historical event, identical. The word
"history" means both writing about the past and past events, and so
it challenges the distinction between language and world. At the
same time, the Chorus is playing a game, calling attention to the
limits as well as to the potentialities of the theater. He is facing the
audience while he is turning away from it. Speaking of time and
history, the Chorus, on one level at least, appears to be trying to
erase the difference between past and present. Historians identify
with the past but also must distinguish the present from it. The
Chorus does both. After flattering the audience with the greatness
of "nought," the Prologue continues to elevate the audience by
belittling the playwright and the actors: "And let us, ciphers to this
great accompt, / On your imaginary forces work." Rosalind's epilogue in *As You Like It* is another begging chorus that plays games
with the spectators. By exalting the audience, the actor praises its
imagination as an integral part of the play, but by being crafty
Shakespeare has the Prologue pun on "accompt" (which, like its
modern form, "account," means both a story and numbers on a
balance sheet), so that the playwright and company become ciphers
who add value to history as a zero can make a hundred thousand a
million. They are profiting the audience! They advocate the value of
history.[36]

Playing the fox, Shakespeare's Prologue defines the role of the
audience by making it more or less important than it is. The
Prologue asks the audience to "Suppose" two armies "confin'd" in
the "girdle of these walls" and to "Piece out our imperfections with
your thoughts." With "imaginary puissance," the audience will
think the few players great armies, turn their playwright's described
horses into actual ones, and deck and carry the player-king from
place to place, skipping and telescoping time. Here, the Prologue is
acknowledging the importance of the audience, for he needs its
cooperation and humors it with compliments and conceits it will

enjoy. He also calls attention to the conventions of the play, exhorting the playgoers: "Admit me Chorus to this history; / Who pro-
logue-like your humble patience pray, / Gently to hear, kindly to
judge, our play." Not only does the Prologue portray himself as a
mediary between playwright and audience but he also pokes fun at
the conventions of humble, begging prologues. If the actor asks the
audience to hear gently and judge kindly the play, it may observe
whether the characters in the play are patient and generous in their
judgments. Shakespeare isolates the phrase "our play" at the end of
the Prologue as if to remind the audience, by a double use of "our,"
that the company's play has become a joint effort of the audience
and the Lord Chamberlain's men.

The other choruses complicate and contextualize this one. With
an irony that calls attention to the conventions of time and space,
Shakespeare begins act 2 (fulfilling the promise, and amplifying the
effects, like direct address, of the Prologue) with the Chorus condensing time by describing the actions of Henry and his enemies and
addressing the audience directly, telling it that the king is transported
to Southampton, which "is the playhouse now," and hoping not to
"offend one stomach with our play." Because the Chorus shifts the
locale of scenes with such uncertainty, editors suspect textual problems or revisions. He informs the audience that the change to
Southampton will not occur until the king appears, which is in scene
2 and not in scene 1.[37] The Chorus of act 2 gives a narrative
description full of heroic images and apostrophes that reaffirm the
power of language to coincide with theatrical representation. He
apostrophizes England, appealing to the audience, calling particular
attention to the relation between inside and outside, to England's
"inward greatness, / Like little body with a mighty heart," and to
the traitors, who from the inside have betrayed their country to
something outside, for the gilt of France—"O guilt indeed!" The
audience is supposed to be carried away with the Chorus's representation but also to recognize the difference between inside and outside, this and the other. Just when the Chorus most wants to catch
the audience in the illusion, he reminds them that they are in a
playhouse, a touch of Brechtian alienation *avant la lettre*. As J. H.
Walter notes in his New Arden edition, lines 41 and 42 contradict
the shift of scenes that lines 35 and 36 promise, but neither accurately

describes what will happen. Walter suspects that Shakespeare made additions to the Chorus, changes that, no matter how pleasing the Chorus wants to be to the audience, cause the reader some bafflement and a realization that textual traces, like those in a palimpsest, complicate interpretation. The material conditions of the theater, where revisions were made under extreme time pressure and where the text was not the author's but the companies' property, produces a play that will not always allow for neat and unified readings. This resistance encourages a measure of hermeneutical humility and discourages a mania for textual organicism.

The Chorus to act 3 challenges the imagination of the audience: "Thus with imagin'd wing our swift scene flies / In motion of no less celerity / Than that of thought." Once again, the Chorus asks the audience to "Suppose," "Hear," and "behold" the men and scenes in his description as existing on stage. He challenges the playgoers to do the literally impossible so that they exercise their imaginations as fully as possible. They become part of the meaning of the play and of history. The Chorus realizes the complexity of historical shaping.[38] He repeats commands: "think," "Grapple your minds," "Work, work your thoughts, and therein see a siege," and (again!) "behold" and "Suppose." Words are also actions and have their existence inside and outside the theater, so that the pale shadows of the "modest" Chorus (and the playwright who is grinning behind him) may be as actual as any physical action. This crafty tension between the "profession of modesty" and the "claim to fame" also resides in the juxtaposition of these commands with the words "Still be kind, / And eke out our performance with your mind." History is, in a sense, a performative act, a mutual shaping between author and audience, past and present, not to mention the complication of characters in historical fiction. After a "battery" of commands, Shakespeare has the Chorus add the slight counterpoise of a polite and humble request. The audience is participating, but under a choric guidance that grows stronger the more resistance it meets. The resistance might take the form of an unwillingness to suspend disbelief among the sophisticated members of the audience or at least those trained in rhetoric, which focuses on the relation of speaker or writer to audience. The audience may have enjoyed the game of manipulation and seen it as a way of revealing assumptions behind theater and world, fiction and history. Unfortunately, we do not have the response of contemporary London audiences to the Chorus, and we can only judge from the increasingly extensive critical response since the Restoration to specific passages in Shakespeare and, especially, from those we are most familiar with, our own. The absence of these passages in the first quarto suggests that they were either added or not always used.

The Chorus's description at the opening of act 4 once again creates an atmosphere and action that are too precisely evocative and telescoped for an equivalent acted out on the stage. Attempting to manipulate the response of the audience, the Chorus exhorts anyone (the generality of his address breaks down the distinction between character and playgoer) who watches Henry visiting his soldiers to cry "Praise and glory on his head!" Some part of Shakespeare probably wanted and liked to represent the heroic side of Henry, just as another part desired the qualification of heroism. Paradoxically, here and throughout his speeches, the Chorus will order the imagination of the audience to be free. Armed with the modest accomplishment of the theater, the Chorus commands the audience to behold, "as may unworthiness define," Henry among his troops at night, the "disgrace" of "four or five most vile and ragged foils" representing the armies at Agincourt (cf. Jonson's Prologue to *Every Man in His Humour* and Sidney's *Apology*). With this amplification, or at least repetition, the Chorus elaborates evocative images of war in all their concreteness, the busy hammers of the armorers "closing rivets up" and the French playing for the English at dice, which almost translates the audience to the very scene and juxtaposes them with the estrangement effects (to steal a term from the Russian formalists) of a few ragged foils for an army. This synecdoche, which makes—in the Prologue's words, a "ridiculous brawl" of the Battle of Agincourt—recalls Hal's reduction of Falstaff's state to a joint-stool, golden scepter to leaden dagger, and rich crown to bald crown when they perform together in the tavern (*1HIV*, II.iv.373–77). As part of the formula that the audience should expect by now, the Chorus speaks the final couplet: "Yet sit and see; / Minding true things by what their mock'ries be." The stage, the Chorus implies, is a mockery of the outside world, but perhaps a mockery in a double sense. The choruses create epic similes and seem to extend the tropic irony of saying one thing and meaning the opposite (or something different) to a theatrical, if not philosophical, stance. The French soon learn to take seriously the political roles of Henry, the supposed mock king, and any audience would become victims of literal-mindedness if it took literature at face value, particularly the rhetorical games the Chorus plays. But then this is a history play, and history asks for a literal, as well as a literary, connection to the world. The problem of the relation between poet and historian will not go away so easily.

Nor does the Chorus tire of repeating his view that the play is unable to express the actual historical events. He does so again at the beginning of act 5. This repetition draws attention to itself and stresses the problems of the history play, limiting the genre as being inferior to the world but, at the same time, raising it above the chaos of the world with strong and precise description, ordered couplets, and the assumption (from the author's point of view at least) that poetry is more lasting than the memorials of princes. The Chorus also dispels the notion of a monolithic Elizabethan audience, promising to prompt "those that have not read the story" and asking pardon of those who have because this play is a poor copy of life. Perhaps Shakespeare, who produced this imitation, is being ironically modest in relation to other sources of this period of history. The repetition of the topos of inexpressibility may be a sign of elegant variation, of a dramatic irony shared by the playwright and audience, as the Chorus "doth protest too much" or is growing too polite. This irony coexists with polished apology and heroic description. Once more, the Chorus repeats his ordinances to the audience, commanding it to use imagination to flesh out the action of the play by telescoping time and space. The very commands may, however, limit the audience's imagination. The Chorus also splits the acting company ("we") for the audience ("you") from the audience ("you"), but he tries to show a close relation in command and action (V.CH.8–9, 23). If the Chorus invoked a "Muse of fire" at the beginning of the play, he now appeals to the smithy and workshop of the imagination of the audience, a fire of a more earthly kind (not the "brightest heaven of invention").

The self-conscious theatricality emphasizes Shakespeare's conscious problems of representing time in *Henry V* and in the history play. But the theater is in the world and Shakespeare does not try to seal his history from classical Rome or from contemporary London. The comparison of Henry, first to Caesar and then to Essex—as Walter glosses it—(and of Romans to Londoners to theatergoers) in a few lines breaks down the divisions of time and space, for the Chorus likens dead rulers of different ages to a living Englishman but subjects the nobility of Essex to Elizabeth. Here is an actor who is aware of the world "out there" playing a character who is not, speaking of historical players who represent men who actually lived and a character who represents a man who is now "making history" in Ireland. With the allusion to Essex, Shakespeare shows the Chorus interpreting the present and future through the past: just as Caesar and Henry were celebrated, so too will Essex be after he defeats the Irish rebels. But Essex will rebel and be executed, just as Henry dies at the peak of his power, which shows that it is easier to predict the past than the future; while Shakespeare can represent the ironies of Henry, it is for time and for future audiences to see the limitations of history and of all interpretation, including their own. Shakespeare and his audience did not know in 1599 that in 1601 the Lord Chamberlain's men would put on *Richard II* during the Essex Rebellion and would be questioned for this act. The writing of history becomes history, and Shakespeare loses control over future events as much as Henry did and we do. The Chorus to act 5 explicitly states one of his dramatic functions, consciously calling attention to a dramatic aim of the history play: "and myself have play'd / The interim, by remembering you 'tis past." He mediates between the audience and past events, helping it to interpret, to shape history.

Shakespeare increases the ironic complexity when the Chorus plays the Epilogue. "Our bending author" has him discuss the story that the playwright has pursued "with rough and all-unable pen," "confining" men to a "little room," "Mangling by starts the full course of their glory," and provides him with the orderly form, the tight confines, of the sonnet to tell his tale that moves from order to chaos. The sonnet telescopes historical time in the extreme, calling attention to the difficulty of representing history at all. The repetition of the posture of modesty and the topos of inexpressibility in six choruses also creates a sense of synchrony, but the orderly sonnet begins to emphasize the ruin of time—a favorite theme of Shakespeare's sonnets—and the return to chaos once more. The fall of Henry the Sixth is once again the fall of time and language. The playwright also has the Chorus transfer the now-familiar topoi of modesty and inexpressibility to the "bending author," explicitly extending the scope of the elegance, irony, and shared joke that come with the convention of prologues, epilogues, and, to a lesser extent, choruses. As in a peripeteia, the sonnet moves from an accolade of Henry's triumph to a lament of waste under Henry the Sixth. The contradiction pushes at the confines of the sonnet and of the history play, qualifying events in *Henry V* with those in the *Henry VI* plays and *Richard III*, which the audience has already seen.

Irony of theater reveals intertextuality, as well as showing the playfulness with which Shakespeare represents the problems of the theater and history in the last of his second group of history plays. The choric scenes and choruses are self-reflexive theatricality that draw as much attention to the stage and playhouse as to the world the history plays are supposed to represent. This self-conscious theater makes us more aware of the problems of the history play, its coexisting dilemmas of time and theater being located in it. Drama and history collide in a creative and destructive mode, raising questions enough about the genre of the history play that by the time we reach *Henry V* the problems have become acute.

The fall of time is closely related to the fall of language. Shakespeare represents characters who are caught in a temporal dilemma between overview and participation, synchrony and diachrony, eternity and now. Many of the characters, especially the kings, think that they can control time, but even the most successful in temporal power— Hal—is one of time's subjects. The reaction to the rejection of Falstaff is not unanimous. Bates and Williams challenge Henry's view of responsibility in earth and heaven, and Henry the Fifth dies at the height of his power, the fall of his son returning England to a state of chaos similar to that after Richard's fall. Hal may redeem time more than Richard, Bolingbroke, Hotspur, and Falstaff can, but, being human, he too cannot transcend language and time. The characters cannot have power over past, present, and future, although at times their actions, interpretations of the past, and prophecies lead us to expect such active and interpretative potence. The theater, a temporal art, calls particular attention to the limits of time and the stage. In *Richard II* the garden scene is allegorical, and the Aumerle conspiracy (or "The Beggar and the King") is tragicomic if not comic, so that it creates some generic friction in the play. The satiric and self-consciously theatrical nature of the tavern scenes, as well as the nature of parody in the play, also modifies the comic thrust of *1 Henry IV*. The Induction and Epilogue of *2 Henry IV* emphasize the theatrical nature of a satiric play and make us aware of the role of rumor and plan in history. The rejection of Falstaff in Part Two also creates a crisis in the history play that is prolonged into *Henry V*, namely, that Henry's private and public selves are at strife and that the integrity of kingship is still in doubt when it is supposed to be most evident. By emphasizing the representation of history, the Chorus in *Henry V* helps broaden the focus of the play by introducing problem elements that later occur in the problem plays and questions of time, its shape and its interpretation, the relation between author and audience. But the division between problem elements and problems of time is tenuous, and they become increasingly bound up in each other. In the next chapter, we shall examine how the Second Tetralogy moves toward the problem play, questioning the genre of the history play, but not being able to resolve with satisfaction the problems and dilemmas that *Henry V* and the tetralogy raise, and unable to repair the ruins of fallen language and time.

FOUR

*Toward the
Problem Play*

F *RICHARD II* TENDS TOWARD TRAGEDY BUT extends that tragic fall from the individual to the state, if *1 Henry IV* develops the comic communal element but also contains the germs of satiric isolation and self-criticism, if *2 Henry IV* represents the negative discipline, blind fallenness, and increasing incommunication of satire but also includes a mixture of the tragic and the comic (as well as a crisis in the relation between fiction and history in the rejection of Falstaff), *Henry V* continues this generic friction that is characteristic of the problem play, its crisis being especially apparent in the disjunction between the structurally comic marriage of Henry and Katharine and the tragic fall that the Epilogue describes.

Although this chapter will concentrate on *Henry V*, it will also look at the generic friction that is the primary characteristic of the problem play in the three earlier plays of the tetralogy. The controversy or confusion over whether *Richard II* is a tragedy or a history began in Shakespeare's day. Even though in 1598 Francis Meres extolled the play as a tragedy, he also praised the *Henry IV* plays for the same reason. Much of the confusion since has arisen from the printers of the quartos calling *Richard II* a tragedy and the editors of the First Folio classifying it as a history play. Based mainly on this discrepancy, critics still argue contrary positions.[1] No classification will please everyone, and it is perhaps comforting to realize that the difficulty in defining the relation between history and tragedy was seen as long ago as Aristotle.[2] *Richard II* does reflect the basic *de casibus* tragic pattern of a central and illustrious character falling from power because of pride. The analogue in Greek tragedy occurs when a character falls through hubris and hamartia (a flaw in character). Part of the tragic pattern may consist in a good but secondary character reestablishing order at the end of the play. It is debatable whether this flaw represents an excess of Richard's virtue or his particular vice.[3] As soon as we try to sketch the main tragic pattern as a simple *de casibus* fall or in terms of Greek tragedy, we observe that the individuality of *Richard II* qualifies the classification. Here are some of the objections.

Although, as king, Richard is undoubtedly important, his personal character seems scarcely of a tragic stature, at least in the first half of the play, and what may appear only a weakness in his private behavior produces too serious consequences on the public level—in the misgovernment of England—to be interpreted merely as a flaw. Bolingbroke can hardly be defined as a "secondary" character, nor by the end of the play is the audience confident of his goodness. The order that he reestablishes is immediately revealed to be as precarious as Richard's. Similar reservations occur when we examine the play in the light of tragic irony. Theorists tend specifically to associate irony with the tragic reversals of peripeteia and anagnorisis.[4] Ever since Connop Thirlwall, many critics have also equated tragedy with Sophoclean, or dramatic, irony.[5] As we have seen, irony operates in *Richard II* in a much more pervasive way than either a concentration on Richard's central character or a structural irony of peripeteia or verbal irony can accommodate. With this pervading irony, Shakespeare creates a multiplicity of points of view, which, in turn, widens the response to the play beyond the personal, tragic fall of Richard to the broader comment on the plight of England and the political behavior of people in a fallen world. This widening pushes the play into generic territory that is considerably more diffuse and less defined than traditional tragedy. Irony destabilizes the boundary between public and private, history and tragedy, while shaping the play through a rigorous redefinition of those oppositions. The allegory of the garden scene, which redirects the symbolic reflection of mimesis into another emblematic realm, encourages another view of England, one that strays from realism, which has become increasingly associated over time with the writing of history. "The Beggar and the King," as Bolingbroke calls the dramatic pleading of York's family, qualifies the tragedy with comedy and creates a friction with the tragic images of Richard, Isabel, and Exton that precede and follow it. Another way of complicating the representation of this tragic history or historical tragedy occurs in the use of self-conscious theatricality, for it calls attention to the dramatic and fictional nature of the history play and questions its ability to live up to traditional notions of historical truth. Poetry and history clash as well as interpermeate the first play of the Second Tetralogy and continue, if not intensify, their tension and mingling throughout the tetralogy.

Whereas in *Richard II* Shakespeare uses irony to explore tragedy more than comedy, in *1 Henry IV* he reverses this strategy. Any definition of "comedy" is notoriously elusive and multifarious. Although Shakespearean comedies differ considerably from one another, they do show some similarities: the use of disguise and a movement toward communal harmony, toward a happy ending. Shakespearean comedy, as I define it, moves toward social integration and reconciliation and celebrates a harmonious community of individuals.[6] Irony in comedy represents the similarities between characters at least as much as their differences, creating a community of characters, emphasizing the tensions between individuals and society, the multiple and various experiences in this relation.[7]

The comic components of *1 Henry IV* complicate the idea of history, as well as the idea of comedy, in the Shakespearean corpus.[8] Irony shows a close relation among "historical" characters like the king, "comic and historical" characters like Hal, and "fictional or unhistorical" characters like Falstaff. These classes by necessity seep one into the other in historical fiction. It is a commonplace that Falstaff probably was originally called Oldcastle, that his descendants may have complained, and that the figure's name was changed to Falstaff, someone found in *1 Henry VI* who was apparently based on a historical person.[9] But Shakespeare's Sir John Falstaff of the *Henry IV* plays is different from his first Sir John Falstaff. Even in naming and invention *1 Henry IV* is ironic. Irony reveals the many sides of an event and of character and the relations between characters. Besides an irony of structure that shows similarities between the worlds of the court, tavern, rebel camp, and Wales (which is actually a part of the rebel camp), the ironic use of the imagery of food and drink is festive and reminds us of the comic feast that celebrates community, while the images of clothing are also comic, for they emphasize the motif of disguise and identity that recurs in Shakespeare's comedies. Irony of words also demonstrates unexpected similarities between the worlds and characters of Part One, such as those between Sir John, the taverner, and Henry, the king. The irony of theater, especially the playacting of Falstaff and Hal, makes the relation between history and comedy, between "fact" and "fiction," more intricate. In part this acting illustrates the likeness between king and clown and establishes a bond of affection between Hal and Sir John. Many of the characters parody other characters and enjoy their own acting, so that the audience enjoys being part of the community of the theater with them. The many ironic surfaces of structure, language, and theater reflect off one another to create a complex and prismatic view of history that is mainly comic in effect.

Not all the ironic reflections in *1 Henry IV* are comic. The structure also manifests an ironic reversal that begins with hope for peace and ends with a certainty of continued warfare. This warlike ending modifies our response to Falstaff's comic resurrection. History is often not content with the happy ending of comedy. Hal's early promise to reject his "comic" companions and his mock rejection of Sir John while playing the king also qualify the festivity at the Boar's Head and of the whole play. Images of gluttony, hanging, judgment, death, and blood remind the audience of the grim experience of a historical period given to war. The different modes of acting differentiate among and divide the characters: Henry is a political actor; the poetic Hotspur plays the unpoetic soldier of honor; Falstaff acts many parts, but none is political, except perhaps when he plays the captain for profit and when he pretends to be dead to obtain reward; and Hal, as usual, straddles the political and comic worlds, acting politically as well as for "entertainment." It is Hal's dissimulation for political ends that eventually defeats Hotspur and Falstaff, who, like Henry, let themselves be deceived by the role that the prince has chosen for himself. For the most part, however, the audience shares in his theatrical and comic communion with Falstaff.

Even though much of the thrust of this play is comic, it begins to show an ironic relation among the reward of Falstaff, the fall of the rebels, and the limited victory of the house of Lancaster, the first being comic, the second a tragic reflection of the tragic fall of England, and the third a combination of, or friction between, comedy and tragedy. Although not as marked as it will be in *2 Henry IV*, this play also represents a satiric friction in structure, words, and theater. An ironic tension occurs between the comic ending and the historic—the "tragic continuance" of chaos and war. Shakespeare uses ironic images of gluttony, so often associated with satire. The stripping bare of each world or character through acting and parody also helps the satiric isolation: Hal particularly exposes such rivals as Hotspur and Falstaff. Thus, *1 Henry IV* can be seen as a history play that celebrates the comic achievement of community while also showing the fallen world of politics and war and looking ahead to the "crowded isolation" and darker satiric tones of *2 Henry IV*.

Even though it is often difficult to distinguish between satire and tragedy on the one hand and between satire and comedy on the other, and though it is generally admitted that satire itself stubbornly resists definition, I shall attempt to define satire and to argue that the relation between satire and history contributes to a fuller understanding of *2 Henry IV* and that the friction between these genres helps push this play and the tetralogy as a whole toward the problem play.[10] This relation between history and satire is by no means the only one in the play. The close relation among satire, tragedy, and comedy begins in what the Elizabethans thought was the origin of the word "satire," which, like irony, entered the English lexicon in the first decade of the sixteenth century. Although most theorists concede that "satura" (mixture, medley) is the proper derivation of "satire," the Elizabethan preference for "satyr" (a mythological creature, half man, half beast, that was associated with the tragicomic play performed with Greek tragedies) as the root of the word had a strong effect on the practice of satire in the Renaissance.[11]

Educated Elizabethans may have associated satire, even if indirectly, with the satyr play, which accompanied and complicated three Attic tragedies by a single author with a rough, lewd, sometimes solemn burlesque that showed moral and artistic license. As we have only one extant tetralogy in ancient Greek, it is difficult to generalize about the nature of the satyr play even if Elizabethans in the universities and in literary circles might have been aware of them. It is more likely that the idea of "man" and beast combined in mythological creatures was more widespread in Elizabethan England and related to the traditional idea that man is part beast, part angel. The satyrs were the sons of Hermes and were associated with Dionysus, or Bacchus, who represented the vital and intoxicating powers of nature and fertility and was the god of tragedy. Like Marlowe's poetry, Shakespeare's displays a deep familiarity with classical mythology, and so it is likely that he was somewhat conversant with satyrs and satire. It is a commonplace that the Renaissance had rediscovered Greek and Roman mythology. Titian's painting *Bacchus and Ariadne,* for instance, shows a detailed knowledge of the Bacchic, or Dionysian. In their tetralogies the Greeks apparently explored the mixed divine and beastly nature of human-kind just as Shakespeare does in *2 Henry IV*. The satire in this play is more complicated than something confined to Falstaff and Hal.[12]

Dramatic satire multiplies and complicates the focus of formal satire, whose voice is usually that of the satirist in the work, though books like *Utopia* and *Gulliver's Travels* have extended nondramatic satire through dialogue or shifting points of view and have suggested how oblique, ironic, and convoluted the relation is between the narrator, protagonist, and author.[13] If satire is, as I contend, at its most powerful a satire on itself, a playwright achieves this in different ways from the satirist who writes verse or prose narratives. Whereas the narrative satirist plays with the reader by making him or her feel superior to the satiric victim only to turn the satire against the reader's pride—the worst of all sins in a Christian view—the play-wright uses dramatic irony to draw the audience into a superior comic community but then reminds it of its humanity through its pride, and so creates division in the communion or communication between author and audience. Paradoxically, however, the godlike playwright assumes that he or she is human and thereby satirizes his or her own pride. Arrogance and pride in character, audience, and playwright become a primary problem in satire. Hal, the playgoers, and Shakespeare face the potential for divine aspiration, a proud *katascopos,* in themselves. Shakespeare's sympathetic detachment al-lows him to detach himself and his audience from the sins and foibles of his characters but also to sympathize with each character enough that he shares their weaknesses. He represents no unalloyed good or evil characters, no character who is a satirist free from the sting or revelations of satire. In *As You Like It,* for instance, Duke Senior makes a similar comment on the satiric Jacques. A satirist or a satirical character cannot be perfect and outside humanity but in-vokes some authority to criticize others. Similarly, a teller cannot be outside the tale, even while erasing himself or herself.

The audience in the theater, especially in historical drama, ob-serves readily the conjunction and separation of actor and character, stage and audience, presentation and representation. Reading creates the fiction of the internalization of the voice, or the theater of the mind, in which the reader filters all voices and parts and seems to receive the words of the author directly. A poet and prose satirist

can address the reader more directly, which in itself can be disingen-
uous (or at least intricate and oblique) in the fiction of sincerity and
directness it sets, whereas Shakespeare's choice not to comment in
his own voice is most often the position of playwrights. In other
words, Shakespeare ironically limits his power through satirical
power, sharing his godlike insight into the fallen nature of his
characters and himself with his audience by also dividing it from
him and dividing each playgoer against himself or herself. The irony
in *2 Henry IV* helps create a multiple perspective that represents a
conjunction and disjunction between the comic and tragic elements
of the play. Rather than relieve the worlds of Gloucestershire and the
tavern on one side and the court on the other, the rejection of Falstaff
illustrates the irresolvability of the rejection between the "comic"
triumph of Henry the Fifth and the "tragic" scapegoating of Sir
John. Rather than deny a satiric catharsis, the ending fosters an
unresolved tension that crystallizes the problems to which satire
addresses itself in this play, so that the ironic juxtaposition of a
"comic" Henry and a "tragic" Falstaff pushes *2 Henry IV* toward the
problem play of *Henry V*.[14] One of the major characteristics of a
problem play is that it presses at the boundary of the genre—in this
case of the history play—and shows a theatrically achieved ending
that seems designed to disturb the audience.

Through irony, satire also achieves an effect distinctive from
comedy and tragedy. Although satire can manifest itself in a definite
form, it is not easy to define what that form is. It seems that satire
has one common element on which theorists agree: its purpose is to
chasten vice and folly.[15] Part Two of *Henry IV* creates a complex
representation of human folly and vice (as well as virtue) and asks
for an understanding that we are all fallen into a tangled and
inscrutable world inside and outside the theater. Another aspect that
is specifically found in satire—the isolation of characters in a
crowded tapestry—also occurs in the play. This disorderly scene, as
Kernan notes of satire in general, is "packed to the very point of
bursting," is choked with people bearing such objects as money,
jewels, and fashions, who group, break up, then regroup, and so
on.[16] Pieter Brueghel's *The Battle between Carnival and Lent* (ca. 1525–
60) is an especially appropriate gloss on an important conflict in Part
Two, Hal choosing the sober Chief Justice and Lancaster over the

antics of Falstaff and Poins. Sin and vice cause isolation among individual characters in the bursting scenes of *2 Henry IV* in which the worlds of court, tavern, rebel camp, and Gloucestershire group and dissolve in intricate patterns. Another central concern of satire is the ruin of an ideal city or society.[17] Through multiplicity, Shakespeare creates a satire that represents a fallen personal and political world, the isolation that sin and vice "cause" in the ruins of England. In this play the limitations of human knowledge and the greed for power often isolate the characters from one another, making an almost tragic mockery of a fragmenting community, set against the memory or fiction of some prelapsarian unity. Nothing is permanent in *2 Henry IV*: oaths, friendships, alliances, the configuration of the characters and their social worlds, all are unreliable.

The most noticeable separation occurs between Hal and Falstaff, who do not have as close a relation as they do in Part One, for they meet only once before their permanent parting: the rejection. Characters in the play do not communicate—and hell, as Kierkegaard asserts, is incommunication. Nor can the rejection mask the continued fragmentation of the "comic" community of *1 Henry IV*. Part Two is a play that transforms the imagery of jolly fat, which at least occupied the surface of Part One, into images of disease and decay that are often associated with satire. Falstaff's sweat is growing rancid; the sexual jokes are becoming drier, sadder, and more obscene; death is nearer at hand for the comic characters; the rebels are cheated into execution; and the old king dies.[18]

Although the relation between history and satire helps show the distinctiveness of *2 Henry IV*, it is not adequate to describe the whole effect of the play. The characters in Part Two are not simply humor characters or caricatures spun out to illustrate a particular vice or folly. With irony, Shakespeare complicates the representation of character and society beyond the isolated crowd of one-sided characters that satire often comprises, thus creating a historical setting where similarities among characters help make a complex and imperfect community of intricate and mixed personalities. Shakespeare has made satire more subtle, as he does with most genres, and makes comedy and tragedy, history and satire collide, so that *2 Henry IV* tends toward the problem play. The likeness among characters might create a comic community, but isolation and ignorance thwart its achievement, though not entirely obliterating it. If, as Frye says, "satire is militant irony" whose "moral norms are relatively clear," whereas irony with little satire conceals the author's attitude, then Part Two also represents a tension or disjunction between ironic satire and unsatiric irony.[19] This later "unsatiric" irony merely shows the complex nature of public life without establishing an obvious satiric point of view, thus complicating character and creating a fallen world in which the genres mix together in one play. In *2 Henry IV* it becomes dangerous to talk about "unsatiric" and "satiric" irony, for, like Jonathan Swift, whose narrator in the Preface to *A Tale of a Tub* (1697) claimed—with some irony—that he was not writing a satire, Shakespeare creates an irony that broadens and deepens satire to an intricacy well beyond the established limits of the traditional definition of satire.[20] The irony in *2 Henry IV* keeps the audience off balance, eliciting a more complex response, which is at once denser and more diffuse than that of satire itself. The ironic discomfort makes the audience particularly uneasy at the end of the play and helps it to question the nature of public life and history. Falstaff's rejection above all demonstrates that the ending of the play creates problems that are not resolved and continue into *Henry V*. The satire is becoming a problem play, and *Henry V* itself partly explores and does not quite answer the problems of kingship and history that begin with Richard's fall, continue as rebellion in Falstaff and in the body politic, and question authority until the rejection of Falstaff creates a rebellion by some members of the audience against the authority of Henry the Fifth, if not of Shakespeare himself. The longer the problems of the fall of language and time, which destabilize kingship and history, persist, the more problematic the plays become. If *2 Henry IV* is almost a problem play, *Henry V* is one, partially because it inherits even more half-answered questions, some of which, like the rejection of Falstaff, occur in Part Two.

In part, *Henry V* attempts to sum up the earlier plays of the second group of histories. It represents the problems of unity and division, offering a problematic ending to the Second Tetralogy, attempting to give its "many-kinded" histories a unified shape.[21] The history play is an unstable genre, partly because history is a continuum of time and therefore hard to capture within the limits of a work of art and partly because the history play is always tending toward something else or, at least, is always incorporating other genres—such as tragedy in *Richard II*, comedy in *1 Henry IV*, and satire in *2 Henry IV*. Although each of these plays contains less prominent aspects of other genres, it is *Henry V* that balances or, rather, makes the different genres collide more equally. By doing this, it pushes out the boundary of its genre in a way that many critics would agree to be a primary feature of the "problem play."[22] Critics mix the terms "problem comedies" and "problem plays," admitting the difficulty of defining them, and do not always concur on which plays come under these headings. Even though some critics include *Hamlet* (1600–1601), *Antony and Cleopatra* (1606–7), and *Timon of Athens* (1607–9), the usual "problem" triad is *Troilus and Cressida* (1601–2), *All's Well That Ends Well* (1602–3), and *Measure for Measure* (1603–4). Shakespearean scholars recognize several other aspects—which I take to be subsidiary to pressing at the bounds of the genre—that characterize problem plays.[23] These elements are numerous: incongruities of generic conventions and structure, especially endings that are theatrically achieved or do not answer the "problems" the play poses; the relation between appearance and actuality or reality, often illustrated through acting and disguise; an involved and intellectual language and discussion in which the debate and probing of ideas (often about the relation between sex and war or politics) are conducted apparently for their own sake; and the raising of complex problems that do not have easy answers—all contribute to the vexed enigma of the problem plays. As William Witherle Lawrence says, these plays demonstrate that "human life is too complex to be so neatly simplified" and show an antiheroic, dark, and critical side to life and to human nature in ways that perplex the audience.[24] Irony has already been used to cause the audience perplexity in the earlier plays of this tetralogy by showing the black humor of tragedy and the dark sides to comedy and satire in a complex view of history. *Henry V* goes beyond its predecessors in this respect and is the play in the Second Tetralogy that most resembles a problem play.

Although no critic seems to have developed an interpretation of the strong elements of the problem play in *Henry V*, a few scholars have pointed to *1* and *2 Henry IV* as containing the origins of the problem play, or at least some of its effects.[25] Closer inspection shows, however, that *Henry V* pushes much more radically at the bounds of the history play. In this work tragedy, comedy, and satire collide with one another. The language of debate appears to exist for itself or, perhaps, to emphasize the problems of the play, as in the clerical debate on Henry's claim to France in the second scene of the first act or the debate between Henry and his soldiers in act 4, scene 1. The antiheroic and the heroic constantly qualify each other, the relation of sex to war is uneasy, and the public and private personalities of the king seem to lack integration. The "tragic" death of Falstaff, Henry's violent sexual imagery, and the satire on war (especially the objections of Bates and Williams, and Burgundy's description of devastated France) all serve to modify the heroic king and his comic marriage to Katharine. Other subsidiary resemblances to the problem plays also occur in *Henry V*. Like *Troilus and Cressida*, this play shows the seamy side of war and questions the kind of heroism that had been exalted since classical times—Fluellen comically likens Pistol to Mark Antony and Henry to Alexander the Great (III.iv.15). Some problem elements in *Henry V* also anticipate those in *All's Well That Ends Well*: most notably, the relation of sex to war and a theatrically achieved ending to what begins and proceeds well into the play as a tragic action. *Troilus* also explores sex and war, whereas *Measure for Measure* looks at the relation between sex and government. *Measure*, too, has a theatrically achieved ending, and, although not comic, the ending of *Troilus* also appears unable to resolve the preceding action. Like the Duke in *Measure*, Henry is a disguised ruler who manipulates other characters, but by doing so is brought to a more profound idea of his own responsibility.[26] The audience and critics of *Henry V* are as divided and perplexed over its forms and ideas as they are over similar matters in the problem plays.

The complicating irony of *Henry V* is compatible with its "problem" elements.[27] *Richard II* and *1* and *2 Henry IV* reveal aspects of the generic friction that characterizes the problem play, but it is the last play of the tetralogy where that friction reaches its highest pitch. The fall of Richard creates problems, and the fall of Falstaff creates more. Other falls over the course of these plays also represent the difficulty of a human redemption of history. Multiplicity in *Henry V* complicates the lines between appearance and actuality, heroism and antiheroism, conscious and unconscious motive, and intention and profession, so that this play "ends" the Second Tetralogy ironically by pushing the history play in the direction of the problem play, extending or bursting (depending on one's view) the bounds of the genre itself.

By inverting, reversing, contrasting, and blending tragic, comic, and satiric conventions and tones, Shakespeare also raises questions about the multiple, ambiguous, and, therefore, ironic nature of history itself. Henry the Fifth would be the hero Richard was not, but he cannot achieve unmitigated heroism. No one can be such a hero, and that is the problem in drawing a portrait of the "mirror of all Christian kings." Henry's own violent thoughts and Shakespeare's ironic use of imagery and theatricality and the juxtaposition of comic marriage and tragic Epilogue modify the king's heroic part. In the end is the beginning. As in *Finnegans Wake*, the cycle of history begins again, "falls to" again, for the informed audience knows the fate of Henry the Fifth before *Richard II* begins. Even if the playgoers do not, the Epilogue tells them, thereby shaping the meaning of the action of the Second Tetralogy (including Richard's fall) and looking ahead to the reign of Henry the Sixth (who falls, and after whom Richard the Third also falls), which Shakespeare had already shown on the stage in the First Tetralogy. The irony in *Henry V* represents the history play as problem play because it depicts the problem of writing history not only in this play but also in the Second Tetralogy (with gestures back to the First Tetralogy). This irony has implications for writing and for writing history generally, for the complex relation between and interpenetration of history and fiction. As in the earlier plays of the tetralogy, multiplicity in *Henry V* extends beyond the established limits of the genre to which each history play is most closely related—in this case the problem play—and explores the study of history and historiography, as well as the nature of the history play itself. Although the problem element cannot include all the implications of *Henry V*, it is important for an understanding of the play. More specifically, we should turn to the ways irony of theater, structure, and words, as well as Henry's debate with Bates and Williams (IV.i), help create the generic friction that makes this history play a problem play.

IRONY OF THEATER

We have seen that the Chorus in *Henry V* elaborates self-conscious theatricality in the earlier plays of the tetralogy. He examines the relation of theater and world, history play and history to such an extent that he raises the audience's awareness of the problems of representing history on stage. That the main action and the Chorus qualify each other also raises questions about the relation between narrative and represented action in the history play. Other aspects of the irony of theater complicate *Henry V*. We become more aware of this complexity through a character's consciousness of "acting" and through an audience within the play watching an actor playing the part. A subsidiary element in this problem play is such self-referential role playing, so that once again the irony of theater shows the close relation of *Henry V* to that kind of drama. The other histories in the tetralogy, however, also show this characteristic, but the self-conscious sense of theater supplements in *Henry V* a choric presence that is stronger than anything in the previous plays.

Through irony, Shakespeare also qualifies and complicates other subsidiary elements of the problem plays found in *Henry V*. The themes of appearance and actuality, as well as acting, deception, and plainness, also contribute to the irony of the theater in this play. These elements also occur in *Richard II* and in *1* and *2 Henry IV*, and although they are central to the problem plays, they are also important to history plays that do not primarily resemble this kind of drama or do so only in an embryonic way. The theater is a world of appearances and illusions in which the audience watches characters contend with dissembling. Throughout *Henry V*, the characters use cognates of the words "appear" and "seem," and disguise is at the heart of this play, as it is in the problem plays, for it engenders a debate that underscores the dilemmas of Henry as king and Shakespeare as an author of historical drama. Ely, for example, asks how Henry "seemed" to receive Canterbury's offer of a great sum of money for the wars in France and thus acknowledges the world of appearance (I.i.82, cf. 27, 72). In giving the background to the Salic Law, Canterbury tells the king what "appears" to be the right interpretation (I.ii.54, 88). From the beginning, the audience wonders whether the priests are dissembling because they expect others also to play roles or whether they are able to approach truth more nearly by understanding the importance of appearances. Irony traps other characters. Cambridge, Scroop, and Grey "appear" (present themselves, dissemble) before Henry, who, unknown to them, has seen through their deception and has trapped them in a "play" he directs himself (II.ii.56, 76, 128–37). The Dauphin and Montjoy speak of appearances but seem to be blind to them (II.iv.43–44, cf. 70; III.vi.123–24; IV.ii.43). The Chorus uses the word "appears" to describe the presence of the fleet, but he does so in a description in which his words create the illusion of action, which, ironically, he does not fully understand, especially as it relates to Henry's heroic stature (II.CH.16; cf. V.CH.13). Henry knows much about acting and semblances: for him, Fluellen only appears to be out of fashion, and he knows that, as a king, he should not show any "appearance of fear" to keep from disheartening his army (IV.i.83–84, 111–13). The words "seem" and "appear" occur most in the courtship scene, one that deals with the split between inward and outward, flattery and plainness (V.ii.21, 62, 241, esp. 309–71). Although Katharine is bashful and charming and Henry is gruff and direct, the courtship has an air of role playing that goes beyond wooer and wooed. The king only appears to love Katharine (which he well may), but he makes it clear that he wants political gains from this marriage. How plain the love and the nature of its motives are questions that the audience may consider for both lovers. No matter how tentative, the answers will help determine how problematic the ending is. As in *2 Henry IV*, Hal proves that he rules and wins partly because he is the most successful political actor, although the rejection of Falstaff and the reign of Henry the Sixth modify his victory.

With dramatic irony, Shakespeare continues to show the complex relation between the role and the man, "conspiring" with the audience against ignorant characters by making it more knowledgable than they. Dramatic irony helps constitute the irony of theater, especially when it arises from the relation of appearance, deceit, and disguise to actuality. Henry's distinction between the outward and the inward is closely related to the king's awareness of acting. He contrasts the private man with the public monarch, calls the pomp of ceremony a "proud dream." Whether or not Henry or any other king or person can hermetically seal private from public, inside from outside, is debatable. Ironically, Henry finds himself in a similar predicament to that of his father (*2HIV*, III.i.4–31). Both act, putting on a good public face.[28]

Shakespeare's theatrical irony shows that deceit is another disguise, revealing with it the problems of private and public and of government. The history plays, especially, share this concern with *Measure* and, to a lesser extent, with *All's Well*. In *Henry V* deceit and disguise test Henry as a ruler (or potential ruler for that matter) more directly and more critically than in *1* and *2 Henry IV*. Shakespeare ensures that the playgoers will appreciate the dramatic irony of the condemnation by Scroop, Cambridge, and Grey of a man who insulted the king when, unknown to them, Henry knows that they have conspired to murder him (II.ii). The king is self-consciously theatrical. In order to punish the rebels most and to achieve the greatest effect so that he may appear just when sentencing them, Henry pretends to reward them with commissions when he hands them a list of their crimes. By way of this dramatic irony, Shakespeare links Henry with the audience and thus appears to seek its approval of the king. Deceit and disguise, such as Pistol's deceit and Henry's disguise, relate closely to each other. The ancient's great voice and seemingly "gallant service" fool Fluellen until Pistol curses the Welsh captain for not intervening to prevent Bardolph's death and until Gower remembers Pistol as an "arrant counterfeit rascal." Henry the Fourth had dressed counterfeits in battle to protect his life, so that kings and knaves are not always so different in their theft and deceit. According to the English captain, the ancient will pretend to be a war hero, learning his part, playing the "roles" of other soldiers, and describing the "scenes" of the battles to be convincing (III.vi.12–82). To compare and contrast this deceit ironically with Henry the Fifth's disguise, the playwright has Henry assume a part among his soldiers before Agincourt and interweaves the incidents of the gloves and the leek. After encountering Bates and Williams, private soldiers, the king complains about the burden of the public man and the irresponsibility of the private man (IV.i). This problem of the relation between public and private lies at the heart of kingship from *Richard II* to *Henry IV*. With the help of the Boy, Pistol, who did not recognize the disguised king, deceives the French soldier (as

Falstaff had Colevile in *2 Henry IV*) into thinking him a great warrior. In a soliloquy the Boy exposes Pistol's empty acting to an already suspicious audience (IV.iv). If Pistol is a hollow man, is Henry? Later, Shakespeare shows Henry "playing" with Williams as Fluellen does with Pistol, so that the playwright once more compares king and Welsh captain and complicates the ironic connections between characters. Henry shares the dramatic irony with the audience at the expense of Williams as well as Fluellen, who is equally ignorant (like Pistol) of the king's earlier disguise and the exchange of gloves and whom Henry asks to be a proxy in a fabricated quarrel with "a friend of Alençon," which is an actual disagreement with Williams (IV.vii, viii). Shakespeare uses disguise and deceit so extensively that *Henry V* seems to foreshadow *Measure*, except that Bates and Williams more obviously turn the disguise against Henry than the characters in *Measure* turn it against the Duke.

Even though Henry complains about the trials of kingship, he uses his "directorial" powers, like Duke Vincentio and Prospero, to arrange events and to manipulate others.[29] After Henry's good-natured fun is over and Williams and Fluellen have stopped fighting (each having the other's glove), the king rewards Williams, who claims that Henry is at fault for having disguised himself and for not having expected abuse in that guise; he then asks pardon of the king (IV.viii.1–74). It is Henry's power as king that keeps the conflict over the glove from getting out of hand. Whereas the king pretends to be less than he is, Pistol feigns that he is more. The glove gives way to the leek. The hyperbolic and out-of-fashion Fluellen punishes the boasting and antique-tongued ancient. Although Pistol likens himself to a horse leech and is called vicious, on stage he does little to warrant the punishment he receives, except that, if the Boy is to be believed, he is a devil from the old morality plays and must be beaten.[30] In any event, the Welsh captain is less merciful than the king, who, nonetheless, may not have learned as much from Williams as he might have. The taverners continue to raise questions about the nature of kingship and about Henry's dilemmas as king, but they also reveal their own limitations. Henry's tricks as an "actor" and "director" show that he is still enraptured by the robes of office, even if he sometimes sees the shortcomings of pomp and protocol.

If, most importantly, the irony of theater in *Henry V* reveals Shakespeare's problematic use of the Chorus, consciously making the audience aware of the limitations and potentialities of the theater and of the history play, that irony also represents other subsidiary elements from the problem plays—theatrical ending, debate, and disguise. *Henry V* often uses these aspects in ways that recall their occurrence in *Richard II* and *1* and *2 Henry IV*, as well as looking ahead to their use in the problem plays, which I consider to be the three that most critics agree on: *Troilus and Cressida, All's Well That Ends Well,* and *Measure for Measure.* Although the irony of theater affirms the close relation between history and the problem play in *Henry V,* it also shows that comparisons that are too close are odious. For instance, the disguised Henry is much like the disguised Duke, but Vincentio is more allegorical and shadowy, more of a god out of the machine than Henry is. On the other hand, Henry must deal with a wider range of public and historical experience, and his directorial side (although central to his character) is only one part of a complex character who seems to taste blood, feel desire, and laugh more readily than the illusive Duke. Theatrical irony raises our awareness of the problems of the history play, and so *Henry V* is a problem play with a difference.

IRONY OF STRUCTURE

The structure of *Henry V* is ironic and displays affinities with that of the problem play.[31] A choric envelope modifies the heroic feats of Henry the Fifth in the main action, for the Epilogue shows that the mortal body lies behind the divine body of a king because Henry, like other mortals, cannot control the future—his son, who, born of the marriage to Katharine, later lost France and then England. Shakespeare makes structural use of debates, such as the clergy's consideration of Salic Law (among themselves and with Henry); the discussion between the king, Bates, and Williams about the nature of warfare and of kingship; and the conversation between Henry and Katharine about love, marriage, and politics. The main action ironically qualifies the patriotism, optimism, and hero worship of the Chorus, and the ways in which the "low-life" scenes modify the words and deeds of Henry and his party. In other words, a friction occurs between Chorus and main action. The worlds of the captains and of the French also provide other ironic perspectives in a complex play. After a general discussion of structural irony, we shall examine the low-life scenes, the captains, and the relation of English threats and French boasting. An investigation of the ironic relation of some scenes in *Henry V* to the first three plays of the tetralogy casts the eye of the audience backward, making it a historian, enabling it to observe a modified Henry and to find that in one regard history appears as fallen as humanity, a circle more like the wheel of fortune than the circle of perfection. Henry the Fifth is more like Richard than he would like to think. People change but also stay the same and—relying too much on similarity between past, present, and future—find themselves caught by and in time. Shakespeare uses references to the past structurally to create an irony that shows the many limited views of people, the collision of worlds, the forgetfulness and ignorance of characters regarding the past as they move in the unstable present into the uncertain future.

The general structure of *Henry V* represents an ironic reversal. The play begins with the Prologue telling a tale of warlike Harry and the glory of Agincourt and ends with an Epilogue that speaks of the loss of France and the return of England to civil war. This choric envelope qualifies the rising fortunes Henry experiences in France during the main action. Although Shakespeare did not divide the play into acts and scenes, the choruses punctuate it in such a way as to suggest that a brief examination, act by act, of the friction in the structure can be helpful. Each act begins with the Chorus, whose simple patriotism becomes modified by complex scenes.[32]

The structure of *Henry V* reveals aspects of the problem play and also the characters' special concern with the nature of time and history. The design of the play emphasizes an ironic treatment of problem elements—extensive debate about love, marriage, and politics, an especially self-conscious tension between appearance and actuality and between the heroic and the antiheroic, and the theatrically achieved ending that does not seem to "answer" the play. Critics find something missing in this type of ending, as if it does not fit with the previous play or does not address with satisfaction the issues or problems that the play raises. An extreme instance of this kind of response is Eliot's view that *Hamlet* lacked an objective correlative. After the Prologue's examination of the relation between history and drama, the first two scenes display a prolonged interest in debate itself. Canterbury complicates the question of how just the war is when he gives a detailed interpretation of the history of the Salic Law, in order to show that Henry is the rightful king of France. Through irony, Shakespeare qualifies Canterbury's position. Henry the Fourth recommended this foreign war to his son, Lancaster had predicted it, the Prologue in *Henry V* confirms it with patriotism, and Exeter and Westmoreland call for war, so that the clergymen are not the only war hawks and should not be held solely responsible for the designs on France (I.ii, see *2HIV*, IV.v.212f.; V.v.105–10). Debate is very important to Canterbury and Henry as a means of justifying the invasion, but the war becomes a tangle. If Henry's advisors are corrupt, the unjust war qualifies the heroic stance; if the invasion is just, Henry's inability to acknowledge that he makes, and is answerable for, the ultimate decisions of government modifies his heroism in France. Shakespeare calls Henry's judgment into question, raising the problem of measure for measure that occurs in *Richard II, 1* and *2 Henry IV*, and in *Troilus, All's Well*, and *Measure*. Although nearly identical to its representation in the problem plays, this problem has a history in the Second Tetralogy and, consequently, also becomes a problem of time and succession. On the whole, *Henry V* examines judgment from a more public point of view than do the problem plays. If reports of earlier actions or the earlier plays in the tetralogy, especially at the end of *2 Henry IV*, provide one part of the context for act 1, the subsequent acts in *Henry V*, and even the pretext (but postscript) of the First Tetralogy, furnish the other part.

Acts 2 through 5 show a similar pattern. The problem elements in act 2 occur mostly in Nym's and Pistol's qualification of the Chorus—who praises Henry as "the mirror of all Christian kings," extols England, and denounces the traitors—when they are involved in verbal combat because the treacherous ancient has stolen Nym's betrothed, Mistress Quickly. She also reminds us that Henry rejected Falstaff (II.i, iii). The king is a modified mirror. Henry's judgment of the conspirators in the second scene of act two may be just, but it is also reminiscent of his rejection of Falstaff. By bracketing Henry's judgment of the conspirators with the taverners' discussion of Falstaff's death and the king's responsibility for it, Shakespeare emphasizes the wider implications of Henry's "trials." The ironic structure of act 3 particularly emphasizes the relation between sex and war, but brings out the tension between private and public more fully than the problem plays. *Troilus* reduces the public to the private. *All's Well* and *Measure* look at the public domain in personal terms. Achilles sulks in his tent and would make war a personal act of revenge. Bertram escapes to the wars to leave Helena, his unwanted wife. Angelo turns government to lust, and Duke Vincentio would make marriage the culmination of his experiment in justice and government.

The Chorus begins act 3 by saying that Henry rejects as insufficient the French king's offer of his daughter and a few petty dukedoms. Shakespeare qualifies Henry's heroic call to his men at the opening of the act's first scene with the savagery before Harfleur in the opening lines of act 3, scene 3, where Henry once again threatens the French in violent images, likening the siege of the town to the rape of its women. What makes this verbal assault even more uneasy is the introduction of Katharine, who is innocently learning a new language (III.iv). Shakespeare further complicates the relation between men and women, private and public, in the fifth scene of act 3, when he represents haughty Frenchmen, including their king, insulting the English, partly because the French women think the French men effeminate. Act 4 continues to qualify heroism, showing the complexity of war and human nature. The playwright makes the problem element a part of his representation of a historical event and, therefore, asks the audience to avoid oversimplifying history. He also uses the motif of the disguised ruler, a motif that occurs later in *Measure*. The Chorus extols Henry for bravery, warmth, and generosity, but the disguised king soon encounters the criticism of Bates and Williams, who try to make Henry responsible for the justice or injustice of the war, a responsibility that he has attempted to shirk from the opening of the play. Other problems arise. When Fluellen reports that the enemy has killed the defenseless boys, the French confirm what the original audience might think of an enemy of England and lose the sympathy of the modem audience. On the other hand, Henry has *already* ordered the killing of the French prisoners because they are reinforcing their scattered men, a cruel action, although Gower praises him for ordering these killings as a reprisal for the slaughter of the boys (IV.vi.35–38, vii.1–11). The reason for the order is ambivalent. Even if the audience perceived the Boy's portentous words that the other boys and he will guard the luggage and that "the French might have a good prey of us if he knew of it," it knows only that this event occurred and not its relation to the king's order (see IV.iv.76–80). Even though the audience probably cannot untangle this problem, it witnesses a king who may think that he has to be ruthless in defending his outnumbered army or prefers revenge to turning the other cheek. Henry's action tempers the sympathy of the audience, keeping it off balance and focusing its attention on the king and his difficulties.

The problem elements that irony stresses in act 5 are appearance and actuality and a theatrically achieved ending. In a charming part of the second scene of this act, Henry woos Katharine, so that if he seemed like a basilisk in war, he appears to be a shy lover in peace (7, 99f.). Nonetheless, the marriage is a theatrical solution, though it is a historical event, a public and political union under the guise of an entirely personal love that cannot mend the animus between England and France.[33] Henry is the actor still, for, having spoken so eloquently throughout the play, he now plays the "plain king," unless he is fluent in war and halting in love: this difference or discontinuity of roles makes it difficult to read his personality (V.ii.121–73). Amid this awkward tenderness, other ironies arise. Even a heroic king can be sadly wrong in his predictions or grimly foiled in his hopes. Henry says to Katharine: "Shall not thou and I . . . compound a boy, half French, half English, that shall go to Constantinople and take the Turk by the beard? shall we not?" (V.ii.216–19). This wish for a crusade is as ironic as the similar desire of Henry the Fourth. The last question—"shall we not?"—which is a negative acting as an intensive affirmative, provides an answer to the king's hopes: Henry and Katharine will not produce such a conqueror. (Even though Henry claims modesty, he breaks custom and kisses Kate.) The Epilogue notes that Henry's son will not fulfill the king's hopes and that the Elizabethan stage has often represented these events.

Like a problem play, *Henry V* shows incongruities of generic conventions and structure, especially in an end that is theatrically achieved and does not respond to the problems that the play raises. The sheer amount of discussion about the legitimacy and responsibility of kingship, much of it for its own sake, threatens to frustrate the historical action of the play and the very survival of the genre itself, pushing it into new regions (the First Tetralogy and beyond) and into new problems—such as when a representation can properly end, and, if history is in part circular (for *Henry V* also turns back to *Richard II*), how it can end at all. One of the major problems of *Henry V* is that its ending threatens to unravel the play and therefore the Second Tetralogy as a whole and also the Shakespearean history play as a genre because of this tension between centrifugal and centripetal forces. Like theater and words, structure is a measure of time, of the diachronic and the synchronic. Each author represents the problems of time in a different way.³⁴ Here, Shakespeare chooses to look at origins and ends differently, using irony of structure to represent a relation between past, present, and future that strains between order and chaos.

Other structural relations are ironic and modify the analysis of the general structure as well as stressing the problem elements in the play.³⁵ In *Henry V* Shakespeare lessens the role of the so-called low-life scenes, although they remain important. As we observed, the taverners appear in two scenes, which raise questions about the king's relation to Falstaff and envelop the trapping of the conspirators (II.i–iii). (Nym, Bardolph, and Pistol will appear subsequently but in new locales.) Pistol later does not blame the king for the execution of Bardolph. The audience, however, sees that the king could have remitted the penalty. The playgoers' sympathy for the executed probably increases when the Boy reports the deaths of Bardolph and Nym, thieves whom the king (who fears that he is descended from a thief of the crown) does not pardon but of whom he says that they were better men than the ancient (III.vi.100f.; IV.i.298f., iv.69f., vii.1f.). The French slaughter of the Boy and his fellows creates sympathy and complicates the response of the audience. Ultimately, Pistol is all that remains of the tavern world, whose satiric dissolution has continued from *2 Henry IV*, and he swears he will return home a thief. Perhaps, more importantly, Shakespeare ironically links Pistol with Henry. The three scenes that make humorous use of the relation between the French and English languages involve Katharine, Pistol, and Henry. Alice gives her ward English lessons (III.iv); the French soldier cannot understand English and thinks Pistol a mighty soldier (IV.iv); and Henry and Katharine claim little knowledge of the other's language and shyly muddle in love (V.ii). Pistol may represent the other side of England and of Henry that sucks the blood of the French until they offer sufficient reward (IV.iv.45–66). Like Falstaff, Pistol is thrown on the scrap heap, not by Henry directly but by Fluellen, who makes him eat a leek and plays a game with him similar to the one Henry plays with Williams (V.i). Henry also requires ample reward: he shows his mercy but will not marry Katharine until he is made heir of France (V.ii.15–20, 343–47; see III.CH.29–34). The low-life plot complicates the audience's response to Henry, the captains, and the French. That plot invites the playgoers to probe such problem elements as appearance and reality (which is also prevalent in other Shakespearean plays besides the problem plays), the relation of sex and marriage to war or politics, and the tug between the heroic and the antiheroic. The alternate plots also raise questions about the nature of kingship and about the right to the throne and succession, all of which Shakespeare represents extensively in his histories.

The playwright makes the world of the play more ironic by adding the perspectives of the captains of various nationalities as well as those of soldiers skeptical about Pistol or about Henry and kingship. These points of view leave the audience with unresolved questions. Fluellen may not be right about Pistol, but is Gower (III.vi.61f.; IV.vii.5–11)? When Pistol is being beaten, is he the Vice or the remnant of the comic tavern world? In small, we find ourselves with another rejection. Pistol was so popular with the Elizabethan audiences that he made it to the title page, so that their reactions to his humiliating lesson, now vanished, would be of great interest. The humor of the play and the dissension among the "English" increase with the representation of the various accents of the captains, as in Fluellen's disputes with MacMorris and Pistol. Shakespeare uses debates structurally—the solemn debates of the clergy, the humorous ones of the captains, and the challenging one between Bates, Williams, and Henry. They show us the many sides of war: the rationalization and self-interest; the loyalty, rivalry, and diversity of soldiers; and common soldiers asking who is responsible for war. The glove incident, which begins in act 4, scene 1 and ends in the eighth scene of the act, shows Fluellen's loyalty to Henry, who holds him in high regard but who uses him as part of the dramatic trick he constructs to surprise Williams, as well as the bravery of Williams, who says: "what your highness suffered under that shape [the disguise], I beseech you, take it for your own fault and not mine." When Williams asks Henry's pardon, the king shows him mercy and generosity (although Henry is still up to his sly tricks), and the Welsh captain, always agreeing with the king, also praises Williams (IV.viii. 51–65, cf. i, vii). The reconciliation between Henry and Williams is still ambivalent, however, for whereas both show their mettle, the soldier says only that he would not have stated his criticisms to the king if Henry had presented himself as the king. To complicate matters, Shakespeare ironically compares Fluellen and Henry through the parallel development of the glove and leek incidents.[36]

Some of the scenes in *Henry V* show a close affinity to others in *Richard II* and *1* and *2 Henry IV*, so, for an audience that sees these plays in succession, the irony of the scenes in *Henry V* becomes more complex in light of the earlier scenes. The idea of judgment arises out of an intricate ironic pattern between different scenes in these plays, an intertextuality, and is both important to the histories in their assessment of kings, kingship, succession, order, and rebellion and to the problem plays, especially in *All's Well* and *Measure*, in which human judges are shown to be so fallible, particularly in personal relations, that they compromise their public duty or office. The audience, but especially readers, directors, and critics, will find another vantage from which to judge, to understand, Henry's treatment of the conspirators in the second scene of act 2 if it compares his judgment with Richard's sentencing of Bolingbroke and Mowbray, with Bolingbroke's handling of Bushy, Greene, Richard, Aumerle, and the conspirators, with Henry the Fourth's condemnation of Vernon and Worcester, and with Lancaster's "trial" of Scroop and the rebels (*RII*, I.i, iii; III.i; IV.i; V.iii, v; *1HIV*, V.v; *2HIV*, IV.ii). The primary irony of these scenes is that a human judge may be judged as he judges others. Henry the Fifth self-righteously condemns rebels, though his father was an insurgent and his brother used treachery to condemn Scroop, a relative of the man Henry vilifies most. The execution of Nym and Bardolph, petty thieves, can be viewed in relation to Bolingbroke's theft of the crown and summary execution of Bushy and Greene, as well as Henry's use, then rejection, of Falstaff. Even if Fluellen's argument for military discipline were entirely convincing (and it does show merit), Henry forgets that his father's illegal actions did not meet with capital punishment. The rules of the game are ad hoc, discontinuous, and serve those who have power to enforce them. For a moment, if we assume that time is a continuum, we might judge judgment in *Henry V* a little differently, although it resembles the judging in earlier plays in the tetralogy as well as in the problem plays, which come after it. On these grounds of interpretation, Henry is breaking the same rules that his father did and for which he feels insecurity if not shame. He punishes others for the faults he shares with them. But discontinuity persists with continuity: the judgment in this play also differs from the problem plays because it occurs in the context of history in which it participates along with *Richard II* and *1* and *2 Henry IV*.

An ironic use of structural references to the past invites us to look at the nature of history in these plays, individually and as a group, not in the temporal isolation of a "pure" problem play. In the opening scene Ely and Canterbury praise Henry's reform from a wild youth and Canterbury also refers to the titles in France that Henry derives from Edward the Third—the king's private and public histories. It becomes apparent from Canterbury's historical account of the Salic Law that wars, depositions, and usurpations characterize the history of France as much as of England. By telling Henry to go to the tombs of Edward the Third and the Black Prince to gain inspiration from classical times to the present, Canterbury provides moral exempla. Ironically, the Black Prince was the father of Richard, whom Henry's father had deposed, so that this reference can also remind us that Henry's claim to the English crown, let alone to the French crown, is tenuous. Characters use history selectively. Gaunt had invoked the spirit of Edward the Third to shame Richard into better government (*RII*, II.i.104–8). Even if Canterbury invokes the glorious past of England, his motives are not clear—how much does he want to protect the church from taxation? This comment is not meant as a kind of carping, because human motives are never clear, simple, and entirely selfless, but interpretation must determine how this is so and what is at stake. Interpretations of history affect present actions, and they can be as mythical as factual. Henry, Canterbury, Ely, and Exeter debate past strategies of fighting the French and the Scots that seem to affect both Henry's decision to invade (or at least give him a rationale for it) and the manner in which he will do it (I.ii). There is a part of Henry's personal past that comes to a close: Falstaff is dead (II.iii.5). The king has forgotten the clown, for the audience never knows whether he is aware of the death, as he never refers to it on stage. This is a past, if the taverners can be believed, that qualifies Henry's heroic nature.[37] We have seen that Henry, like his father and the rebels, interprets Richard's role in history as a way of coming to terms with his own part. The memory of Richard is a locus for Henry's doubt over, and assertion of, his own authority and the idea of kingship.

The irony of structure shows the history as problem play, for the fall of England once more at the end of *Henry V* and the failure of the English to reach a lasting heroic age (even in fallible human terms) create a crisis in history because instability in human events threatens to defy or render false any principle of artistic order or any genre applied to (or perhaps imposed on) the chaos of human time. And this instability and chaotic flow of time, which occurs in all ages (another attempt to order time), makes the temporal art of historical writing especially vulnerable. Do history play and historical narrative falsify by imposing order on chaos, or do they shape necessary myths that stem from the will to order and meaning that may arise from the very nature of syntax and the human brain itself? I am not blaming Henry the Fifth, either the historical figure or character, nor am I faulting Shakespeare. Instead, I am calling attention to these problematic history plays because they so superbly raise issues that will be with us in one historically modified form or another. And are these forms or structures themselves myths and impositions? Such are the quarrels between structuralists and post-structuralists. The playwright is caught between a view of his task as supplement to nature, something that fills the gap between humanity and nature after the Fall, and as a reflection or representation of the fallen world. Whatever the solution, it is symbolic because the word can never be the world. It seems, however, that history demands a representational muse because there is a tradition that the language and structure of history conform more closely to conventions of what was long called realism and because there is a supposition that historical representation relates directly to past events and an outside world. Shakespeare explores the relation between invented speeches, characters, and events (the actions of Pistol, Bardolph, Williams, and Fluellen) on the one hand and those taken from the chronicles, from "real life" (Ely, Henry the Fifth, and Katharine) on the other. Through irony of structure, Shakespeare represents temporal instability and temporal patterns, shapes and unshapes history, and asserts and questions the existence of history. It is the unresolved tensions between unity and dissolution, between history and fiction, heroism and skepticism that make *Henry V* difficult to interpret but that ultimately give the play its interest and vigor.

THE IRONY OF WORDS

Henry's violent images and Burgundy's description of France as a ruined garden most clearly show *Henry V* pressing at the bounds of the genre of the history play, for they reveal a qualification of the "comic" marriage at the end and modify Henry's heroism. Besides developing aspects of the problem play in *Henry V*, the irony of words complicates such historical patterns as the question of time, much as verbal irony has done in *Richard II* and the *Henry IV* plays. The problem and historical elements overlap. In this section I shall discuss in *Henry V* only examples of verbal irony that I have not yet touched on.

Ironic images of war and peace best illustrate the problematic attributes of the play. As we saw earlier, the major speech that modifies Henry's gentleness in war is the threat against Harfleur (III.iii). Both in love and in war Henry uses violent images. In his conversations with Burgundy and the King of France, Katharine becomes a sex object and joke about siege and rape (V.ii.309–47). Even the imagery of peace involves strife and ruin, as may be observed in Burgundy's image of France as a ruined garden (V.ii.23f.). If this personal violent language spills over into Henry's public conduct of the war and makes his kingship more problematic, references to time also call attention to a crucial question for the history play: How can we best represent and re-create time?

We have looked at the prince's view of time in the *Henry IV* plays and his views of temporality when, in *Henry V*, he becomes king. Here, in exploring the problem of representing history in historical drama, we shall concentrate on the views of time expressed by the Chorus and other characters in *Henry V*, although these views share many ideas with characters in the first three plays of the tetralogy and although we shall glance at Henry's Crispin Crispian speech. These shared problems help unite the tetralogy, even if the difference in ironic emphasis and in treating problem elements also distinguishes each play. Once again, irony creates a tension between centrifugal and centripetal forces in a history play. In addition to the Chorus's conscious references to history, the views that the characters hold of the past spur them to ironically limited actions. When the Prologue asks the audience to make leaps of imagination, to turn "the accomplishment of many years / Into an hour-glass: for the which supply, / Admit me Chorus to this history," he offers to act as an intermediary in presenting the history play, especially in making the audience aware of the difference between "historical" and "dramatic" time (PR., 30–32). For the Prologue, then, the telescoping of time is important enough to mention at the beginning, suggesting that the representation of this historical period, or, more specifically, a play about this reign, demands a radical selection of events and swift representation through narrative foreshortening.

The views of time reflect or refract a divided and fallen world. Shakespeare qualifies the triumph of time that the Chorus proclaims and raises questions about the nature of history. When the Chorus invites the audience to help re-create a specific time, each production creates a novel relation between the eve of Agincourt, the performances of 1599 and their references to Essex, and each new audience (IV, V: CH). The words of the Chorus take on different meanings as time passes. If the playgoers take up the invitation to use their historical imaginations, to participate, they will involve themselves in the interpretation of history (which, with past events and the author's representation, is history) and in the change of history, not as it happened but as people perceive it to have happened. All history is thus, but the Chorus's speeches bring this idea into relief. The Chorus talks about other written representations of history and asks the audience, with some irony, to accept the limitations of the theater in representing historical time (V.CH.1–9). The audience can admire the representation of Agincourt while realizing that it is not the battle as it happened but an interpretation of it. Playgoers can extrapolate from this limitation the shortcomings of their own interpretations. Paradoxically, Shakespeare's version of the reign of Henry the Fifth is for many the only or the primary representation of that period, even if it calls attention to its limitations. *Henry V* resembles Shakespeare's sonnets, which are aware of the desolation and constraints of time while defying time with a representation that will survive its human subjects.

Shakespeare modifies the Epilogue's praise of the glory of Henry's "Small time." The playwright helps achieve multiplicity by creating a tension between the form, rhythm, and musical time of the sonnet that the Epilogue speaks and the ruin he must announce for time ahead. The sonnet is also a coda in a score that not only sings the praises of Henry but also criticizes him. Shakespeare's ironic use of time shows the problems of the genre of the history play, especially in the relation between Chorus and the main action, but, perhaps above all, it reveals a common ground between the four plays by representing their shared concerns about human limitations in time.

Nor is history one-sided. For the French, but not for Henry and Fluellen, Cressy represents the "memorable shame" that Edward the Third inflicted on them at the height of his power and reminds them of Henry, Edward's descendant, who now threatens France (II.iv.53–64). Although the French king states a particular lesson of history—that the Dauphin should learn to respect the English—he later does not follow it himself and rejects Henry's "memorable" pedigree that would give him the French crown (II.iv.88). Memory also fails the characters. It takes Gower a while to remember that Pistol is "a bawd, a cut-purse" (III.vi.61–62). Here, Shakespeare causes an "unhistorical" character to judge another "unhistorical" character as if to complicate history through the supposition of how things might have been. To inspire his own soldiers in the Crispin Crispian speech, Henry reminds them that although as old men they will forget other events, they will remember this great day, each man recalling his own feats with exaggeration, passing on the story of English honor to his son, who will teach his son, so that Crispin Crispian will never be forgotten until the "ending of the world" (IV.iii.40–66). Henry shows a subtle understanding of subjectivity, embellishment, and mythmaking, of the difficulty of keeping history from becoming an epic or romantic narrative, and of the advantages to his situation and to heroism that the difficulty allows. Oral history is important to Henry for reasons of self-interest, patriotism, and heroism, even as he understands its departure from fact and truth. For Henry, as for many of us, the truth is never plain and rarely simple. The truth of fiction and the fiction of truth interact to the very end of the tetralogy. Irony of words—as we saw in appeals to God, self-trapping images, and Henry the Fifth's view of time—helps reveal the problem play in *Henry V*, which presses at the bounds of its genre, including from more problematic "images" such as those of war and peace as well as more commonly historic ones like "time."

THE PROBLEMATIC CHALLENGE TO THE KING IN ACT 4, SCENE I

This scene represents appearance and actuality, acting and disguise, and a friction between heroism and antiheroism, all of which are problematic and complicate the idea of history in *Henry V*. It is a scene that looks at the relation between religion and politics, a theme that helps bind together the plays of the Second Tetralogy. Time being once more the thief, I have concentrated my analysis on the debate that Henry has with his soldiers and with himself rather than looking at the whole scene. The debate between Henry and Bates and Williams raises problems about the responsibility and legitimacy of kingship. Henry also admits his doubts about his relation to Richard and about regal succession and authority.

It is ironic that in a "godlike" disguise Henry finds even his humanity questioned. Presenting himself as a common soldier serving under Captain Erpingham, Henry, who is playing yet another role, answers Bates that Erpingham should not tell "the king" his despairing thought, for the monarch—and here Shakespeare wrings the dramatic irony for all its worth—"is but a man, as I am: the violet smells to him as it doth me; the element shows to him as it doth me." This speech of Henry's echoes Richard's musings on the "death of kings" after he learns that Bolingbroke has not only invaded the country but has also executed Bushy, Green, and Wiltshire: "I live with bread like you, feel want, / Taste grief, need friends" (cf. *RII*, III,ii. 171–77). Like Richard, Henry wants others to see the man beneath the regal ceremony (99–106). It is ironic that Henry, like any person in his position, still faces the problem of the king's two bodies that Richard experienced and that he is drawn to talk about it in the same terms. In light of Bolingbroke's deposition of Richard, irony also arises when Henry expresses this tension in an image of rise and fall. The memory of Richard throughout the tetralogy affects the action and the characters' notions of kingship. Although the king's "affections are higher mounted than ours, yet when they stoop, they stoop with the like wing" (106–8). This description can be applied to both Henries as well as to Richard, for Bolingbroke was "base" in deposing his predecessor and Henry descends from and not only maintains a stolen crown but seeks to mount a new throne in France. From a self-interested English vantage, Henry the Fifth is most successful because he helps stop civil war and exports strife to France.

The debate with Williams and Bates brings kingship and the Shakespearean history play to another crisis, for Henry the Fifth, the hero at the culmination of the Second Tetralogy, finds his judgment and policy questioned and wins a limited and not entirely convincing debate with his soldiers. Henry then admits that a king must be an actor, hiding his fears from his men so that they will not be disheartened. His acting is political and recalls his father's dissembling more than Richard's histrionics of self-expression. However attractive we find the later Richard, it may be a cultural bias that values this kind of sentimental and theatrical acting over the acting skills of a politician, whose very acting, our culture seems to assume, is insincere and dangerous. Most of us reading Shakespeare's plays are more drawn to the theater than to "politics," although this last word resonates throughout the register of contemporary Shakespearean criticism. This may explain the return of the repressed, Richard and Falstaff, no matter how much critics and readers think they have dealt with the "sentimental" defenses of these characters by those who lament the death of the one and the rejection of the other.

Bates takes the king to task on one of his favorite topics through-out the play—the difference between the inward and the outward man—saying that no matter what courage Henry "shows" the world, the king wishes himself home in England (e.g., cf. V.ii). Inside and outside often interpenetrate. In another reminder of dramatic irony, Shakespeare has the disguised king speak the "con-science of the king" and say that Henry would wish himself only in France. "Conscience" is also an important word in the king's view of responsibility and of the inward and the outward (cf. 8, I.ii). Having shaken Henry's confidence in the authority of, and popular consent in, his rule, Bates shakes him some more. He says that the king should be fighting alone so that he might be ransomed for sure and might save the lives of innocent men, a statement that Henry answers with another intense moment of dramatic irony: "methinks I could not die any where so contented as in the king's company, his cause being just and his quarrel honourable." Williams grumbles: "That's more than we know." As in a dark night of the soul, Henry must reexamine his assumptions, for here are men who view war with France in an opposite way to his position or to the one he professes.

Like Richard, who plays many roles and none contented, the judge is being judged. Henry's example has not resurrected the spirits of the soldiers but has, instead, caused Williams to use the image of the Resurrection against him (135f., cf. 18–23). Whereas Henry had tried Falstaff and the conspirators, he is now on trial himself (*2HIV*, V.v; *HV*, II.ii). Whereas Bates says that, owing to the obedience of the soldiers, the king will assume the responsibility for the crime if the war is unjust, Williams describes the dismem-bered bodies of the soldiers in battle crying at the Day of Judgment when Henry will answer if the war was wrong, for the soldiers fought as obedient subjects doing their duty whether their monarch was right or wrong. The literally dismembered body politic takes on theological as well as teleological meanings. The play and the group of history plays are also in danger of flying apart, as the tetralogy's own unity is the multiple questioning of kingship. Inter-pretations clash. Human judgment and design are fallible. Playing at

God is a game no human can win, but without trying to achieve a god's eye view, people, including playwrights and audiences, can slip into solipsism and lapse into incommunication. Judge not but the judge. Where Henry has found a righteous crusade in Christianity, Williams finds pacificism: "I am afeared there are few die well that die in battle; for how can they charitably dispose of any thing when blood is their argument?" (143–46). Nor will the king accept this accountability, although he used a similar argument to remind Canterbury that his conscience is answerable to God (cf. I.ii.14–32). It appears that Henry's response shows false logic for Williams because he does not share the same premise as Henry, that the war in France is just. A son sent to sea on business who dies in a sinful state is not the same as a man fighting an unjust war who dies in his sins, for only when the business is criminal and unjust is the case the same. But in Henry's public thoughts the war is just, although in his private meditations he is not so sure. Even as the father is not responsible for the state of sin in which the subject dies, he is answerable for the death, if one places the problem in the context of the play and the tetralogy, which is at least in part Christian. Eschatology is at the center of a central debate in the Shakespearean history play. The question of what is criminal and what is just is not such a simple one, and to live by the logician's rule is not easy. The king does not give the voyage or the boy a bad cause, or at least a cause that doubts its own justice, even when it might be just and so create a narrative that better reflects the complexity of the king's bodies, motives, politics, and psychology. A general knows that the probability of death for his soldiers is greater in battle than in peace even if he does not "purpose" their deaths. The king is evading the point. Bates had said that the monarch assumes the crime of the wrong cause and not the personal sins of the men (see 131–33). But then the king is playing a role and, like a playwright, manipulates the scene. In an unwanted discussion (the king had wanted to walk alone unengaged in the night), Henry has played one of Erpingham's captains, and he is and is not the king.[38]

In this self-consciously theatrical situation, the king continues his line of argument. He says that even a king with a spotless cause in war will be fighting alongside some vicious soldiers, whose violent crimes Henry enumerates, including the seduction of virgins, an image (like that of rape) he appears to repeat, if not relish, perhaps unconsciously. Henry may be no better than the spotted soldiers in his example (cf. III.iii.20–21, 35; V.ii.318–19, 330–32, 343–47). The king continues to talk about men who have committed violent crimes, saying that if they outstrip human justice "they have no wings to fly from God," for whom war is a vengeance against such sinful men. The confident appeal to God characterizes the public king, even in disguise. Henry also fails to consider the good men who perish in an unjust war or to think about the justice of his cause: he wants to have it both ways—"Every subject's duty is the king's; but every subject's soul is his own." Returning to the idea of individual "conscience," Henry argues that the soldier should prepare his soul for God because, if he dies so, he gains a life in Christ, and if he lives, he has benefited from such a spiritual exercise (135–92). If in our interpretations of this and the other plays of the tetralogy we still owe a debt to Tillyard, we cannot neglect Shakespeare's Christian and medieval heritage and his increasing use of debate and discontent with genre and form, both of which lead to the problem plays.

Williams and Bates concede the argument, but Williams continues to take exception to Henry's words. This time he does not believe that the king will be ransomed. Shakespeare again plays up the dramatic irony as Henry replies that if the king is ransomed, "I will never trust his word after." He is a king and no king. Nor can Williams tolerate the pomposity of the caped soldier, scorning that "perilous shot" from a popgun, that impotent private displeasure against a monarch, that vain peacock's feather trying to turn the sun of the king to ice with fanning. Williams seems to be getting to Henry. Although there may be some truth in what Williams says soldier to soldier, Henry appears to be taking offense as a king. When Henry expresses "potential" anger, Williams suggests that there will be a quarrel between them and then they exchange gages. As Henry's answers are problematic, the comic resolution of this challenge in the last two scenes of act 4 should perplex the audience. The glove incident is resolved comically, but, rather than cowering before the king, Williams appeals to decorum. The king, Williams says, came disguised as a common soldier and was answered as one. He did not offend the king but asks pardon still, his reward a glove full of gold crowns, as well as a royal pardon. Even though the resolution shows Henry's sense of humor, power, generosity, and "mercy," and catches the aggressive Williams, who boasts like the French, in a dramatic irony, it does not remove the difficult problem of responsibility in war and makes the comic ending of the plot an uneasy one. Like the theological, political, and military debates in the first two scenes and like the debates on military history in which Fluellen finds himself, this dispute resolves itself in the English victory but with the irresolution of dissent and fallen nature.

Shakespeare now represents Henry's private considerations of the nature of kingship. After Bates and Williams exit, Henry is finally "alone with his thoughts," but they are now more disturbed than before (193–235). In a soliloquy the king speaks about the burden of kingship as Richard and Henry the Fourth had before him (*RII*, III.ii.155f.; *2 HIV*, III.i.4f.). Even though, when speaking with Bates and Williams, Henry had described the king as a just man, he now differentiates between the king and private men, particularly fools who feel nothing but their own "wringing," or pain, especially intestinal.[39] Like Richard, whom Bolingbroke soon deposes, Henry the Fifth curses "ceremony" for its emptiness. Both Richard and Henry wrestle with the tension between the private and public aspects of kingship. Whereas Richard said, "throw away respect, / Tradition, form, and ceremonious duty," Henry apostrophizes ceremony, recalling the nought, the *O*, the nothing in something that the Chorus conjures. Henry would personify his troubles and doubts and blame them, calling the inside out and censuring it for not being inside, for its alienation. He also apostrophizes the king's two bodies, "Twin-born with greatness," and personifies "thrice-gorgeous ceremony" in a moral allegory of king and man, vilifying it for being pompous and for being a royal burden a common man does not have to endure. Henry asks ceremony, "Art thou aught else but place, degree and form, / Creating awe and fear in other men?" He questions the very order he has asserted. Although he also discovers the same kind of flattery Richard did, he has more might than Richard, is able to suppress rebellion and can be more concerned with the fear that power causes and how the powerful thus grow unhappy (cf. *RII*, IV.i.305–10). Like his father before him, Henry also apprehends the idea that Gaunt tried to teach Richard: a king has limited power because he cannot improve the health of another man (262–63; cf. *RII*, I.iii.226; IV.i.302f.; V.iii.78). Just as his father spoke about the cares and troubled sleep of kingship, so too does Henry (cf. *2HIV*, III.i.4f.). Neither the regal clothes nor the titles nor the "tide of pomp / That beats upon the high shore of this world" makes the king sleep as soundly as the "wretched slave." The tidal imagery may reveal Henry's recognition that time waits for no one. Henry also implies that the king is like Phoebus, who rises to light the world with the help of the private man who, like a lackey, bears no responsibility for the rise and fall of the fortunes of governments and nations. The king illuminates the world and keeps the peace for men. If, as Henry told Bates and Williams, each man must show the king duty but answer for his own soul, then no king should be overburdened. To rise or fall, a king needs private men, so that they are more important than Henry says and suffer more than he admits in his idyll of the common man. Subjects can suffer exile, death in battle, and poverty. Although Henry inveighs against royal power (namely, ceremony), he does not mind using it to advantage with Williams, Fluellen, Katharine, and the French king (see IV.vii; V.ii, iii).

In private Henry now doubts his relation to God, whereas in public he proclaims his special status. After Erpingham enters, tells Henry that his nobles want to see him, and leaves, the king speaks a second soliloquy in which he prays to the "God of battles" to keep the hearts of his men from fear and from counting the superior numbers. Henry would take from them their sense of "reckoning," which can also mean judgment, as if the soldiers would judge Henry harshly. After all Henry's echoes of Richard's thoughts, Shakespeare seems to be showing that the heroic king is losing his confidence in his special relation with God, asking God's pardon for his father's fault in acquiring the crown, and telling what penance he has done for Richard. Lastly, Henry promises to do more penance than he has done for Richard's death, but realizes this repenting—imploring pardon—"comes after all" (or "ill" as Taylor emends the text). Depending on the reading ("all" or "ill"), the meaning is either that the sins of the fathers are visited on the sons or that, having himself done ill, Henry the Fifth's penitence is worth little. The asking of forgiveness, if deeply felt, is the first step to absolution. How sincere

Henry is, we can only wonder. We may be willing to grant him his new understanding of his own limitation, or ask why he waits such a long time to pray that God not punish him ("Not to-day, O Lord! / O not to-day"), why he is so concerned about the day of battle, why he implies that punishment is something that he can only stave off, and whether he is, like Everyman and Mankind, trying to bargain with God (231–311). This scene follows the patriotic and adulatory Chorus and precedes the French denunciations of the English, so that the context displays the ironic qualification I have been speaking of throughout. Here are different views of history modifying one another. The problem elements of disguise and debate and the historical aspects of time and interpretation are in constant and creative friction. Perhaps most of all, the collision of official and unofficial history, of private and public selves (and other roles that challenge this opposition) make us aware of how much strain persists in the genre of the history play. The idea of kingship helps relate this scene to the rest of the play and to the tetralogy. Irony, here especially, creates a situation for the history play and the Second Tetralogy that mediates between unity and disunity without resolution.

It would be foolish to forget the heroic aspects of Henry's character. Because I am assuming that my audience knows the important contributions of critics from Dryden through Johnson to Tillyard to the discussion of this king and the history plays plays generally, I have emphasized a view of Henry that, while having gained greater acceptance since World War II, remains, historically, a minority position until the 1960s. Unlike the new historicists and the cultural materialists, whose work I have found helpful and provocative, I think it unironic and one-sided to condemn Tillyard and the tradition he represents wholesale. F. R. Leavis's attack on A. C. Bradley, while having some salutary effects in shifting attention from a tired paradigm of character to a new paradigm of theme, will in the long run fail to overshadow Bradley's criticism. Leavis's Shakespearean theme is itself in the shadows, for the moment. (Like Chaucer so will Dryden be / Like Dryden so will Pope be / Like Pope so will _____ be. And so on. But they are still read). Thus, the eclipse of

Tillyard continues with a strange disdain, even though Rossiter began it so long ago now, and Tillyard has been long on the wane. Rossiter's "ambivalence," the new historicists' many metaphors for the multiple, and my use of "multiplicity" and cultural pluralism cannot overshadow that we reside, as Shakespeare did, in a dialectic between material conditions and ideal constructions. None of us, the fictional Henry or the real critic, can escape this irony.

Irony qualifies and complicates but does not undercut Henry's personality. *Henry V* possesses the chief attribute of the problem play: it pushes at the boundaries of its genre, in this case of the history play. The Aumerle conspiracy, especially, represented comedy ab ovo in the tragic history of *Richard II*. The promises of Hal to redeem time at the expense of others like Falstaff (and Sir John's promises that he will reform and his parodies in *1 Henry IV*, mainly a comic history) begin the satire, with its attendant isolation, that predominates in *2 Henry IV*. In Part Two the rejection of Falstaff stresses the problems of kingship that Richard's fall began and looks forward to the problem play in *Henry V*. Although in the last play of the Second Tetralogy different types of irony reveal many of the same problems, irony of structure stresses the tension between the Chorus that praises heroism and the main action that is partly antiheroic; irony of theater particularly calls attention to Henry's uses of disguise and acting and to the Chorus's emphasis on the problems of writing and viewing a history play; and irony of words uniquely uncovers the images of war and peace that modify Henry's heroic character, a heroism that has been amply documented by Tillyard and others. The examination of act 4, scene 4, looks at the combination of these ironies and especially the problematic debate between Henry, Bates, and Williams. These kinds of irony, as well as the analysis of the representative scene, reveal common subjects among the four plays, such as kingship (right, responsibility, and succession), that help mold these plays into a tetralogy. Paradoxically, the problems of the history play serve not only to perplex the audience and induce a crisis in understanding history but also to unite the plays in a coherent pattern. Chapter 5 will make a few further suggestions about the perplexities of the relation between history and literature in these plays and, briefly, will mention Shakespeare's Spanish and French contemporaries and near contemporaries in order to counter the illusion in the English-speaking world that Shakespeare stands alone in his great achievement. I shall also say a little about other kinds of historical representation that Shakespeare helped to enable in a world that becomes ever more radically different from his with each decade.

FIVE

Conclusion

I N SAMUEL DANIEL'S LAST MAJOR WORK, A prose history from the Romans to Edward the Third entitled *The Collection of the History of England (1612–18)*, he asks:

Pardon us Antiquity, if we mis-censure your actions, which are ever (as those of men) according to the vogue, and sway of the times, and have onely their upholding by the opinion of the present: We deale with you but as posterity will with us (which ever thinkes it selfe the wiser) that will judge likewise of our errors according to the cast of their imaginations.

Here, one of Shakespeare's contemporaries, who shared with the playwright a keen interest in English history, shows an ironic awareness of the comings and goings of intellectual fashions. It is easy for us to reconstruct the Renaissance and think we know better and have done better than Davenant, Cibber, and Tate in adapting Shakespeare to our age. Tate's comic ending for *King Lear* is scornworthy, but reading *Troilus and Cressida* as an antiwar pamphlet is not. A Restoration playwright's presumption is comic, but a postwar theorist's redaction of Shakespeare as the poet of material anxiety is not. Our imaginations are somehow more equipped coming in a latter age. This hubris may be an antidote to yearning for a golden age when our ancestors lived pastorally and without the threat of tedium and disease, war and privation, anxiety and injustice. Nonetheless, in the historical imagination the past and present place restraints on each other, the past leaving its traces biologically, socially, and textually in the present, the present using the past to persuade contemporaries to critical, theoretical, and political causes in literature and in society. We make Shakespeare our contemporary whether he likes it or not (the tongues of the dead are textual traces we read), but his last will and testament, his complete works, have been so influential that it may be Shakespeare who reads us. Francis Bacon observes, "Dramatic poetry is like history made visible, and is an image of actions past as though they were present." Historical understanding, no matter how difficult, is important for literary studies and for living in the world. To try to comprehend Shakespeare's complexity is a daunting task that involves an assumption of historical difference between his period and ours, within a frame-work that allows for a cultural meaning of the category of difference itself. To say that understanding is impossible, even if it is provisional, is to abdicate the sharing of textual and theatrical pleasure, as well as historical and political responsibility. To say that understanding is self-evident opens us to other potential literary and social dangers from those who would read history and literary texts too transparently and naïvely. Irony complicates literary and theatrical response and increases awareness of the complexity of representation.

The fall of language creates problems for the characters in these plays and their assertions of authority for their words in representing the world, kingship, and God as they are caught in contradiction and self-trapping images. The Fall as metaphor interrogates the efficacy of metaphor and language generally in representing truth. By observing the problems and dilemmas of the characters in these four plays, we learn more about our own, the relation of godlike knowledge and human ignorance. Irony—which is multiple and overarching and consists of the irony of words, theater, and structure—makes us more conscious of our situation in language and temporality, as we yearn for overview while we participate in time. The Shakespearean history play, particularly the four that we have been discussing, goads us to understand better our complex fallenness in history. Shakespeare's irony also complicates the history play, the relation between history and drama. If history is preoccupied more exclusively than any other human study with time, the history play is a good way to study temporality. In looking at the relation between drama and time, Shakespeare and his audiences can explore the subtle problems of language and time in life and art until they can question the nature and effectiveness of history and the history play. The fall of language and time is also the fall of kingship because when Richard loses his authority, there are two kings—Bolingbroke and Richard—and this condition destabilizes the word "king" and represents a division of experience. The rebels in the *Henry IV* plays question the new king's right to rule, and even Hal, who promises to redeem time, cannot control temporality and finds that there are challenges to his kingship. Irony of words, theater, and structure reveal that there is a movement in the tetralogy toward the problem play because these history plays call attention to the difficult relation between drama and history. Kingship, language, and time, as well as the history play itself, are subjects of which we become increasingly aware. The fall of Richard, the Aumerle conspiracy, Hal's pact with the audience to redeem time, the use of Rumor as an induction, the rejection of Falstaff, the debate between Henry, Bates, and Williams, and the Epilogue to *Henry V* are some of the features in the Second Tetralogy that call attention to the compounding problems of language, theater, and structure.

The study attempts to make clearer than before the complex nature of the problems and dilemmas of the Second Tetralogy. In chapter 1 I make problematic the relation between the terms "theater" and "world" by yoking them at close quarters. The second chapter argues that critics and characters use a language that cannot correspond to the world that they describe. Chapter 3 discusses how drama and its language make us particularly aware of the nature of time and the human predicament of infinite desire and finite performance. Chapter 4, which at another time I might call "Undoing the History Play," analyzes the problems of representing history and the difficulties of genres, especially in relation to *Henry V*, which is a problem play that questions itself and the whole tetralogy, the genre of the history play, and its ability to end this group of histories. The study argues that in the Second Tetralogy Shakespeare represents something akin to what in *The History of the World* Ralegh called the realm of secondary causes, a fallen world in which the search for meaning and the relation between cause and effect remain forever uncertain. A large part of the Fall is the human predicament in time. A specific application of these critical dilemmas is the way that the individual plays and the tetralogy become increasingly like a problem play.

The Afterword supplements the main body of the study by discussing how our historical context has changed, and how in the past decade or so the interpretations of Shakespeare's history plays have changed significantly. The Afterword discusses irony, the material conditions of Shakespeare's theater, narrative and dramatic history, and recent critical developments such as new historicism, cultural materialism, and feminism, all in direct and indirect relation to the Second Tetrology. Although I agree with Moody Prior's observation in *The Drama of Power*—that we cannot reduce Shakespeare's histories to his sources and his society when posterity has considered these plays greater than this reduction—I think that the return to historicism has been an important corrective to Bardolatry and Shakespeare-the-only-Elizabethan and the-Text-is-the-Thing. The dialectic between the contextual and the textual should provide a more ironic and less absolutist view of Shakespeare. We are Shakespearean contexts and certainly would not want to do away with ourselves in the representation of his plays. Shakespeare-the-only-Contemporary is also an interpretative death wish. From these concerns with Renaissance contexts, the Afterword proceeds to issues that charge Renaissance studies today, however much or little posterity will regard them: historical materialism and gender. These concerns are not unified within themselves but are contested and ever changing. They make the critical and theoretical dialectic in Shakespearean studies more vital because the women and material conditions of Shakespeare's theater were idealized or neglected. The terms for historical and gender studies are already in a flux. The Afterword should help make my readings of Shakespeare's Second Tetrology more contextual.

This tetralogy points backward to plays that Shakespeare wrote a few years earlier but that portray the reigns following the rule of Henry the Fifth. Even though the First Tetralogy does not represent the rule of Edward the Fourth in a separate play, it incorporates Edward in the first and second acts of *Richard III* (ca. 1593) and is as distinct in its periods as the Second Tetralogy. It culminates with the ascension of Henry the Seventh and the dawn of Tudor stability. Later, Shakespeare was to write, or help write, *Henry VIII* (ca. 1613), in which Cranmer prophesies the greatness of Elizabeth in a pastoral vision in which the future predicts the past and in which Shakespeare gives to his last English history play a comic ending against the wishes of the Prologue, thereby complicating history-as-romance with irony (*HVIII*, V.iv.14–55, esp. 33–47). All is not literally true or stable under the Tudors. Each character has his or her own truth. Shakespeare tempers history with romance and romance with history, challenging the audience with the relation between story and myth in history while giving it a pattern of history that interrogates itself, so that although Elizabeth is like the "maiden phoenix" of peace rising out of its own ashes, she is not as clearly redemptive as Hermione at the end of *The Winter's Tale* (ca. 1610–11) (*WT*, V.iii.98–99ff.). History qualifies genre, in this case the convention of romance. Shakespeare does not appear to have worked chronologically in a grand redemptive plan, beginning with *Richard II* and ending with *Henry VIII*. Only with force can *King John* (ca. 1591–98) and *Henry VIII* be placed in an unmodified epic frame. The Second Tetralogy points back to the despair in the *Henry VI* plays and in *Richard III* as well as to the fall of Richard the Second. Even if it is argued that years later, after having traveled exhaustively through melodrama, tragedy, comedy, satire, romance, and other genres, Shakespeare answered this doubt with Cranmer's messianic vision of Elizabeth, it is doubtful that we can convince many to see the ten histories as a piece. There are too many gaps in the reigns and too much distance dividing *Henry VIII* from the rest in the time of composition and *King John* from the rest in historical time. This objection is not based simply on Shakespeare's intention but on the strain that the critic or audience must experience to enforce a unity. A consideration of the English history plays, even if they are not a monolith, is valuable, just as a discussion of their relation to the Roman plays, the tragedies, and the romances often produces fruitful results.

Even if this national epic were a convincing whole, the history plays imply that Shakespeare expected England to rise and fall many times over the the centuries. The end of the Second Tetralogy supports this view, for the ruin of England after Henry the Fifth resembles its decline during and even after Richard's reign. Falls also involve rises and rises, falls, as *Richard II* illustrates. Patterns are never plain and exactly repetitive in human time. If, like a helix (which combines a linear view of time with a cyclical one), the Second Tetralogy loops backward and forward to the First Tetralogy, this second group also makes time a circle, showing that there is little progress in a fallen world, in which all things human are subject to decay, for Shakespeare turns the mind of the audience back to Richard the Second, who becomes a type of future kings. He is their destiny, no matter how successful they are, because kings have not kept and perhaps cannot keep chaos from being part of experience. Historians, historical poets, and historical dramatists find patterns of hope and despair, sometimes cycles that recur and can only be redeemed by hope, sometimes a world in time that changes in similar patterns or that remains as unchanged in its essence as a circle. Shakespeare wrote *Henry VIII* some fourteen years after *Henry V*, and he seems to have left his audience for a long time with the Epilogue of *Henry V* promising chaos and with the memory of the grim character of the First Tetralogy, which has been tempered with the brief appearance of Richmond, uniting the white and the red rose, at the end of *Richard III* (*RIII*, V.v.1f.). We may wonder how much like Richmond's triumph Bolingbroke's is. Today, we cannot neglect the difficult relation between performance and reading texts, so that it would be naïve to keep critics, readers, and playgoers (who so often read Shakespearean texts) from thinking about the relations among the English histories. Although I do not believe it wise to discuss the form of the Second Tetralogy as if it were part of the English epic that A. W. Schlegel and others saw in Shakespeare's ten history plays, history has kept this debate open ended.

The last lines of the Second Tetralogy point in many directions, but they mention the fall of England and remind us, at least in their immediate sense, of the chaos that helps comprise history. In history there is a wish for order and an anxiety over disorder for those who support the status quo and the reverse for those who oppose it, but most of us are not kings or rebels and never seem to inhabit these extremes. Most characters also have mixed desires and anxieties. Bolingbroke wants and does not want to seize power and is glad and guilty when he does. Shakespeare molds the Second Tetralogy into an apparent unity, binding it through linear time, which represents the reigns of three successive kings, and, analogically, through cyclical time, which reminds the audience that in the England of Henry the Fifth kings and kingdoms are as apt to fall as during the reign of Richard. The playwright enriches this irony by showing the diverse and multiple forms in which history occurs and in which it may be cast, emphasizing discontinuities as much as continuities, showing the limited view that characters and people have of history, which neither repeats itself entirely nor creates itself anew in each generation. Although the end of *Henry V* is open, it does not only point to the First Tetralogy (which was written before, but whose events happened after in historical time). Shakespeare's attitude to time itself is unifying and multiple and presents an ironic view of history. Historical context and form qualify each other, so that the pressures of censorship, the response of the audience, and the growth of the genre of history itself modify Shakespeare's experimentation as it modifies them. Without a keen interest in Elizabethan England and without genres like tragedy, comedy, and satire, Shakespeare would not have been able to forge these four plays. Through the limits of history, Shakespeare uncovers its potentialities and, through the potentialities, the limits, a shaping and enabling irony that the Schlegels, Hegel, Kierkegaard, and we can appreciate.

As irony invites serial qualification and the tension between synchrony and diachrony, overview and participation, and as history in the drama demands sequels and balances precariously between stability and instability, shape and the questioning of shape, the Second Tetralogy interrogates form while it represents it. In its vanishing presence this group of history plays asks that our reason create patterns and question them, even challenging us to consider the possibility of history itself. The choruses in *Henry V* especially break down the simple authority of intentionality by asking the audience to use its imagination and become part of history. In many ways the history play is a mutual creation of playwright and audience, one that includes reason but also extends beyond it. Historical drama is presentation and representation, the play on the stage creating the illusion of presence through the body of the actors and represence because the play is a past text about the past in the present. In the fallen world and word of history, irony reveals the interpermeability of opposites that informs and unforms, joining and disjoining uniformity and multiformity. Shakespeare complicates with and through us the fall, communal celebration, fragmentary isolation, and the friction between actuality and fiction in kind. Here, Shakespeare has begun to give us history and antihistory, the probability and improbability of historical mimesis that he later displays in *Henry VIII*. The very end of *Henry V* may illustrate the difficult task of history. There, he rubs together the problems of structure, self-conscious theatricality, and words, juxtaposing the "comic" marriage of Henry and Kate and the language of sexual exploitation with the politics of triumph and conquest, and joining and disjoining them with the future premature death of Henry the Fifth and the fall of Henry the Sixth in the radically reduced temporal form of the sonnet. Conclusions about irony and history are as tentative as their representation. In the end, both limit and enable.

If this book has contributed something, it may have suggested that irony in the Second Tetralogy is qualification and not simply undermining, multiple and not only double. The study has also tried to argue and demonstrate that form and history interact, that genre is mixed, so that the boundaries between history and literature permeate. Genre involves flexible general conventions and individual innovation. Although other studies have considered dramatic irony in Shakespeare's histories or philosophical irony more generally or in his other plays, this book has attempted to bring into the discussion of the Second Tetralogy German romantic irony and the critiques that Hegel and Kierkegaard have of that irony. This was the second great development in the theory of irony (centuries after the first in Plato and Aristotle), and the Schlegels and others placed Shakespeare at the center of their discussion. Thomas Nashe and Robert Burton may have begun to see in theory what Shakespeare and others observed in practice—that irony explored the disjunction of the ideal and the actual, the divine and the human, synchrony and diachrony, and that the katascopic tradition found in writers like Lucian was useful for understanding literature. The study has also attempted to discuss briefly Thirlwall's contribution to the theory of irony in English, especially as it applies to the drama and to Shakespeare, to give some sense of the intellectual and dramatic context of the four histories, and to broaden our view of history and form. It has also attempted to argue that rationality and irrationality are both part of history and that no simple deprecation of reason is true to the way we set out, discover, and test patterns. Imagination, I have contended, is also important for the writing and interpretation of truth and illusion in history and literature. The author and the audience work together to make history, so that intentionality and response engage or interact and cannot exist one without the other. However modestly, the study has also tried to join others that are breaking down rigid barriers between dramatic and nondramatic literature in Renaissance studies. Theater and world permeate still. Reading and viewing must interact no matter how much difficulty we have discovering a proper dialect to talk about this relation. There is always a gap between desire and performance in life, drama, and criticism.

With this and other caveats in mind, perhaps hoping to find something solid beneath mutability and relativism but knowing how difficult that is, I shall make a few suggestions about Shakespeare's representation of history. Whereas since World War II we have been increasingly questioning the assertion that history should be or is scientific (an inquiry that has rid itself of myth and rhetoric), in Shakespeare's day writers like Camden, Stow, and Bacon were shifting history away from rhetoric and myth toward scientific inquiry and the use and rules of evidence. This inversion and difference can be instructive for us. Although Shakespeare's history plays are not scientific, they use their medium to represent history with great effect. The plays make an innovative use of sources, give a complex shape to history other than a simple linear chronological structure, focus on what are seen as primary problems while avoiding verbiage and extraneous detail, and help create a dramatic form that increases popular interest in history. Shakespeare brings to history a powerful historical imagination. He represents the complex private, social, and political relations between people and makes a contribution to psychology as well as to political science. Through ironic relations among language, structure, and performance, the Second Tetralogy also develops a complex and multiple attitude toward human character, time, and experience. Shakespeare represents the predicament of characters in their limited fields of knowledge and how they fight their war with time, and, by intricate interpretation, how we read our relations to those characters. There is a relation between theater and world, but it is refracting and refractory. Epistemologically or religiously or metaphorically, in history humankind lives in a fallen world and, though in many ways it seeks to repair the ruins, in politics it too often seeks power too selfishly and perpetuates a broken nature.

Because Shakespeare does not see life as being of a piece, he represents a multiplicity of characters in all their moods. Each period and character has its individuality, its diversity and unity in time. Characters experience history in many ironic forms, feeling in the theater of the world and the world of the theater an ironic strain between public and private selves and the problems of continuity and discontinuity that characterize human life in society in time, as well as the history play as a unique, mixed, and interpenetrating genre. Shakespeare also represents mutability in history by showing that history itself is mutable. He examines the death of Richard from many angles and shows how attitudes, including perhaps his own, change throughout the four plays. He implies with irony that the dramatists and the audience become part of the historical process. Through a subtle use of the irony of words, theater, and structure within and between these four plays, Shakespeare creates a depth of character, a multifold view of the past, a use of form so various and engaging that it has been rarely seen before or after. The plays of the Second Tetralogy have a care and complexity that express the world better than mortals can speak in daily life, but they are somehow more actual, somewhere near the ever-elusive truth, both poetic and historical. All of us, being human, are both fallen in and from history; and even Shakespeare, for all his greatness, cannot do more than give us a shard of knowledge, a suggestion of the past. The final irony, if there are final ironies, may be that, though he was acutely aware of his human limitations, in representing history in the Second Tetralogy Shakespeare took a godlike stance.

There are many Shakespeares. The Shakespeare of the Second Tetralogy is one. These history plays mix with other genres. In a different study I might emphasize some of the following aspects of genre, with, of course, the realization that time can make the seemingly fashionable seem permanent and the seemingly permanent seem fashionable. As the once uncanonized Shakespeare becomes, paradoxically, canonized in an age whose most famous Shakespearean critics are set against Bardalotry, we speak of the new aspects of old genres with a seriousness that many critics in their graves would find bewildering. In tragedy, the violence of *Titus Andronicus* is no longer the comic incompetence of a young playwright making his way but a deadly serious parable of female dismemberment. But our rediscoveries are not always as new as we might like. Others before us may have found that the ingratitude in *Timon of Athens* is no less interesting because it represents it from another, less spectacular point of view than that in *King Lear*. Those great proto-rewriters, the Restoration dramatists, found *Timon* fascinating. Thomas Shadwell's *History of Timon of Athens, the Man-*

Hater (1678) added two women characters and a love interest and held the stage for a long time. The issue of aristocracy versus democracy, as well as the relation between mother and son, probably made *Coriolanus* popular for the adapters during the Restoration and the eighteenth century. In comedy, another Duke of Milan (this one in *The Two Gentlemen of Verona*) introduces more anxieties that the pastoral works to dispel. This play, as Herbert Farjeon mentions in 1925 (see *The Shakespearean Scene* [collected 1949]), foreshadows at least six other plays and is related to some of the sonnets. It is as prospective as the tragicomedies or romances are retrospective in their use of earlier comic conventions. In tragicomedy, what seems to be Shakespeare's last collaboration with John Fletcher, *The Two Noble Kinsmen*, relates to the pageantry of the court masque but was not included in the First Folio. (In 1664 William Davenant adapted it as *The Rivals*. John Aubrey said that when Davenant was drunk, he called himself Shakespeare's illegitimate son.) The original play, which disappeared from the stage between the late 1660s and the 1920s, represents a dynastic marriage like the one that gives a comic structure to *Henry V* and also provides another perspective on romance for the romantic history on which Shakespeare probably collaborated with Fletcher in *Henry VIII*. But these are musings on matters, along with Shakespeare's narrative and short poems beyond the more canonical sonnets, that I have written as might be set down later. The absence of these plays in my discussions and definitions of genre in relation to the history play is the kind of omission that occurs regretably but by necessity in a study.

The history play, like irony, has a context, no matter how much we textualize it. Although Lindenberger, Wikander, and others have discussed the history play since Shakespeare, I want to say a few words about his contribution. If Shakespeare's histories were influential in future historical genres in Europe, they were only partly responsible for the interest in historical fictions. Historical elements occur, for instance, in the following sixteenth- and seventeenth-century plays: Miguel de Cervantes's *El cerco de Numancia* (ca. 1585–87); Lope de Vega's *Lo fingido verdadero* (ca. 1605), *Fuenteovejuna* (1611–18), and *El caballero de Olmedo* (ca. 1615–26); Calderón de la Barca's *El principe constante* (1629), *La vida es sueño* (ca. 1631–32), and *El alcalde de Zalamea* (1640–44); Pierre Corneille's *Le Cid* (1637),

Cinna (1640), *Horace* (1640), *Polyeucte* (1641–42), *Rodogune* (1644–45), and *Nicomède* (1650–51); Jean Racine's *Britannicus* (1669), *Bérénice* (1670), *Bajazet* (1672), *Mithridate* (1673), *Phèdre* (1676), *Esther* (1688), and *Athalie* (1690–91). Although innovative and distinctive, the German tradition, perhaps calling on the interest Schiller and Goethe had in English Renaissance drama, drew on Shakespeare, Marlowe, and others. The contribution of Schiller and Goethe to historical drama and fiction is great. Goethe's *Egmont* (1775–87) and Schiller's *Maria Stuart* (1800), *Die Jungfrau von Orleans* (1801), and *Wilhelm Tell* (1804) represent some of their important history plays. In *Dantons Tod* (1835) Georg Büchner represents the French Revolution, and he also translates Victor Hugo's *Lucrèce Borgia* (1833) and *Marie Tudor* (1833). Brecht, who was familiar with the historical fictions of Schiller and Goethe, has made some of the most daring adaptations of the works of Shakespeare, Marlowe, and Shaw in our century. Coriolanus, Edward the Second, and Saint Joan are as much Brechtian creations as re-creations, and stand beside Galileo, Mother Courage, and Arturo Ui as kinds of historical characters. Brecht understands the political and social uses of ironic alienation, in addition to the theatrical uses.

In the English-speaking tradition, besides the playwrights like Marlowe and Jonson, George Chapman, who is most famous for his translation of *The Iliad*, represents heroism in *Bussy D'Ambois* (ca. 1604) and helps to forge the tradition of history in *The Conspiracy and Tragedy of Charles, Duke of Byron* (ca. 1608). Samuel Daniel writes a closet drama, *Cleopatra* (1594–1623). As Irving Ribner has examined in detail the history plays of the Renaissance, I shall not linger. Dryden takes a more French classical view of drama and shapes his history accordingly, so that he transforms *Antony and Cleopatra* into *All for Love* (ca. 1677). Dryden is attempting something very different from Shakespeare. His plays are heroic without the same complex qualifications. *The Indian Emperor* (ca. 1665), *The Conquest of Granada* (ca. 1670–71), *Aureng-Zebe* (ca. 1675), and *Don Sebastian* (ca. 1689) owe more to the romance of Beaumont and Fletcher than to Shakespeare's Second Tetralogy. Nineteenth-century English closet historical drama, such as Shelley's *Charles I* (1819–22) and Tennyson's *Queen Mary* (1876) and *Becket* (1893), borrow more from Shakespeare's blank verse than from his sense of theater. Shaw's history plays, *The Man of Destiny* (1895), *Caesar and Cleopatra* (1898), and *Saint Joan* (1923) are more theatrically astute and may be more able heirs, with a Shavian difference, to Shakespeare's histories, especially in *Caesar and Cleopatra,* where he characteristically challenges Shakespeare openly while assuming that he is the only one worth challenging.

In the twentieth century historical drama has become more international. Even though British history plays persist with great variety, they do so in a new context. Here are only a few examples. In *Murder in the Cathedral* (1935) T. S. Eliot makes a conscious effort to avoid Elizabethan blank verse and the pitfalls of Tennyson's *Becket.* He also attempts to sidestep the tired imitation of Shakespeare by seeking classical Greek models as well as imitating Shaw's *Saint Joan.* Sean O'Casey's *Juno and the Paycock* (ca. 1923–24) represents the British in history from an Irish point of view. John Arden writes political and historical plays, the most notable of which may be *Sarjeant Musgrave's Dance* (1959) and *Armstrong's Last Goodbye* (1964). Edward Bond critically adapts Shakespeare's *King Lear* and gives it more historical distance by placing it centuries beyond Bond's era. He also writes a historical drama about Shakespeare called *Bingo* (1973), which reflects a kind of historical importance that the playwright could only have dreamed of because no one in the 1590s was writing historical plays about dead dramatists. But Bond, as much as he is indebted to Shakespeare, is critical about Shakespeare's investments. Tom Stoppard's *Travesties* (1974), where he mixes characters from *The Importance of Being Earnest* (1895) with seemingly historical figures, is a kind of modernist collage that verges on a postmodernist sensibility about the relativist construction of history. Caryl Churchill and other younger playwrights are representing issues that have historical and political implications. Other European playwrights like Jean Anouilh, Luigi Pirandello, and August Strindberg have written potent historical drama. The historical drama, in this age of other new imperialisms, which is also hopefully called the postcolonial era, has spread through the former colonies of Spain, Portugal, France, Britain, the Soviet Union, and other powers.

Nor is there any need to duplicate the work of critics like Georg Lukács on historical novels. Besides the legacy of epic and romance, of *The Iliad* and the various versions of the Arthurian legends, the rise of the novel complicates and partly displaces the play as the major representation of history. Many of Shakespeare's sources are prose tales and histories. As early as *Don Quixote,* historical questions like the nature of chivalry are being raised. The vast novels of Walter Scott, Feodor Dostoevsky, and Leo Tolstoy, as well as the novel of political ideas—like those of Thomas Mann—all are new and different kinds of fictional worlds to represent history. In our century, film and television epics and satires on historical subjects like Napoleon, the American Civil War, the Russian Revolution, World War II, Hitler, the Korean War, and Vietnam have supplemented, if not overtaken, the popularity of the historical novel. Newsreels in World War II, the grim live footage of Vietnam, and, most recently, the satellite transmissions of the dumbfounding Armageddon of the bombing of Baghdad and the almost surreal press conferences on precision bombing have created genres that make fiction, especially written fictions, seem removed and symbolic. The point of view of the camera pretends to be natural more than naturalism ever could. This camera-ready history challenges us all to find words for these images, as most of us do not speak daily with visional signs. Perhaps an experience of Shakespeare's history plays, which give us words in print and in the visual and aural medium of the theater, can help us to make sense of the perplexing nature of history, this history that is past lived experience, its representation, and the present experience of that representation.

Shakespeare's English history plays have become suggestive political works beyond that small kingdom in the 1590s. Like *The Tempest,* they engage us in a political debate in which our concerns and those of Renaissance England interact. The Second Tetralogy has been controversial at least since the Essex Rebellion of 1601. These are dramas that play upon the ancient conventions of rhetorical history. They do so, however, with such ironic complexity that generations will return to the Second Tetralogy and find new problematics of history from the shifting perspectives of their historical moments. And each shift, if Daniel is to be believed, becomes part of the history of these histories.

Afterword

ITH THE RECENT MOVEMENT TOWARD HIS-
tory in literary studies, it is not surprising that
critics would once again turn their attention to
some of the most famous representations of history in English, Shakespeare's history plays. When
I began this study about eleven years ago, Shake-
speare's historical dramas seemed relatively neglected, but, in retrospect, they were subject to a pause between two productive periods,
the reaction to E. M. W. Tillyard's important work from A. P.
Rossiter to Henry Kelly and beyond and the further reaction in the
1980s led by Stephen Greenblatt, Jonathan Dollimore, and others.
The neglect was relative because critics rarely neglect Shakespeare as
they do other writers. Earlier critics and editors had paid considerable attention to the history plays. While Dr. Johnson, Friedrich and
August Wilhelm Schlegel, Adam Müller, and Coleridge concentrated their considerable talents on Shakespeare's histories, Thomas
Courtenay was the first to write extensively on Shakespeare's history
plays and in 1840 had his two-volume commentary published. Only
Tillyard and his successors matched Courtenay's zeal and output in
producing long critical assessments. Tillyard owed much to A. W.
Schlegel's view that Shakespeare's histories constituted an English
epic. *Theater and World* could not have been written without a vast
amount of work by men and women over the centuries on these
history plays. Their interpretations, or those we have left in writing,
become part of the history of the history plays themselves and
cannot be separated from the texts. Performances and criticism
cannot be shorn from a text to make it "pure." This Afterword
must also address the paradigm shift away from a textual criticism
(New Criticism, structuralism, deconstruction, and metadrama) toward a contextual criticism (feminism, new historicism [or cultural
poetics], cultural materialism, and cultural studies). To rewrite this
study to forget the textual nature of much valuable criticism would
be to deny the period in which I produced *Theater and World*.
Although I have revised the text and brought my notes and bibliography up to date, I have chosen not to try to digest each new article
and book that has come out in the past few months and make it a
vital part of my argument. Given the important work being done in
Shakespearean, literary, and cultural studies, I should always be

revising the work. This study would, then, be rewritten annually as a ritual celebrating its own limitations. Instead, I hope to suggest here the importance of the most recent criticism and theory to *Theater and World*, leaving more development to a related volume, "Translating Shakespeare."

If history can contextualize texts, texts can textualize history. History requires writing as much as writing requires history. It is a matter of emphasis whether a critic tends more to textualizing or to contextualizing. I make these statements tentatively and heuristically and not as dogma or total truth. In the Afterword I want to make a few observations about form, irony, theatrical matters, narrative and dramatic history, new historicism and cultural materialism, and gender in the Second Tetralogy, the four plays—*Richard II*, *1* and *2 Henry IV*, and *Henry V*—that provide the focus of my study. The brief suggestions I make on these subjects constitute an intertext to the main body of *Theater and World*, which concerns itself with the relation among language, temporality, and structure in these history plays. In other words, this study focuses on the relation of genre to history as mediated through irony. If there were time and space enough, I should foreground the material in the Afterword, but I leave that for another argument. To leave it altogether would be a form of malpractice. In assuming that history involves the present interpreting the past by attempting to use the material conditions and textual traces of the past to interpret the present, I am also assuming that the interpreter is situated between himself or herself as self and subject and finds a place that shifts between free will and determinism. By advocating cultural pluralism—which I take to be the assumption that different methods and practices can be used more successfully in different contexts at different times and that history and all temporal practices like critical theory and criticism depend on cultural change and the exchange between an ever-changing present and a receding past—I am presuming that the critical concerns over Shakespeare's histories and what critics perceive as problematics change over time and may endure over time but not for all times. Shakespearean forms and histories rely on the interests of the present as well as the productions of the past.

FORM

An apparent division exists in literary studies between formalism and historicism, idealism and realism that manifests itself in new historical contexts but has ancient and medieval antecedents. Duns Scotus, William of Ockham, and others, for instance, debated the differences between realism and nominalism. Realism is an extreme formalism that assumes that conceptual maps exist that are not heuristic fictions, whereas nominalism assumes that concepts have no existence, like the character in *Gulliver's Travels* who carries a chair because language cannot represent it. Neither realism nor nominalism explains formalism fully.[1] Each formal system or textual practice needs to have perspective on itself and can build self-reflexivity into itself. Without some abstraction, explanation or making sense is impossible, so that the current preference for particulars is one of emphasis. Some formality is required for comprehension, but too much abstraction, as in arcane mathematical formulas, may mean that only six people in the world can understand what is being asserted.[2]

Directions to a stranger in one's neighborhood, including the names of the inhabitants of houses and other details, can confound him, but if the local person makes too many assumptions that the stranger knows more than he does, the guide imparts a sketchy and abstract description that is of no help. In history form is already always there. A plurality of forms governs the way we make sense of words and world. Formalism and idealism held sway under the New Criticism, and some critics of deconstruction like to accuse deconstructionists of continuing the formalist enterprise. The new *doxa* is historicism and realism or conventionalism. Historical critics are now reversing and reshaping the New Critical repudiation of the so-called old historicism by contextualizing and historicizing the newer formalists, the deconstructionists. Nevertheless, a residue of New Criticism and deconstruction remains in new historicism. Literary critics must textualize history and historicize texts. We use narrative and argument to make sense of history through texts and cannot escape history, even if sometimes implicitly, because we bring present historical conditions to bear on a text from the past. I am not sure one can reconcile Derrida's *mise en abîme* and Foucault's *mise en discours*, but both are important for a clear critical position. Derrida claims that *il n'y a pas d'hors texte*, whereas Foucault says that textuality relates to a plurality of texts, to history, society, power, and knowledge. Here are a textual and a historical deconstruction. Both rely on texts. From Derrida to Foucault, who is one of the sources for new historicism, the distance may be great, but that distance is not a simple movement from formalism to history.[3]

This study of Shakespeare's major history plays is by necessity at least implicitly textual. The friction between the textuality of history and the historicity of texts should be enabling rather than disabling. By using a model of irony that depends on historical change beyond the Renaissance to the nineteenth and twentieth centuries and creates a gap between Shakespeare's age and our own, *Theater and World* assumes that a study of history must especially acknowledge the difference between one historical period and another. To use an irony that was simply topical, as it is in Puttenham, Peacham, and their contemporaries, would ignore the great changes that have occurred in the theory of irony since the 1790s and would negate the response of a late twentieth-century interpreter as part of the historical encounter with Shakespeare's history plays. The Brechtian alienation effect is historical in another sense. By applying German romantic irony to Shakespeare's histories, I am doing something the German romantics did not do, except perhaps for Müller, who did not do so systematically. I am using a critical tool not available in theory to Shakespeare, whose practice helped the German romantics to take the concept of irony beyond the Socratic and rhetorical irony of the ancients. Brecht's alienation effect, not to mention Barthes's double sign (which seems indebted to Brecht), is deeply historical but descends from so-called formalist theories. The alienation effect is a descendant, through Erwin Piscator and others, of the "estranged" language, or defamiliarization, of the Russian formalists and of Roman Jakobson's "poetic word." Jakobson connects the Russian formalists and the Czech structuralists, who inspire French structuralism and poststructuralism, theoretical movements to which Barthes contributed.[4] Like Brechtian alienation, my multivalent irony makes this formal distancing serve the purposes of history. Irony destabilizes literal and totalizing meaning, but even the material conditions of irony cannot keep a text from settling, from becoming partially abstract and idealized, even if only temporarily. Ever since Socrates was sentenced to drink hemlock, irony has been considered dangerous to the state, or at least to textual integrity. The New Critics have tried to tame it, but irony becomes a critical means of uncovering ideological contradictions in the text. Through irony, the vast complexity of Shakespeare's Second Tetralogy as a verbal and historical construct becomes apparent. One voice, one party line will no longer do within the text and in response to it. Irony brings out the jostle of voices. It enables pluralism. Irony needs to be examined historically. It underpins my method. Other contexts relate to irony, to which I now turn. The following sections of the Afterword touch briefly on the historical ground of the theater in Shakespeare's day and, to distance us from that ground, the classical, medieval, and Renaissance views of history as antecedents to those during the Renaissance. I also make a few observations about recent views of history, such as new historicism and cultural materialism, as well as gender in the Second Tetralogy. To discuss these problematics at length is beyond the scope of this study, but to ignore them would be foolhardy.

IRONY

Cultural materialism and new historicism have attracted such interest in Renaissance studies that it is possible to neglect other contributions. The German romantics and critics like Gerald Gould and William Empson have contributed to an understanding of the complexity and possible subversiveness of Shakespearean irony.[5] Irony destabilizes the text, which is not stable and permanent, even if some New Critics wanted it to be that way and even if the text creates as part of its own myth the illusion of its own stability and permanence. The text is and is not stable and permanent. Ambiguity represents the unsettling of the literal into the figurative, so that even amidst a rage for order and a unified text a certain contingency paradoxically arises.[6] Irony is one of the tropes that New Criticism appropriates from rhetoric and, in this case, from the German romantics. Many modern critics, and not necessarily New Critics, have spoken out against the dangers of German romantic irony. In 1940 David Worcester warned that Friedrich Schlegel and his followers had shifted the meaning of irony from something objective found in the work to a subjective quality present in the author's mind and in doing so had opened the gates to mysticism and ego worshiping. This charge echoes Hegel's and similarly neglects the objective side of romantic irony and the difficult question of objectivity. If philosophers, historians, and literary critics cannot agree on the relation of subject to object, it is not self-evident that objectivity is something easily definable and controllable.[7]

"Multiplicity," my overarching term for irony, argues for a multiple, rather than simply a double, view of irony, though, at the level of trope, its doubleness cannot be denied. It comprehends various aspects that work in concert but that, for the sake of clarity, have been examined separately in this study—irony of words, theater, and structure. Multiplicity occurs in the relation between playwright and audience or reader. This multiple irony happens when the playwright and the godlike audience share a sympathetic detachment from all characters, when they juxtapose ironically the comic and the serious, when they attempt to understand the complexity of the play and of the world for which it is an intricate analogue and disjunction. Multiplicity can indicate multileveled effects—that is, not only does it juxtapose ironically many different events, characters, and situations, but it can also contrast ironically levels of techniques such as themes, acting, words, images, and the arrangement of scenes. This multiple irony results from the audience or reader engaging Shakespeare's method of representing a postlapsarian world where questions must be asked, where answers must be tentative, where loose ends proliferate and nothing is categorical, simple-minded, or dogmatic. The metaphor of the Fall, or fall into language, is important for the Second Tetralogy.

That a desire for identification, for unity between word and world, persists may be observed in contemporary discussions in philosophy, psychology, anthropology, and literary criticism. Ironic language shows the hard struggle for selfhood in the world, but it does so in language, which is in the world but separate from it. Richard Rorty suggests that we need to distinguish between the claim that the world is out there and that the truth is out there, because nature encompasses causes that do not include mental states, while truth exists in human sentences that are human creations. Descriptions of the world, and not the world itself, are true and false. The boundary between word and world is porous and seemingly indeterminate, and traditionally in European culture the view prevailed that the world and truth were out there. Only in the past two hundred years has the view that the truth is human made gained any credence.[8] As Richard Waswo notes, attempts in the past thirty years to make maps of meaning by relating signs to the psychology of the users or by describing mathematically the rules of their combination into properly formed and deviant utterances repeats, on the one hand, part of classical rhetoric, and, on the other, part of medieval nominalism.[9] The theory that discourse is a set of discrete signs that correspond to specific ideas, events, or objects has constituted the model of language that has dominated Western thinking. In what Waswo calls the "semantic shift" from the referential to the relational, some theorists in the fifteenth and sixteenth centuries came to doubt this model and to offer alternatives to it. Waswo suggests a magical connection between words and things that endures from preliterate cultures to our own notions of poetry.[10] Irony destabilizes the illusion of unity, order, and authority. Waswo aptly observes that the obsession with time during the Renaissance was partly grounded in the changing views of language because humanist philologists had discovered in language time as history. Change occurred in all languages, so that such a historical observation made it possible to dignify the vernaculars and treat them as equal to Greek and Latin. Finally, a sense of history weakened the faith in the enduring power of spoken language that it had raised.[11] This is an ironic view of the relation of philology to "modern" history, the one giving rise to the other only to have it question the very foundations of language.

Irony has changed from a rhetorical trope and from Socratic role playing to a philosophical or theoretical concept. Its constituents, in my scheme, are irony of words, irony of theater, and irony of structure. If irony of words is closely associated with posing or acting (and thus with the irony of theater), it is mainly because the first use of *eironeia* occurs in Plato's *Republic* when Thrasymachus abuses the consummate actor and poseur, Socrates, by associating him with the term. Both the friends and adversaries of Socrates think of irony as involving deceit, mockery, and hypocrisy, even though Plato makes it the center of Socrates himself and the very structure of the dialogues. Unlike Aristophanes in *The Clouds*, Aristotle dignifies Socrates as *eiron* and prefers his understatement to the overstatement of the *alazon*. For Aristotle, however, the middle way is the way to truth. He recommends irony as a useful rhetorical strategy, although again with some displeasure. In Demosthenes and Theophrastus the deceptive and self-effacing *eiron* becomes a social and political dissimulator, shirking duty and responsibility. Beginning with Cicero, however, Socrates and irony begin to gain acceptance. Cicero asserts that Socrates' urbane pretense acts as a mask of ignorance only in order to penetrate truth. Cicero inaugurates the distinction between irony as a figure of speech and irony as a habit of discourse. Although Quintilian names only two categories, the trope and the schema, he distinguishes three aspects of irony: a brief figure of speech (trope), an entire speech or case presented in a tone of voice contrary to the content (schema), and, finally, the whole life of a man (schema). He also views irony as a strong weapon that Socrates has given the orator and the satirist—the ability to blame by praise and praise by blame—a definition that first appeared in the *Rhetoric of Alexander* by Anaximenes of Lampsacus.[12]

During the fourteen centuries between Quintilian and the first appearance of the word in English in the *Ordynarye of Crystyanyte* (1502), nothing much happened to it. The definition of blame-through-praise passes on from rhetorician to rhetorician. Following the rediscovery of Lucian (Loukianos) in the Renaissance, an irony unlike that in Plato, Aristophanes, and the Greek tragedians resurges in literature as a form of raillery and, especially, in the ironic use of the ancient rhetorical exercise of composing an imaginary speech for some legendary or historical figure. Early in the sixteenth century, More, Rabelais, and Erasmus all use Lucianic irony. Of the three, Erasmus exerts the most influence, using irony for moderation's sake. This rediscovered classical irony blended well with ironic elements already present in the vernacular tradition, although theory, as usual in this period, lags behind practice.[13] In the *Ordynarye*, "irony" ("yronye"), which first appears as a supplement to other forms that the educated reader would encounter in the sixteenth

century like *ironia* and *ironie*, is a feigned humility that is to be
avoided as much as *jactaunce*, or excessive boasting. This work also
makes the distinction between moral and immoral postures and
makes this rhetorical device of irony Christian. It resembles Quintilian's view while retaining the moral disapproval the term held with
Aristotle and his predecessors. Often without this disapprobation,
irony means to the sixteenth-century reader the verbal device of
saying the opposite of what one means. This sense is found in
Thomas Hoby's translation of *The Book of the Courtier* (1561),
George Puttenham's *Art of English Poesie* (1589), Henry Peacham's
Garden of Eloquence (1593 ed.), John Florio's *Worlde of Wordes* (1598),
and Richard Perceval's *A Dictionary* (1599). A second and less popular
definition—saying something other than one means—also appears in
rhetorical handbooks like Richard Sherry's *Treatise of the Figures of
Grammer and Rhetorike* (1555) and Thomas Wilson's *Arte of Rhetorique*
(1566). The third and least popular definition is, according to John
Marbeck's *Notes and Commonplaces* (1581), "calling the foule which
is faire, or that sweete which is sowre."[14] These Renaissance rhetoricians add nothing new to the theory of irony, but they begin to
arouse an interest in the device.

Despite the illustrious practice of irony in England between 1500
and 1750, this period, according to Norman Knox, makes only one
theoretical contribution—it introduces certain classical ideas of irony
into the mainstream of English culture and develops them slightly.
This epoch represents part of a theoretical hiatus between the fertility
of the term among the ancients and the nineteenth-century renewal
of it. Nevertheless, a few interesting points arise between 1500 and
1750. The English do not stick entirely with the classification that
Cicero and Quintilian gave to "irony," as a type of jest that derides,
but refer to the word as any mock or scoff regardless of the rhetorical
structure. Until the early eighteenth century, most people view irony
as a brief and taunting trope, although Wilson and Fraunce borrow
Quintilian's figures, which extend irony through a whole speech or
an entire life. Knox thinks that isolated passages of Thomas Nashe's
Unfortunate Traveller (1594) and of Robert Burton's *Anatomy of Melancholy* (1621) anticipated Connop Thirlwall's identification of Sophoclean, or dramatic, irony, the first such connection in English and

one that marks the beginning of a wider and more speculative use of the word.[15] In the period after the Second Tetralogy (ca. 1595–99), "irony" becomes a more accessible term, and one of its cognates first appears in the title of a book, *Essays and Characters Ironicall and Instructive* (1615). In the last decade of the eighteenth century and in the first half of the nineteenth, irony develops philosophic and tragic connotations.

Not until the German romantics did the theory of irony occupy a central place in intellectual history. When discussing irony these romantic critics emphasize paradox, objectivity, and the mixture of the comic and the serious. Friedrich Schlegel calls paradox the soul and source of irony and asserts that only through irony's recognition of the world as paradoxical can people understand fully the contradictions of life. He also introduces the term "romantic irony" and complicates the theory of irony by emphasizing the human predicament as a finite being in an infinitely complex and contradictory world that the godlike artist justly represents through an acceptance of the limitations of his human art.[16] For his brother, A. W. Schlegel, irony balances the comic and the serious, the fanciful and the prosaic, but cannot be reconciled with tragedy. Goethe says that irony raises people above subjectivity—and thus beyond good and evil—and Karl Solger maintains that earthly irony means a vision similar to God's. Real irony, Solger states, begins by contemplating the fate of the world in large. The German romantics are the first to advocate in any systematic way Shakespeare's artistic objectivity, his apparent refusal to judge his characters, as a type of irony and to argue that irony is the very principle of art. They do, however, owe a large debt to Goethe, J. G. Herder, and Schiller, who wrote about the importance of Shakespeare's art.[17] By objectivity, they mean the artist's critical detachment from and conscious power over his own creations. And Shakespeare is at the center of their theory of irony. Although the German romantics make the greatest contribution to the theory of irony—by expanding its dialogical and rhetorical role as found in Plato's Socratic dialogues and in Aristotle's *Rhetoric* to a worldview and a method of writing and reading—they can mystify the role of the writer as a god and can, perhaps to satisfy their critics, make their enterprise seem more orderly and balanced than it always is. In some ways the German romantics begin to limit their own views of irony as paradox, instability, and negativity by advocating balance, the paradoxical negation of negation, and the potential objectivity of humans.

When discussing romantic irony, Hegel accuses the German romantics and their followers, those "chattering" after Friedrich Schlegel, of empty egotism and negativity masquerading as objectivity. For Hegel, irony does not qualify but completely undercuts, representing "the self-annihilation of what is noble, great and excellent," contradicting and "overreaching" itself. Because such irony discourages taking a stance, according to Hegel, it destroys character and becomes the antithesis of art rather than, as the purveyors of romantic irony suggest, *the* principle of art. However, Hegel thinks that Karl Solger found a way to avoid this negativity by postulating "the dialectical phase of the Idea" or "the infinite absolute negativity," which represents this negative idea negating itself as infinite and universal in order to pass into finitude and particularity. The Hegelian dialectic must master irony as a constituent. Even though this criticism of the predominant theory of irony in his time may help to demonstrate its abuses, Hegel's limitation is that he does not observe that his predecessors often argue for an irony that represents a complex human experience and accounts for the limits of human perception and action before infinity, an infinite Maker, or history.[18]

Kierkegaard praises and continues Hegel's criticism of romantic irony but also criticizes Hegel's postion. He agrees with him that romantic irony, while asserting its objectivity, tends toward the subjective. He also borrows Hegel's borrowed phrase (it was originally Solger's) "infinite absolute negativity" when talking about irony, concurs with Hegel that irony resides in a dialectic—irony can only be a part and not the end of the Idea—and sees him correcting what was deceptive and sentimental in Schlegelian irony. Kierkegaard criticizes Hegel as one-sided because he concentrates mostly on one kind of irony, especially that of the Schlegels, as if it were the central part of irony, thus neglecting other important aspects of the subject. If Kierkegaard fails to see the positive side of Friedrich Schlegel's theory, he does describe his own version of a complex and "positive" irony. Kierkegaard notes the ability of the Roman Catholic church of the middle ages to conceive of itself ironically in the Feast of the Ass, the Feast of Fools, and the Easter Humor and also describes the role of irony as buoying the contraries of appearance and actuality. Just as a person uses irony in life for protection against overwhelming impressions, Kierkegaard says, Shakespeare's ironic art does the same. Kierkegaard also gives Shakespeare an important place in his scheme for irony. Shakespearean irony is the instrument of objective realism, creating a balance, controlling or mastering the material so that one opposition does not influence unduly another, freeing the poet not to take sides.[19] Kierkegaard's notion that irony is critical and self-critical helps make it a tool of cultural, political, and psychological critique, and his idea that irony helps to structure our works becomes especially useful in explaining Shakespeare's shaping of genre in the Second Tetralogy. But Kierkegaard's use of metaphors of discipline, law, and order presents one side to irony, one that can imply too much order, stability, and even repression.

Hence, ever since the 1700s implicit and explicit versions of ironic criticism of Shakespeare's histories occur. When discussing Falstaff, Maurice Morgann says that we must consider the contrasting juxtaposition of characters. Although the German romantics, Connop Thirlwall, and Kierkegaard develop this irony of character and praise Shakespeare's ambiguous structural design or his ability not to take sides with his characters, only Adam Müller provides a complex view of the histories. His ideas are brief and suggestive. For Müller, Shakespeare's plays are dialogical, formed out of complex relations in which our sympathy is not just for the hero but for the whole world in which he lives. In the history plays, especially, Müller finds the dialogical method in its clearest form.[20] Analysis of irony, ambiguity, and ambivalence in Shakespeare develops further in the twentieth century. Verbal, structural, character, and theatrical ironies in Shakespeare's plays interest critics after World War I.[21] In 1919 Gerald Gould discovered verbal irony in *Henry V,* where the king's brutal speeches help turn the play into a satire on war. Empson, Brooks, and Heilman emphasize the sympathetic detachment of the audience, as well as parallels and contrasts between characters in *1 Henry IV,* while Rossiter argues that in the Second Tetralogy Shakespeare uses ambivalence or a dialectical method in which two opposed value judgments are valid. Although Anne Righter (Barton) does not explicitly mention irony of theater, she says that the Elizabethans were aware that "life tends to imitate the theater" and observes how Henry the Fourth, Falstaff, and Pistol all play roles that evoke a comparison between life and art. John Barton demonstrates that for director and actor, as well as for the critic, irony enriches as it makes interpretation more unsure: "Talking about irony has led us inexorably to talking about interpretation. . . . We'll find that there are many knotty questions here and few certain answers. So we must always go on searching." Irony opens up rather than closes down interpretative possibilities. It brings us to the most important aspect of criticism, to questioning.

THEATRICAL MATTERS

Although the classical Greek theater possessed material conditions quite different from those of its Elizabethan counterpart, both fulfilled a more direct role in the community than our theaters do. Shakespeare and his contemporaries experienced less political openness than Aristophanes did. Except for the Epilogue in *2 Henry IV* and the choruses in *Henry V,* Shakespeare does not come close to speaking in his own person to the audience. He does not use the *parabasis* as Aristophanes does or overtly take sides. The *parabasis* occurred in the intermission, when the chorus—alone, without a mask, and out of character—came forward in the orchestra to face the audience and to deliver the dramatist's views on religion, politics, and other controversial subjects. The renowned Shakespearean ambiguity, seen long before Keats so aptly called it "negative capability," may owe something to the political and religious censorship in Elizabethan England as well as to Shakespeare's artistic openness.

The metaphor of the world as a stage occurs from classical antiquity and among the early Christian writers through the middle ages to the Renaissance. As Ernst Robert Curtius notes, the proverbial metaphor of the person as a puppet, the *mimus vitae,* can be found in Plato's *Laws,* the philosophical lectures of the Cynics, Horace's *Satires,* and Seneca's *Epistles.* He also locates the idea of the show of life, or *scena vitae,* in Petronius, 1 Corinthians 4.9, Boethius, John of Salisbury's *Policraticus* (1159), Luther, Ronsard, and others. During the sixteenth and seventeenth centuries, as Curtius says, the metaphor of the theater of the world, or *theatrum mundi,* which

developed from the *scena vitae* as early as John of Salisbury, prolifer-
ates. Ronsard's epilogue to a comedy that was played before the
court in the year of Shakespeare's birth contains the line "Le monde
est un théâtre, et les hommes acteurs" ("The world is a theater, and
men actors"), and that includes stock expressions of the *theatrum
mundi* in which men are actors, Fortune is the stage director, and the
heavens and fates resemble spectators. Ronsard's epilogue is like
Jaques's famous speech in *As You Like It,* as well as the motto for the
Globe Theatre, which opened in 1599. The motto—"Totus mundus
agit histrionem"—derives from John's *Policraticus,* except, as Curtius
says, it exchanges "agit" for "exerceat." The "agit," from the verb
"agere," plays on its double meaning of conducting one's life and an
actor acting. The metaphor also occurred frequently in Spain. When
Don Quixote tells Sancho how similar a play and life are, the squire
praises the comparison but also mocks it as a cliché, which it seems
to have been in the *siglo de oro.* Calderón makes great use of the
theatrum mundi in his canon. Unlike Curtius, Jonathan Crewe shares
Johan Huizinga's view that the notion of the theater as the world in
the Renaissance represented an effete Neoplatonic topos even in the
worldly guise of political theater. Crewe wonders quite rightly
whether we have become prisoners of the trope even as we are
relentless in our political analyses of Elizabethan and Jacobean
drama.[22]

Both Spain and England developed a permanent, public, and
commercial theater in the last quarter of the sixteenth century.
Walter Cohen considers the public theater as the mediation between
drama and society in the two countries. While distinguishing them
before 1600 (Spain had an extensive empire, England did not;
England was making the transition to capitalism, Spain was not)
Cohen defines their common features in the last two or three decades
of the 1500s—they are internally stable, externally imperial, and
possess an incomplete absolute monarchy. He considers Henry the
Fourth's advice to his son near the end of *2 Henry IV* "to busy giddy
minds / With foreign quarrels," the younger Henry's prosecution of
that advice in *Henry V,* and similar impulses in Spanish history plays,
like Lope de Vega's *Arauco domado* (1599?) and *El asalto de Mastrique*
(1600?–1606?) as celebrations of foreign conquests. Cohen properly
warns against an oversimplification of the heterogeneous theater

because it was influenced by a "multiplicity of forces," which he characterizes as economic, social, political, and ideological. In order for a critic to avoid "one-sidedness" in discussing the public theater, Cohen notes, he or she can look at the ruling-class control of the theater through patronage, licensing, and censorship; at the profit-motive and capitalistic structures of the theater that coincide with bourgeois interests (a position Christopher Hill also takes in *Reformation to Industrial Revolution*); and at the physical structures, playwrights, audiences, and actors that relate closely to popular culture. The theater was "a socially composite organization."[23]

The Elizabethan audience is difficult to construct. We do so as an extrapolation on evidence about Elizabethan staging or as an act of imagination. No number of empirical or thick descriptions will obscure this problem. The audience, like the actors and playwright, make a performance and can only be ignored at our peril. We can only reenact, and not recover, the material conditions of the Elizabethan theater, including its audience. Although the recent archaeological finds of the Rose and Globe playhouses will give us more evidence about the physical nature of the theaters, even they will not provide conclusive proof within that one sphere of the imaginative historical reconstruction of the performance of Elizabethan plays in the playhouses. Historical reconstruction involves the present as much as the past.[24] In the 1580s and 1590s playgoers began to pay money to hear poetry and, as Gurr notes and as I have argued in my study, the plays composed between about 1590 and 1610 largely explore this new and direct relation between playwright and playgoer. The metatheatrical aspects, those that highlight the *theatrum mundi,* would be more apparent in the daylight, where the Elizabethan actors could see the audience, which observed itself.

When John Brayne opened the first professional theater in London, the Red Lion, in 1567, a new era began in the history of theater in England. Brayne and Burbage replaced this building in Whitechapel when they built the Theater in Shoreditch in 1576. The Blackfriars also opened in the same year. The terminology that split public from private theaters did not occur until 1600. The professional theater provided fixed venues and a demand for new plays, as well as giving impresarios more control over their revenues, and established a more direct relation with their audiences than before, when the impresarios had relied on the goodwill of a mayor or an innkeeper.[25]

The social classes in London differed from those in the country and were reflected in the theater audiences. Urban workers were mostly literate, rural workers mostly illiterate. Throughout the country, the illiteracy rate among women was about 90 percent and did not drop until the last quarter of the seventeenth century, so that Elizabeth the First, whose education owed something to the consequences of the humanism of More's circle and who in her youth read Greek and Latin daily with Roger Ascham for almost two years, represented one of the exceptions. Gurr suggests that the oral nature of the plays accounts for the high proportion of women in the audience and thinks that the three women who answered Joseph Swetnam's notorious attack on women, his *Araignment of lewde, idle, and unconstant women* (1615), were privileged in their educations. Some men attacked women who attended the theater as unvirtuous and praised those who stayed away from the performance of plays. *A third blast of retrait from plaies and Theaters* (1580) and Samuel Rowlands's *The Bride* (1617) exhibit such attitudes.[26]

Hieronymo, Tamburlaine, and Faustus are, according to Gurr, representative characters of the period between 1588 and 1599, the wake of the defeat of the Spanish Armada and the war against Spain in the Netherlands. These characters are historical or quasi-historical figures who speak wonderful verse, possess strong personalities, and face great challenges. They are also men. The first embodies revenge to restore justice in an unjust world, the second social mobility and military power, and the third religious doubt. Gurr associates these male characters with male interests, and he concludes that no other decade between 1567 and 1642 supplied plays that concentrated so much on war and military history and on bawdy clownings, and showed less concern for female members of the audience, than did the 1590s.[27] This is an interesting hypothesis that needs more testing, but it seems that the examples I discuss in the Second Tetralogy at least establish the interest in militarism and the treatment of women as sexual objects in the *Henry* plays. Nonetheless, bawdry does persist in *Hamlet, Troilus and Cressida, King Lear, Othello,* and other plays in the next decade, and the treatment of women in the romances or tragicomedies, such as Prospero's control of Miranda, Posthumus's betrayal of Imogen to Pisanio, and Leontes' jealous mistreatment of Hermione, may not represent much better treatment of women and seem to show a mistreatment that crosses the bounds of genre. Nor is the idealization of female characters, like that of Imogen and Miranda, flattering to many women today, a reaction that might differ from the responses of Elizabethan women, although our relative lack of direct evidence from early modern women makes it difficult to say.

More generally, in the 1590s London had only two amphitheaters, so all classes made up the audience. When in 1599 the hall playhouses and boy companies were revived, the gentry probably attended the amphitheaters less often. Gurr argues that the two adult companies, Alleyn's and Burbage's, which had a monopoly on plays in London from 1594 to 1599, the period of the Second Tetralogy (4 of the 145 plays from this five-year span), presented a remarkably similar repertoire that reflected the tastes of the citizen class, including plays about English history. Both rival companies staged plays about Henry the Fifth, Hieronymo, Owen Tudor, King John, Jack Straw, Richard the Third, and Troilus and Cressida. They also offered prodigal plays, to which the *Henry IV* plays are related, heroic romances, and citizen comedies, of which *The Merry Wives of Windsor* is a good example. Both companies produced Oldcastle plays, which probably led Burbage's company to change Oldcastle to Falstaff as a response to political pressure and Alleyn's to make Oldcastle in the image Foxe does in *Acts and Monuments*.[28]

In representing self-conscious theatricality, Shakespeare creates characters who both celebrate and are wary of the theater. Quite possibly, this is what a life in the theater engendered for Shakespeare. His plays were produced on the margin and at the center but not in the "Puritan," or at least anti-theatrical, middle ground. Until the dismantling of the Theater and its reconstruction and modification as the Globe, Shakespeare's plays may have been produced in the Theater and the Curtain in Shoreditch to the north of the city, outside the jurisdiction of the merchants who spoke out against plays. James Burbage built "the Theater" in Shoreditch in 1576, and soon after the Curtain was put up nearby. On Bankside the Rose was built in 1587, the Swan in 1595. When the Globe was erected in 1599, it too was at the margin in Bankside, beside a baiting house and brothels, but the first productions of the second group of Shakespeare's histories probably did not occur at the Globe but may have been produced at the Theater and the Curtain.[29] About 1600, the Fortune was erected in Cripplegate and the Red Bull in Clerkenwell. The court commanded performances, paid for them, and protected the companies.

In this period Shakespeare's company was under the patronage of the lord chamberlain, under the protection of a member of the privy council who exerted influence over the master of revels, although this did not always prevent the players from facing censure. The notorious incidents of *Sir Thomas More* and *The Isle of Dogs*, the latter almost precipitating in 1597 the suppression of the theaters in and about London with the consent of the queen, the lord chamberlain, and the lord admiral (all of whom liked and protected the theater), demonstrate that sedition in the theater was taken very seriously. *Richard II* was printed without the deposition scene until after Elizabeth's death.[30] As Shakespeare moved into the middle of his career with the Second Tetralogy, he seems to have spent less time on nondramatic poetry and more on the theater.[31] The theater was good to Shakespeare, but when he began writing for it, it was not as prestigious as poetry. Gerald Eades Bentley says that although the professional status of the playwright increased between 1590 and 1640, it was lower than many modern readers assume.[32] In this relatively new professional public theater and dramatic form, the English history play, Shakespeare seems to have experimented but also to have doubted the very medium. Even as he moved deeper into the theater, Shakespeare explored the world, for the history play calls attention to a larger polity than the stage. In these plays he represents the theatricality of the world and the world of theatricality. If the theater had not been firmly in the world and had some influence on it, then it would never have provoked attacks from at least the time of Plato, a controversy that Jonas Barish has looked at so ably.[33] Shakespeare's age involved numerous attacks on the defenses of the theater, and it was in this divided world that he wrote the histories. He was born into the controversy, and it did not die with him.

PLAYING WITH THE WORLD: SHAKESPEARE
AND THE HISTORY PLAY

The tradition of attempting to define the history play, which includes efforts by Thomas Percy, Dr. Johnson, Coleridge, Tillyard, Madeleine Doran, Irving Ribner, and others, will continue.[34] Shakespeare inherited various kinds of history play with diverse conventions and expectations that had not yet hardened and was able to experiment and alter the rules of the game. Later the game shifted, for whatever reasons, from English to Roman history, though, as Chambers shows, plays on Roman history occurred well before Shakespeare came to London.[35]

Genre, in this case the history play, need not be rigid and unporous. Historiography is one of the biggest problems of genre. Shakespeare reworked the history play and changed its critical context. His use of genre is experimental and open, the boundaries seeping and overlapping, the rules and conventions something against which to differentiate the experimentation and motivation. Some deconstructionists and Marxists distrust form in literature, although for different reasons. Jacques Derrida sees fixed form as necessarily limiting free play. Paul de Man observes the false desire to link intrinsic form and an external, referential, and nonverbal world. Raymond Williams characterizes genre as an earlier stage in historical dialectic, a feudal and neoclassical system of abstract rules. This system leads, in his view, to an empirical and relativistic celebration of individual genius in a mechanical proliferation of genres and subgenres until they are subsumed by Marxism, which relates generic classification at its separate levels—literary form, subject matter, and intended readership—to the "social material process."[36] If genre were truly dead, then its opponents would not still be discussing it. Rather, it is rigid formalism that has come under attack.

Genre need not be a fixed form or seal inside from outside or neglect historical context or be merely mechanical. Leonard Tennenhouse, for instance, discusses the affinities that *Hamlet* and *Henry VIII* have with the chronicle history plays and examines the similarities among the popular genres of the 1590s—Petrarchan poetry, romantic comedy, and history plays—and attempts to explain why they hastened to obsolescence together after 1600.[37] As I have said, Chambers cites evidence that may substantiate the general drift of Tennenhouse's assertion but that qualifies it. Tennenhouse's examination of genre is viable but is also subject to an assumption that politics is subject to form as much as form is subject to politics. As criticism is metonymic and synecdochic, as literature and history are, critics must select a way of talking about their subject. Genre is one of these ways, but it can be mixed with, or contextualized by, other methods. It is not just a matter of the dominant ideology, as new historicism suggests, absorbing the rebellions against it, for, if there is such a thing as a dominant ideology, it changes from time to time and place to place, and the audience brings another set of social conditions to the text than the author did. On the other hand, Stephen Greenblatt and others are right to challenge us with history, just as formalism should ask historical critics to prove that history is not context in the sense of being made up of many texts and interpretations, as Hayden White has suggested. History and form qualify each other. De Man was interested in form but talked about romanticism, which may be an example of the historical genre of periodization, whereas Lukács began with history but wrote about such forms as historical fiction and Shakespeare's plays.[38] Shakespeare's irony of theater, his exploration of the relation between theater and world, of their interplay, is meant as an engagement of context and text, audience and author, society and individual. The audience and the reader participate in meanings, so that the authoritative author is figuratively dead, as Barthes and Foucault have suggested.[39] If Shakespeare is dead, his textual practice lives on, and the Shakespeare we imagine, we infer from the text in ways that are as much produced by history as by genre.

DRAMATIC HISTORY

The representation of central stories, or *mythoi*, in the trilogies and tetralogies of the Greek tragedians; the Senecan reworking of the story of the house of Atreus, which Aeschylus, Sophocles, and Euripides had represented earlier; the miracle and morality plays; the humanist drama about politics; and the history plays from about 1580 to the closing of the theaters in London all contributed, in conjunction with many others, a general context for Shakespeare's histories. In some cases this dramatic tradition may be obliquely related to Shakespeare's representation of history, and it is best not to take cause and effect to extremes. But Shakespeare's plays are situated in this dramatic field or inheritance.

If the only classical trilogy we have left is Aeschlyus's *Oresteia* (*Agamemnon, The Choephori* [*The Libation Bearers*], and *The Eumenides*), and we have only one extant satyr play related to another trilogy, then it is difficult to generalize about the nature of trilogies, tetralogies, and satyr plays. Scholars have, however, fragments and commentaries to examine, and it seems that tetralogies were sometimes loosely constructed, sometimes closely, and that the satyr plays contained heroic and comic characters. The satyr play, with its mixture of genres, the implied Aristotelian allowance for mixed genres like the history play, the Ciceronian insistence on the literary qualities as well as the truth of history, the use of invented speeches by classical historians that demands the attention of those interested in the relation between history and fiction, the biblical and Augustinian notions of the Fall and the human tragedy made comic, the chroniclers' attention to detail, fact, and myth, and the historical sweep of the Corpus Christi plays all find vital reverberations in the Second Tetralogy.

Shakespeare's history faces the difficulty and obtains the advantages of dramatic representation, so that although it may share characteristics with epic and other nondramatic representations it can never face identical problems. Originally, dramatists who competed at the City Dionysia in Athens had to provide three tragedies and a satyr play to be performed in succession on the same day. Aeschylus appears to be the first playwright to view this loose tetralogy as a whole, making the three tragic plays successive steps in the story and concluding with the satyr play as a humorous scene from the same legend. The general form was flexible, the plays sometimes being closely related, sometimes distantly. A. E. Haigh says that the connection in the *Oedipodeia* was most distant, the *Oresteia* (the only extant trilogy) in between, and the *Lysurgeia* closest. Aeschylus does not always seem to have used the trilogic or tetralogic forms.[40] We should keep in mind this formal flexibility when thinking about the term "Second Tetralogy" that Tillyard made current. The term is valuable for this group of plays that may or may not be as closely related as the *Oresteia*. The satyr plays appear to have mixed refinement and grossness, heroes and satyrs, seriousness and humor but could occasionally involve burlesque of tragic myths.[41] The Second Tetralogy incorporates a mixture of serious and comic elements.

The *Oresteia* may have influenced Tillyard's notion of a tetralogy and strengthened his conviction about the Tudor myth, in which England is punished for the deposition of Richard the Second until Richmond can unite the Red and White Roses and so redeem the broken country. Aeschylus's trilogy represents the curse of the house of Atreus, and similar curses were familiar enough for medieval and Renaissance chroniclers to embed then in their narratives. Undeniably, Shakespeare uses this aspect of his sources, but it is his characters who invoke divine Providence in England, and the theme of the visitation of the sins of the fathers on the sons is a contributary pattern and not the predominant one for Shakespeare, who balances different points of view.[42] I am not saying that the *Oresteia* is a model or source for the Second Tetralogy, but I am observing analogues that are mediated through Seneca and others to Shakespeare and his contemporaries. These analogues have powerful resonances for critics of Shakespeare's histories, especially those, like Tillyard, who were well aware of the classics. Both the Second Tetralogy and the *Oresteia* represent the familial and internecine nature of the original wrong and revenge and how subsequent generations suffer strife and grief. Aeschylus's plays treat the immediate family and the taboo of incest and adultery. Agamemnon is a historical and mythical character and is subject to a curse that reaches back through Pelops to Tantalus, who, favored of the gods, abused them in a horrible banquet with a pride beyond the dreams of Adam. Shakespeare explores another, more overtly historical and less mythical, fallen world. History and myth are both stories and so cannot be entirely different. Whereas Aeschylus involves the gods directly, Shakespeare does not.

Unlike the Corpus Christi plays, the histories in Shakespeare's Second Tetralogy do not contain constant reassurances of Christ's agency. If one were to argue for a providential view in the Second Tetralogy, which I contend is only part of the historical representation, then one would say that, if Richmond redeems the civil strife of a fallen England at the end of *Richard III*, his redemption of Richard and England, of Adam and Israel, is typological because, like the Old Testament in relation to the New Testament, *Richard III* was written before *Richard II*, so that history is made prophetic. From this point of view, it was as if Shakespeare wrote his New before his Old Testament, which he then interpreted in relation to his knowledge of the "end." The providential plan of Shakespeare's history—the ten-play epic to which A. W. Schlegel, Tillyard, and others subscribe—includes the Second Tetralogy, which combines tragic falls and comic redemptions, the First Tetralogy, and the wider context of the Bible and Christian beliefs, which include the great comic movement of history for those who are saved. But in the Second Tetralogy Shakespeare qualifies the providential view. In these plays he often focuses on immediate political and human concerns, implies that English history will continue, and suggests that all literature can be seen as a fall or series of falls when observed from the point of view of the Bible, so that all unbiblical writing is comic, secular scripture, or demonic parody of the Bible. In other words, if the Bible is viewed as the supertext, literature is subsumed in the triumph of humankind in the mercy and grace of Christ. My focus assumes the irony of human ignorance or blindness, the middle earth or Augustine's sixth age. No direct divine intervention or participation occurs in the Second Tetralogy. Ultimately, the premise, the frame of reference, origin and end determine meaning in history.

Nonetheless, some traces of a medieval dramatic heritage occur in the Second Tetralogy. The Corpus Christi plays are not concerned primarily with secular matters. They are eschatological and teleological and span the time from Creation to the Last Judgment. They use typology to foreshadow Christ and to look back on a world before and after the Incarnation and, in biblical terms, most often involve a reflection of the Old and New Testaments in a double mirror. The Second Tetralogy is more secular than the Corpus Christi cycles, but it does contain, especially in *Richard II*, allusions to the sacramental nature of kingship. The whole tetralogy also contains a network of prospective and retrospective allusion (a kind of typology of prophecy and memory or nostalgia). It contends with the appeal to and the disintegration of the king's two bodies, which is, after all, founded on the human and divine body of Christ. Ultimately, for the Christian, the shape of history is comic for the chosen, so that in the widest sense all literature, including the second group of histories, is subsumed in the divine comedy (and human "tragedy" for the damned). This framework would end all generic discussion, which was lively in Elizabethan England, a place where Christianity was much more overtly and extensively a part of education and public debate than it is today in most Western countries. The sweep of public history, the many figures of biblical history, preoccupies the Corpus Christi cycles, whereas the struggle of the individual and representative Christian to find salvation, his proper place in human history, is most often the object of the morality play. The anxiety of Richard the Second, Henry the Fourth, and Henry the Fifth over their responsibility to themselves, their state, and their God resembles this *psychomachia* as well as the conflicts for the individual in Senecan tragedy and in early English attempts at the tragic form like John Bale's *Kynge Johan* (1530–36), Thomas Norton's and Thomas Sackville's *Gorboduc, or Ferrex and Porrex* (1561), John Pickering's *Horestes* (ca. 1567), and Thomas Legge's *Richardus Tertius* (1579–80). Some of the themes of *The Castle of Perseverance* (ca. 1405–25) may be found in Shakespeare's second group of histories (not to mention in the work of his contemporaries like Marlowe): the struggle of the human soul between virtue and vice, the coming of death, and the debate of body and soul. The kings of the Second Tetralogy all wrestle with their consciences. Comic boasting, slapstick comedy, scatalogical language, physical abuse—the comedy of vice—characterizes the Deadly Sins and is akin to the comedy of Falstaff and the taverners. *Mankind* (ca. 1465–70) emphasizes the body and knockabout comedy even more than *Castle*. Unlike Shakespeare, these morality playwrights point their lessons.

Some of the playwrights of the mid sixteenth century and Shakespeare are in the process of secularizing history. In examining some sixteenth- and seventeenth-century contexts for Shakespeare's representation of history in the Second Tetralogy, I shall resist the temptation of discussing at length the First Tetralogy (*1, 2, 3 Henry*

VI, Richard III), which others have done well elsewhere. Whereas in
John Skelton's *Magnyficence* (1516) morality figures participate in an
allegory not of the salvation of a representative Christian soul but of
the secular struggle of politics, later history plays begin to shed
moral abstractions in their exploration of statecraft. The shift in
titles from *Magnyficence* to *Kynge Johan* demonstrates the beginnings
of a movement from the general to the specific, from historical
morality to moral history. By the 1530s, as David Bevington has
shown, historical drama was even more overtly political. Plays like
John Bale's *Kynge Johan* were apparently sanctioned by Thomas
Cromwell and Henry the Eighth's government. Bale was on Cromwell's payroll and translated Archbishop Kirchmayer's *Pammachius*
(1538), a Protestant polemic that was dedicated to Cromwell, and
rewrote *Kynge Johan* with Kirchmayer's play in mind. In 1539 Bale's
play was performed at Cromwell's house during the Christmas
holidays. But Bale's case is not so simple, for after Cromwell's
death, he revised the ending of *Kynge Johan* to represent his opposition to Henry the Eighth's policies, such as the political use of
confiscated monastic property, and, as Bevington has also noted, in
the play Bale finds fault with many different parties, in England and
in Rome, past and present. Bale's next revised version, which was
played before Elizabeth at Ipswich in 1561, still showed a concern
for Catholic threats to Protestant England and makes extensive use
of English chronicles.[43] The king is a protagonist of the Reformation
in which the thirteenth century points a lesson for (and throughout)
the sixteenth. *Kynge Johan* is a transitional play because morality
characters coexist with historical figures. It is history with an ideological purpose, in which the past serves the present, far from the
mouse-eaten records of Sidney's caricature of the historian in the
Apology. The historical dramatist is involved in rewriting history and
trying to affect ruler and ministers over three decades. This is a play
that responds directly and fearlessly to changes in historical context.

Like Bale, Norton and Sackville used their play to point an
unambiguous political moral to their monarch. *Gorboduc* was written
the same year that *Kynge Johan* was revised and played before the
queen, and it was performed by the Inner Temple for Elizabeth on
18 January 1562 at Whitehall Palace. Unlike *Respublica*—which was
performed by boys at court during the Christmas holidays of 1553

and which, among other things, advocated Catholicism under Mary and criticized the greed for power of Protestant counselors under Edward—*Gorboduc* is the work of two counselors who were advising Elizabeth.[44] Both Norton and Sackville spell out the moral lessons of their play, which is a tragedy and a history play. Whether Norton wrote the first three acts and Sackville the last two, as tradition has it, is not my main concern. Sackville may have subscribed to the so-called Tudor myth and Norton may have been a "Puritan," but what is particularly interesting for us is the didacticism, the denotative technique, and the tension in the text between obedience to and defiance of the authority of the monarch. Shakespeare did not inhabit the same social class as Norton and Sackville and wrote later in Elizabeth's reign, so that he would encounter different constraints on his political language, but this tension or disjunction also occurs in the Second Tetralogy.

Cambises and *Richardus Tertius* also bear on the questions of kingship and history that Shakespeare later interrogates so fully. Part One of *Henry IV* includes a parody of the rant in Thomas Preston's *Cambises* (1569), which is a play that represents the divine punishment of a tyrant, far removed in time and space from Elizabeth and someone whose tyranny and madness rivals Herod but is less comic than the rendition of Herod in the Corpus Christi plays. Like *Gorboduc*, *Cambises* is much concerned with good advice for princes, so much so that the first line of the Prologue broaches this subject. Preston attempted to remove his play from the immediate geographical and historical contexts, although Egypt, Persia, Greece, and Rome in history plays relate to England. A three-part Latin play, produced at St. John's College, Cambridge, in 1579–80, Thomas Legge's *Richardus Tertius* offered a transformation of Senecan tragedy on the subject of the fall of an English tyrant, Richard the Third. More's portrait in *The History of Richard III* of the king as a tyrant was incorporated into the chronicle tradition, including Hall and Holinshed, and Shakespeare seems to have used both in his portrait of the crook-backed king. Legge appears to combine the Senecan tragedy and native chronicle tradition, which is interesting from our point of view because Shakespeare pays close attention to the chronicles. Legge also moralizes in the typical manner on the destruction of the tyrant. The Senecan elements in *Gorboduc* and *Richardus Tertius* have long been noticed and had a vital effect on the English history play. Another revenge tragedy, Thomas Kyd's *Spanish Tragedy* (ca. 1584–89), represents, among other subjects, the deleterious effects of private feuds on the body politic. Revenge in this play is private but has public effects because it involves the nobility. Although this kind of revenge is related to the conflicts within the extended royal family in the Second Tetralogy, it probably exerts a greater influence on *Titus Andronicus* (ca. 1594), *Romeo and Juliet* (ca. 1595), and *Hamlet* (1600–1601).

Too often Shakespeare's ability blinds critics to the contributions of his predecessors.[45] Those, especially, who wrote in the 1580s and 1590s gave him his first lessons in mixing the comic and the tragic, creating linked plays that had great scope and described history, focusing on representative protagonists or monstrous villains, and using chronicles. Several oppositions of ideas that occur in the Second Tetralogy recur in these anonymous plays—*The Famous Victories of Henry the Fifth* (ca. 1586–88), *The Troublesome Raigne of John, King of England* (ca. 1588), *The Raigne of King Edward the Third* (ca. 1590), and *Woodstock* (ca. 1590–94)—justice and injustice, order and change, heroism and cowardice, Englishness and Frenchness (or foreignness), the making and breaking of oaths, victory and defeat, love and war, free will and fate, ignorance and prophecy, and kingship and rebellion, to name a few. Shakespeare explores their interplay more rigorously.

Marlowe and Jonson, Shakespeare's great contemporaries, raised the quality of the London theaters. Except in *Edward II,* Marlowe does not represent English history directly. In about six years, from 1587 to 1593, Marlowe transformed the London stage radically, his characters' ideas of heroism, policy, and history challenging his audience and fellow playwrights. Tamburlaine is a character whose great rhetorical voice echoes throughout the Elizabethan repertoire. In *Tamburlaine* Marlowe represents the power of strength, the rise of a shepherd in spite of class differences, a hero and a tyrant, who believes that might is right. In what may have been Marlowe's last play, *Edward II,* he represents more taboos: powerlust, greed, homosexuality, the abuse of knowledge, and blasphemy. Most of these subjects, except perhaps for sodomy, could have easily been found in the miracle and morality plays. It is the way Marlowe handles the subjects that puts his audience off guard and off balance. The exuberance of language and the seeming successes and lack of penitence that Tamburlaine and other Marlovian characters display apparently made some of the dramatist's contemporaries wonder whether he was an atheist, homosexual, Catholic, and so on, although some of his acquaintances seem to have condemned him posthumously to save themselves from the law. Marlowe does not avoid exploring dissembling or the relation between religious and political crisis and controversy. If he examines the relation of gentile and Jew before *The Merchant of Venice,* he also experiments with polemic and propaganda before Shakespeare does in *King John.* Like Barabus in *The Jew of Malta,* Guise in *The Massacre at Paris* is a plotter and a poisoner. He attempts to justify his own actions and says that he has subdued religion with policy (ii.34-36, 64-69). He is also aware that language is action. Guise, the Admiral, the Protestants, Ramus, Charles, Navarre, the Duchess, and Henry all apostrophize and dramatize themselves in order to try to identify themselves with the world (as if they can equate word and world) and control it with speech, fit it into their story. Hence, they behave like Tamburlaine and display a like penchant for intertextuality, especially with classical poetry. Texts can become part of historical context. Like Tamburlaine, Guise dies defiantly. Although Marlowe did not explore English history in a systematic fashion, he brings a radical and experimental view of language, character, and history to the English stage, from which Shakespeare seems to have learned, although as early as *1 Henry VI* he is experimenting. *Edward the Second* describes the burden of kingship as Shakespeare's *Richard the Second, Henry the Fourth,* and *Henry the Fifth* will (IV.v.12-16, 25f., vi.9–62).[46] Like Shakespeare, Marlowe represents the king's two bodies, how kingship is divided between heaven and earth, ideal and material. Edward says: "Two kings in heaven cannot reign at once" (V.i.58). The end of *Richard II* seems to have borrowed much from that of *Edward II.* Even if Shakespeare beat Marlowe to English history, he had already learned much from him.

Whereas Shakespeare moved on to Roman history in about 1599 or 1600 and only returned to English history in about 1612 or 1613 with *Henry VIII,* Ben Jonson appears to have preferred Roman history. In the first decade of the seventeenth century, he wrote

Sejanus and *Cataline*, and at his death his only English history play, *Mortimer, His Fall,* was unfinished. The only complete scene of *Mortimer,* which may have been influenced by Marlowe's *Edward II,* is Mortimer's Machiavellian speech. As a pupil of Camden and as a humanist, Jonson took history seriously and even annotated the 1605 edition of *Sejanus.*[47] Jonson thought highly of history and did not subordinate it to poetry as Sidney did. When his library burned in 1623, a nearly completed manuscript of the history of Henry the Fifth was said to be among the writings lost. For Jonson, history meant truth and memory, a community that explores evidence and value. He also made the history play a more scholarly endeavor than Shakespeare did.

Nor is Jonson the poet entirely suppressed, for he teaches his moral lesson by leaving out details of character, as in the representations of Sejanus and Tiberius, making characters into types just as he did in his comedies of humor and in his satires. Perhaps ironically, Jonson places the trial of the historian, Cordus, at the center of *Sejanus,* right after the suicide of Silius, thereby telescoping Tacitus, showing the violence of truth and virtue and placing before the audience the old notion of historical events as moral *exempla.*[48] Although Jonson may have wanted to demonstrate the solid and truthful sources of antiquity, as opposed to the popular chronicles that Shakespeare used, the lack of complexity in his characterization and his poetic manipulation of the sources in places may be more inimical to Jonson's own standard of scholarly history, for it oversimplifies human action in time and works against the truth it proclaims, planting fables among notation. On the other hand, Jonson sticks to the best historians and does not play with legends and invented characters. *Sejanus* may have commented on state authority at the end of Elizabeth's reign, particularly in relation to the Essex Rebellion, but it might be an exaggeration to compare Elizabeth with Sejanus and Tiberius, and topical allusions are indirect and discreet, so that the censor cannot discover, or at least prove, the allegory. Shakespeare often qualifies his characters with irony when they point morals from history, but the end of *Sejanus* does not seem ironic. Terentius says: "Let this example move th'insolent man / Not to grow proud and careless of the gods. / . . . For whom the morning saw so great and high, / Thus low and little, 'fore the even doth lie" (V.899-900, 902-3). The fall of pride is an old Christian lesson, while the wheel of Fortune is implicit. Whereas Shakespeare qualifies the notion of the *de casibus* pattern and the moral fables of *A Mirror for Magistrates,* Jonson embraces and then complicates them. His history plays are more overtly moral than Shakespeare's. Both explore the relation between tragedy and history, and it may be that for all its accomplishment and scholarship *Sejanus* approaches *de casibus* tragedy more closely in its pattern than *Richard II* does.

Like *Sejanus, Cataline* is a conspiracy play, which might also illuminate such contemporary conspiracies as the Essex Rebellion and, especially, the Gunpowder Plot. *Cataline* calls attention to its moral tone and lesson, whereas the Second Tetralogy eschews an authorial view, or at least the authoritarian voice of a character, and is more playful and multiple in its representation.[49] Nor does Jonson represent in detail the range of classes and characters that Shakespeare does. Jonsonian satire in his histories deals in types, Shakespearean satire is often complicated with irony in which some characters can be limited by the complexities of their personalities and situations. Whatever preferences we have, the style of history that Jonson gives us has been at least as influential and important as Shakespeare's. Possibly, while many professional historians would prefer Jonson as a "historian," most "common" readers would not, but even this division is probably too simple and may be changing as the disciplines of history and literature change. Shakespeare himself acted in Jonson's historical tragedy, a play of which Jonson was proud but that was not popular at the Globe.[50]

The history play was various and resilient, though its popularity waned between the domestic, or romantic, history of Thomas Dekker's *Shoemaker's Holiday* (ca. 1600) and John Ford's *Perkin Warbeck* (ca. 1623–34). An interesting development in the form is Elizabeth Cary's historical plays *Mariam* (1602–4) and *The History of Edward II* (1627). Here, especially in the second play, a female playwright constructs historical characters of both genders in ways that embody and challenge the gender values of the age in which she wrote. As Herbert Lindenberger has shown, historical drama has been alive and well enough to survive ever since the Renaissance.[51] Shakespeare's last consideration of history is the romantic *Henry*

VIII. Cranmer's paean to the Virgin Queen is the future reading itself back on the past. It provides a comic ending that is like the phoenix, Cranmer's description of Elizabeth, for out of sorrow it gives joy, good rising from the tragic falls of the illustrious. Henry, who has sought a male heir and power and claimed conscience, should, perhaps, be forgiven as the Lord Chamberlain and Katherine forgave Wolsey. If Elizabeth, in Cranmer's words, shall be "A pattern to all princes living with her," the play urges itself as a pattern of virtue and happiness (V.iv.22).[52] The trouble is that the Prologue did not want the play to be comic and that more strife was to follow in the reign of Henry the Eighth, that "truth" and "honor" have been difficult and changeable words in the course of the action. The structure of the play, so long relying on Wolsey, who asked and received the greatest forgiveness, asks for charity. Once forgiven, Cranmer does not seem to bear grudges but celebrates with Henry Elizabeth's birth. It is as if mythology and the desire for reason, for a pattern of virtue, has taken over. Either Shakespeare, and possibly Fletcher, decided to allow the imagination of the audience freer play than in any of the English history plays, or thought that there was no pattern to events in human time without the moral and aesthetic senses of the audience, or realized that religion and mythology have as much to do with history as fact and evidence. There are, of course, other alternatives. The pastoral tribute to Elizabeth is as touching in its nostalgia as it is in its frankness when it makes the past future and the future past. The Epilogue is about "naught" and is being naughty, using wit to ask for happy applause—like the conventional appeal in Latin comedy *Plaudite, spectatores, et valete,* which includes the audience in the resolution of the play—and, like the epilogues to *As You Like It* and *2 Henry IV,* encouraging but manipulating interpretation.

For whatever reason, Shakespeare returns to the old episodic chronicle play and supplements it with pageantry and masque. The influences of Beaumont, Fletcher, and Jonson may be apparent here. Perhaps with Fletcher's help, Shakespeare cuts the play loose from the closer mimesis of some of his earlier English histories, leaving his audience to follow the promptings of the Chorus to *Henry V* to fill out the historical action with imagination. Long before reader-response theory, Shakespeare knew that writing, and in this case historical representation, demanded more than intention. The tragic and the comic aspects of *Henry VIII* rub together in a creative way that proclaims the variety of history and the problematics of its writing and interpretation. *Henry VIII* is both historical and antihistorical. Its brilliant surface calls into question patterns of history while asserting them. The play is simple historical pageant full of complexity and contradiction. What the Boy says about Pistol in *Henry V* might apply to *Henry VIII*: "I did never know so full a voice issue from so empty a heart; but the saying is true, 'The empty vessel makes the greatest sound.' " If the desire for reason in history remains strong, reason itself recognizes that desire is infinite but performance is not. As an experienced playwright, Shakespeare, with or without Fletcher, understood the limits of performance even as he celebrated its beauty and power. If, on earth and in time, Henry can wish "That when I am in heaven I shall desire / To see what this child does, and praise my maker," the audience shares his predicament but also has the benefit of the backward look and the overview of history.

NARRATIVE HISTORY

Time and history are not identical. History is human action in time, its representation and interpretation. One of the large questions is where to begin and where to end, for history as writing (as much as an Aristotelian plot, or *mythos*) must have a beginning, middle, and end. Time may flow endlessly, but human reason, the translating of fact, and the necessity of narrative all demand a shape, even as the author, whether an annalist or chronicler, may deny it and try to give to time the shape of time. History as action and writing shares an open territory with mythology on the one side and science on the other, with imagination and with empiricism. To deny science in history is a romantic dream, but to shun the literary part of history is not to dream at all. If Camden, Stow, Bacon, Sprat, and others ushered science into history in England, they had precedents among the ancients, especially Thucydides. In the past twenty years or so, the recuperation of the literary and rhetorical heritage of history has been as necessary as the earlier assertions of its scientific nature. The root of "history" includes story as much as inquiry.

Shakespeare is a remarkable innovator in historical drama and so makes a contribution to the imaginative, mythological, literary, and rhetorical part of history. He is not lacking inquiry, but his is not the patient archival work that has given rise to the view of history that grows in strength from the Renaissance to the present until its dominance was only recently questioned with any vigor and collective purpose. It is necessary to limit Shakespeare's ironic view of history ironically. He makes us want to inquire into the nature of history and, for some of us, into the history of our ancestors. For others, he makes them want to observe the silence and powerlessness of women in history, the views of ordinary people, the decline of feudalism, or the representation in history of an imperial Western power. The present engages the past as we move into the future, so that, at least in part, Shakespeare's history is our own, whatever our background. We interpret ourselves as we interpret him. Shakespeare's multiplicity has given us more room to explore these histories than if he had identified with one character or point of view. This openness, however, has its perils. If we are qualifying a polemic position, we should be sure about what past we are engaging, but when the positions are katascopic, shifting, sympathetically detached, and invoke a complex relation between reader and audience response we are not as certain. Shakespeare is protean and ironic and invites us to explain and translate histories as much as History. Irony is inextricably connected with Shakespeare's representation of history, but it is also important to survey the contexts of epic and narrative history to suggest (not exhaust) the historical situation in which he found himself when he produced the Second Tetralogy.[53]

A danger in historical overviews or indeed with any history is the impression that they contain their subject. To state the obvious— "history" is a difficult term. The best historical discussions can do is to sharpen the definitions of the terms and to limit the examinations ironically. Irony is temporal and temporality is ironic. Shakespeare worked in an environment sensitive to history and literature and to the vast amount of work that had been and was being done on the subject. Although he did not use Aristotle's *Poetics* or Aristotelian prescriptions for drama, it is now a commonplace that Shakespeare was much aware of the classical and native traditions. What he did not study was transported and transformed over time through Latin and vernacular imitations of classical genres like tragedy, epic, comedy, satire, and epyllion.

The Greeks, Romans, and early Christians provided a context for the interest in history in Renaissance England. The Homeric exploration of Greek history or myth through the stories of Achilles and Odysseus; the Aristotelian differentiation between, but likening of, history and poetry in the *Poetics* (because what happened in history is what is possible, which is the domain of poetry); the attempts at objectivity and truth, the use of invented speeches, the relation between human and divine, cause and effect, and the examination of critical times in Greek and Roman history in historians like Herodotus, Thucydides, Polybius, Diodorus, Sallust, Livy, and Tacitus; the Ciceronian insistence on style, as well as truth, in history; the distinction that Quintilian makes between the fiction of poetry and the truth of history, which should interest the orator; the Virgilian reinterpretation of myth and history as it relates to Rome; the detailed biographical interests of Plutarch, who downplays the importance of biography in relation to history but who tries to show that a chance remark or gesture can tell us more about a historical figure than his public plans and comportment; the division of history into the city of God and the earthly city in Augustine; the biblical typological tradition in which the virtuous are rewarded at the Last Judgment in the final act of a human tragedy turned divine comedy through the mercy and grace of Christ; the medieval chronicle tradition that foreran Hall and Holinshed, who provided important sources for Shakespeare; and the dramatic sources I have already outlined, all these contributory factors provided, in conjunction with many others, a context for Renaissance historiography, of which Shakespeare's histories are a great part.

When Shakespeare read More, North, Montaigne and others, he was often reading Renaissance readings of the classics. Shakespeare's small Latin and less Greek are not so small or less today, and the years of practice in the grammar schools of translating from the original to English and back again, sometimes to the exact meter in the case of poetry, helped the literary education of boys like Spenser, Marlowe, Shakespeare, Jonson, Milton, and others. Education in the middle and late 1500s in England still owed much to Colet, Erasmus, and More, all of whom were steeped in classical poetry, rhetoric, and history. It seems that in grammar school Shakespeare read more than a few Latin poets and historians and may have been exposed to some of their Greek predecessors.[54] Beyond grammar school, Shakespeare read widely and so well that his use of sources has been a marvel to each new generation.

Shakespeare and most of his contemporaries wrote within the rhetorical tradition of classical history, of what Aristotle described when discussing the universal truth of the poet, inventing speeches that did not occur but might have happened under similar circumstances.[55] Few of Shakespeare's contemporaries—excepting Spenser, Daniel and, perhaps, Ralegh—shared his concern for the structure of history, being content, for the most part, to chronicle events or to place everything into the *de casibus* pattern.[56] Possibly above all his contemporaries, Shakespeare concerned himself with the form of history, differentiating each reign with a "genre" appropriate to the events of the time. William Camden and others began to establish criteria for evidence and to divide history from fiction, developing an area of research in which Shakespeare's history made little or no contribution. In the Second Tetralogy Shakespeare's view of history is multiple, ambiguous, and complex, achieving this effect mainly through irony. The multileveled language ironically reflects and refracts the multiple structure that, in turn, makes the characters more complex and creates a sense of multifold time. Shakespeare complicates but does not negate the ideas of reason and truth, but his representation of history makes us work hard for truth and understand our limits and potential for history, justice, and truth. These goals refract our desires for transhistorical values, while being subject to contingency and historical change. We are in and apart from nature: this is our fall and challenge. To shape our events and narratives, we cannot have a facile notion of reason and imagination or keep them separate. History needs both.[57]

If in Shakespeare's day a movement began that initiated the change in history from a branch of literature to an aspiring science, in our century historiographers like Hayden White have attempted to reverse this movement. Metahistory has rhetoricized history just as deconstruction has literature and literary criticism and theory. Metahistorians, or narrativists, assert the importance of the relation between form and history, history and literature. In White's view, the tropes of metaphor, metonymy, synecdoche, and irony determine history, and the historian must be ironically conscious of history's formal nature, its likeness to fiction. The ironic mode, White says, has been the predominant one since the nineteenth century, so that Shakespeare may be "modern" in the self-critical language and form of his history plays. White's metahistory has its critics, but it is valuable in suggesting the use of "literary" genre in the writing of history.[58] If Shakespeare derives a great deal from the rhetorical history that comes down to him from the classics, he also uses his native dramatic and historical traditions. He transforms the historical and dramatic tradition, the relation between history and poetry.

NEW HISTORICISM AND CULTURAL MATERIALISM

An interest in new-historicist and cultural-materialist positions has supplemented that in metahistory. Hayden White's concern with the textuality of history influences the new historicists. Perhaps more readily than they, White refuses to say that the context is concrete and accessible whereas a text is not. The new historicism is about ten years old. In the turmoil of contemporary theory, new methods do not predominate for as long as they once did. As I have discussed new historicism in detail elsewhere, I shall only mention briefly the changes to it and its use of anecdote and analogy.[59] Although in 1980 Michael McCanles was the first to use the term "new historicism," in 1982 Stephen Greenblatt gave it currency. New historicism has recently undergone three great changes. First, in the United States it has become the dominant discourse of studies of the English Renaissance. Second, it has extended its range of practitioners to include those interested in feminism, deconstruction, Marxism, and other discourses. Third, it has moved outside the Renaissance to other periods, just as deconstruction came to range beyond romanticism.[60]

Female theorists and critics often question the maleness of new historicism. Jean Howard, Carol Thomas Neely, Jane Marcus, Judith

Newton, and others find suspect the way Greenblatt and other male new historicists assume the representativeness of much-studied Renaissance male writers for all those living in Renaissance England and for female Renaissance scholars of the late twentieth century. Neely thinks that, consciously or not, the male material historicists in Britain and the United States have produced work that has oppressed women, repressed sexuality, and subordinated gender issues. Male material historicists can, in the view of Neely, Howard, and Linda Boose, reproduce patriarchy by focusing on power, history, politics, and the monarch instead of on marriage, women, sexuality, and the "masterless," thus driving women's subversion away. Like Nancy Miller, Neely warns that decentering the subject calls into question the notion of gender and takes away from women the opportunity to be self-possessed subjects, thereby denying them the privilege that men have traditionally enjoyed.[61] Edward Said makes a similar point about colonized peoples. Most of all, these male materialist historicists do not refer to the work of their predecessors, especially to their female progenitors. For Gayatri Spivak, the politics of history is not the politics of new historicism: the state of criticism seems pale beside the state of the world. Catherine Gallagher, however, thinks that new historicism will continue to study the complexity of the modern subject and will be as oppositional as Marxism, even if Marxists do not always think so.

The anecdote is one of the methodological practices of new historicism. Like Joel Fineman, I think that the anecdote only seems casual and accidental; it actually represents the literary and referential, affects historically the writing of history, and provides an opening into the teleological and the form of beginning, middle, and end. Anecdote opens and destabilizes the context of a larger historical narrative that can be seduced by the opening anecdote— the characteristic rhetorical practice of many new historicists. Fineman is perceptive in characterizing the writing practice of new historicism as a "Baconian" essay that introduces history, an amplification, a moralizing conclusion that puts an end to history, and, sometimes, another anecdote. The anecdote appears incidental to history but becomes its basis. Although Fineman's argument asks us quite rightly to take new historicism even more seriously, its assumption that the anecdote is the *historeme*, or smallest unit, of historiographic fact, like any search for the ground or origin, becomes one of conjecture, fiction, and myth. We are free to choose this or any other mythology about the nature of history, so that Fineman's own argument is its own story or anecdote. To dismiss the new-historicist anecdote is to be blind to its subtlety, to make it a ground is to give it unnecessarily an originary authority. Some theorists fault new historicism for denying that texts are products of, and participants in, a history that remains a structured set of social, political, and gender relations, whereas others assert that these historical codes are actually textual.[62] Another recent position is that new historicism is not radical enough.[63]

In turning to another important method of new historicism—the use of analogy—I shall concentrate on Stephen Greenblatt's *Shakespearean Negotiations* as an illustration. At the core of his theoretical and critical techniques lies the power of analogy. This is an old philosophical issue that informs new historicism. In the philosophical tradition idealists have thought that analogies demonstrated the connectedness of things, but nominalists have seen them as showing the futility of human thought. Aristotle condemns the use of poetical and metaphorical language in philosophy. If Aquinas defends the use of metaphor in the scriptures because it renders spiritual realities more accessible (as knowledge begins with sense experience), he avoids too much use of pictorial language. William of Ockham, the nominalists, and skeptics like Hume all discuss the importance of analogy.[64] Argument by analogy occupies an important place in theological and philosophical discussions on the existence of God, and, coincidentally, in Greenblatt's comparison of Harriot to Henry the Fifth in light of religion and atheism. This discussion occurs in "Invisible Bullets," an essay that Greenblatt includes in another form in *Shakespearean Negotiations*, the work I want to discuss in detail because, like my study, it focuses on Shakespeare's genres and his use of, and relation to, history. Although Greenblatt, the leading new historicist, also uses story, autobiography, biography, a Foucauldian analysis of power, and a deconstructive notion of marginality, his method relies on such types of analogy as inference, metaphor, and simile. Even though anecdotes appear in *Renaissance Self-Fashioning*, the opening of "Invisible Bullets" can provide a paradigm for the openings to Greenblatt's essays—the telling anecdote. He then compares the introductory tale with a literary text and, from that comparison, generalizes about Renaissance culture. By selecting a marginal or atypical example to compare with a more central or typical one, Greenblatt calls attention to new insights about his subject, but he also risks converse accident and hasty generalization. In discussing the marginal, Greenblatt, like Derrida, is challenging traditional philosophical notions of evidence—that one usually only looks at some cases and therefore one should generalize from typical rather than atypical ones.[65]

Even if Greenblatt attempts to revive history in literary studies, he takes a largely rhetorical view of the historical. His intricate use of analogy, metaphor, and narrative often relies on the ability to persuade and to forge a new myth about Shakespeare and the Renaissance rather than appeal to a systematic presentation of evidence. Greenblatt's Renaissance is fragmentary, recalcitrant, and pluralistic: it is another displacement of E. M. W. Tillyard's more unified, normative, and monolithic Elizabethan world picture.[66] Whereas Tillyard observes the rule, Greenblatt seeks the exception. As Hayden White suggests in *Metahistory* and in subsequent works, history is a story, a narrative act, an emplotted discourse.[67] At the extremes, rhetorical historians and historiographers break with the traditional notion that form and content interact and argue that the form is the content. The shape of history, the genre it adopts, and the effectiveness of its tropes govern its meaning and success. The virtuoso analogical and anecdotal performance gives the new history its narrative drive. Its pleasure becomes its instruction. If there can be no truth, or if that truth remains so refractory as to seem darkness invisible, then the delight of the myth seduces the reader into further delights.

Rhetorical history passes beyond fact and data, and appeals to the activity that departments of English, if not of literature, have long prized—interpretation. This imaginary license might begin with the close relation among poetry, rhetoric, and history in classical Athens and Rome. Thucydides and Tacitus imagined and invented speeches when the evidence was not at hand. Aristotle related poetic invention to universals: poets create according to what might happen or be said in a given situation, not necessarily what did happen or was said.[68] The historian, poet, and rhetor had to know his audience and the situation in which he or his characters participated. Greenblatt might not admit that it is possible to tell what happened, so that he enhances the idea that rhetorical history represents the best we can do. Since antiquity, notions of evidence have changed many times. We are in a period that is reacting against a positivistic and social-scientific practice in history; for polemical purposes, advocates of rhetoric may have swung too far in suggesting that fact and evidence are themselves myths or biases. While the writings of Derrida, White, and Greenblatt act as correctives to a twentieth-century practice of philosophy, history, and literary criticism that has under-valued rhetoric and overvalued its own grasp of evidence and truth, these discourses can lead to an irrationality, know-nothingness, self-contradictory skepticism, and myth building that abdicates social responsibility, abjures rule of law, and ignores the positive contri-butions of science. While pleasure deserves praise, because dullness always demands a *Dunciad*, pleasure has, historically at least, not seemed enough. Like Homer's epic similes, Lyly's euphuistic com-parisons, and Wilde's aphorisms, Greenblatt's analogies must do more than please. And they do. Wilde's play on names in *The Importance of Being Earnest* shares much with nominalism. Whereas Plato knew the dangers of image, metaphor, analogy, and allegory, he used them with great power and provided the pleasure he so loved and feared. The rhetorization of philosophy, history, and literary studies, as C. S. Lewis suggests in regard to the latter, has meant that the whole story has had to be retold. After standing back from rhetoric and observing its new insights, we should ask whether the story is all we can negotiate from nature, culture, and the world.[69]

Are Greenblatt's analogies as helpful as they are powerful? The brief and paradigmatic introductory tale in "Invisible Bullets" shows the power of Greenblatt's analogy of the story about Thomas Harriot and his tale of colonization in *A Briefe and True Report of the New Found Land of Virginia* (1588) to the story about Shakespeare and the accounts in his major history plays. The potency of narratives derives from their memorability. Stories often stay in the mind—at least the literary mind—longer than arguments. Greenblatt derives much of his rhetorical power from the assumption that his reader will find narrative appealing and that he or she will assent to his point because of an admiration for his connective narrative or the anecdotal analogy by which he connects the marginal and central narratives under discussion. To "argue" by analogy, image, and plot is to complicate the illusion of logicality that some earlier criticism desired. To clarify this statement, I appeal to a longtime standard introduction to logic in North American universities—Irving Copi's.[70] Even though logic texts are not the entire measure of theory, criticism, and literature, some of Copi's basic distinctions help to illuminate some of the disjunctions, tensions, and powers of Greenblatt's new-historical discourse. In discussing analogy and probable inference, Copi reminds us that not all arguments are deductive, do not demonstrate that the truth of their conditions follows necessarily from their premises. Instead, many arguments are inductive and intend to establish conclusions as probable. The argument by analogy, in which two or more entities are compared to show one or more similarities, is probably the most common inductive argument. In "Invisible Bullets" (page 40) Greenblatt calls attention to his analogy between Harriot and Shakespeare.

As suggestive as literary criticism and theory is, its analogical arguments are not certain or demonstratively valid, but more or less probable. Analogies, as Copi notes, are often used nonargumentatively, especially for lively description and in metaphor and simile to create a vivid image in the reader's mind. Analogy is also an aid to explanation when it makes intelligible something unfamiliar by comparing it to something familiar. The literary attack on logic occurs after logic's self-examination. As Copi states, "the use of analogies in description and explanation is not the same as their argument, though in some cases it may not be easy to decide which use is intended" (p. 353). The power of Greenblatt's method, as a deconstructionist might see it and as Greenblatt might admit, is the conflation or confusion of argumentative and nonargumentative types of analogy. Even if Greenblatt wants to bring back history into literary studies after decades of New Criticism, structuralism, and deconstruction, he shares with Derrida the exploration of analogy, metaphor, and rhetoric in all texts, not just literary ones.[71] Is Greenblatt using a story-argument or a story to illustrate his argument? Is there any argument at all? Are all arguments nonarguments?

Greenblatt's "new historical" method deserves close scrutiny. New historicism shares with deconstruction an unmasking of the manipulation of texts and the destabilization of binary opposites like center and margin. It shares with Marxism a concern with the collective and a qualification of the role of the individual. It also draws on Michel Foucault's analysis of power and institutions and explores subversion. It also uses the work of sociologists and cultural anthropologists like Edward Shils, Clifford Geertz, and Michel Leiris to decenter traditional assumptions about European culture, colonization, and power.[72]

Cultural materialism is a similar, but distinct, movement. It owes much to Raymond Williams, and its practitioners relate the past—often Renaissance England—to modern Britain. There is an urgency and an optimism for social change, as well as a more unabashed relation to Marxism, in cultural materialism than in its American counterpart, new historicism. In cultural materialism the politics of the Renaissance often becomes overtly focused on the politics of the modern era as a means of enacting change. Even though cultural materialism is difficult to define (for instance, my associating it with Britain is over-simple), Jonathan Dollimore, a leading theorist and practitioner, provides a good summary of it:

> The term "cultural materialism" is borrowed from its recent use by Raymond Williams; its practice grows from an eclectic body of work in Britain in the post-war period which can be broadly characterized as cultural analysis. That work includes the considerable output of Williams himself, and, more generally, the convergence of history, sociology and English in cultural studies, some of the major developments in feminism, as well as continental Marxist-structuralist and post-structuralist theory, especially that of Althusser, Macherey, Gramsci and Foucault.[73]

While Dollimore acknowledges the influences of Marxism, post-structuralism, and feminism more openly than does Greenblatt, his use of the term "cultural materialism" is elastic. This shows that it is also a loose confederacy, as new historicism is, but that, like Foucault's notion of power, it threatens to become diffuse and without a specific location.

Dollimore says that cultural materialism has come later to the study of Renaissance literature than new historicism did. Cultural materialism has related literary texts to the oppression of the rural poor and to enclosures (Williams), state power and resistance to it (Lever, Moretti), reassessments of dominant ideologies and the "radical countertendencies" to them (Aers, Hodge, Heinemann, Sinfield, Dollimore, Axton, Holderness), witchcraft and the carnivalesque (Stallybrass and Allon White), feminist recovery of the actual conditions of women and their relation to literary representation (Shepherd, Lisa Jardine), and class fractions and nonmonolithic conceptions of power (Sinfield and Dollimore). Although much of this work examines power, Dollimore says that new historicists in the United States have paid the most attention to representations of power in Renaissance literature. New historicism, in his view, is a perspective concerned with the interaction in the Renaissance between state power and cultural forms, more specifically those genres and practices, like pastoral, masque, and patronage, where state and culture most noticeably merge. This new-historical analysis also asserts that power in early modern England was theatrical and that the theater was an important location for its representation and legitimation. Two main emphases in cultural analysis occur on both sides of the Atlantic: Dollimore says that some critics concentrate on culture as the making of history, thereby allowing much to human agency and human experience, while others focus on the unchosen conditions that constrain and inform that making, thereby opening the question of autonomy by examining the formative power of ideological and social structures that are prior to, and in some ways determine, experience.[74]

New historicism and cultural materialism share many concerns: a refusal to privilege literature, a recontextualization of literature (of text with context), looking at social processes that lead beyond literary idealism (with its universals and transhistorical human essence), and replacing that idealism, which was declining well before cultural materialism arrived on the scene. In addition to setting out these shared concerns, Dollimore thinks that materialist criticism examines ideology. He sums up the complex ideology of Renaissance England: "This combined emphasis on universal interests, society as a 'reflection' of the 'natural' order of things, history as a 'lawful' development leading up to and justifying the present, the demonizing of dissent and otherness, was central to the age of

Shakespeare" (p. 7). The social and political perspective of materialist criticism can help to recover the political dimension of Renaissance plays. Dollimore expresses the two major attitudes to the theater in Shakespeare's day: it was good for the populace, as Thomas Heywood thought, and, in an opposite view, it demystified the power of rulers, as Samuel Calvert said.[75] Other attitudes existed. It is important that we do not fall into a simple binary thinking. Materialist criticism also discusses three processes: consolidation (the ideological ways that a dominant order uses to perpetuate itself), subversion (the upsetting of that order), and containment (the immobilization or enclosure of subversive pressures). Dollimore cites the example of feminist criticism of Shakespeare to show how important perspective is to the use of these terms. One group of critics says that Shakespeare partook in patriarchy and misogyny (summarized in Kathleen McLuskie), and another group argues that Shakespeare and others participated in the resistance to social constructions of women (Dusinberre, Gayle Greene, Shepherd, Lisa Jardine, Woodbridge), both of which differ from a nonmaterialist view that Shakespeare's women exemplify the transhistorical nature of "woman."[76]

A materialist feminism, Dollimore says, does not co-opt or write off Shakespeare but follows the unstable constructions of patriarchy and gender back to the contradictoriness of the historical moment at which Shakespeare derived his authority, which will then be better understood and challenged. In discussing the subversion-containment debate, Dollimore aptly observes that theory needs history and history, theory, or else both lose perspective. One person's sense of containment may be another's view of subversion, and what seemed like a movement toward containment at a given historical moment may in retrospect appear to be an act of subversion. The ruling culture does not constitute all of culture, and all marginalized, alternative, and oppositional cultures help in the ever-changing process of reshaping culture.[77]

When Carolyn Porter asks in the title of her essay "Are We Being Historical Yet?" she answers, after the swerve of her own argument, no, but that with more effort we should be able to make strides toward understanding what Raymond Williams called "language in history: that full field."[78] But history is too important to abandon and to be satisfied with our textualization of it and our refractory views of texts. We have needed a sophisticated rhetoric of history to question the hermeneutic of certainty, but in our sophistication we cannot stop at treating the drawings of the children dead in the holocaust as traces and museum pieces rather than lived experiences that remind us of the outrage of their deaths. For all our rhetorical sophistications and philosophical arguments about history, how do we translate "Never Again" into a history we can recognize and live with?

GENDER IN THE SECOND TETRALOGY

New historicism has been criticized for not taking into account enough the marginal, especially the role of women, in history. Jonathan Dollimore has suggested strategies for a feminist cultural materialism, or at least for a cultural materialism cognizant of, and sensitive to, women and history. Although I touch on some of the issues of the role of women in these four history plays, especially in *Henry V,* have discussed these issues for more than a decade, and will include an essay on this subject in another study of Shakespeare, I want to add some brief comments on gender in these four history plays.

The role of women, the silence of women, the impotence of women in the Second Tetralogy—the height of the English history play—is striking yet has not received systematic treatment.[79] The interdependence of genders as well as classes represents a point that Natalie Zemon Davis made about fifteen years ago when speaking about historians: "Our goal is to discover the range in sex roles and in sexual symbolism in different societies and periods, to find out what meaning they had and how they functioned to maintain the social order or to promote its change."[80] History, in Davis's view, should look at men and women, just as it should examine all classes. Women have a plural nature. Race, class, and other factors do not allow for a singular and all-inclusive definition of woman.

Characters are not people, to state the obvious that is so obviously elided and disregarded so often in textual practices, but they bear a refractory relation to people. Some female characters in the comedies, and Joan of Arc in *1 Henry VI*, dress as men and challenge gender codes.[81] Joan Kelly's question—"Did women have a Renaissance?"—is particularly appropriate when considering the most influential representations of history in Renaissance England, if not of Europe in the sixteenth century: the Second Tetralogy. During the past twenty years, feminist criticism has questioned the marginalization, abuse, and neglect of women in the Roman and English histories and among male critics. But feminist critics, such as Angela Pitt and Marilyn French, have considered Shakespeare's First Tetralogy much more than his Second Tetralogy.[82] Many male characters in Shakespeare and Shakespearean critics seem to have to tell themselves stories about women in authority, and to make them more and less than men, in order to accept female political power. Phyllis Rackin, who focuses on *1 Henry VI* and *King John*, describes the role of female characters in Shakespeare's histories as that of antihistorians. Patricia Parker has expanded on Lisa Jardine's comments that the pregnant woman in Renaissance England represented fertility and a threatening sexuality to discuss the copiousness and unruliness of the "body" of female rhetoric. Like Gayle Whittier, Parker discusses Falstaff as a Renaissance "fat lady," looking at Shakespeare's means of associating him with effeminacy and the pregnant earth in *1* and *2 Henry IV* and of actually representing the fat knight as a fat lady in the transvestite scene (at IV.iv) of *The Merry Wives of Windsor*.[83] In *1 Henry IV* Hal says to Poins: "I prithee call in Falstaff; I'll play Percy, and that damned brawn shall play Dame Mortimer his wife" (II.iv.106–8; Arden ed. here and in subsequent citations and quotations). This scene is never played out. Shakespeare does, however, feminize Falstaff in the imagery of the play. At length, Falstaff and Hal act the patriarchal drama of the king and his son. Women are now rewriting the Renaissance by disrupting the male narrative of the great rebirth of classical learning and European culture. My project is to discuss the problematics of Shakespeare's history, and this is one problematic.

Whether one accepts Joan Kelly's assertion, taking up Ruth Kelso's view that the Renaissance was not a revolution for women, that medieval aristocratic women were freer in their sexual and social relations than their counterparts in the Renaissance, one should not ignore the exploration of the hypothesis.[84] Like Kelso, Kelly herself opposed the view, as set out by writers as disparate as Jacob

Burckhardt and Simone de Beauvoir, that men and women were equal in the Renaissance. Although the Second Tetralogy is a symbolic representation of history in the 1590s of the period from about 1399 to 1422, it seems to support Kelly's view of the Renaissance, although it may not tell as much about the middle ages. Even as a fictional reconstruction of the past that bears a complex relation to the world, the tetralogy, like its sources, keeps women on the edges of power and politics. Possibly, Andreas Capellanus's *Art of Courtly Love* represents an ideal version of the role of aristocratic women in the twelfth century while treating the lower orders with indifference and contempt, so that Kelly's reading of the work may be as optimistic as Michel Foucault's idealization of the *épistème* in the Renaissance.[85] Whether Kelly, like Foucault and many of us, yearns for a golden world to criticize our fall into exploitation, ideology, or co-optation, one to which we can return or from which we can draw to transform our brazen world, she raises an issue wholly appropriate for the Second Tetralogy. I might now translate her famous question into something more mundane and specific: Why don't the women have power in Shakespeare's best-known history plays? If women experienced equality with men in the Renaissance, why do Shakespeare's symbolic representations of history deny an equal place to his female characters?

The Renaissance does not seem to grant women equal status with men. As Kelly points out, Baldassare Castiglione's handbook for the nobility, *The Book of The Courtier*, equates men and women except at one important level: the men are to be trained to take up arms, the women to be charming. Thomas Hoby's translation of this work in 1561 spread Castiglione's ideas into England. Kelly praises Castiglione for rejecting the unfair views that Plato, Aristotle, Ovid, and Aquinas held, but says that he helped to establish a connection between love and marriage that included an implicit sexual double standard for men because he includes too many hortatory tales about female chastity in addition to his disapproving comments on male infidelity. In an ultimate Neo-Platonic flourish, Castiglione represents the idealization of love of woman and prince, a displacement of actual love into a private and imaginative creation of pure beauty. The power of the woman and ruler are in the image of God: both demand service. Kelly is right to suspect an emblematic smoke screen here. While, as she suggests, the courtier dominates his beloved and the prince on a symbolic level, he subjects his beloved and takes on "women's ways" in his relation to the prince. Even though Castiglione defends the courtier against charges of effeminacy, the man at court could take on feminine characteristics to manipulate his prince. The male power of the prince controlled the constructed female roles of the men and women of the aristocracy. The ultimate agent of power and "love" was maleness, in what Kelly implies is a homosocial, if not homoerotic, relation that leaves women out of the equation. Here, the aristocratic men lose their public power and, as a consolation prize, gain private power over their wives, whose bodies they clothe and suppress as their own influence is suppressed while being clothed in ceremony and title. The noblewoman becomes dependent on her husband and her prince.[86]

A few brief comments on women in the Second Tetralogy and the openings of the individual plays may provide illustrations to suggest that the position that Kelso, Kelly, Maclean, and others have arrived at—that women are not equals to men in Renaissance Europe—is true for the female characters in Shakespeare's major histories. The Duchess of Gloucester cannot persuade Gaunt to take revenge on Richard, and Queen Isabel cannot sway Richard the Second. Hotspur will not listen to Kate or tell her anything about his political and military plans, and Mistress Quickly must put up with Falstaff's control and lies. Bolingbroke is wifeless, and Falstaff tells Doll that "You make fat rascals," or accuses her in a misogynistic fashion of tempting men to loose living, to make lean dear bloated (*2HIV*, II.iv.41). *Henry V* begins with a long debate on the Salic Law, which disinherits women from the right to the French crown, and ends with the promise of marriage between Henry and Katharine, when France, Burgundy, and Henry speak about her as a town ready to be entered by force. This political marriage is set out in male terms in which the male characters construct Katharine within their language of "love" and politics. Women characters are private, men characters public. The male characters also control the private domain.

Richard II begins with the king's address to his uncle and patriarch, "Old John of Gaunt, time-honoured Lancaster," in a play that represents few female characters. No woman speaks in the first scene, and, if the stage directions are reliable, no woman appears until the second scene. In the opening scene Mowbray declares to Bolingbroke: " 'Tis not the trial of a woman's war, / The bitter clamour of two eager tongues, / Can arbitrate this cause betwixt us twain" (I.i.48–50). This declaration reveals what Coppélia Kahn calls the "maternal subtext" of Shakespeare's plays, "the imprint of mothering on the male psyche, the psychological presence of the mother whether or not mothers are literally represented as characters."[87] Mowbray's appeal to deeds as opposed to words is in keeping with the popular saying current in Elizabethan England—"Women are words, men deeds"—that Patricia Parker has discussed. In the world of *Richard II* and of the Second Tetralogy, manly action takes precedence over the femininity of words. It is as if the male characters are afraid of appearing effeminate and so, as Chodorow and Kahn point out, must consciously and unconsciously oppose the maternal and the feminine. This male preference for action does not prevent Mowbray from continuing to answer at some length Bolingbroke's long accusation. The male characters do not always follow their own advice regarding words and seem to use the ploy of denouncing speech even when there is no conflict. Amid their mutual recriminations, Bolingbroke and Mowbray will not listen to Richard and Gaunt, who want to resolve the conflict with words of forgiveness rather than with combat (I.i.152–205).

Like *Richard II*, *1 Henry IV* begins with the king's speech. Both opening scenes exclude women and involve talk about physical conflict. After Henry the Fourth's speech about going on a crusade to expiate Richard's murder, Westmoreland gives him news about the civil war in England. Westmoreland focuses on the thousand dead English soldiers, "Upon whose dead corpse there was such misuse, / Such beastly shameless transformation, / By those Welsh-women done, as may not be / Without much shame retold or spoken of" (*1 HIV,* I.i.42–46). Westmoreland's narrative strategy uses *occupatio,* or paralepsis, which allows Henry and the audience to imagine whatever barbarities it wishes. The "transformation" to which Westmoreland alludes is "mutilation." It also occurs in Holinshed, who reports, "the shameful villanie used by the Welsh-women towards the dead carcasses, was such, as honest eares would be ashamed to heare, and continent toongs to speake thereof."[88] Henry's only reaction is that his plans for the crusade must be broken off. This reticence may have to do in part with the nature of Westmoreland's *occupatio,* which appeals to the honest (and, by implication, the civilized) to note the enormity of the women's crime by being brief or silent in the face of it. In part, Henry's silence may have to do with his own mutilation of Richard, his inability to get beyond his guilt over it, and his desire to atone for his sin with a crusade. This response helps to suspend the issue of the Welshwomen as exotic enemy. Instead, the king talks about a long list of noblemen and compares his son unfavorably to Hotspur. This apparently aberrant fact—which equates women with dishonor, cowardice, and mon-strosity—is lost in the rolls of military honor and the king's anxieties over his heir's ability to succeed him. Fortune is feminine: her pride is Hotspur, not Hal. In the absence of women in this opening scene, the allusion to "transformation" implies an endless monstrosity to the Welshwomen because of their foreignness and their gender. Falstaff, as Gayle Whittier suggests, becomes a kind of Welshwoman.

The second part of *Henry IV,* like the first, minimizes the role of women and represents male characters who worry about their man-liness. Rumor, who begins *2 Henry IV,* resembles Virgil's Fama, a female figure who possesses many eyes, ears, and tongues and speaks about truth and falsehood. During the English Renaissance, the gender of Rumor, and the related figures of Report, Supposition, and Fame, is not so clear. Whereas Stephen Hawes represents Fame as "A goodly lady, envyroned about / With tongues of fire," Holinshed writes about one of Henry the Eighth's pageants in 1519: "Then entered a person called Report, appareled in crimsin sattin full of toongs."[89] Rumor is self-consciously monstrous but, using *occupatio,* will and will not blazon its anatomy. After characterizing itself as "a passive pipe on which the blunt monster" can play, Rumor asks, "But what need I thus / My well-known body to anatomize / Among my household?" (*2HIV,* IN.20–22).[90] The Eliz-abethan audience—the theater being one of Rumor's households—already knew what to expect from that figure. From one interpreta-tive vantage, that assumes Rumor to be a female character played by a boy actor, the falsity of rumors in this male world has been displaced onto the feminine through the "effeminate" medium of a boy.[91] This point, although not certain, is in keeping with Virgil's use of Fama in book 4 of the *Aeneid* and with the general attempt in the Renaissance to separate the manly realm of deeds from the effeminate and feminine realm of words. Even though Shakespeare shows his power through visual images on stage, like Rumor itself, he often represents deeds through words, and much of his art arises from his verbal power. The anxiety over the status of words and much of his art arises from verbal power. The anxiety over the status of words, even their relation to gender, may help comprise a larger concern with values in Renaissance England. Shakespeare should not be equated with his characters, but they are refractions of their author's psyche and participation in his culture. The characters are a site for the debate over gender, which refracts a debate over the value of the theater and of poetry, which can be seen in the many attacks on the theatrical and poetic and the defenses against them throughout Shakespeare's life. Are poetry and the theater unmanly and sinful? This is a central question in the debate. Poetry and theater must be moral and teach men to act morally, even if they must do so with the much-questioned temptations of pleasure. If Rumor is not a female figure, it still uses "false" images of a personified war, making the year pregnant, and speaks about itself as a passive pipe. These traits in conventional terms of the Renaissance would be identified with the female and effeminate. This emphasis on gender, though potentially important, does not seem to be here Shakespeare's conscious rhetorical concern.

In beginning obliquely with the suggestion that Elizabeth I was an important implied or potentially actual audience for Shakespeare when he wrote *Henry V,* I do not mean to ignore my interpretation of the play in the body of my study, but to provide other grounds for it. I am not advocating a simplistic moral allegory in which Henry is really Elizabeth, but I am suggesting that ideas of gender and of governance in the play would be considered in terms of those in Elizabeth's England. Censorship is a commonplace of the Elizabethan playhouses, experienced by Shakespeare, Ben Jonson, and others. Shakespeare was probably the script doctor for the censored and troubled *Sir Thomas More.* His plays were often performed at Elizabeth's court. The connection between the queen's gender and her ability to rule recurs in the debates of Elizabethan politics. Should a woman rule? Should a woman ruler marry? Should a female monarch rule her country and be ruled by her husband? Was Elizabeth primarily a "prince" or a woman? Henry the Fifth defeated the French against great odds; Elizabeth routed the great Spanish Armada. *Henry V* opens with the clergy afraid for clerical interests and consequently advocating a foreign war based on Henry's right to the crown as a result of their interpretation of the Salic Law, which came to be the rubric under which those who argued for the exclusion of women from the French throne rallied. The issue of gender in this play, and in the tetralogy of which it is the culmination, becomes more vital than it first appears. This is an issue that almost all male critics have failed to address seriously (many are charmed by and with Katharine) and that no female critic of whom I am aware has examined in detail. The relation of Elizabeth to a king dawned on the queen herself in 1601, when she is said to have referred to herself as Richard the Second after the performance of Shakespeare's *Richard II* at the same time as the Essex Rebellion. When portraying Elizabeth in *If You Know Not Me, You Know Nobody* (1604), a two-part play, Thomas Heywood takes lines from Shakespeare's Richard the Second and Henry the Fifth and gives them to Elizabeth, thereby making her masculine through ventriloquy and textual interplay.[92]

These comments on irony, form and genre, theater, history and the history play, and gender provide different perspectives on the argument of the main body of my study. The backgrounds are "supplements" to what has gone before, so that they are not necessary for an understanding of the argument, but, I hope, will enrich it. For some, the supplement should be developed, but to them I can only say that is one of the projects of which I am in the midst. What has preceded is a relation between theater and world, the problematics of Shakespeare's representation of history in his most powerful sequence, the Second Tetralogy. The contradictions and complexities of these plays provide a challenge that is as intricate as it is pleasurable.

NOTES

NOTES TO CHAPTER ONE

1. For some views of the Fall, see Augustine, *Concerning the City of God against the Pagans,* trans. Henry Bettenson (Harmondsworth: Penguin, 1972), esp. 13, chs. 1– 3; 14, chs. 10–13; *Lydgate's "Fall of Princes,"* ed. Henry Bergen (Washington: Carnegie Institute, 1923); John Calvin, *Institutes of the Christian Religion,* ed. John T. McNeill and trans. Ford L. Battles (Philadelphia: Westminster Press, 1960), 1. ch. 15: 4, 6, 8, chs. 16: 15; 2. ch. 6; 3. ch. 10: 1, ch. 23: 7; William Perkins, *Of the Symbol or Creede of the Apostles* (Printed by John Legate, University of Cambridge, 1597), pp. 146–57; Godfrey Goodman, *The Fall of Man* (London: imprinted by F. Kyngston, 1616), esp. F2, F3. Dramatic irony displays some of the aspects of the Fall, for it often shares the author's superior knowledge with the audience at the expense of one or more characters, who are unaware of their predicament. See Thirlwall, "On the Irony of Sophocles," in *Remains Literary and Theological of Connop Thirlwall,* ed. J. J. Stewart Perowne (London: Daldy, Isbidster, 1878), vol. 3, pp. 1–57. Thirlwall's pioneering essay on dramatic irony, which owes much to German romantic irony, was originally published in *Philological Museum* in 1833. Romantic irony also shows some affinities to the overview of God and the blindness of humanity, which help comprise the idea of the Fall. See, for instance, Karl Solger, *Erwin, or Four Dialogues on Beauty and Art* (1816), in *German Aesthetic and Criticism: The Romantic Ironists and Goethe,* ed. Kathleen Wheeler (Cambridge: Cambridge University Press, 1984), p. 148. For recent views of the Fall in Shakespeare's histories, see John Wilders, *The Lost Garden: A View of Shakespeare's English and Roman History Plays* (London: Macmillan, 1978), esp. pp. 10–11, 26–30, 74–80, 125–39; and James Calderwood, *Metadrama in Shakespeare's Henriad: "Richard II" to "Henry V"* (Berkeley: University of California Press, 1979).

Other important books that provide broader perspectives on classical and biblical versions of the Fall in the Renaissance are A. Bartlett Giamatti, *The Earthly Paradise and the Renaissance Epic* (Princeton: Princeton University Press, 1966) and Harry Levin, *The Myth of the Golden Age in the Renaissance* (New York: Oxford University Press, 1969), esp. pp. xv–xxiv, 59–61, 75–79. The classical idea of *katascopos*, which we shall examine later, also relates to the Fall, and the analogous relations among author, audience, and character in the theater has parallels to God and humanity in the world. Some theorists still find the Fall useful. See, for example, Paul de Man, "The Rhetoric of Temporality," in *Blindness and Insight: Essays in the Rhetoric of Contemporary Criticism* (1971; Minneapolis: University of Minnesota Press, 1983), p. 214.

2. In addition to notions of the Fall, ideas of genre are central to an understanding of the Second Tetralogy. See Rosalie Colie, *The Resources of Kind: Genre-Theory in the Renaissance*, ed. Barbara K. Lewalski (Berkeley: University of California Press, 1973), esp. pp. 7–9, 76–80, 95–102; Alastair Fowler, *Kinds of Literature: An Introduction to the Theory of Genres and Modes* (Cambridge, Mass.: Harvard University Press, 1982), p. 264, see pp. 54–74; Marjorie Garber, " 'What's Past Is Prologue': Temporality and Prophecy in Shakespeare's History Plays," in *Renaissance Genres: Essays on Theory, History, and Interpretation*, ed. Barbara K. Lewalski (Cambridge, Mass.: Harvard University Press, 1986), pp. 301–31; and, in the same volume, Barbara K. Lewalski, "Introduction: Issues and Approaches," pp. 1–14. For more general views on genre, see Paul Hernadi, *Beyond Genre: New Directions in Literary Classification* (Ithaca: Cornell University Press, 1972), esp. pp. 1–38, 76–84; *Theories of Literary Genre*, ed. Joseph P. Strelka (University Park: Penn State University Press, 1978), esp. pp. vii–3, 17–57, 254–69; and Heather Dubrow, *Genre* (London: Methuen, 1982).

3. Walter Ralegh, Preface to *The History of the World*, in *Selections: From His Writings and Letters*, ed. G. E. Hadlow (Oxford: Clarendon Press, 1917), p. 42, see pp. 40–45. See John Hooker, "The Epistle Dedicatory" (to Sir Walter Ralegh), in *Holinshed's Chronicles of England, Scotland and Ireland: Volume 6: Ireland* (1808; New York: AMS Press, 1954), p. 102. For other perceptive views of the contexts of Christian historiography, see C. A. Patrides, *The Phoenix and the Ladder: The Rise of the Christian View of History* (Berkeley: University of California Press, 1964), and F. Smith Fussner, *Tudor History and Historians* (New York: Basic Books, 1970), pp. 263–64.

4. For other points of view, see Pierre Lefranc, *Sir Walter Ralegh: Écrivain: l'oeuvre et les idées* (Paris: Librairie Armand Colin, 1968), pp. 308–15; see pp. 254–307, 316–34; Stephen J. Greenblatt, *Sir Walter Ralegh: The Renaissance Man and His Roles* (New Haven: Yale University Press, 1973), pp. 140–54,

and his *Renaissance Self-Fashioning: From More to Shakespeare* (Chicago: University of Chicago Press, 1980), pp. 168–69. See also Henry A. Kelly, *Divine Providence in the England of Shakespeare's Histories* (Cambridge, Mass.: Harvard University Press, 1970), esp. pp. 205, 304–5.

5. Friedrich Schlegel calls paradox the soul and source of irony and introduces the term "romantic irony." [See F. Schlegel, *Literary Notebooks, 1797–1801*, ed. Hans Eichner (Toronto: University of Toronto Press, 1957), p. 114, and his *Notebooks, fragmente* A, 121, cited in Anne K. Mellor, *English Romantic Irony* (Cambridge, Mass.: Harvard University Press, 1980), p. 12; see Mellor, pp. 21–25; D. C. Muecke, *The Compass of Irony* (London: Methuen, 1969), pp. 9, 229, and his *Irony* (London: Methuen, 1970), p. 20; and the Afterword to this volume, p. 228.] Goethe, Solger, and the German Romantics focus on the relation between subjectivity and objectivity in their discussions of irony. [See Johann Goethe, *Dichtung und Wahrheit*, quoted in Erich Heller, *The Ironic German: A Study of Thomas Mann* (1958; New York: Appel, 1973), p. 30; and Karl Solger, quoted in Josef Budde, *Zur romantischen Ironie bei Ludwig Tieck* (Bonn, 1907), pp. 18–19, 23, cited in G. G. Sedgewick, *Of Irony: Especially in Drama* (1935; Toronto: University of Toronto Press, 1948), p. 17. See also René Wellek, *A History of Modern Criticism: The Romantic Age* (New Haven: Yale University Press, 1955), p. 330; Alan Reynolds Thompson, *The Dry Mock: A Study of Irony in Drama* (Berkeley: University of California Press, 1948), pp. 63–64; and the Afterword to this volume, p. 228.] J. G. Herder and Schiller, who influenced the romantics, wrote about the importance of Shakespeare's art. The romantics, led by F. Schlegel, did not agree with Schiller's view that Shakespeare, like Homer, was a naïve artist and called Shakespeare *the* "romantic," a term that soon absorbed the classical for the romantic ironists and that signified all great art. Schiller admired Shakespeare for his objectivity but also observed passion in his works; see Friedrich Schiller, *Naive and Sentimental Poetry*, trans. Julius A. Elias (1793; New York: F. Unger, 1966), pp. 106–7. Tieck was a Shakespearean scholar as well as a romantic ironist. See Wheeler, pp. 3–4, 7; F. Schlegel, "Athenaeum Fragments" (1799), trans. Peter Firchow, 253, and "Letter about the Novel" (1799), in Wheeler, pp. 50, 77–78, and his "Dialogue on Poetry," trans. Ernst Behler and Roman Struc, in *German Romantic Criticism*, ed. A. Leslie Willson (New York: Continuum, 1982), pp. 93–94; and Ludwig Tieck, "Tony—A Drama in Three Acts by Th. Korner" (date uncertain), trans. Mark Ogden, in Wheeler, pp. 116–18, as well as another of his discussions of Shakespeare in Wheeler, pp. 120–23, and his *Das Buch uber Shakespeare*, ed. H. Ludeke (Halle, 1920), cited in Wheeler, p. 249. Solger gives Shakespeare a prominent place in the dialogue *Erwin*, saying that Shakespeare conceives a historical subject as a given, reconciling

opposites, avoiding one-sidedness, and seeing that irony is embedded in existence and the contemplation of existence. In *German Romantic Criticism*, ed. A. L. Willson, see other appreciations of Shakespeare: Jean Paul Friedrich Richter, "School for Aesthetics," trans. Margaret R. Hale, pp. 39, 48; Novalis (Friedrich Hardenberg), "Aphorisms and Fragments," trans. Alexander Gelly (from 158 of "Logological Fragments"), p. 72; and Adam Müller, " 'Lecture VII' of Twelve Lectures on Rhetoric," trans. Dennis R. Bormann and Elizabeth Leinfeller, p. 256; see also A. Müller, "Fragmente uber William Shakespeare," in *Ueber die dramatische Kunst* (1806), in Roy Pascal, ed., *Shakespeare in Germany, 1740–1815* (Cambridge: Cambridge University Press, 1937), pp. 153–63; see also Pascal's Introduction, pp. 1–36. The ideas of the German romantics prefigure Thirlwall's on irony and A. P. Rossiter's on Shakespeare's histories, except on *Henry V*, which Rossiter considers a one-eyed propaganda play ("Ambivalence: The Dialectic of the Histories," in *Angel with Horns and Other Shakespeare Lectures*, ed. Graham Storey [London: Longman's, 1961], p. 51, see pp. 47–61). *Katascopos*, or the Greek idea of an overviewer, was a commonplace in the Renaissance and may have lain behind romantic irony. The discussion of Shakespeare's ironic genius has led "I" in Solger's *Erwin* to an earthly vision of an eternal art that would hover between consciousness and unconsciousness when the tendencies interpenetrate: "And because the ironical standpoint has exactly the same attitude towards both tendencies [the conscious and the unconscious], and is present and real everywhere at the same time, this can take place with equal truth towards both sides. This art would be the first to unite perfectly freedom with necessity and contemplation with wit, and thus realize its entire scope from the purest concept of art. But perhaps our temporal weakness makes that unattainable in real life, and it is reserved for only the Godhead itself, or, it may be, for an imitation of the Godhead's actions—which may be granted us only if we reach a higher world" (Solger, *Erwin*, trans. Joyce Crick, in Wheeler, p. 149, see p. 150, and also his exchange of letters with Tieck (trans. Mark Ogden) on pp. 155–57; for a discussion of *katascopos* in the Renaissance, see Douglas Duncan, *Ben Jonson and the Lucianic Tradition* [Cambridge: Cambridge University Press, 1979], pp. 15–16). In addition to following Dr. Johnson in the observation of Shakespeare's mixture of the comic and the serious, A. W. Schlegel also has Shakespeare hovering objectively over his creation (August Wilhelm Schlegel, *Lectures on Dramatic Art and Literature*, trans. John Black, 2d. ed., rev. [London: George Bell and Sons, 1900], pp. 368–72; see this work also in Wheeler, pp. 215–17. For a related view of irony, see Maurice Morgann, *An Essay on the Dramatic Character of Sir John Falstaff*, ed. W. A. Gill (1777; London: Frowde, 1912), pp. 11–13, 58–62, and Gill's Introduction, pp. xii-xiv.

6. William Empson, "Double-Plots: Heroic and Pastoral in the Main Plot," in *Some Versions of Pastoral* (London: Chatto and Windus, 1935), pp. 64–65. See Thirlwall, "On the Irony of Sophocles," pp. 8–9.

7. See Mellor, pp. 5, 22; de Man, "Temporality," pp. 222, 228, and "Criticism in Crisis," in *Blindness and Insight* (1971; Minneapolis: University of Minnesota Press, 1983), pp. 12–13. For other views on the stability, instability, and flexibility of irony, see Geoffrey Hartman, *Criticism in the Wilderness* (New Haven: Yale University Press, 1980), p. 278; and Wayne Booth, *The Rhetoric of Irony* (Chicago: University of Chicago Press, 1974), esp. pp. 1–31. Richard Levin considers irony to be undercutting, not modification and qualification as in this study: see *New Readings vs. Old Plays: Recent Trends in the Reinterpretation of English Renaissance Drama* (Chicago: University of Chicago Press, 1979), pp. 78–79. For the relation between the author and reader in irony, see Kenneth Burke, *A Grammar of Motives* (New York: Prentice-Hall, 1945), pp. 512–17; John McKee, *Literary Irony and the Literary Audience: Studies of the Victimization of the Reader in Augustan Fiction* (Amsterdam: Rodopi, N.V., 1974), pp. 1–2; and Wayne Booth, *Irony*, p. ix.

8. For a discussion of irony in Peacham, as well as in More, Hoby, Florio, Perceval, Coverdale, Day, Nashe, and Burton, see Norman Knox, *The Word "Irony" and Its Context, 1500–1755* (Durham: Duke University Press, 1961), pp. 5, 30–31; see also 7–8, 22–24, 59, 93–94, 141. Soren Kierkegaard, *The Concept of Irony: With Constant Reference to Socrates*, trans. Lee Capel (London: Collins, 1966), pp. 47–50, 260–89. Kierkegaard considers Hegel's dialectical view of irony and Hegel's reaction to romantic irony; see G. W. F. Hegel, *The Philosophy of Fine Art [Aesthetics]*, trans. F. P. B. Osmaston (1920; New York: Hacker, 1975), pp. 8–94.

9. Samuel Johnson, "Preface to Shakespeare, 1765," in *Johnson on Shakespeare*, ed. A. Sherbo, Yale ed. of *Works*, vol. 7 (New Haven: Yale University Press, 1968), pp. 68, 75. Samuel Taylor Coleridge, "Notes on Shakespeare's Plays from English History," in *Lectures and Notes on Shakespeare and Other English Poets* (London: Bell, 1883), p. 256.

10. Jonas Barish, *The Antitheatrical Prejudice* (Berkeley: University of California Press, 1981), p. 2; see also pp. 1–37, 80–191. William Bavande's *The Good Ordering of a Common Weal* (1559), translated from the Latin of Montanus, also stresses moral lessons and examples and says that lewdness has no place in the theater (Marvin Carlson, *Theories of the Theatre: A Historical and Critical Survey, from the Greeks to the Present* [Ithaca: Cornell University Press, 1984], pp. 76–84). In attacking the theater, John North-brooke forgets Plato's injunction against poetry and admonishes the reader in verse, and his treatise is itself in a dramatic form, the dialogue, possibly

in imitation of Plato. Northbrooke uses Augustine extensively and inveighs against ungodly idleness ("Treatise wherein Dicing Dau[n]cing, Vaine plaies or Enterludes . . . are reprooved by the authoritie of the worde of God and auncient Writers" [1577], in *Early Treatises on the Stage; Viz. Northbrooke's Treatise Against Dicing, Dancing, Plays, and Interludes; Gosson's School of Abuse; and Heywood's Defence of Stage Plays* [London: Shakespeare Society, 1843], esp. pp. 3–7, 35, 49, 76, 83, 100).

11. Carlson, p. 80; Stephen Gosson, "Schoole of Abuse," in *Early Treatises*, pp. 7–34, esp. p. 12. See also J. Leeds Barroll, "The Social and Literary Context," in *The "Revels" History of the Drama in English: Volume III, 1576–1613*, gen. eds. Clifford Leech and T. W. Craik (London: Methuen, 1975), p. 29. Barroll says that the lord mayor of London and the city counselors did not mind theater in its right time and place, with the right content, that control and views of morality were the issue and not the existence of theater itself. Barbara D. Palmer discovers civic pageantry in these four histories: see " 'Ciphers to This Great Accompt': Civic Pageantry in the Second Tetralogy," in *Pageantry in the Shakespearean Theater,* ed. David M. Bergeron (Athens: University of Georgia Press, 1985).

12. See, for instance, Thomas Blundeville's *Of Wryting and Reading Hystories* (London, 1574: facsimile—Amsterdam: Theatrum Orbis Terrarum, 1979), which adapts and abridges two treatises by Franceso Patrizi (1560) and Giacomo Acontius (ca. 1564), and is the first book in English to be devoted entirely to historical theory and tries to dignify history partly in the vein of Cicero. Blundeville prefers philosophers and historians to poets, for the former make as much as the thing is, but the poet augments or diminishes events. For Blundeville, the three ends of history are to acknowledge the Providence of God; to learn from the wise to act wisely in private and public, peace and war; and to be stirred by good example to be good and by evil example to flee evil (F1^r-F3^r). More conspicuously than Shakespeare's historical representation, Blundeville's view is that history is past politics, especially *res gestae*, military actions or battles. See Arthur B. Ferguson, *Clio Unbound: Perception of the Social and Cultural Past in Renaissance England* (Durham: Duke University Press, 1979), pp. 7, 24–35, 432, and Herschel Baker, *The Race of Time: Three Lectures on Renaissance Historiography* (Toronto: University of Toronto Press, 1967), pp. 19, 51, 88–89.

13. Carlson, pp. 80–81. Philip Sidney, "An Apology for Poetry," in *English Critical Texts: 16th to 20th Century*, ed. D. J. Enright and Ernst de Chickera (London: Oxford University Press, 1962), p. 17; see Aristotle, "On the Art of Poetry," in *Classical Literary Criticism*, ed. T. S. Dorsch (Harmondsworth: Penguin, 1965, rpt. 1975), pp. 43–44. For an interesting view of Sidney in a comparativist context (du Bellay and Tasso) that takes

into account Freud's concept of defense, see Margaret W. Ferguson, *Trials of Desire: Renaissance Defences of Poetry* (New Haven: Yale University Press, 1983), esp. pp. 1–17, 137–93.

14. Sidney, p. 31, see p. 18; see also Oscar Wilde, "The Decay of Lying," in *Essays by Oscar Wilde*, ed. Hesketh Pearson (London: Methuen, 1950), pp. 36–38.

15. Sidney, pp. 13–21. See F. J. Levy, *Tudor Historical Thought* (San Marino, Calif.: Huntington Library, 1967), pp. 235–44; and F. Smith Fussner, *The Historical Revolution: English Historical Writing and Thought, 1580–1640* (London: Routledge and Kegan Paul, 1962), p. 46.

16. George Puttenham, *The Arte of Englishe Poesie*, ed. Gladys D. Willcock and Alice Walker (1936; Cambridge University Press, 1970), esp. pp. 24–41.

17. Ibid., pp. 83–84, 127. Apparently, between 1585 and 1600, the number of defenses outweighed attacks. On the surface, this can be interpreted as the triumph of the theater or, conversely, as the attackers feeling more secure that their views are shared by many, so that the poets and theater people are growing defensive over this threat from the community. Two of the more significant attacks during the time Shakespeare would have been writing history plays are *A Mirror of Monsters* (1587) by William Rankin and *Th' Overthrow of Stage-Playes* (1599) by John Rainold, the last of which still attacks religious drama as a parody of the liturgy. Like Puttenham's *Arte*, William Webbe's *Discourse of English Poetrie* (1586) defends poetry. See Carlson, p. 81.

18. Edmund Spenser, "A Letter of the Authors . . . To . . . Sir Walter Raleigh etc.," in *The Faerie Queene: Book One*, in *Works* (variorum), ed. Edwin Greenlaw et al. (Baltimore: Johns Hopkins University Press, 1932), 1:168–69; see also pp. 167, 170. For other views, see Andrew Fichter, *Poets Historical: Dynastic Epic in the Renaissance* (New Haven: Yale University Press, 1982), esp. pp. 1–23, 156–211; Page duBois, *History, Rhetorical Description, and the Epic: From Homer to Spenser* (Cambridge: Cambridge University Press, 1982), pp. 1–4, 95; and Thomas M. Greene, *The Light in Troy: Imitation and Discovery in Renaissance Poetry* (New Haven: Yale University Press, 1982), esp. pp. 4–27, 171–96.

19. Thomas Heywood, "An Apology for Actors," in *Literary Criticism: Plato to Dryden*, ed. Allan H. Gilbert (Detroit: Wayne State University Press, 1962), p. 558.

20. Ralegh, pp. 56–57, 61; and William Baldwin, "Love and Lyve etc." (Baldwin's Dedication), in *A Mirror for Magistrates* (1559), ed. Lily B. Campbell (Cambridge: Cambridge University Press, 1938), pp. 65–66. Other editions of Baldwin appeared in 1563, 1578, and 1587 (in which the editors made additions).

21. Thirlwall, "On the Irony of Sophocles," p. 9; G. G. Sedgewick, pp. 22–23, 32–33. Ralegh's "On the Life of Man" expresses the relation between theater and world, seeing life from womb to grave in terms of the beginning and close of a play, a comedy that is serious from tiring house to curtain (quoted in Alvin Kernan, "Plays," in *"The Revels" History of the Drama in English: Volume III, 1576–1613*, gen. ed. Clifford Leech and T. W. Craik (London: Methuen, 1975), pp. 247–48).

22. For perceptive views of the relation between history and literature, see Hayden White, "The Structure of Historical Narrative," *Clio* 1 (1972), 5–20; *Metahistory: The Historical Imagination in Nineteenth-Century Europe* (Baltimore: Johns Hopkins University Press, 1973), esp. pp. 1–33, 426–35; "The Historical Text as Literary Artifact," *Clio* 3 (1974), rpt. in *Tropics of Discourse* (Baltimore, 1978), in *The Writing of History: Literary Form and Historical Understanding*, ed. Robert H. Canary and Henry Kosicki (Madison: University of Wisconsin Press, 1978), and in *Critical Theory since 1965*, ed. Hazard Adams and Leroy Searle (Tallahassee: Florida State University Press, 1986), pp. 395–410; "The Politics of Historical Interpretation: Discipline and De-Sublimation," in *The Politics of Interpretation*, ed. W. J. T. Mitchell (Chicago: University of Chicago Press, 1983), pp. 119–45; and "The Question of Narrative in Contemporary Historical Theory," *History and Theory* 23 (1984), 1–33. For some of Lionel Gossman's recent work, see "History and Literature: Reproduction of Signification," in *The Writing of History: Literary Form and Historical Understanding*, ed. R. H. Canary and H. Kozicki (Madison: University of Wisconsin Press, 1978), pp. 3–39, and "Literature and Education," *New Literary History* 13 (1982), 341–71. For a questioning of White's idea that form is metahistorical and for an assertion that history and form depend on each other, see Suzanne Gearhart, *The Open Boundary of History and Fiction: A Critical Approach to the French Enlightenment* (Princeton: Princeton University Press, 1984), esp. pp. 4–28.

23. For different views of genre and its possibility, see Jacques Derrida, *Of Grammatology*, trans. Gayatri C. Spivak (1967; Baltimore: Johns Hopkins University Press, 1976), pp. 4, 59, and his "Law of Genre," in *On Narrative*, ed. W. J. T. Mitchell (Chicago: University of Chicago Press, 1981), pp. 51–79; Paul de Man, "Semiology and Rhetoric," in *Allegories of Reading* (New Haven: Yale University Press, 1979), pp. 3–5; Raymond Williams, *Marxism and Literature* (Oxford: Oxford University Press, 1977), pp. 145–50, 173–99; and Stephen J. Greenblatt, Preface to *Allegory and Representation*, ed. S. J. Greenblatt (Baltimore: Johns Hopkins University Press, 1981), pp. vii–xiii. On the definition, role, and possibility of the author, see Roland Barthes, "The Death of an Author," in *The Discontinuous Universe*, trans. Richard Howard (New York: Basic Books, 1972), pp. 7–13; and Michel Foucault,

"What Is an Author?" in *Language, Counter-Memory, Practice: Selected Essays and Interviews*, ed. Donald F. Bouchard (Ithaca: Cornell University Press, 1977), pp. 113–39. See also Richard Lanham, *The Motives of Eloquence: Literary Rhetoric in the Renaissance* (New Haven: Yale University Press, 1976), pp. 27, 143, see pp. 28–35, 130–34. Tennenhouse argues that, like romantic comedy, the history play represents patriarchy in a state of disorder. Even more so than romantic comedy and the Petrarchan lyric of the 1590s, the history play in the same decade idealizes the state. This constitutes Tennenhouse's new historical position on genre, in which he tries to be very specific in his historicizing of the genres. See Leonard Tennenhouse, *Power on Display: The Politics of Shakespeare's Genres* (New York: Methuen, 1986), pp. 72–101; for more on Tennenhouse's position, see the Afterword to this volume. Although I approach the problem from another angle, I make a similar argument. Shakespeare's wrestle with the content of history translates into a formal dilemma that strains the history play to the extent that it transforms the genre so utterly or questions its very possibility that Shakespeare moves on to Roman history and represents English history very differently when he returns to it in *Henry VIII*. The history play and its historical context modify each other.

24. Aristotle, "On the Art of Poetry," pp. 43–44; Sidney, pp. 9, 13–20; see B. L. Ullmann, "History and Tragedy," *Transactions and Proceedings of the American Philological Association* 73 (1942), 20, 40, 53.

25. For poetry, see Puttenham, pp. 81, 115–16, 161–62; for nondramatic, especially epic, see pp. 39–45 ; for dramatic genres, see pp. 26, 34, 58; for history, see pp. 21, 39–41, 148, 157, 191. Dympna Callaghan has asserted that class preferences in Elizabethan England placed tragedy over comedy. See *Women and Gender in Renaissance Tragedy: A Study of "King Lear," "Othello," "The Duches of Malfi," and "The White Devil"* (Atlantic Highlands: Humanities Press International, 1989), esp. p. 37.

26. Anne Barton, "Shakespeare: His Tragedies," in *English Drama to 1710* , ed. Christopher Ricks (London: Sphere, 1971), pp. 215–16; Madeleine Doran, *Endeavors of Art: A Study of Form in Elizabethan Drama* (Madison: University of Wisconsin Press, 1954), pp. 112–13; and Philip Brockbank, "Shakespeare: His Histories, English and Roman," in Ricks, p. 166.

27. Heywood, p. 560.

28. Northrop Frye, *Anatomy of Criticism: Four Essays* (Princeton: Princeton University Press, 1957), pp. 283–84, 289; for a similar view of the word "history," see Ralegh, Preface to *The History of the World*, p. 57, and Tom F. Driver, *The Sense of History in Greek and Shakespearean Drama* (New York: Columbia University Press, 1960), p. 5. Thomas Percy, *Reliques of English Poetry* (1765), in *Shakespeare: The Critical Heritage: Vol. 4, 1753–54*, ed. Brian

Vickers (London: Routledge and Kegan Paul, 1976), p. 544. Anne Barton, "Troilus and Cressida," *The Riverside Shakespeare*, ed. G. Blakemore Evans (Boston: Houghton Mifflin, 1974), p. 444.

29. David Worcester, *The Art of Satire* (New York: Russell and Russell, 1940), p. 124. For those with a similar view, see Hegel, pp. 88–91. For a different position, see Muecke, *Compass*, p. 183, and Mellor, pp. 24–25. The problems of irony that the German romantics, Hegel, and Kierkegaard explored persist. Where does irony reside? Who controls it? Does it shape or encourage chaos? See G. G. Sedgewick, p. 49; Thompson, p. 24; Eleanor Hutchens, *Irony in "Tom Jones"* (Tuscaloosa: University of Alabama Press, 1965), p. 22. For other important works on irony, see J. A. K. Thomson, *Irony: An Historical Introduction* (London: Allen and Unwin, 1926); Lilian Furst, *Fictions of Romantic Irony* (Cambridge, Mass.: Harvard University Press, 1984), esp. pp. 1–49, 225–40; and Kierkegaard, *Irony*, p. 336, for a view of Shakespeare's ironic objectivity. For a discussion of *katascopos*, see Duncan, pp. 14–16. For discussions of *peripeteia*, see Aristotle, "On the Art of Poetry," pp. 38–42; Bert O. States, *Irony and Drama: A Poetics* (Ithaca: Cornell University Press, 1971), pp. xviii, 6, 28–31, 57, 69; Rossiter, pp. 47–62; Empson, *Some Versions of Pastoral*, pp. 27, 43; Thompson, p. 2; and Hutchens, p. 13.

NOTES TO CHAPTER TWO

1. For works related to the Fall, language, and public and private, see Thomas Norton and Thomas Sackville, *Gorboduc; or Ferrex and Porrex*, in *Chief Pre-Shakespearean Dramas: A Selection of Plays Illustrating the History of the English Drama from Its Origin Down to Shakespeare*, ed. Joseph Quincy Adams (Boston: Houghton Mifflin, 1924); Ernst H. Kantorowicz, *The King's Two Bodies: A Study in Mediaeval Political Theology* (Princeton: Princeton University Press, 1957), pp. 7–41; and Joseph Porter, *The Drama of Speech Acts: Shakespeare's Lancastrian Tetralogy* (Berkeley: University of California Press, 1979).

2. C. T. Onions, *A Shakespeare Glossary*, 2d ed. (Oxford, 1919), cited in William Shakespeare, *King Richard II*, ed. Peter Ure, Arden ed. (London: Methuen, 1961, rpt. 1978), p. 68. All quotations and citations, unless otherwise indicated, will be to the Arden editions of the plays. For the other Arden editions, see *The First Part of King Henry IV*, ed. A. R. Humphreys (London: Methuen, 1960, rpt. 1965); *The Second Part of King Henry IV*, ed.

A. R. Humphreys (London: Methuen, 1966, rpt. 1977); and *King Henry V,* ed. J. H. Walter (London: Methuen, 1954, rpt. 1977).

3. Shakespeare uses stage images or symbols to reinforce and focus verbal images; in *Richard II,* see the stage images of the garden (III.iv), crown, face and mirror (IV.i), death (Exton) (V.iv, vi), prison, and music (V.v).

4. For another treatment of the Fall, see Stanley Maveety, "A Second Fall of Cursed Man: The Bold Metaphor in *Richard II,*" *Journal of English and Germanic Philology* 72 (1973), 175–93. A specific treatment occurs in Robert P. Merrix, "The Phaeton Allusion in *Richard II:* The Search for Identity," *English Literary Renaissance* 17 (1987), 277–87. For a recent view of the opening of *Richard II,* see Harry Berger, Jr., "Psychoanalyzing the Shakespeare Text: The First Three Scenes of the *Henriad,*" in *Shakespeare and the Question of Theory,* ed. Patricia Parker and Geoffrey Hartman (New York: Methuen, 1985), pp. 210–29.

5. *The Oxford English Dictionary (OED),* especially definition 4. The Arden, Cambridge, Pelican, and Signet editions do not refer to the political and legal definition of the word.

6. I have in mind Barish's work on antitheatrical views. See also Leonard Dean, "*Richard II:* The State and the Image of the Theatre," *PMLA* 67 (1952), 211–18. Later studies of the state theater have made this subject popular among Renaissance literary critics. Here are a few examples. Stephen Orgel wrote a suggestive and influential work on the relation between the monarch's political and theatrical power in the court masque. See *The Illusion of Power: Political Theater in the English Renaissance* (Berkeley: University of California Press, 1975). Leah S. Marcus focuses on the traditional popular pastimes related to seasonal holidays—marginal ceremonies associated with the rites of church and state but practiced sporadically in the seventeenth century. See *The Politics of Mirth: Jonson, Herrick, Milton, Marvell, and the Defense of Old Holiday Pastimes* (Chicago: University of Chicago Press, 1986). Christopher Pye discusses the relation of theater to power in *Richard II, Henry V,* and *Macbeth* and argues that although the public stage was subject to pressures from the monarch and from popular sources, it was shaped by the rise of absolutism. See *The Regal Phantasm: Shakespeare and the Politics of Spectacle* (London: Routledge, 1990). Pye has an interesting and opposite interpretation of irony in Shakespeare's plays to Robert Ornstein's, who thinks that the irony is obvious. Pye holds that in *Henry V* Shakespeare presents us with an ironic paradox: the play "seems to offer back in the place of a tale of conquest a mocking reflection of the hermeneutic pursuit itself" (Pye, 14; see Robert Ornstein, *A Kingdom for a Stage: The Achievement of Shakespeare's History Plays* [Cambridge, Mass.: Harvard University Press, 1972], pp. 176–77). For an interesting discussion of theatrical effect, or

epideictics, as well as the relation of ideology and theatricality in the Second Tetralogy, see Joanne Altieri, "Shakespeare and the Imperial Myth," in *The Theatre of Praise: The Panegyric Tradition in Seventeenth-Century Drama* (Newark: University of Delaware Press, 1986), pp. 39–73. The background she gives on readings wary of Henry the Fifth (Hazlitt), the rejection of Falstaff (Johnson), and ironic readings in general is useful. She suggests for interpreters a medial way between irony and romance, like Hal's between Falstaff and Henry. See esp. pp. 48–58.

7. *The Plays and Poems of William Shakespeare*, ed. Edmond Malone (London, 1790), cited in William Shakespeare, *The First Part of King Henry IV*, ed. A. R. Humphreys, Arden ed. (London: Methuen, 1960, rpt. 1965), pp. 3–4; see Genesis 4.11.

8. Oscar G. Brockett, "Satire in English Drama, 1590–1603," dissertation (1953; Ann Arbor: University Microfilms, 1981), pp. 57–58, 272, and Alvin Kernan, *The Cankered Muse: Satire of the English Renaissance* (New Haven: Yale University Press, 1959), p. 34.

9. See Kernan, *Cankered*, p. 11, and Frye, *Anatomy*, p. 235, for general remarks on satiric imagery.

10. For similar imagery, see Job 24.13–17; Edmund Spenser, *The Faerie Queene,* III.iv, stanzas 58–59; and I.ii.190–96 in *1 Henry IV*, cited in Ure, ed., *Richard II*, p. 96.

11. For an evaluation of the sun imagery, see, for example, Kathryn M. Harris, "Sun and Water Imagery in *Richard II*: Its Dramatic Function," *Shakespeare Quarterly* 21 (1970), 157–65. See the story that the Groom tells Richard about Bolingbroke riding his old horse (V.v.76f.). A detailed discussion of horse imagery occurs in Robert N. Watson, "Horsemanship in Shakespeare's Second Tetralogy," *English Literary Renaissance* 13 (1983), 274–300. For more on the use of "reign," "rein," and "rain," see I.ii.1–8 and III.iii.43–44. For a general view of language, see George R. Hibbard, *The Making of Shakespeare's Dramatic Poetry* (Toronto: University of Toronto Press, 1981).

12. Dover Wilson's note in William Shakespeare, *The First Part of the History of Henry IV*, ed. John Dover Wilson (Cambridge: Cambridge University Press, 1946), p. 166. Janet Adelman has said that food is the foundation of class conflict in *Coriolanus,* so that the food imagery of satire and of *1 Henry IV* probably also has an economic and a social basis. Keith Wrightson says that there were forty recorded food riots between 1585 and 1660 in England. See Adelman, "Feeding, Dependency, and Aggression in *Coriolanus,*" in *Representing Shakespeare: New Psychoanalytic Essays,* ed. Murray M. Schwartz and Coppélia Kahn (Baltimore: Johns Hopkins University Press, 1980); and Keith Wrightson, *English Society, 1580–1680* (New Bruns-

wick: Rutgers University Press, 1982). In an interesting discussion, Phyllis Rackin examines food in *2 Henry VI* (and refers to Adelman, Wrightson, Charney, Whigham, and others). See *Stages of History: Shakespeare's English Chronicles* (Ithaca: Cornell University Press, 1990), pp. 211–16.

13. Gerald Gould, "A New Reading of *Henry V*," *English Review* 29 (1919), 42–55, rpt. as "Irony and Satire in *Henry V*," in *Shakespeare. "Henry V": A Casebook*, ed. Michael Quinn (London: Macmillan, 1969), pp. 81–94; C. H. Hobday, "Imagery and Irony in *Henry V*," *Shakespeare Survey* 21 (1968), 107–13. Christopher Marlowe, *Tamburlaine, Parts One and Two: Text and Major Criticism*, ed. Irving Ribner (Indianapolis: Bobbs-Merrill, 1974), V.i. 1–132. If Shakespeare parodies Tamburlaine with Pistol's tags here and in *2 Henry IV*, is he modifying the heroic view of Henry by causing him to use images like Tamburlaine's before virgins and cities? For another view, see Roy Battenhouse, "The Relation of Henry V to Tamburlaine," *Shakespeare Survey* 27 (1974), 71–79.

14. Walter's notes in *King Henry V*, ed. J. H. Walter, Arden ed. (London: Methuen, 1954, rpt. 1977), p. 66.

15. Kantorowicz, esp. pp. 7–41. I thank the law librarians at the University of Alberta and Garry Sherbert for their suggestions and assistance in regard to bibliographical matters in medieval and Renaissance legal theory. For a discussion of a king's titles, see Joseph Candido, "The Name of King: Hal's Titles in the *Henriad*," *Texas Studies in Literature and Language* 26 (1984), 61–73.

16. Umberto Eco, "Language, Power, Force," in *Travels in Hyperreality*, trans. William Weaver (1986; London: Pan, 1987), pp. 239–55. See also Roland Barthes, "Inaugural Lecture," in *A Barthes Reader*, ed. Susan Sontag (New York: Hill and Wang, 1982), and Michel Foucault, *Discipline and Punish*, trans. Alan Sheridan (New York: Random House, 1979), pp. 16–17, and *The History of Sexuality: An Introduction*, trans. Robert Hurley (New York: Pantheon, 1978), 92–94. Rather than rely on a pun to establish, as Barthes and others do, the writer as *auctor* and political *auctoritas*, I suggest the analogy between king and author, subjects and audience as an imaginative force and not as an irrefutable connection in the world. Like Aristotle's audience in the *Poetics*, the audience sympathizes with the characters, but, like Brecht's audience, it also experiences an alienation effect and realizes that differences exist between the king and subjects, playwright and spectators. In the very language and conventions of the drama, the audience is reminded at times that the theater is not the world. Possibly, the audience experiences the empathy and the distancing that culminate in Aristotle's idea of catharsis. The audience, like subjects, can sometimes relate to the playwright's godlike and human attributes. If, by analogy, the king has lost

his right to rule and control meaning in history, perhaps the author has forfeited the sway of his intended meaning over reader and audience in the history play. Paradoxically, however, subjects and audience seem to want to return to order, meaning, and an authority even as they are caught up in a fallen world or hermeneutical uncertainty. They want to limit the authority they have given to the playwright but recognize that to take that authority back is to call into question the possibility of a stable power. In other words, by analyzing the word "king" in these plays, I am assuming, at least in part, that Shakespeare and his text have some stability and meaning even if I am saying at the same time that the term "king" is questioning the possibility of meaning and possibility. Questioning the author's authority and assuming the rights of readers—which Roland Barthes, Michel Foucault, Wolfgang Iser, and others have advocated—may suggest why the fight over kingship has not died down in Renaissance and Shakespearean studies even (at the time of this note's composition) forty-five years after Tillyard's book and more than fifty years after Arthur Lovejoy's work on the great chain of being. How free is the reader or audience and how absolute or relative is the meaning are questions that are as political as they are interpretative. The critical and theoretical debate in Shakespearean studies centers on the nature of kingship and authority and is related to the authority of the playwright over his audience. The playwright is both theatrical presenter and author; like the king, he has two bodies, just as the person who receives a play is both a member of the audience and a reader. See Roland Barthes, "The Death of the Author," pp. 7–13; Michel Foucault, "What Is an Author?" pp. 113–39; Wolfgang Iser, *The Implied Reader* (Baltimore: Johns Hopkins University Press, 1974); Umberto Eco, *The Role of the Reader* (Bloomington: Indiana University Press, 1979); and Stanley Fish, *Is There a Text in This Class? The Authority of Interpretive Communities* (Cambridge, Mass.: Harvard University Press, 1980), esp. pp. 87–97, 135–38, 208–10. See Arthur Lovejoy, *The Great Chain of Being: A Study of the History of an Idea* (Cambridge, Mass.: Harvard University Press, 1936).

17. Marie Axton, *The Queen's Two Bodies: Drama and the Elizabethan Succession* (London: Royal Historical Society, 1977). One way that subsequent critics have used this political theory has been to relate it to Elizabethan constructions of gender and to discuss their relation to Elizabeth's power. Katherine E. Kelly looks at six roles in Shakespeare's plays where a female character dresses herself temporarily in the clothes of a boy, roles that Harley Granville-Barker called "the boy actress" (*Prefaces to Shakespeare*, vol. 3 [Princeton: Princeton University Press, 1946], p. 12). See Kelly, "The Queen's Two Bodies: Shakespeare's Boy Actress in Breeches," *Theatre Journal* 42 (1990), 81–93. The debate over gender in theater and society (state) in

Elizabethan times and our times is charged. See, for instance, Linda Bamber, *Comic Women, Tragic Men: A Study of Gender and Genre in Shakespeare* (Stanford: Stanford University Press, 1982), esp. ch. 1; Lisa Jardine, *Still Harping on Daughters: Women and Drama in the Age of Shakespeare* (Sussex: Harvester Press, 1983), pp. 9–36; Marianne Novy, *Love's Argument: Gender Relations in Shakespeare* (Chapel Hill: University of North Carolina Press, 1984); Simon Shepherd, "Women and Males," *Marlowe and the Politics of Elizabethan Theatre* (Brighton: Harvester Press, 1986), pp. 178–207; Sue-Ellen Case, *Feminism and Theatre* (New York: Methuen, 1988); and Lorraine Helms, "Playing the Woman's Part," *Theatre Journal* 41 (1989), 190–200. As Kelly mentions, Case criticizes feminists for performing aesthetic analyses of the convention of the boy actor that legitimate the exclusion of women from the Elizabethan stage (Case, 21–24, in Kelly, 81).

18. Edmund Plowden, *Commentaries or Reports* (London, 1816), 212a, quoted in Kantorowicz, p. 7, see pp. 1–23.

19. Richard Waswo, *Language and Meaning in the Renaissance* (Princeton: Princeton University Press, 1987), p. 70, see p. 60.

20. *The Collected Papers of Frederic William Maitland*, ed. H. A. L. Fisher (Cambridge: Cambridge University Press, 1911), 3: 249, or *Maitland: Selected Essays*, ed. H. D. Hazeltine, G. Lapsley, and P. H. Winfield (Cambridge: Cambridge University Press, 1936), p. 109. For a different legal focus from my own, see Edna Z. Boris, *Shakespeare's English Kings, the People, and the Law: A Study in the Relationship between the Tudor Constitution and the Engish History Plays* (Cranbury, N.J.: Associated University Presses, 1974).

21. Anne Barton, "The King Disguised: Shakespeare's *Henry V* and the Comical History," in *The Triple Bond: Plays, Mainly Shakespearean, in Performance*, ed. J. G. Price (University Park: Pennsylvania State University Press, 1975), pp. 92–117; and Barton, "He Who Plays the King," in *English Drama: Forms and Development: Essays in Honour of Muriel Clara Bradbrook*, ed. Marie Axton and Raymond Williams (Cambridge: Cambridge University Press, 1977). Katherine E. Kelly looks at the relation between the queen's two bodies and the breeches parts in Shakespeare's plays, where female characters dress up temporarily in the clothes of a boy, which is a different but analogous kind of theatrical moment. Both the king's disguise and the female disguise depend on the relation between theatrical and political power, but the one relates obliquely to Elizabeth because she is the ruler, the other because she is a woman. Neither form of disguise represents Elizabeth directly. See Kelly, pp. 81–93. In a different kind of discussion of the representation of queens on stage, see Kim H. Noling, "Grubbing Up the Stock: Dramatizing Queens in *Henry VIII*," *Shakespeare Quarterly* 39

(1988), 291–306. In Noling's view, "for anyone dramatizing the reign of King Henry VIII of England, an unavoidable subject is his obsession with begetting male heirs and his repeated substitution of one queen for another as a means to that end. Shakespeare, preparing his *Henry VIII* (1613) under the patronage of James I, created a dramaturgy of queens that, although admitting some dissent against such an expedient use of queens, ultimately endorses Henry's patriarchal will" (291).

22. See Irving Ribner, *The English History Play in the Age of Shakespeare* (New York: Barnes and Noble, 1957, rev. 1965), pp. 1–30.

23. E. M. W. Tillyard, *The Elizabethan World Picture* (London: Chatto and Windus, 1943), p. 88, and his *Shakespeare's History Plays* (London: Chatto and Windus, 1944), p. 19. For a qualification of Tillyard's views on order and Providence in history, see Henry A. Kelly, *Divine Providence in the England of Shakespeare's Histories* (Cambridge, Mass.: Harvard University Press, 1970), pp. viii, 297–98. For a general account of the role of God and order in the Elizabethan age and the critical reaction to Tillyard, see Graham Holderness, *Shakespeare's History* (Dublin: Gill and Macmillan, 1985), pp. 17–26.

24. John Wilders aptly notes: "Indeed it transpires that very few of the appeals or thanks to God which are spoken by Shakespeare's characters are free from ironies created by the dramatist." See Wilders, p. 63, see also pp. 53–64. H. R. Coursen argues that Shakespeare represents a new world in which God is absent, or at least inaccessible. See *The Leasing Out of England: Shakespeare's Second Henriad* (Washington: University Press of America, 1982), pp. 4, 10–11. Jonathan Dollimore and Alan Sinfield relate ideology and God with regard to *Henry V*: "The principal strategy of ideology is to legitimate inequality and exploitation by representing the social order which perpetuates these things as immutable and unalterable—as decreed by God or simply natural. Since the Elizabethan period, the ideological appeal to God has tended to give way to the equally powerful appeal to the natural. But in the earlier period both were crucial: the laws of degree and order inferred from nature were further construed as having been put there by God." See their "History and Ideology: The Instance of *Henry V*," in *Alternative Shakespeares*, ed. John Drakakis (London: Methuen, 1985), pp. 211–12, see 206–15. For a general discussion, see Robert Rantoul Reed, Jr., *Crime and God's Judgment in Shakespeare* (Lexington: University Press of Kentucky, 1984). Other writers have discussed ideology in the individual plays in more general terms. See, for instance, Henry E. Jacobs, "Prophecy and Ideology in Shakespeare's *Richard II*," *South Atlantic Review* 51 (1986), 3–18, and Gunter Walch, "*Henry V* as Working-House of Ideology," *Shakespeare Survey* 40 (1988), 63–68. See also note 92 to the Afterword. A more

general political discussion of Shakespeare in the British and American academies occurs in Walter Cohen's "Political Criticism in Shakespeare," pp. 18–46, and Don E. Wayne's "Power, Politics, and the Shakespearean Text: Recent Criticism in England and the United States," pp. 47–67, both in *Shakespeare Reproduced: The Text in History and Ideology,* ed. Jean E. Howard and Marion F. O'Connor (New York: Methuen, 1987).

25. Jonathan Culler, ed. *On Puns: The Foundation of Letters* (Oxford: Blackwell, 1988); Margreta de Grazia, *Shakespeare Verbatim* (Oxford: Clarendon Press, 1991); Jonathan Goldberg, *Writing Matter: From the Hands of the English Renaissance* (Stanford: Stanford University Press, 1990), esp. pp. 241–42.

26. For "scot," see Humphreys, ed., *1 Henry IV,* p. 31; for "sol" or its variant, "soul," see the *OED,* s.v. "sol" (sun, gold, soul), definitions sb¹ (a and 2a) and sb³; see also Volpone's opening speech.

27. Humphreys, pp. 113, 118.

28. Ibid., p. 145. Shakespeare most often connects the devil and hell with the comic world, though Falstaff's fear of damnation, seeing a *memento mori* in Bardolph's face, has solemn aspects. The playwright also places his characters in ironic relation to fortune or Fortune. The use of money imagery, which "debt" helps comprise, is ironic; see II.iv; III.ii.103, iii.75–77. "Death" also conjures images of violence and hunting, mixing the solemn and the comic. Hal parodies Douglas as one who could never hit a sparrow with a pistol (II.iv.341–44). Although the rebels accuse Henry of being predatory, they sometimes use hunting images and act like predators themselves. Hotspur employs such hunting terms as "rouse" and "start" when he resolves to pursue the king (I.iii.195–96). When the Hostess is telling the prince the truth about Sir John's backbiting and boasting, Falstaff answers her that there is "no more truth in thee than in a drawn fox," a hunted fox forced from cover. Hal says that Sir John used sugar to keep himself long-winded, a practice employed for fighting cocks and perhaps for fat and fighting men (Humphreys, pp. 115, 117). Falstaff uses hunting imagery while he preys on his naked recruits (IV.ii.18–20). If Sir John is a "lugged bear," he is as well a hound, which also baited bears, ensnaring the game and looking for the scraps while waiting with servility for his master to break up the catch: "I'll follow, as they say, for reward." "Follow" and "reward" represent hunting terms that apply to the behavior of hounds during the hunt as well as having religious connotations (Humphreys, p. 162). Hunting imagery is equivocal because the rebels, the king, and Falstaff say they are hunted while they also hunt.

29. No one in the play, except Mowbray and Scroop, judges John's act nor does anyone at court show any knowledge of it. In more general terms, Falstaff condemns John (IV.iii.84f.).

30. For a general view of kingship, see Clifford Geertz, "Centers, Kings, and Charisma: Reflections on the Symbolics of Power," in *Culture and Its Creators: Essays in Honor of Edward Shils*, ed. Joseph Ben-David and Terry Nichols Clark (Chicago: University of Chicago Press, 1977), esp. p. 160. For background on the king as God's deputy and on succession and sovereignty, see Moody E. Prior, *The Drama of Power: Studies in Shakespeare's History Plays* (Evanston: Northwestern University Press, 1973), pp. 83–100. Prior mentions that in *A Conference about the Next Succession to the Crowne of Ingland* (1594), Robert Parsons, a Catholic, argued that hereditary succession was a legal matter and so could be changed and that a king could be deposed. Thomas Hooker condemned as unnatural the idea that succession could be determined by the will of the people and the qualities of the claimant (pp. 88–89). The complexity, if not the contradictory nature, of the Elizabethan views of kingship appears in Prior's lucid account. Compare, for instance, three of his generalizations: "The sixteenth-century idea of kingship implied as a necessary corollary that the king may not be resisted" (p. 89); "A more important consideration is that for most English writers the monarchy of England was circumscribed by Parliament and by law" (p. 94); "It is also a commonly held opinion that the king should regard himself as subject to the law" (p. 95, see p. 96). The divine right of kings, or the doctrine of the king's two bodies, and the idea of the king as subject to the law (*lex facit regem*) oppose each other. Shakespeare represents this conflict in the Second Tetralogy. John W. Blanpied discusses the king as actor, antic, and machiavel. See his *Time and the Artist in Shakespeare's English Histories* (Newark: University of Delaware Press, 1983), pp. 13–15, 20–29. For an interesting consideration of the two bodies of Queen Elizabeth that is based on the work of Kantorowicz and Axton, see Leah S. Marcus, *Puzzling Shakespeare: Local Reading and Its Discontents* (Berkeley: University of California Press, 1988), pp. 53–66. In opening a chapter entitled "The 'Godly' Queens," John N. King says: "Because Mary I and Elizabeth I were the first regnant queens of England, their apologists faced the unprecedented problem of defending the authority of women to govern. Tudor artists addressed this political issue by rehabilitating the iconography of late medieval queens, who until this time had fulfilled no more than an ancillary role as the wives and mothers of kings" (p. 182). See John N. King, *Tudor Royal Iconography: Literature and Art in an Age of Religious Crisis* (Princeton: Princeton University Press, 1989), pp. 182–266.

31. For the complexity of the various claims of kingship in Shakespeare's histories, see E. W. Talbert, *The Problem of Order: Elizabethan Political Commonplaces and an Example of Shakespeare's Art* (Chapel Hill: University of North Carolina Press, 1962), pp. 66–67; and Prior, p. 99. For various

myths—Lancaster, York, and Tudor—in the histories and their relation to kingship and Providence, see Henry A. Kelly, pp. vii-viii, 1–83, 203, 305–6. Robert Ornstein discusses the Tudor myth, which makes the Tudor defeat of Richard the Third redeem Richard the Second's fall, and examines kingship, which includes a discussion of the weakness of the king. See *A Kingdom for a Stage*, pp. 14–22, 29. C. G. Thayer thinks that Shakespeare's stage subverts the Tudor myth. See *Shakespearean Politics: Government and Misgovernment in the Great Histories* (Athens: Ohio University Press, 1983), esp. p. viii.

32. Freud argues that humans in primitive and modern societies surround their leaders with taboos designed to protect and punish the rulers: "The ceremonial taboo of kings is *ostensibly* the highest honor and protection for them, while *actually* it is a punishment for their exaltation, a revenge taken on them by their subjects. The experience of Sancho Panza (as described by Cervantes) when he was governor of his island convinced him that this view of court ceremonial was the only one that met the case" (*Standard Edition*, vol. 13, p. 51, quoted in Paul Roazen, *Freud: Social and Political Thought* [New York: Vintage, 1968], pp. 148–49). That Freud relates life to a literary work from the Renaissance is instructive. The position of Elizabeth in her society complicates Freud's representation of patriarchal ruler and subject. Freud likens the relation between king and subject to that between father and son, which has its foundations in primitive society: "much of a savage's attitude to his ruler is derived from a child's infantile attitude to his father" (ibid., p. 52, quoted in Roazen, p. 149). For a discussion of the ruler-subject relation, see Judith K. Shklar, *Legalism* (Cambridge: Harvard University Press, 1962), esp. pp. 70–80. Such anthropological musings as Freud's raise the question of an ethnocentric and gender-specific (in this case, male) attempt to universalize according to its own position and advantage. A current debate between some proponents of feminism and of postmodernism is being engaged over the subject of anthropology. See, for instance, Frances E. Macia-Lees, Patricia Sharpe, and Colleen Ballerino Cohen, "The Postmodernist Turn in Anthropology: Cautions from a Feminist Perspective," *Signs* 15 (1989), 7–33. This debate is also related to the questioning in postcolonial studies, for instance in Edward W. Said's work, of anthropology and to new historicism, which has for one of its influences the anthropological work of Clifford Geertz.

33. *The Reports of Sir Edward Coke*, 2d ed. (London: H. Twford, etc., 1680), pp. 438–39. For another edition, which includes *Calvin's Case*, see *The Reports of Sir Edward Coke*, ed. John Farquhar Fraser (London: Joseph Butterworth and Son, 1826), 4: Pt. 7, 1–48.

34. Louis Nafla, *Law and Politics in Jacobean England: The Tracts of Lord*

Chancellor Ellesmere (Cambridge: Cambridge University Press, 1977), pp. 60, 65–76.

35. Stephen Greenblatt discusses the manipulation of God and religion during the Renaissance in colonizing the New World; relates the collapse of royal power in *Richard II* with "the discovery of the physical body of the ruler"; likens the audience to king and subject, colonizer and colonized; argues that the audience creates Henry the Fifth as the ideal king; and maintains that although the representation of power in the theater absorbs the audience, it does not allow it to participate with "deep intimacy" in that power or to control its "significance and force." See his "Invisible Bullets: Renaissance Authority and Its Subversion, *Henry IV* and *Henry V*," in *Political Shakespeare: New Essays in Cultural Materialism*, ed. Jonathan Dollimore and Alan Sinfield (Ithaca: Cornell University Press, 1985), esp. pp. 21–24, 40–44. For a discussion of the ideology of ceremony in this speech, in which they argue that Henry is afraid of deceptive obedience because it is disruptive to state power, see Dollimore and Sinfield, "History and Ideology," pp. 219–23.

36. See Wilde, "The Decay of Lying," pp. 33–72, esp. pp. 46, 70–72, and, in the same volume, see his views of Shakespeare's history plays, "The Truth of Masks," pp. 15–28. See Hamlet's reaction to the First Player's performance in his speech on the relation between life and fiction—"O what a rogue and peasant slave am I"—at II.ii.543–601 in *Hamlet*, ed. Harold Jenkins (London: Methuen, 1982). See also James L. Calderwood's perceptive discussion of language and lying in *1* and *2 Henry IV* in his *Metadrama in Shakespeare's Henriad*, pp. 6, 30–88. For a thorough analysis of lying in relation to speech acts in *2 Henry IV*, see Joseph A. Porter, *The Drama of Speech Acts*, pp. 94–115.

NOTES TO CHAPTER THREE

1. Examination of Gelly Meyricke, 17th Feb. 1600 (*Domestic State Papers, Elizabeth*, vol. 278, no. 78), and of Augustine Phillips, 18th Feb. 1600 (ibid., no. 85); William Lambard, in John Nichols, *Progresses and Processions of Queen Elizabeth* (1823), vol. 3 all quoted in *The Shakespeare Allusion-Book: A Collection of Allusions to Shakespeare From 1591 to 1700 . . .* , vol. 1, compiled by C. Ingleby et al., re-ed. and rev. J. Munro (1909; Freeport, N.Y.: Books for Library Press, 1970), pp. 81–82, 100.

2. John Orrell, *The Quest for Shakespeare's Globe* (Cambridge: Cambridge University Press, 1983), esp. p. 157; pp. 8–16, 121, 140–50. See also Francis

Yates, *Theatre of the World* (London: Routledge and Kegan Paul, 1969), pp. 92–136, 159, 168; for Vitruvian figures, see plate 2, and for *Theatrum Vitae Humanae,* see plate 23. For the *Theatrum Mundi,* see Glynne Wickham, *The Medieval Theatre* (1974; London: Weidenfeld and Nicholson, 1980), pp. 64, 89. See also the views of Richard Hosley, Glynne Wickham, and Bernard Beckerman in *The Third Globe: Symposium for the Reconstruction of the Globe Playhouse, Wayne State University, 1979,* ed. C. Walter Hodges, S. Schoenbaum, and L. Leone (Detroit: Wayne State University Press, 1981), pp. 130–63. For other views of the Renaissance theater, see Stephen Orgel, *The Illusion of Power,* and Kent T. van den Berg, *Playhouse and Cosmos: Shakespearean Theater as Metaphor* (Newark: University of Delaware Press, 1985), esp. pp. 11–85. On the whole, scholars do not think that the first performance of *Henry V* was at the First Globe: see, for example, E. K. Chambers, *The Elizabethan Stage,* vol. 2 (Oxford: Clarendon Press, 1923), p. 203, and Peter Thomson, *Shakespeare's Theatre* (London: Routledge and Kegan Paul, 1983), pp. 60–64. Richard Hosley, however, thinks that *Henry V* was written for the Globe, where it was performed in 1599; see his "Playhouses," in *The "Revels" History of the Drama in English: Volume III, 1576–1613,* gen. eds. Clifford Leech and T. W. Craik (London: Methuen, 1975), p. 181. For a close consideration of the Theater, see *The First Public Playhouse: The Theatre in Shoreditch 1576–1598,* ed. Herbert Berry (McGill-Queens University Press, 1979). For pictorial evidence, see R. A. Foakes, *Illustrations of the English Stage, 1580–1642* (London: Scholar Press, 1985), esp. pp. xiii–xviii, 46–55, see chs. 24–26. For more information on the Theatre, Curtain, and Globe, see Chambers, pp. 383–404; Hosley, esp. p. 132; Michael Hattaway, *Elizabethan Popular Theatre: Plays in Performance* (London: Routledge and Kegan Paul, 1982), esp. pp. 11–14; and Glynne Wickham, *Early English Stages, 1300–1660,* vol. 2: 1576–1660, part 2 (London: Routledge and Kegan Paul, 1972), esp. pp. 63–78, pp. 110–17. For works on acting and playwrighting, see John Barton, *Playing Shakespeare* (London: Methuen, 1984); Michael Goldman, *Acting and Action in Shakespearean Tragedy* (Princeton: Princeton University Press, 1985); and Gerald Eades Bentley, *The Professions of Dramatist and Player in Shakespeare's Time, 1590–1642* (Princeton: Princeton University Press, 1986). Whereas Andrew Gurr's and John Orrell's *Rebuilding Shakespeare's Globe* (New York: Routledge, 1989) looks at the reconstruction of the most illustrious Elizabethan theater, Steven Mullaney's *Place of the Stage: License, Play, and Power in Renaissance England* (Chicago: University of Chicago Press, 1988) provides a materialist reading of Shakespeare's stage. It is sad that Shakespeare's fame can, admittedly after many efforts and centuries, save the Globe but condemn the Rose (a much more complete archaeological find). The political reason given for not saving the Rose was that it was not Shakespeare's theater. Whereas Alan T. Bradford argues for a seeming lack of parallelism between the architectural and literary situations in Elizabethan England ("Drama and Architecture under Elizabeth I: The 'Regular' Phase," *English Literary Renaissance* 14 [1984], esp. 3–7), Mullaney takes a different view when he asserts that it was the playhouses' location, and not their facilities and design, that impressed Elizabethans. He discusses the public playhouses in terms of their place, both as status and locale, and tries to discuss the material conditions of the Liberties, the places beyond the walls of London, as the context for the physical, moral, and ideological "architecture" of Shakespeare's theater (pp. 26–59, esp. 30). Jean Howard examines the material nature of the relation among dress, theater, and gender in early modern England: "Dramas in which women dress as men . . . are my main concern, and the question is: do they present constructions of woman that challenge her subordinate place in the Renaissance sex-gender system and so, perhaps, lead to the transformation of that system? Or do they recuperate, countervail, the threat the figure posed in the streets of London and in the symbolic economy of the period?" See "Crossdressing, the Theatre, and Gender Struggle in Early Modern England," *Shakespeare Quarterly* 39 (1988), 430. In discussing George Puttenham's *Arte of Englishe Poesie* (1589), Jonathan Crewe says: "His own *Arte* testifies as strongly as any document of its time to the intense theatricality of Elizabethan courtly-political life, and hence to the possible constitutiveness of the theatrical 'metaphor.' Yet Puttenham doesn't lose sight of the phenomenon of theater as one material institution among others in the world." See Jonathan V. Crewe, "The Hegemonic Theater of George Puttenham," *English Literary Renaissance* 16 (1986), 71. In the Afterword I use the discussion of the cultural materiality of the theater to provide a further context for the metaphor of theater and world.

3. "A Preface of Simon Grineus to the Reader as concerning the profite of reading Hystories"—that is, *De utilitate legendae historiae* (1531)—prefixed to Golding's translation of *Thabridgment of the Histories of Trogus Pompeius* (1564) sig. a1r, quoted in Herschel Baker, *The Race of Time*, p. 47. Baker notes: "Grynaeus' popular treatise was also included in Thomas Lodge's translation of Josephus (1602) and in George Wilkins' of Justin (1606)" (pp. 103–4). For some recent revisionist discussions of history in Shakespeare and in the Renaissance, see Jonathan Dollimore, "Introduction: Shakespeare, Cultural Materialism, and the New Historicism," in *Political Shakespeare: New Essays in Cultural Materialism*, ed. J. Dollimore and A. Sinfield (Ithaca: Cornell University Press, 1985), pp. 2–17; in the same volume, see Leonard Tennenhouse, "Strategies of State and Political Plays: *A Midsummer Night's Dream, Henry IV, Henry V, Henry VIII*," pp. 109–29; Louis Montrose,

"Renaissance Literary Studies and theSubject of History," *English Literary Renaissance* 16 (1986), 5–12, and, in the same issue, Jean E. Howard, "The New Historicism in Renaissance Studies," 13–43. See also A. D. Nuttall, *A New Mimesis: Shakespeare and the Representation of Reality* (London: Methuen, 1983), esp. pp. 1–51, 143–63; *Alternative Shakespeares*, ed. John Drakakis (London: Methuen, 1985), in relation to the histories, especially Drakakis's Introduction and the articles by Terence Hawkes, Christopher Norris, and Dollimore and Sinfield, pp. 1–67, 206–28; and Ekbert Faas, *Shakespeare's Poetics* (Cambridge: Cambridge University Press, 1986), esp. pp. 28–79, 144–49. Calls are now arising for a history and historiography that differs from those that new historicism offers. A. R. Branmuller, for instance, says that Holinshed, Shakespeare, and Hayward all reimagined their historical sources "by removing text from its original (fictive) conceptualization and embedding it in a new one." See *"King John* and Historiography," *English Literary History* 55 (1988), 327, see 309–32. Leeds Barroll calls for the new history to avoid a postmodern form of positivism and "to deal with the profound problems posed by the notion of the historical 'event.' " See "A New History for Shakespeare and His Time," *Shakespeare Quarterly* 39 (1988), 464, see 441–64.

4. Thomas Heywood, *An Apology for Actors*, London, 1612 (London: Shakespeare Society Reprint, 1841), p. 13, cited in Yates, *Theater of the World*, pp. 164–65: here corrected. I thank G. Blakemore Evans for informing me that this reprint is untrustworthy. Kernan aptly points out the paradox of the relation of the theater to the world in the Renaissance; playing and theater expressed the greatest hopes of humanity for freedom and change but also represented a sense of human helplessness and the transience of life and world ["Plays," in *"The Revels" History of Drama in English*, vol. 3, pp. 247–48].

5. See, for instance, Augustine, *The City of God*, (trans. Bettenson), esp. 13, chs. 1–3, and 14, chs 10–13; and de Man, "Temporality," in *Blindness and Insight*, pp. 187–229.

6. Richard calls attention to logic, self-conscious theatricality, and metaphor. For a more general discussion of these matters, see Gordon Teskey, "Theatrical Self-Reference in Shakespeare," *College English Association Critic* 46 (1984), 27–37.

7. As I argued in a paper to the Marlowe Society of America at the MLA in 1986, many of Marlowe's protagonists or antagonists die with the word "die" and so try to use their language to gain power over nature or at least to attempt to conflate word and world.

8. Henry's view of time is related closely to those about him. In *2 Henry IV*, as in *Richard II*, Shakespeare ironically connects time and necessity. An

important word in two scenes (III.i; IV.i), "necessity" represents the inevitability of events. The king claims that he has no intention of ascending the throne, but he "had" to because of Richard's misrule. How much can we trust Henry? In *Richard II* Shakespeare appears to qualify Bolingbroke's success through an ironic use of images such as those of rain, and in *2 Henry IV* he causes the king to admit that the crusade was a political diversion rather than an act of religious atonement. Whereas George Steevens (1793) says that Henry's memory is treacherous because at the time he is describing he had already ascended the throne, Edmond Malone (1790) interprets the lines "I had no such intent / But that necessity" as a conditional "*I should have had* no such intent" and asserts that Shakespeare (and not Bolingbroke) forgets his former play. Nonetheless, Matthias Shaaber (1940) maintains that although other editors have followed Malone's reading, "no one states positively that the clause is conditional." A. R. Humphreys (1966), however, thinks that Henry's view of necessity "should be taken as fact, not as hypocritical extenuation." (The editions of Steevens and Malone are cited in *The Second Part of Henry the Fourth,* ed. Matthias A. Shaaber, new variorum ed. (Philadelphia: J. B. Lippincott, 1940), p. 227, where his opinion is also found. Humphreys, p. 93; see also "Henry and Necessity" in the Introduction to his edition of *2 Henry IV*). Throughout the three plays in which Henry appears, Shakespeare represents a character torn between care and guilt on the one hand and policy and ruthless action on the other. To hide the politician in Henry, as Humphreys sometimes seems to do, is to represent only a part of his character. When the king is concerned with Richard's prophecy about Northumberland, Warwick claims that in "the hatch and brood of time" Richard could see the "necessary form" of events or, in other words, the "inevitable pattern" of cause and effect because he had studied past examples to interpret the present and the future (III.i.80–92) (Humphreys, p. 93; see my section on prophecy). By studying history, Warwick asserts, men may predict that a rotten acorn will grow to a rotten oak, but he neglects Richard's prediction that Bolingbroke's suspicion would increase the breach between Northumberland and the new king. Henry finds comfort and resolve in Warwick's idea of necessity and now views it as a cause of strength and action in fighting the rebels. It is Warwick's interpretation of history that enables the king to meet the immediate future with an unwavering will (III.i.93–94).

The second discussion of time and necessity in *2 Henry IV* occurs when Mowbray the younger maintains that Henry bruised the rebels into rebellion and that he now causes them to "suffer the condition of these times" with unequal honors. Westmoreland replies: "Construe the times to their necessities, / And you shall say, indeed, it is the time, / And not the King, that doth you injuries" (IV.i.104–6). He asks Mowbray the younger to consider the inevitability of the times—Westmoreland is arguing for determinism against free will—and, therefore, to blame time (and thus the times) and not Henry for the wrongs the rebels have suffered (*The Second Part of the History of Henry the Fourth,* ed. John Dover Wilson (Cambridge: Cambridge University Press), p. 183; Humphreys (New Arden ed.), p. 121; Shaaber (new variorum ed., p. 294) quotes Dr. Johnson [1765]: "Judge of what is done in these times according to the exigencies that overrule us." With conflicting interpretations, Mowbray the younger and Westmoreland cast their minds back to the events of the opening act of *Richard II.* Whereas Westmoreland reminds Mowbray the younger that Bolingbroke restored Norfolk's lands, Mowbray the younger curses the day Richard stopped the battle between Hereford and Mowbray the elder (IV.i.107–59). As in *Richard II,* there is no simple resolution to these complicated events. Necessity, then, may be the ineluctable force that spurs the free will into action or a determinism that excuses that will from responsibility. Ironically, two men of the king's party, Warwick and Northumberland, use both positions to justify Henry's actions, past and future. Time is a many-headed beast, showing more than satiric isolation, for it makes the audience look backward and forward to history and tragedy and comedy on the one hand and to history and the problem play on the other.

For additional discussions of the shapes of time, see B. T. Spencer, "*2 Henry IV* and the Theme of Time," *University of Toronto Quarterly* 13 (1944), 394–99; L. C. Knights, "Time's Subjects: The Sonnets and *King Henry IV, Part II,*" in *Some Shakespearean Themes* (London: Chatto and Windus, 1959); Paul A. Jorgensen, " 'Redeeming Time' in Shakespeare's *Henry IV,*" *Tennessee Studies in Literature* 5 (1960), 101–9; Ricardo Quinones, *The Renaissance Discovery of Time* (Cambridge, Mass.: Harvard University Press, 1972); David Scott Kastan, "The Shape of Time: Form and Value in the Shakespearean History Play," *Comparative Drama* 7 (1973–74), 259–77; David Scott Kastan, *Shakespeare and the Shapes of Time* (Hanover, N.H.: University Press of New England, 1982), esp. pp. 3–79; David Scott Kastan, " 'To Set a Form upon that Indigest': Shakespeare's Fictions of History," *Comparative Drama* 17 (1983–84), 1–16; and Peter Munz, *The Shapes of Time: A New Look at the Philosophy of History* (Middletown, Conn.: Wesleyan University Press, 1977), esp. pp. 1–22, 246–301.

9. See "mete" definition v⁴ in *OED* and Carter (1905), p. 282, cited in Shaaber (new variorum ed.), p. 349.

10. Whereas Dover Wilson (p. 171) cites Plutarch's *Lives* and *A Mirror for Magistrates* as examples of this doctrine, Shaaber (p. 228) refers to Walley (1748), who quotes book 7, section 49, of the *Antonius* of Marcus Aurelius. However, Aurelius may not have been known to Shakespeare.

11. *2 HIV*, IV.iv. 125–28. Holinshed, iii. 540; Stone, p. 158, cited in Dover Wilson, p. 193. Shaaber (p. 89) supports the attribution of this echo when he refers to Ax (1912), who located the passage in Holinshed. Nonetheless, Humphreys says that none of the chronicles "connect[s] such an occurrence with Edward III's death" (p. 145). Perhaps Shakespeare's echo and alteration of the chronicles reflects his ironic view of the "making" of history, although he could have made the changes for many reasons.

12. Nevertheless, history is dramatic, and drama shares much with history. See R. G. Collingwood, *The Idea of History*, ed. T. M. Knox (Oxford: Clarendon Press, 1946, rpt. 1948), esp. pp. 214–15, 219, and Driver, esp. pp. 5–17, 204–11.

13. Shakespeare then has Ely utter the proverb "If you will France win, / Then with Scotland first begin," which is found in Hall and Holinshed, who both assign this speech to Westmoreland (I.ii.166–67). In the details Shakespeare is once again changing "history." See Branmuller, note 3, above, who reminds us that Holinshed did the same thing.

14. See, for instance, Anne Righter, *Shakespeare and the Idea of the Play* (London: Chatto and Windus, 1962); Lionel Abel, *Metatheatre: A New View of Dramatic Form* (New York: Hill and Wang, 1963); and James Winny, *The Player King: A Theme of Shakespeare's Histories* (London: Chatto and Windus, 1968). For a more specific analysis of acting and military action, see James Black, "Counterfeits of Soldiership in *Henry IV*," *Shakespeare Quarterly* 24 (1973), 372–82. A related but different kind of theatricality occurs in the Tudor cult of chivalry. See, for instance, Julia Briggs, *This Stage-Play World: English Literature and Its Background, 1580–1625* (Oxford: Oxford University Press, 1983), and Arthur B. Ferguson, *The Chivalric Tradition in Renaissance England* (Washington: Folger Shakespeare Library, 1986). As we shall observe, the cult of Elizabeth was not without its theatrical possibilities.

15. Through the ironic use of garden imagery, Shakespeare generalizes the fall of Richard to the fall of England. It is as if Richard and England have fallen before the action of *Richard II*, as if the murder of Gloucester were an echo of original sin or, in the memories of the characters, when words and things no longer coincided. The characters speak about England as this "other Eden" suffering a second Fall (II.i.42, 59–60). See the section on garden imagery in chapter 1.

16. Humphreys, *1 Henry IV*, p. 56.

17. Dover Wilson, *1 Henry IV*, pp. 153–54; Humphreys, p. 77; J. C. Maxwell, "Appendix V," in Humphreys, pp. 199–200.

18. George Peele (Malone Society, lines 584–618), cited in Humphreys, *2 Henry IV*, p. 74; Dover Wilson, *2 Henry IV*, pp. 162–63.

19. Peele's *Battle of Alcazar, Alphonsus,* and *The Turkish Mahamet and*

Hyrin The Fair Greek, cited in Humphreys (pp. 73–74), who credits Malone with hearing the echo from *Alcazar*. See Dover Wilson, pp. 161–62. Is Hyrin the Hostess's Hiren?

20. Righter, pp. 139–43. See Barish. In a complementary study to Barish's, Michael O'Connell explores "the contrasting ways Shakespeare and Jonson defined their dramaturgy in response to this post-Reformation alteration of perceptual values." "The Idolatrous Eye: Iconoclasm, Anti-theatricalism, and the Image of the Elizabethan Theater," *English Literary History* 52 (1985), 282, see 279–310.

21. Hawkins, *History of Music* (1776), iii.30, attributes the poem to Anne, but F. M. Padelford, *Early Sixteenth-century Lyrics* (pp. 102, 148) to George, cited in Humphreys, p. 76.

22. See Sonnet 87.13–14: "Thus have I had thee as a dream doth flatter: / In sleep a king, but waking no such matter" (lines 13–14), quoted from *Shakespeare's Sonnets*, ed. Stephen Booth (New Haven: Yale University Press, 1977), p. 76; see Stephen Booth, ed., *Shakespeare's Sonnets*, p. 291, for commentary on the dichotomy between substance and illusion; see also Walter, ed., *Henry V*, p. 104. For a discussion of ceremony in a Roman tragic history or historical tragedy, *Julius Caesar*, in relation to authority in the year that Shakespeare probably wrote this play and *Henry V*, see Mark Rose, "Conjuring Caesar: Ceremony, History, and Authority in 1599," *English Literary Renaissance* 19 (1989), 291–304.

23. This relation between inside and outside occurs in the Chorus's use of apostrophe in *Henry V* and in Marlowe's plays.

24. For a detailed view of these scenes, see Sheldon P. Zitner, "Aumerle's Conspiracy," *Studies in English Literature, 1500–1900* 14 (1974), 239–57; see also Waldo F. McNeir, "The Comic Scenes in *Richard II*," *Neuphilologische Mitteilungen* 73 (1972), 815–22; Leonard Barkan, "The Theatrical Consistency of *Richard II*," *Shakespeare Quarterly* 29 (1978), 5–19; Phyllis Rackin, "The Role of the Audience in Shakespeare's *Richard II*," *Shakespeare Quarterly* 36 (1985), 262–81.

25. Ure, *Richard II*, p. 163; Humphreys, *2 Henry IV*, p. 174.

26. Dover Wilson, *2 Henry IV*, p. 127. For a discussion of personification and Rumor, see Richard Abrams, "Rumour's Reign in *2 Henry IV*: The Scope of Personification," *English Literary Renaissance* 16 (1986), 467–95.

27. Humphreys, p. 186.

28. Ibid. The Oldcastle controversy might also make the audience aware of the close relation between history as event and history as writing. The disclaimer may show Shakespeare getting around censorship while using the contrast between Oldcastle and Falstaff for ironic purposes: whereas the martyr was a Lollard, Sir John mocks Puritans ("heretics") and dies of a

sweat. Perhaps Shakespeare suspects that to kill a popular comic character like Falstaff may be akin to making a martyr and possibly sacrificing a popular play. See Humphreys's note, p. 186. In his Introduction to *1* and *2 Henry IV* in *The Riverside Shakespeare*, ed. G. Blakemore Evans (Boston: Houghton Mifflin, 1974), Herschel Baker mentions the evidence for revision in Parts One (I.ii.41) and Two (I.ii.20) in the traces of the name Oldcastle in the texts. In an apparent addition to the Epilogue to *2 Henry IV*, Baker argues, Shakespeare distinguishes between the historical Oldcastle (Lord Cobham) and the characters Oldcastle and Falstaff, the latter once called after the Oldcastle of *Famous Victories*. Taking up the traditional view of Shakespearean scholars, Baker also suggests that in deference to the contemporary Lord Cobham Shakespeare changed Oldcastle to Falstaff, as well as Harvey and Russell to Peto and Bardolph (*1HIV*, I.ii.162; *2HIV*, II.ii.0.s.d) (843). The prologue to *Sir John Oldcastle* (acted in 1599 and printed in 1600), by Drayton, Munday, Wilson, and Hathaway, alludes to Shakespeare's distortion of Lord Cobham's character (843).

29. For recent views, see G. P. Jones, "*Henry V*: The Chorus and the Audience," *Shakespeare Survey* 31 (1978), 93–105; Anthony S. Brennan, "That Within Which Passes Show: The Function of the Chorus in *Henry V*," *Philological Quarterly* 58 (1979), 40–52; and Lawrence Danson, "*Henry V*: King, Chorus, and Critics," *Shakespeare Quarterly* 34 (1983), esp. 27–33. See also Anne Barton, "The King Disguised," p. 92. For a more general view of the theater, including the Chorus, see van den Berg, "Heroism, History, and the Theater in *Henry V*," in *Playhouse and Cosmos*, pp. 102–25. For a textual discussion, see Warren D. Smith, "The *Henry V* Choruses in the First Folio," *Journal of English and Germanic Philology* 53 (1954), 38–57.

30. Alvin Kernan, *The Playwright as Magician: Shakespeare's Image of the Poet in the English Public Theater* (New Haven: Yale University Press, 1979), esp. pp. 157–58.

31. Walter, p. 5; Taylor, p. 91. See Edward P. J. Corbett, *Classical Rhetoric for the Modern Student*, 2d. ed. (New York: Oxford University Press, 1971), pp. 16, 33–36, 45; see also Sidney, quoted in Walter, p. 5.

32. See Taylor, p. 91.

33. See Sonnet 55: "Not marble, nor all the guilded monuments / Of princes shall outlive this pow'rful rhyme" (lines 1–2), quoted from *Shakespeare's Sonnets*, ed. Stephen Booth, pp. 48–51. In connection with this idea, Booth (p. 227) follows earlier critics when he quotes from Horace, *Odes*, III.xxx.

34. William Shakespeare, *King Henry V*, ed. John Dover Wilson (Cambridge: Cambridge University Press, 1947), p. 122; see Walter, p. 6; Taylor, p. 92. For a different emphasis, see David Willbern, "Shakespeare's Noth-

ing," in *Representing Shakespeare: New Psychoanalytic Essays*, ed. Murray Schwartz and Coppélia Kahn (Baltimore: Johns Hopkins University Press, 1980), esp. 255–57.

35. Jonathan Culler, "Apostrophe," in *The Pursuit of Signs: Semiotics, Literature, Deconstruction* (Ithaca: Cornell University Press, 1981), pp. 135–55. For a different view of apostrophe and the lyric, see Barbara Johnson, "Apostrophe, Animation, and Abortion," *Diacritics* 16 (1986), 29–49. Puttenham, pp. 237–39. Aristotle and Quintilian are instrumental in conveying notions of apostrophe in antiquity and influence those that occur in the Renaissance.

36. Dover Wilson, *Henry V*, pp. xiv–xv, 123; Taylor, p. 92.

37. Dover Wilson, pp. 113–14; Walter, pp. xxxvi–xxxvii, 30. I shall heed Kristian Smidt's advice about basing interpretation on especially garbled texts, realizing that—to our knowledge—Shakespeare did not "authorize" any of his plays, so that we must interpret with what we have; see *Unconformities in Shakespeare's History Plays* (London: Macmillan, 1982).

38. The complexity of Shakespeare's history plays can be seen by the diverse response to them. Because I have assumed a thorough knowledge of earlier criticism, without which our present debates would not be possible, I have not referred previously to some of these works. See, for instance: Thomas Courtenay, *Commentaries on the Historical Plays of Shakespeare* (1840; New York: AMS Press, 1972), vols. 1 and 2; Tillyard, *Shakespeare's History Plays*; Leonard F. Dean, "Tudor Theories of Historical Writing," in *University of Michigan Contributors to Modern Philology* 1 (1941), pp. 1–24, and "From Richard II to Henry V: A Closer View," in *Shakespeare: Modern Essays in Criticism*, ed. L. F. Dean, rev. ed. (New York: Oxford University Press, 1967); John Dover Wilson, *The Fortunes of Falstaff* (Cambridge: Cambridge University Press, 1943); Lily B. Campbell, *Shakespeare's "Histories": Mirrors of Elizabethan Policy* (San Marino, Calif.: Huntington Library, 1947); Josephine Pierce, "Constituent Elements in Shakespeare's English History Plays," in *Studies in Shakespeare*, ed. A. Matthews and C. Emery (1953; New York: AMS Press, 1971), esp. p. 150; Derek Traversi, *Shakespeare from "Richard II" to "Henry V"* (Stanford: Stanford University Press, 1957); Ribner, *The English History Play;* M. M. Reese, *The Cease of Majesty: A Study of Shakespeare's History Plays* (London: Arnold, 1961), pp. 159–63; S. C. Sen Gupta, *Shakespeare's Historical Plays* (London: Oxford University Press, 1964); Wilbur Sanders, *The Dramatist and the Received Idea: Studies in the Plays of Marlowe and Shakespeare* (Cambridge: Cambridge University Press, 1968); Robert Pierce, *Shakespeare's History Plays: The Family and the State* (Columbus: Ohio State University Press, 1971); Ornstein, *A Kingdom for a Stage;* Michael Manheim, *The Weak King Dilemma in the Shakespearean*

History Play (Syracuse: Syracuse University Press, 1973), Prior, The Drama of Power; Paul Bacquet, Les pièces historiques de Shakespeare: La deuxième tétralogie et "Henri VIII," vol. 2 (Paris: Presses universitaires de France, 1979); Coursen, The Leasing Out of England; Holderness, Shakespeare's History; and Robin H. Wells, Shakespeare, Politics, and the State (London: Macmillan, 1986). For views of the history play in various periods, see Herbert Lindenberger, Historical Drama: The Relation of Literature to Drama (Chicago: University of Chicago Press, 1975),and Matthew H. Wikander, The Play of Truth and State: Historical Drama from Shakespeare to Brecht (Baltimore: Johns Hopkins University Press, 1986), pp. 13–49.

NOTES TO CHAPTER FOUR

1. For instance, see Anne Barton, "Shakespeare: His Tragedies," pp. 215–16; Doran, Endeavors of Art, pp. 112–13; and Brockbank, "Shakespeare: His Histories," p. 166. For a perceptive view on the importance of Bolingbroke and history to the play, see John R. Elliott, Jr., "History and Tragedy in Richard II," Studies in English Literature, 1500–1900 8 (1968), 253–71.

2. Aristotle, "On the Art of Poetry" (Penguin), pp. 43–44; Ullmann, "History and Tragedy," pp. 26, 40, 53; and Sidney, pp. 5, 14, 17–20.

3. A. C. Bradley, Shakespearean Tragedy: Lectures on "Hamlet," "Othello," "King Lear," "Macbeth" (1904, 1905; London: Macmillan, 1957), pp. 10–26. See Kenneth Muir, "Shakespeare and the Tragic Pattern," Publications of the British Academy 44 (1959), 145–49. For other views of tragedy, see, for example, J. M. R. Margeson, The Origins of English Tragedy (Oxford: Clarendon Press, 1967); Stephen Booth, "King Lear," "Macbeth," Indefinition, and Tragedy (New Haven: Yale University Press, 1983), esp. pp. 5–20; Jonathan Dollimore, Radical Tragedy: Religion, Ideology and Power in the Drama of Shakespeare and His Contemporaries (Chicago: University of Chicago Press, 1984), pp. 49–56, 156–58; and Catherine Belsey, The Subject of Tragedy: Identity and Difference in Renaissance Drama (London: Methuen, 1985), esp. pp. 3–16. Other books on Shakespeare's tragedy are Howard Felperin, Shakespearean Representation: Mimesis and Modernity in Elizabethan Tragedy (Princeton: Princeton University Press, 1977); Phyllis Rackin, Shakespeare's Tragedies (New York: Ungar, 1978); Bertrand Evans, Shakespeare's Tragic Practice (Oxford: Oxford University Press, 1979); P. N. Siegel, Shakespearean Tragedy and the Elizabethan Compromise: A Marxist Study (Washington: University Press of America, 1983); J. Leeds Baroll, Shakespearean Tragedy

(Washington: Folger Books, 1984); and Thomas McAlinden, *English Renaissance Tragedy* (London: Macmillan, 1986).

4. Francis Bolen, *Irony and Self-Knowledge in the Creation of Tragedy*, Salzburg Studies in English Literature 19 (Salzburg: Universität Salzburg, 1973), pp. 5–8. Frye, *Anatomy*, p. 207; and States, *Irony and Drama*, pp. xii, xvii–xviii, 13–15.

5. Thirlwall, "On the Irony of Sophocles," pp. 1–5. See G. G. Sedgewick, pp. 26, 59, 83, 91–92; Worcester, pp. 112–15, 138–41; Thompson, pp. 143–48; and Robert Sharpe, *Irony in the Drama: An Essay on Impersonation, Shock, and Catharsis* (Chapel Hill: University of North Carolina Press, 1959), pp. 65, 84–85.

6. For a similar view of the difficulty of defining comedy, see Madeleine Doran, *Endeavors of Art*, p. 148, and H. D. Howarth, "Introduction: Theoretical Considerations," in *Comic Drama: The European Heritage*, ed. H. D. Howarth (London: Methuen, 1978), p. 1. For a subtle and wide-ranging exploration of comedy, see Harry Levin, *Playboys and Killjoys: An Essay on the Theory and Practice of Comedy* (New York: Oxford University Press, 1987). Levin observes something that applies particularly well to the dark, or problem, comedies, to the problem play: "The most protean aspect of comedy is its potentiality for transcending itself, for responding to the conditions of tragedy by laughing in the darkness" (132). Levin's essay is a tour de force of comparative theory and criticism. His method is pluralistic and exhaustively rather than gesturally contextual. Comedy, like the novel, attracts Levin partly because it is a social institution, partly because Aristotle did not codify its rules, and partly because it complicates our view of realism. He discusses comic drama from its dark, anthropological origins to the various enigmatic spaces of our comic stage. Comedy, Levin says, recycles its oldest conventions. Its first principle is the pleasure principle, whereas its second, and secondary, principle is ridicule, antagonism, and malice. This is the most important study of comedy in years. For a discussion of *Playboys and Killjoys* in relation to the traditions of comedy and realism, see Jonathan Hart, "Playboys, Killjoys, and a Career as Critic: The Accomplishment of Harry Levin," *Canadian Review of Comparative Literature* 16 (1989), 118–35, esp. 126–35. The intractability of defining Shakespearean comedy is a view shared by the following works: Kenneth Muir, Introduction to *Shakespeare: The Comedies: A Collection of Critical Essays* (Englewood Cliffs: Prentice-Hall, 1965), p. 2; Ralph Berry, *Shakespeare's Comedies: Explorations in Form* (Princeton: Princeton University Press, 1972), pp. 3–5; and J. L. Styan, "The Delicate Balance: Audience Ambivalence in the Comedy of Shakespeare and Chekhov," *Costerus* 2 (1972), 159–60. For descriptions of comedy that also stress community, see Northrop Frye,

"The Argument of Comedy" (1948), in *Theories of Comedy*, ed. Paul Lauter (Garden City: Doubleday, 1964), pp. 451–54, and Frye, *Anatomy*, p. 218; Albert Cook, *The Dark Voyage and the Golden Mean: A Philosophy of Comedy* (Cambridge, Mass.: Harvard University Press, 1949), p. 59; Herbert McArthur, "Tragic and Comic Modes," *Criticism* 3 (1961), 36–45; and Robert Tener, *The Phoenix Riddle: A Study of Irony in Comedy*, Salzburg Studies in English 44 (Salzburg: Universität Salzburg, 1979), pp. 45, 199.

7. For a similar view that the ironies serving tragedy and comedy are alike, see G. G. Sedgewick, p. 26. For festive and celebrative views of comedy, see C. L. Barber, *Shakespeare's Festive Comedy: A Study of Dramatic Form and Its Relation to Social Custom* (Princeton: Princeton University Press, 1959), especially the chapter on the *Henry IV* plays; and Mikhail M. Bakhtin, *Rabelais and His World*, trans. Helene Iswolsky (Cambridge, Mass.: MIT Press, 1968), particularly the discussion of the carnival in the Introduction. For a view of genre that relates to that of the German romantics, see P. N. Medvedev and M. M. Bakhtin, *The Formal Method in Literary Scholarship: A Critical Introduction to Sociological Poetics*, trans. Albert J. Wehrle (Baltimore: Johns Hopkins University Press, 1978), pp. 129–41, 151–59, 170–75; see Wehrle's Introduction, pp. xiv, xxi-xxii. Adam Müller's "monologic" and "dialogic" may have influenced Bakhtin.

8. For a similar view, see L. C. Knights, "Notes on Comedy" (1933), in Lauter, pp. 438–43; Frye, "Argument," pp. 458–59; Ralph Berry, *Shakespeare's Comedies*, p. 4. This comic history play may have had a specific historical context. E. K. Chambers notes: "On 6 March 1600 the company had an opportunity of rendering direct advice to their patron Lord Hunsdon, by playing *Henry IV*, still oddly called *Sir John Oldcastle*, after a dinner which he gave to the Flemish ambassador, Ludovic Verreyken, presumably at his house in the Blackfriars" (p. 204, see p. 196). For recent discussions of Shakespearean comedy that provide different emphases, see Linda Bamber; Marianne Novy; Z. J. Jagendorf, *The Happy End of Comedy: Shakespeare, Jonson, Molière* (Newark: University of Delaware Press, 1984); Joseph Westlund, *Shakespeare's Reparative Comedies: A Psychoanalytic View of the Middle Plays* (Chicago: University of Chicago Press, 1984); Catherine Belsey, "Disrupting Sexual Difference: Meaning and Gender in the Comedies," in *Alternative Shakespeares*, ed. J. Drakakis (London: Methuen, 1985), pp. 166–90; Edward Berry, *Shakespeare's Comic Rites* (Cambridge: Cambridge University Press, 1985); Richard Levin, *Love and Society in Shakespearean Comedy: A Study of Dramatic Form and Content* (Newark: University of Delaware Press, 1985); T. W. MacCary, *Friends and Lovers: The Phenomenology of Desire in Shakespeare's Comedy* (New York: Columbia University Press, 1985); J. A. Bryant, Jr., *Shakespeare and the Uses of Comedy* (Lexington: University Press

of Kentucky, 1986); Barbara J. Bono, "Mixed Gender, Mixed Genre in Shakespeare's *As You Like It*," in *Renaissance Genres*, ed. B. K. Lewalski (Cambridge, Mass.: Harvard University Press, 1986), pp. 189–212; W. C. Carroll, *The Metamorphoses of Shakespearean Comedy* (Princeton: Princeton University Press, 1986); Louis Montrose, "*A Midsummer Night's Dream* and the Shaping Fantasies of Elizabethan Culture: Gender, Power, Form," in *Rewriting the Renaissance*, ed. M.W. Ferguson, M. Quilligan, and N. Vickers (Chicago: University of Chicago Press, 1986), pp. 65–87; Robert Ornstein, *Shakespeare's Comedies: From Roman Farce to Romantic Mystery* (Newark: University of Delaware Press, 1986); and M. L. Williamson, *The Patriarchy of Shakespeare's Comedies* (Detroit: Wayne State University Press, 1986). In "Staging Carnival: Comedy and the Politics of the Aristocratic Body," in *Power on Display*, Leonard Tennenhouse asserts: "The drama, too, made love its obsessive concern. . . . From a literary historical viewpoint, perhaps the most important manifestation of the new *ars erotica*, was the rise of the public theater which worked variations within the same problematic of desire" (p. 17; see pp. 17–71). Although Mary Beth Rose chooses not to emphasize "the interlocking connections between literary expression and configurations of political power" (she discusses *Troilus and Cressida* but not the English histories), she examines historically the relation of sexuality to private life, an examination that bears indirectly on the connection between sex and politics and directly on sexual politics in the problem play. See *The Expense of Spirit: Love and Sexuality in English Renaissance Drama* (Ithaca: Cornell University Press, 1988), pp. ix, 1–42, 199–230. For a view of the relation of genre to Elizabethan drama, and to Shakespearean comedy, see Jean E. Howard, "Crossdressing," pp. 418–40, esp. pp. 430–36.

9. E. K. Chambers, II, 196–204. See Dover Wilson, *The Fortunes of Falstaff*.

10. For views of the relation of satire to tragedy, see Northrop Frye, "The Nature of Satire," in *Satura: Ein Kompendium moderner Studien zur Satire*, ed. Bernard Fabian (Hildesheim: Georges Olms, 1975), p. 122 (originally published in *University of Toronto Quarterly* [October 1944], 75–89) and Frye's *Anatomy*, p. 228; Maynard Mack, "The Muse of Satire," in *Satura*, p. 100 (originally published in *Yale Review* 41 [1951], 80–92); and Alvin Kernan, *Cankered*, p. 192. For views of the relation of satire to comedy, see Frye, *Anatomy*, pp. 178, 223–24; Kernan, *Cankered*, p. 150; Charles A. Allen and G. D. Stephens, Preface to *Satire: Theory and Practice*, ed. C. A. Allen and G. D. Stephens (Belmont, Calif.: Wadsworth, 1962), p. v; Leonard Fineburg, *Introduction to Satire* (Ames: Iowa State University Press, 1967), p. 4; and Matthew Hodgart, *Satire* (London: Weidenfeld and Nicolson, 1969), pp. 188–89. For a discussion of the relation of satire,

tragedy, and comedy, see G. L. Hendrickson, "Satura Tota Nostra Est," in *Satire: Modern Essays in Criticism*, ed. Ronald Paulson (Englewood Cliffs, N.J.: Prentice-Hall, 1971), p. 37; (originally published in *Classical Philology* 22 [1927], 46–60); Frye, *Anatomy*, p. 225–29, 239; and Kernan, *Cankered*, pp. 20, 32–33. For a difficulty of defining satire, see O. G. Brockett, "Satire in English Drama," pp. 8, 28–29; Kernan, *Cankered*, p. 34; Gilbert Highet, *The Anatomy of Satire* (Princeton: Princeton University Press, 1962), p. 233; and W. O. S. Sutherland, Jr., *The Art of the Satirist: Essays on the Satire in Augustan England* (Austin: University of Texas Press, 1965), p. 9.

11. David Worcester, *The Art of Satire*, cites the *OED*, saying that the word "satire" entered the English language in 1509. For discussions of the etymology of the term "satire," see B. L. Ullmann, "The Present State of the Satura Question," *Studies in Philology* 17 (1920), 379–401; J. Wight Duff, *Roman Satire: Its Outlook on Social Life* (Berkeley: University of California Press, 1936), p. 20; Oscar J. Campbell, *Comicall Satyre and Shakespeare's "Troilus and Cressida"* (San Marino, Calif.: Huntington Library, 1938), pp. viii, 24–29; Brockett, p. 10; and Highet, *The Anatomy of Satire*, pp. 231–32. For a view maintaining that "satire" derives from the word "satura," but that "satirize" and "satirical" come from the Greek word "satyr," see Robert C. Elliott, *The Power of Satire: Magic, Ritual, Art* (Princeton: Princeton University Press, 1960), pp. 101–2.

12. O. J. Campbell, *Comicall Satyre*, passim, and his *Shakespeare's Satire* (New York: Oxford University Press, 1943), pp. x, 18–21; and Alice L. Birney, *Satiric Catharsis in Shakespeare: A Theory of Dramatic Structure* (Berkeley: University of California Press, 1973), pp. 15–16, 47, 53–64, 75–77. For a view suggesting that Falstaff is not a satirist, see Wyndham Lewis, "The Greatest Satire Is Nonmoral," in *Satire: Modern Essays in Criticism*, ed. Ronald Paulson (Englewood Cliffs, N.J.: Prentice-Hall, 1971), p. 72, excerpted from *Men without Art* (London, 1934).

13. For a similar view, see Kernan, *Cankered*, pp. 142–43. For a different approach, see David Bevington, "Shakespeare vs. Jonson on Satire," in *Shakespeare 1971: Proceedings of the World Shakespeare Congress, Vancouver, August 1971*, ed. Clifford Leech and J. M. R. Margeson (Toronto: University of Toronto Press, 1972), pp. 116–21. See also Michael Seidel, *Satiric Inheritance: Rabelais to Sterne* (Princeton: Princeton University Press, 1979), esp. p. 23. For recent discussions of Elizabethan satire, see Ian Donaldson, "Jonson and Anger," in *English Satire and the Satiric Tradition*, ed. Claude Rawson (Oxford: Basil Blackwell, 1984), pp. 56–71; John N. King, "Spenser's *Shepheardes Calender* and Protestant Pastoral Satire," in *Renaissance Genres*, ed. B. K. Lewalski (Cambridge, Mass.: Harvard University Press, 1986), pp. 369–98; and James S. Baumlin, "Generic Context of Elizabethan

Satire: Rhetoric, Poetic Theory, and Imitation," in *Renaissance Genres*, ed. Lewalski, pp. 444–67.

14. Birney, pp. 60–61, 76–77; see Frye, *Anatomy*, p. 66; Barber, ch. 8, and his "Saturnalia in the Henriad," in *Shakespeare: Modern Essays in Criticism*, ed. Leonard F. Dean (New York: Oxford University Press, 1957, rpt. 1975), pp. 176, 182, cited in Birney, p. 77. For a general view that concentrates more on the relation between carnival and ideology, see Michael Bristol, *Carnival and Theater: Plebeian Culture and the Structure of Authority in Renaissance England* (New York: Routledge, 1985).

15. Brockett, pp. 57–58, 272.

16. In *The Cankered Muse* Kernan mentions as satiric exempla Juvenal's *Satires* and Hieronymus Bosch's *Carrying of the Cross* and *The Temptation of Saint Antony*.

17. Hodgart, pp. 126–29; Earl Miner, "In Satire's Falling City," in *The Satirist's Art*, ed. H. James Jensen and Marvin R. Zirker, Jr. (Bloomington: Indiana University Press, 1972), pp. 3–5. In *Anatomy* (p. 234) Frye also observes fragmentation and disintegration in satire.

18. See Kernan, *Cankered*, p. 11, and Frye, *Anatomy*, p. 235, for general remarks on satiric imagery.

19. Frye, *Anatomy*, p. 223, see p. 177. See also Worcester, pp. v–vi; Brockett, p. 70; and Hodgart, p. 131.

20. Jonathan Swift, Preface to "A Tale of a Tub," in *"Gulliver's Travels" and Other Writings*, ed. Ricardo Quintana (New York: Modern Library, 1958), pp. 273–74.

21. Although I find Norman Rabkin's view provocative, I think that *Henry V* is a both/and play rather than an either/or play. Richard Levin's positions also contribute to the debate, but he thinks of irony too much as undercutting. Unlike Levin, I would say that William W. Lloyd's view of irony (1856) is ironic. See Rabkin's "Rabbits, Ducks, and *Henry V*," *Shakespeare Quarterly* 28 (1977), 279–96, and his "Either/Or: Responding to *Henry V*," in *Shakespeare and the Problem of Meaning* (Chicago: University of Chicago Press, 1981), pp. 33–62. See Richard Levin's *New Readings vs. Old Plays*, esp. pp. 4–5, 90–142, and his "Hazlitt on *Henry V*, and the Appropriation of Shakespeare," *Shakespeare Quarterly* 35 (1984), esp. 138. For other views, see John Jump, "Shakespeare and History," *Critical Quarterly* 17 (1953), 233–44; Zdeněk Stříbrný, "Henry V and History," in *Shakespeare in a Changing World: Essays on His Times and His Plays*, ed. A. Kettle (London: Lawrence and Wishart, 1964), pp. 84–101; Pierre Sahel, "Henry V, Roi Idéal?" *Études Anglaises* 28 (1975), 1–14; Gordon R. Smith, "Shakespeare's *Henry V*: Another Part of the Critical Forest," *Journal of the History of Ideas* 37 (1976), 3–26; E.W. Ives, "Shakespeare and History: Divergencies and

Agreements," *Shakespeare Survey* 38 (1985), 19–37; Jonathan Dollimore and Alan Sinfield, "History and Ideology," pp. 206–27; and Stephen Greenblatt, "Invisible Bullets," pp. 18–47.

22. Frederick Boas, *Shakspere and his Predecessors* (New York: Scribner's, 1896), p. 345; William W. Lawrence, *Shakespeare's Problem Comedies*, rev. ed. (1931; Harmondsworth: Penguin, 1960), p. 24; Peter Ure, *William Shakespeare: The Problem Plays* (London: Longmans and Green, 1961), pp. 7–8; R. A. Foakes, *Shakespeare: The Dark Comedies to the Last Plays: From Satire to Celebration* (London: Routledge and Kegan Paul, 1971), p. 61; Richard P. Wheeler, *Shakespeare's Development and the Problem Comedies: Turn and Counter-Turn* (Berkeley: University of California Press, 1981), pp. 1–2; and Northrop Frye, *The Myth of Deliverance: Reflections on Shakespeare's Problem Comedies* (Toronto: University of Toronto Press, 1983), pp. 8, 61–63.

23. In addition to these problems of structure and genre, critics have often stated the difficulty of defining a problem play or a problem comedy. For instance, see E. M. W. Tillyard, *Shakespeare's Problem Plays* (Toronto: University of Toronto Press, 1949), p. 1; Ure, *Problem Plays*, p. 7; and Ernest Schanzer, *The Problem Plays of Shakespeare: A Study of "Julius Caesar," "Measure for Measure," and "Antony and Cleopatra"* (London: Routledge and Kegan Paul, 1963), pp. ix, 5–6.

24. For the incongruities of structure, see the references listed in note 22, above. For the relation between appearance and actuality, see A. P. Rossiter, "The Problem Plays," in *Angel with Horns*, pp. 117–20; Terence Hawkes, *Shakespeare and the Reason: A Study of the Tragedies and Problem Plays* (London: Routledge and Kegan Paul, 1964), p. 73; and Frye, *Deliverance*, p. 63. For the difficult language of these plays, see Ure, *Problem Plays*, p. 8; Foakes, *Dark Comedies*, pp. 61–62; and Frye, *Deliverance*, p. 63. For views of the complexity of the problem plays and their effect on the audience, see Lawrence, pp. 21–22; see also Boas, p. 345; Rossiter, p. 128; Schanzer, p. 5; and Wheeler, pp. 1–2. The critics of the problem plays have mentioned their antiheroic, brooding, and dissatisfied nature. See Kenneth Muir and Stanley Wells, eds., *Aspects of Shakespeare's "Problem Plays"* (Cambridge: Cambridge University Press, 1982). In the larger context of a study of Shakespeare's skepticism, Graham Bradshaw uses Troilus's question— "What's aught, but as 'tis valu'ed?" (the terror of which, Bradshaw thinks, escapes the speaker)—as one of his points of departure (p. 1). He also discusses in detail *Troilus and Cressida* and *Measure for Measure*. See *Shakespeare's Scepticism* (Brighton: Harvester Press, 1987), esp. pp. 1–5, 126–218. In the context of a debate over new historicism, Anthony Dawson speaks not of theatrically achieved endings but of theatrical power in one of the problem plays. He observes: "Moretti refers to *Measure for Measure* as a 'deproblematizing' play,

but I am inclined to guard my perhaps old-fashioned notion of the text as problematic" (330). For Dawson's interesting historicizing of new historicism (including its localization in California) and his discussion of the problems of this problem play, see *"Measure for Measure,* New Historicism, and Theatrical Power," *Shakespeare Quarterly* 39 (1988), 330, see 328–41. See also Franco Moretti, "Representing Power: *Measure for Measure* in Its Time," in *The Power of Forms in the English Renaissance,* ed. Stephen Greenblatt (Norman: Pilgrim Books, 1982), pp. 139–56.

25. Lawrence, p. 28; Tillyard, *Problem Plays,* p. 6; Rossiter, pp. 124, 128; and Frye, *Deliverance,* p. 72, see pp. 70–71.

26. Tillyard, *Problem Plays,* pp. 6–7, thinks the two common attributes of the problem play are that a young man gets a shock and that the shock or "business that most promotes the process of growth is transacted at night." The young king, Henry the Fifth, gets such a shock at night when he debates with Williams and Bates.

27. Rossiter almost equates ambivalence in the history plays with the definition of the problem play; see pp. 126–28. Frye thinks that *Troilus* stresses a fallen world and fails to deliver its audience from it, and he connects the division and the collision of different worlds in the *Henry IV* plays, *Troilus,* and *Antony*; Frye, *Deliverance,* p. 72; see Hawkes, *Reason,* p. 73.

28. See the section "The Theater and Its Ironies" in chapter 3 for a more elaborate interpretation of the private and the public for Henry the Fourth and his son.

29. See, for instance, John W. Blanpied, *Time and the Artist*; see also an earlier formulation of his work in " 'Unfathered Heirs and Loathly Births of Nature': Bringing History to a Crisis in *2 Henry IV,"* *English Literary Renaissance* 5 (1975), 212–31. See Alvin Kernan, *The Playwright as Magician* and, more generally, his "Henriad: Shakespeare's Major History Plays," in *Modern Shakespearean Criticism: Essays on Style, Dramaturgy, and the Major Plays,* ed. A. Kernan (New York: Harcourt, 1970), pp. 245–75 (for an earlier version, see *Yale Review* 59 [1969], 3–32), and "Shakespeare and the Abstraction of History," in *Shakespeare: Pattern of Excelling Nature,* ed. D. Bevington and J. Halio (Newark: University of Delaware Press, 1978), esp. pp. 133–34.

30. Fluellen exposes Pistol as a "counterfeit": V.i.69; cf. III.vi.61.

31. For another view, see Brownwell Solomon, "Thematic Contraries and the Dramaturgy of *Henry V,"* *Shakespeare Quarterly* 31 (1980), 343–56. For an analysis of satire in the play, see Allan Gilbert, "Patriotism and Satire in *Henry V,"* in *Studies in Shakespeare,* ed. Arthur D. Matthews and C. M. Emery (1953; New York: AMS Press, 1971), pp. 40–64.

32. For act and scene division, see Introduction, *Henry V,* ed. J. H.

Walter, p. xxxv. For other views of the Chorus, see Barton, "The King Disguised," p. 92; and Danson, "King, Chorus, and Critics," esp. 27–33. For a more general article, see Jean-Marie Maguin, "Shakespeare's Structural Craft and Dramatic Technique in *Henry V*," *Cahiers Elisabéthains* 7 (1975), 51–67. In an interesting discussion of the text of *Henry V*, Annabel Patterson notes that the Chorus to act 5 did not appear in the First Quarto (thus in Shakespeare's lifetime) and that the first scene of act 1, the threats of violence against the citizens of Harfleur, Henry's soliloquy on the hardships of kingship, much of the wooing scene between Henry and Katherine, and a great deal more did not occur in the Quarto. Patterson says, "We simply do not know, in fact, what the performative version of *Henry V* was like" (p. 73), and she challenges the notion of a Bad Quarto, which privileges the First Folio version of this play. See Patterson, *Shakespeare and the Popular Voice* (Oxford: Blackwell, 1989), pp. 71–92.

33. Laurence Olivier's film captures the theatricality of the courtship and plans for marriage by drawing the scene back from the "fields of France" to the stage. For Olivier's consciously patriotic interpretation, see *"Henry V,"* in his *On Acting* (New York: Simon and Schuster, 1986), pp. 90–105.

34. For more general views on time and ending in fiction, see Frank Kermode, *The Sense of an Ending* (New York: Oxford University Press, 1967), esp. pp. 76–89, and Barbara Herrnstein Smith, *Poetic Closure* (Chicago: University of Chicago Press, 1968).

35. For a different view of parts of the structure, see Marilyn Williamson, "The Episode with Williams in *Henry V*," *Studies in English Literature, 1500–1900* 9 (1969), 275–82, and her "Courtship of Katherine and the Second Tetralogy," *Criticism* 17 (1975), 326–34.

36. Another structural complication that irony helps create is the balance between English threats and French boasting. We have observed a similar use of ironic balance in the three previous plays. Here, Shakespeare balances Henry's heroism and shortcomings with French presumption and, to a lesser extent, moderation. By act 3, scene 4, the audience should expect a wavelike pattern of French insult, English threat, and French defeat. Through agents, the Dauphin scorns Henry, and Henry menaces him (I.ii.246f.; II.iv). Henry threatens Harfleur and overcomes the French who resist him (III.iii). The French disdain Henry and he returns their taunts (III.v.122–71). The pattern of insult, threat, and defeat recurs (III.vii; IV.ii, viii; see IV.iii, v, vii). The king's penchant for disguise and tricks also resurfaces, from Boar's Head to glove incident. What is the difference between the king's tricks and Falstaff's playing dead? The disguised king finds kingship questioned. Like Richard and Henry the Fourth, who had also described kingship in images of insomnia, Henry laments the tribulations of being a king (IV.i.236f.; cf. *RII*,

III.ii.155f.; V.i.35f., v.67; *2 HIV*, III.i.4f.). Structural patterns have their history.

37. The French and the captains have views of history. The Constable tells the Dauphin that Henry covers "discretion with a coat of folly," implying that the English king will use the deception to defeat the French as Lucius Junius Brutus had done to save his life from his uncle, Tarquinus Superbus, and to expel the Tarquins from Rome (II.iv.29–40, see III.v) (editions of *Henry V*: Walter, p. 51; Taylor, p. 148; and Dover Wilson, lines 1807–17). Here, the Constable rightly assesses Henry's ability to act and the French blindness to it, deprecating his nation and lauding Henry. Hotspur, Henry the Fourth, and Falstaff had been ignorant of the true scope of Hal's acting and action. The language of classical history dignifies both the Constable and Henry at this point in the play. The French king echoes Canterbury in saying that Henry is descended from a fearful and bloody strain of warriors who had won France (II.iv.48–64; see III.v). The patriotic and epic parts of the play are undeniable. The English and French kings are usurpers, but, not surprisingly, both interpret the Salic Law in a different fashion, seemingly to serve their own present purposes. Henry and Fluellen refer to Alexander without entirely heroic effect. Before Harfleur, Henry exhorts his "noblest English" and likens their fathers to "so many Alexanders" (III.i.17–25). Ironically, this allusion may refer more specifically to Juvenal's treatment of Alexander the Great in "Satire X," in which the author says: "One globe is not enough for the youth from Pella . . . yet he will be contented with a sarcophagus," a statement that will apply equally to Henry and the English (lines 168–72, quoted in Taylor, p. 158; see Walter, p. 59). The king himself is a complex character and is not so reliable in his view of the past. Having been so sure in public that God was defending his right, in private Henry doubts his claim to the English crown, implores God's pardon for his father's murder of Richard, and tells us how he has tried to atone for that "fault" (IV.i.298–311). He still wants to conquer France and can punish Nym and Bardolph without a twinge of conscience. When Fluellen compares Henry to Alexander the Pig, his slip may be in part appropriate, for the king is both kind and ruthless. Fluellen is Welsh and is proud of his kinship with Welsh Henry, but, as the Welsh captain knows more about Alexander than Macedon, the comparison between the ancient conqueror and Henry is not entirely ludicrous, whereas the one between Macedon and Wales is. The foolish content of Fluellen's analogy contrasts ironically with the rigor with which he follows accepted rhetorical order (T. W. Baldwin, *William Shakspere's Small Latine and Lesse Greeke* [Urbana: University of Illinois Press, 1944]), 2:336–38, cited in Walter, p. 124; see Taylor, pp. 44–45; for another, more detailed view, see Robert P. Merrix,

"The Alexandrian Allusion in Shakespeare's *Henry V*," *English Literary Renaissance* 2 [1972], 321–33). Whereas, as the Welsh captain notes, Alexander was drunk when he slew his friend Cleitus, Henry was sober when he rejected Falstaff. Although Henry's self-control is commendable, Fluellen's reference revives the ambivalence of the rejection in *2 Henry IV* and shows that the traces of the controversy remain in *Henry V* and that a crisis in history and the history play informs many aspects of the play's structure and intertextuality.

38. Taylor, p. 208.

39. Taylor, p. 217; Walter, p. 102.

NOTES TO THE AFTERWORD

1. For discussions of nominalism, see F. C. Copleston, *A History of Medieval Philosophy* (London: Methuen 1972), pp. 69–70, 234–46, and Waswo, pp. 33–34. For my treatment of pluralism in relation to fictional world theory and possible world theory, which relates to my assertions above, see "A Comparative Pluralism: The Heterogeneity of Methods and the Case of Possible Worlds," *Canadian Review of Comparative Literature* 15 (1988), 320–45.

2. See Max Black, *Models and Metaphors: Studies in Language and Philosophy* (Ithaca: Cornell University Press, 1962), pp. 219–43; see also Douglas Hofstadter, *Gödel, Escher, Bach: An Eternal Golden Braid* (New York: Basic Books, 1979), and his *Metamagical Themas: Questing for the Essence of Mind and Pattern* (New York: Basic Books, 1985).

3. I have found Edward Said's discussion useful. See his "Problem of Textuality: Two Exemplary Positions," *Critical Inquiry* 4 (1978), 673, see 674–713.

4. I discuss the background to the alienation effect in "Alienation, Double Signs with a Difference: Conscious Knots in *Cymbeline* and *The Winter's Tale*," *CIEFL Bulletin* (New Series) 1 (1989), 58–78.

5. Gerald Gould, "A New Reading of *Henry V*," *English Review* 29 (1919), 42–48, 52; William Empson, "Double-Plots: Heroic and Pastoral in the Main Plot," in *Some Versions of Pastoral,* pp. 64–65. The notes to my first chapter amply document the contribution of the German romantics to an understanding of Shakespeare's irony.

6. This reading of New Criticism differs somewhat from Stephen Greenblatt's when he discusses his training in New Criticism. See his *Shakespearean*

Negotiations: The Circulation of Social Energy in Renaissance England (Berkeley: University of California Press, 1988), p. 3.

7. Worcester, p. 124. For a similar position, see Hegel, pp. 88–91, and Hutchens, p. 22. For those with a position different from Worcester's, see Muecke, p. 183, and Mellor, pp. 24–25.

8. Richard Rorty, *Contingency, Irony, and Solidarity* (Cambridge: Cambridge University Press, 1989), pp. 3–5.

9. Similar psychological and logical consciousness of language with regard to fictional worlds occur in Jerome Bruner, *Actual Minds/Possible Worlds* (Cambridge, Mass.: Harvard University Press, 1986), Thomas Pavel, *Fictional Worlds* (Cambridge, Mass.: Harvard University Press, 1986), and Hart, "A Comparative Pluralism."

10. Waswo, pp. 3–7, 25–36. For a discussion of the dualistic model of language, see Barbara Herrnstein Smith, *On the Margins of Discourse* (Chicago: University of Chicago Press, 1978), and her "Narrative Versions, Narrative Theories," *Critical Inquiry* 7 (1980):213–36. For a discussion of magical language and poetry, see D. W. Winnicott, "Transitional Objects and Transitional Phenomena," *Playing and Reality* (London: Tavistock, 1971), pp. 1–25 (first published in the *International Journal of Psycho-Analysis* 34 [1953]); and Frank Kermode, *Romantic Image* (London: Routledge and Kegan Paul, 1957). See also Francis M. Cornford, *The Origin of Attic Comedy* (Cambridge: Cambridge University Press, 1934), esp. pp. 35–52; Robert C. Elliott, *The Power of Satire;* and Marcel Mauss, *A General Theory of Magic,* trans. Robert Brain (New York: Norton, 1975). I thank Thomas Greene, who taught me a great deal in his seminar "Language, Poetry, and Magic."

11. Waswo, p. 59. See Peter Burke, *The Renaissance Sense of the Past* (London: Edward Arnold, 1969), and Donald R. Kelley, *Foundations of Modern Historical Scholarship: Language, Law, and History in the French Renaissance* (New York: Columbia University Press, 1970).

12. *"The Republic" of Plato,* trans. A. Bloom (New York: Basic Books, 1968), I, 337a, Jerome listing. See the Loeb Classics edition, trans. Paul Shorey (London: Heinemann, 1930; rpt. 1946)—Greek 337 A 3. The *"Ethics"* of Aristotle, trans. J. A. K. Thomson (1953; Harmondsworth: Penguin, 1955; rpt. 1975), book 2, ch. 7, p. 70; bk. 4, ch. 3, p. 124; bk. 4, ch. 7, pp. 131–34; and The *"Art"* of Rhetoric (Loeb), trans. J. H. Freese (London: Heinemann, 1926, rpt. 1959), bk. 2, ch. 2, p. 23; bk. 3, ch. 18, pp. 463–65. See Demosthenes, *The Orations* (Loeb), trans. J. H. Vince (London: Heinemann, 1930), vol. 1, passim; and *The Characters of Theophrastus* (Loeb), trans. J. M. Edmonds (London: Heinemann, 1929), pp. 41–43. Cicero, *De Officiis* (Loeb), trans. Walter Miller (London: Heinemann, 1913), bk. 1, sect. 104, p. 137. The *"Institutio Oratoria"* of Quintilian (Loeb), trans. H. E. Butler

(London: Heinemann, 1921), vol. 3, bk. 9, ch. 2, sect. 43–53. For secondary sources to which I am indebted, see G. G. Sedgewick, 2d ed., pp. 5, 10–11; Knox, pp. 3–5; J. A. K. Thomson, pp. 163, 194–95.

13. See Duncan. For an elegant exploration of the Renaissance use of the classical past, see Greene.

14. Marbeck, quoted in Knox, p. 33, see pp. 5, 30–33.

15. Knox, pp. 7–8, 22–24, 59, 93–94, 141.

16. Friedrich Schlegel, *Literary Notebooks,* p. 114. Mellor, p. 21; see pp. 23–114, where, like many who seek to redeem irony, she asserts that most comentators, such as Hegel, Kierkegaard, and Wayne Booth, ignore the enthusiastic creativity in Friedrich Schlegel's concept of romantic irony and think of it as negative, absurd, or unstable.

17. August Wilhelm Schlegel, pp. 18–19. Johann Wolfgang Goethe, *Dichtung und Wahrheit,* quoted in Heller, p. 30. Karl Solger, quoted in Josef Budde, *Zur romantischen Ironie bei Ludwig Tieck* (Bonn, 1907), pp. 18–19, 23, cited in G. G. Sedgewick, p. 17.

18. Hegel, pp. 88–94.

19. Kierkegaard, *The Concept of Irony,* p. 336, see pp. 47–50, 260–89.

20. Morgann, pp. 11–13, 58–62; *German Romantic Criticism,* ed. A. Leslie Willson (New York: Continuum, 1982); *German Aesthetic and Criticism,* ed. Kathleen Wheeler; Thirlwall, "On the Irony of Sophocles," pp. 8–9, 44–50; Kierkegaard, *The Concept of Irony,* p. 336; Adam Müller, "Ueber die dramatische Kunst: Vorlesungen gehalten zu Dresden, 1806," in *Shakespeare in Germany, 1740–1815,* ed. Roy Pascal (Cambridge: Cambridge University Press, 1937), pp. 153–63; see Pascal's Introduction, pp. 10, 30–33.

21. Gould, pp. 42–48, 52; Empson, "Double Plots," in *Some Versions of Pastoral,* pp. 64–65; Cleanth Brooks and Robert B. Heilman, Introduction and Notes to "Shakespeare, *Henry IV, Part I,*" in *Understanding Drama: Twelve Plays,* ed. C. Brooks and R. Heilman (New York: Holt, 1945; rpt. 1948), pp. 329–30, 383–87; Righter; Rossiter, "Ambivalence," in *Angel with Horns,* p. 51; John Barton, p. 133.

22. J. A. K. Thomson implies that Aristophanes' irony also makes him like a *katascopos,* or godlike overviewer; J. A. K. Thomson, p. 33; Curtius, *European Literature and the Latin Middle Ages,* trans. Willard R. Trask (Bern, 1948; New York: Harper and Row, 1963), pp. 138–44; Crewe, 71; see Johan Huizinga, *Homo Ludens: A Study of the Play Element in Culture* (Boston: Beacon Press, 1955), p. 5.

23. Walter Cohen, *Drama of a Nation: Public Theater in Renaissance England and Spain* (Ithaca: Cornell University Press, 1985), pp. 136–85.

24. For a thorough and sensitive account of the potential and the problems of reconstructing Shakespeare's Globe, see Gurr (with Orrell), *Rebuilding*

Shakespeare's Globe, esp. pp. 13–27, 53–92. Elsewhere, Gurr warns about bending the evidence of Shakespeare's theater to one's own wishes and argues that the political conditions that prevailed encouraged Alfred Harbage to construct a populist audience (*Shakespeare's Audience* [New York: Columbia University Press, 1941]) and Ann Jennalie Cook (*The Privileged Playgoers of Shakespeare's London, 1576–1642* [Princeton: Princeton University Press, 1981]) a privileged audience. See Andrew Gurr's *Playgoing in Shakespeare's London* (Cambridge: Cambridge University Press, 1987), pp. 3–4, 12.

25. Gurr, *Playgoing,* pp. 11–13.

26. Ibid., pp. 55–56.

27. Ibid., pp. 136–37. For a discussion of women in the playhouses, see ibid., pp. 59–64; Howard, "Crossdressing," 439–40; and Richard Levin, "Women in the Renaissance Theatre Audience," *Shakespeare Quarterly* 40 (1989), 165–74.

28. Other versions of the Elizabethan theater have arisen in the past few years. Steven Mullaney tries to relate the ambivalent or contradictory view of the theaters in London—which provided their actors with a living but threatened the companies with closure, as happened in 1597 when the privy council ordered the theaters closed for the first time in fifty years—to the ambivalence and contradiction in *Henry IV,* written then, that is prodigal in its lavishness but whose close prohibits that abundance. Mullaney suggests quite plausibly that in the Second Tetrology the taverns of Eastcheap represent a contemporary scene that displaces history by moving it from the past into the present, by translating Tudor myths into a means of staging the cultural practices and tensions of Shakespeare's time. The tavern companions become the "strange" dramatic surrogates of the popular and marginal cultures of Elizabethan England, bearers of a license that the audience watches critically. The dominant culture makes familiar and absorbs some aspects of the strange and rejects and suppresses others. (Mullaney, pp. vii, 84–85, 129–32). Mullaney extends his guiding metaphor of Walter Cope's wonder-closet, or collection of curiosities from around the world, to the curious spectacle of strangeness, the theater, in his description of cultural negotiation. Here is a suggestive but restrictive metaphor for the complexity of the Elizabethan theater, but one that points to our own estrangement from Shakespeare's period because it resembles the metaphor of the collection that Susan Stewart discusses in relation to postmodernism. See her *On Longing: Narratives of the Miniature, the Gigantic, the Souvenir, the Collection* [Baltimore: Johns Hopkins University Press, 1984], esp. pp. 151–69. For a brief discussion of Stewart and collections, see my "Canadian Literature: In the Mouth of the Canon," *Journal of Canadian Studies* 23 [1988–89], 154–55.) The rejection of Falstaff takes on a new dimension in light of

cultural poetics or cultural materialism and is not, as some might think, a dead issue. Like Franco Moretti, Christopher Pye discusses the role of the theater in shaping political subjects in an age of absolutism. Pye says that feudalism has a religious theater and turns to the monarchy and the public theater only as a way of shoring up feudal social structures when mobile free labor is threatening them. The very vulnerability of royal spectacle alongside its power, Pye asserts, destabilizes the notion of a monolithic royal material power. Either that idea of vulnerability arises from the material limitations of royal power, or the theater increases that vulnerability by representing it, or both alternatives interplay. Robert Weimann's view of Shakespeare's material theater is that it constitutes a bifold authority. Its early modern ways of negotiating authority collide with a mimesis of premodern authorization. Like Mullaney, Weimann says that this theater is a cultural and economic institution that involved some unresolved questions of the Tudor administration and the clash between differing authorities (bourgeois and aristocratic, civic and royal) in the open and transitional rhetorical space beyond the walls in the Liberties of London. (Pye, pp. 5–6, 43–44; Franco Moretti, "A Huge Eclipse: Tragic Form and the Deconsecration of Sovereignty," *Genre* 15 [1982], 20; Robert Weiman, "Bifold Authority in Shakespeare's Theatre," *Shakespeare Quarterly* 39 [1988], 401–4; see Mullaney, pp. 21, 49.)

Jean Howard's material theater has literally to do with material. Her question is an important one: "Did the theater, for example, with its many fables of crossdressing, also form part of the cultural apparatus for policing gender boundaries, or did it serve as a site for further disturbance?" After posing questions about social containment or transformation and about the all-male model of production, Howard says that the plays that include cross-dressing, except for a few works like Middleton and Dekker's *Roaring Girl,* do not comment directly on the cross-dressing debates. She thinks that the theater is a contradictory site of ideological production that can circulate recuperative fables of cross-dressing, which reinscribe the gender system and sexual difference, while making visible in the theatrical practice the interplay of sexual kinds. Howard's view, which includes the assertion that the middle-class female playgoer perhaps called into question the "place" of women more radically than Shakespeare's fictions of cross-dressing did, seems plausible, except that it elides the usual connection, especially in Shakespeare's time, despite all its changes, between title, blood, and money. (Howard, "Crossdressing," 422–25; see note 2, chapter 3. For related works, see Karen Newman, "Renaissance Family Politics and Shakespeare's *The Taming of the Shrew,*" *English Literary Renaissance* 16 [1986], 91–92; Belsey, *The Subject of Tragedy;* Natalie Zemon Davis, "Women on Top: Symbolic

Sexual Inversion and Political Disorder in Early Modern Europe," in *The Reversible World: Symbolic Inversion in Art and Society,* ed. Barbara Babcock [Ithaca: Cornell University Press, 1978], pp. 147–90; and Novy.)

Changes were occurring, but only the rate at which titles were bought or won through battle and marriage might have changed. But Howard's main point about social mobility is sound. New gentry reinforced the class system, so that mobility made it less rigid but maintained its values. Social mobility in the period from 1558 to 1641 was, in Lawrence Stone's estimation, greater than at any time until the nineteenth and twentieth centuries. The aristocracy's wealth shrinks quickly in the last quarter of the sixteenth century. Stone says that vast numbers of people from various social origins, and often from commercial backgrounds, were absorbed into the landed gentry. While the middle classes grew, the values of the landed gentleman remained dominant. (Lawrence Stone, *The Crisis of the Aristocracy, 1558–1641* [Oxford: Clarendon Press, 1965], pp. 36–49.) Change in classes itself, if it involves assimilation to dominant values, can be a form of containment as much as renewal. For those who are upwardly mobile, this kind of containment is easier to bear than exclusion. The theater played with some of these issues.

29. For the most part, scholars do not think that the first performance of *Henry V* was at the First Globe. For views for and against this position, see note 2, chapter 3.

30. Chambers, pp. 106, 202–4, where he also talks about the Oldcastle controversy; Barroll, "The Social and Literary Context," pp. 42–47; Peter Thomson, pp. 3–6.

31. Alvin Kernan has explored in detail this movement from poetry to dramatic poetry: see *The Playwright as Magician.*

32. Bentley, esp. p. 43; see also in the same volume "The Profession of Player in Shakespeare's Time, 1590–1642." Bentley discusses the close relation among the status of playwrights, players, and theaters in this period.

33. Barish, esp. pp. 1–37, 80–191. See Barroll, "The Social and Literary Context," p. 29, where he says that the lord mayor of London and the city counsellors did not mind theater in its right time and place, with the right content, that control and views of morality were the issue and not the existence of theater itself. To substantiate his claim, he cites the pageant of the installation of the mayor.

34. Percy, p. 544. Samuel Johnson, pp. 68, 75. Coleridge, "Notes on Shakespeare's Plays," p. 256. Tillyard, *Shakespeare's History Plays,* pp. 320–21. Doran, pp. 112–13. Ribner, *The English History Play,* esp. pp. 24–29.

35. English history was not entirely neglected after 1599. *Henry V* was played before James at court sometime between 1 November 1604 and 12

February 1605 as part of a revival of Elizabethan drama and *1* and *2 Henry IV* were performed at court during the season of 1612–13, about the time *Henry VIII* was produced at the Globe. Chambers, p. 214

36. Derrida, *Of Grammatology*, pp. 4, 59; see his "Law of Genre," pp. 51–79. Paul de Man, "Semiology and Rhetoric," pp. 3–5. Williams, *Marxism and Literature*, pp. 145–50, 173–99. Rosalie Colie thinks that historiography is one of the greatest problems of genre; see *The Resources of Kind*, esp. pp. 7–9, 76–80, 95–102. Even though Alastair Fowler says much about historical kinds in the Renaissance, he only mentions Shakespeare's history plays as an example of how interest in genres changes over time as the critic and his or her audience change; p. 264, see pp. 54–74. Marjorie Garber sees the irony of temporality in the relation between Shakespeare and his audience, history and prophecy in the history plays, so that the idea of kind in these plays is mutual and challenging and not a stifling authorial dictation; see " 'What's Past Is Prologue,' " pp. 301–31. See in the same volume Lewalski, pp. 1–14. See also Hernadi, esp. pp. 1–38, 76–84; *Theories of Literary Genre*, esp. pp. vii–3, 17–57, 254–69; Dubrow, *Genre*.

37. Tennenhouse, pp. 72–101.

38. See, for instance, Greenblatt's Preface to *Allegory and Representation*, pp. vii–xiii, in which he discusses various representations of representation, including de Man's questioning of it. For assumptions about period classification of a literary "movement" (which itself implies something other than stasis), see Paul de Man, *The Rhetoric of Romanticism* (New York: Columbia University Press, 1984). See particularly the chapter on history plays in Georg Lukács, *The Historical Novel*, trans. Hannah and Stanley Mitchell (1937; Boston: Beacon Press, 1963).

39. Barthes, "The Death of an Author," pp. 7–13. Foucault, "What Is an Author?" pp. 113–39. See Lanham, pp. 27, 143, see pp. 28–35, 130–34.

40. A. E. Haigh, *The Tragic Drama of the Greeks* (1896; Oxford: Clarendon Press, 1925), pp. 96–101.

41. Ibid., pp. 39–45, 389–95; see Tillyard, *Shakespeare's History Plays;* Philip Vellacott, *Ironic Drama: A Study of Euripides' Method and Meaning* (Cambridge: Cambridge University Press, 1975), esp. pp. ix–25, 51–53, 126–36, 153–81.

42. See Henry A. Kelly on the various myths of divine Providence in Shakespeare's history plays.

43. See David Bevington, *From Mankind to Marlowe: Growth in Structure in the Popular Drama of Tudor England* (Cambridge, Mass.: Harvard University Press, 1962), and his *Tudor Drama and Politics: A Critical Approach to Topical Meaning* (Cambridge, Mass.: Harvard University Press, 1968), esp. pp. 97–119, 141–47. Honor McCuskor, *John Bale, Dramatist and Antiquary* (Bryn

Mawr, 1942), pp. 32–47, cited in Ribner, *The English History Play*, p. 34, see pp. 33–39. For discussions of Shakespeare's First Tetralogy, see, for instance, Don Ricks, *Shakespeare's Emergent Form: A Study of the Structures of the "Henry VI" Plays* (Logan: Utah State University Press, 1968); David Riggs, *Shakespeare's Heroical Histories: "Henry VI" and Its Literary Tradition* (Cambridge, Mass.: Harvard University Press, 1971); and Paul Bacquet, *Les pièces historiques de Shakespeare: La première tetralogie et "le Roi Jean,"* vol. 1 (Paris: Presses universitaires de France, 1978).

44. For a discussion of *Respublica* and the unwelcome advice on the succession that *Gorboduc* gives, see Bevington, *Tudor Drama,* pp. 112–19, 141–47, and Ribner, *The English History Play,* pp. 36–49.

45. See F. P. Wilson, *Marlowe and Early Shakespeare* (Oxford: Clarendon Press, 1953), p. 106, and Ornstein, *A Kingdom for a Stage,* pp. 2–6.

46. All quotations and citations from Marlowe's plays will be from *The Complete Works of Christopher Marlowe,* ed. I. Ribner (New York: Odyssey Press, 1963). For other views of Marlowe's history, see Ribner, "The Idea of History in Marlowe's *Tamburlaine,*" *English Literary History* 20 (1953), 251–66; Greenblatt, "Marlowe and the Will to Absolute Play," in *Renaissance Self-Fashioning,* pp. 193–221; and Clifford Leech, *Christopher Marlowe: Poet for the Stage,* ed. Anne Lancashire (New York: AMS Press, 1986). I mention Marlowe's representation of history all too briefly partly because my focus here is Shakespeare and partly because I am in the midst of a manuscript, "Marlowe: Language and History," which examines this subject in more detail.

47. Ben Jonson, *Sejanus,* ed. Jonas A. Barish (New Haven: Yale University Press, 1965; see Barish's Introduction, pp. 1–24). Ribner, *The English History Play,* pp. 290–99; Wikander, pp. 50–64; Lindenberger, esp. pp. 3–5, 30–32.

48. Barish, Introduction, *Sejanus,* pp. 10–18; Wikander, pp. 52–54.

49. Wikander, p. 62.

50. For a perceptive and elegant discussion of the play and its use of Tacitus's *Annals,* see Anne Barton, *Ben Jonson, Dramatist* (Cambridge: Cambridge University Press, 1984), pp. 92–108.

51. My thanks to Margaret Ferguson for discussing Cary with me, for sharing some of her course materials on Cary, and for making me aware of the work of Tina Krontiris on Cary's *Edward II.* Not only does Lindenberger's *Historical Drama* show the importance of Shakespeare in the shaping of the history play, but it also demonstrates the transnational and transtemporal nature of of this kind of play. According to Lindenberger, the history play is far from dead. See also Wikander.

52. William Shakespeare, *King Henry VIII,* ed. R. A. Foakes (1957; London: Methuen, 1968). For a more detailed discussion of this and other

aspects of the play, see my *"Henry VIII*: The Play as History and Anti-History,"* Aevum: Rassegna di Scienze Storiche-Linguistiche e Filologiche* (forthcoming, December 1991). For an illuminating appraisal of *Henry VIII*, see Wikander, pp. 36–49; for an interesting but opposite view, see Alexander Leggatt, *"Henry VIII* and the Ideal England,"* Shakespeare Survey* 38 (1985), 131–43.

53. For a more detailed view on the relation of drama and narrative in European Renaissance drama, see my Introduction to a Special (or topical) Issue of the *Canadian Review of Comparative Literature* 18, no. 2–3 (June 1991 [Renaissance Narrative and Drama]), where I argue that narrative in drama is considerably more important than most critics have thought. In *The Light in Troy,* Thomas Greene discusses imitation and discovery in Renaissance poetry and the complex relation of the poets to their classical predecessors. Greene's work is an example of a sensitive treatment of historical matters.

54. T. W. Baldwin, 2:563–65.

55. Aristotle, "On the Art of Poetry," pp. 43–44; Sidney, p. 17; Fussner, *The Historical Revolution,* p. 46; Nancy S. Struever, *The Language of History in the Renaissance: Rhetoric and Historical Consciousness in Florentine Humanism* (Princeton: Princeton University Press, 1970), esp. pp. 3–8, 21–37, 143–45, 193–99; Marion Trousdale, *Shakespeare and the Rhetoricians* (Chapel Hill: University of North Carolina Press, 1982), esp. pp. 65–78.

56. For history that represents less formal differentiation than that in the Second Tetralogy, see Edward Hall, *Hall's Chronicle* [etc.] (New York: AMS Press, 1965), and Raphael Holinshed, *Chronicles of England, Scotland and Ireland,* 6 vols. (1808; rpt. New York: AMS Press, 1978), and Baldwin, et al., *A Mirror for Magistrates.* (Hall and Holinshed are also found in *Narrative and Dramatic Sources of Shakespeare,* ed. Bullough.) An important question in Samuel Daniel's career is why he changed from historical poetry to history in prose and how this development affected his representation of history and was related to the changes in views of history in the last years of the sixteenth century and the beginning of the seventeenth. See, for instance, William Blissett, "Samuel Daniel's Sense of the Past," *English Studies* (Amsterdam) 38 (1957), 49–63.

57. In "The Rationality of History" (1986), Lionel Gossman questions and qualifies some of the innovative work he did during the 1960s and 1970s in exploring the rhetorical and literary nature of history in the eighteenth and nineteenth centuries. My thanks to Lionel Gossman for allowing me to read his essay in manuscript. It recently appeared in his collection *Between History and Literature* (Cambridge, Mass.: Harvard University Press, 1990), pp. 285–324.

58. White, "Historical Text," esp. pp. 15–20, and *Metahistory,* esp. pp. 1–

42. White's metahistory has attempted to restore imagination and rhetoric to history but has met with resistance. Without reference to the metahistorians, Peter Gay says that "interpretation is an attempt to offer an objective account of an objective past," cites Shakespeare's histories as "a reminder of how readily historical personages lend themselves to myth making," and accepts the invention of speeches in poetry but not in history. But, more recently, he asserts that history is an art and science, argues for "the overpowering variety of possible ways of expressing truths and reaching them," says that in earlier works he wanted to warn "against the facile pessimism of the skeptics and the equally facile simplifications of the dogmatists," and makes some perceptive comments on the relation between reason and the unconscious. See Peter Gay, *Style in History* (New York: Basic Books, 1974), pp. 188–212, and his *Freud for Historians* (New York: Oxford University Press, 1985), pp. vii–ix, 122–27, 133–38. Leon Pompa rejects the metahistorical view as an extreme position and defends the scientific idea of history. He seems to be saying that the metahistorians are dissolving a single objective truth in the external world of the past and are relegating it to the multiple artifacts of the text itself. In an attempt to refine Pompa's rebuttal of White, W. H. Dray claims that the historian is not *"free to interpret the past as he likes"* because his or her choices are at least partly determined by the structure of the events themselves. More recently, Suzanne Gearhart has criticized White for basing his typology on an untenable distinction between figurative and literal language. Leon Pompa, "Narrative Form, Significance, and Historical Knowledge," in *La Philosophie de l'histoire et la practique historienne d'aujourd'hui = Philosophy of History and Contemporary Historiography,* ed. David Carr et al. (Ottawa: University of Ottawa Press, 1982), pp. 143–57. W. H. Dray, "Narration, Reduction, and the Uses of History," in *La Philosophie,* pp. 203–4. Gearhart, pp. 17–18. For views cautious of White's position, see Paul Ricoeur, *Reality of the Historical Past* (Milwaukee: Marquette University Press, 1984), esp. pp. 33–34, and, once again, William H. Dray, "Narrative and Historical Realism," *On History and Philosophers of History* (Leiden: Brill, 1989), ch. 7. A recent and pertinent exchange has occurred between Ankersmit and Zagorin. See F. R. Ankersmit, "Historiography and Postmodernism," *History and Theory* 28 (1989), 137–53, and Perez Zagorin, "Historiography and Postmodernism: Reconsiderations," *History and Theory* 29 (1990), 263–74, and, in the same issue, Ankersmit's "Reply to Professor Zagorin," 275–96.

59. See my "New Historicism: Taking History into Account," *Ariel* 22 (1991), 93–107, and "Stephen Greenblatt's *Shakespearean Negotiations*," *Textual Practice* (forthcoming, Fall 1991).

60. Michael McCanles, "The Authentic Discourse of the Renaissance,"

Diacritics 10 (1980), 77–87; Stephen Greenblatt, "The Forms of Power and the Power of Forms in the Renaissance," *Genre* 15 (1982), 1–4. An interesting collection that demonstrates the changes in this approach is *The New Historicism*, ed. H. Aram Veeser (New York: Routledge, 1989). For earlier accounts, see Jonathan Goldberg, "The Politics of Renaissance Literature: A Review Essay," *English Literary Renaissance* 16 (1982), 13–43; Montrose, "Renaissance Literary Studies," esp. 6; Howard, "New Historicism in Renaissance Studies," 13–43; Edward Pechter, "The New Historicism and Its Discontents: Politicizing Renaissance Drama," *PMLA* 102 (1987), 292–303; and Walter Cohen, "Political Criticism in Shakespeare," in *Shakespeare Reproduced: The Text in History and Ideology*, ed. J. E. Howard and M. F. O'Connor (New York: Methuen, 1987), pp. 18–46.

61. Carol Thomas Neely, "Constructing the Subject: Feminist Practice and the New Renaissance Discourses," *English Literary Renaissance* 18 (1988), 6. See Jean Howard, "Old Wine, New Bottles," *Shakespeare Quarterly* 35 (1984), 236–37; Linda Boose, "The Family in Shakespeare Studies; or— Studies in the Family of Shakespeareans, or—The Politics of Politics," *Renaissance Quarterly* 40 (1987), 707–42. See Nancy K. Miller, "Arachnologies: The Woman, the Text, and the Critic," in *The Poetics of Gender*, ed. Nancy K. Miller (New York: Columbia University Press, 1987). Essays by Gayatri Spivak ("The New Historicism: Political Commitment and the Postmodern Critic," pp. 277–93), Catherine Gallagher ("Marxism and the New Historicism," pp. 37–48), Jane Marcus ("The Asylums of Antaeus: Women, War, and Madness—Is there a Feminist Fetishism?" pp. 132–151), Judith Newton ("History as Usual? Feminism and the 'New Historicism,' " pp. 152–67), and the other critics I discuss appear in Veeser's collection *The New Historicism*.

62. See Joel Fineman, "The History of the Anecdote," in *The New Historicism*, esp. pp. 56–64. In examining the anecdote that ends *Renaissance Self-Fashioning*, which relies on the analogy or similitude between the Renaissance and now, Frank Lentricchia thinks that as a Foucauldian Greenblatt implies that we sustain a dream of free selfhood amid our disappointed liberal imagination because we think we know that the structure of power denies freedom everywhere else. New historicism, Lentricchia says, is a representative story about the contemporary American academic intellectual, who frets about liberalism in the face of presumed totalitarianism, or one that sustains totalitarianism as the denial of freedom except in a dream. See his "Foucault's Legacy: A New Historicism?" in *The New Historicism*, esp. 241–42. In "Literary Criticism and the Politics of the New Criticism," Elizabeth Fox-Genovese argues against the textual position of new historicism, whereas in "New Historicism: A Comment" Hayden White argues for it (see *The New Historicism*, pp. 213–24, 293–302).

63. For instance, Alan Liu says that the new historicists exchange *bricolage* for "the more methodological *narratio* or presentation of facts in history of ideas" ("The Power of Formalism: The New Historicism," *English Literary History* 56 [1989], esp. 721–23, 758). He finds in new historicism borrowings from the lexicon of New Criticism, deconstruction, dialectic, and complementary terminologies in Geertz, Foucault, and Althusser. New historicists, Liu argues, are a rear-guard disguised as an avant-garde as they face the postmodern in which an intellectual effort in the face of history is passé. James Holstun says that new historicism has made it possible in the United States to say what could not be said twenty years ago, "that literature does political work" ("Ranting at the New Historicism," *English Literary Renaissance* 19 [1989], 190–93). While Holstun praises the theoretical concerns of the new historicists, he wonders why their practice has not led them to study the subversive and radical pamphlets of the English Revolution. Holstun has a point. The anecdote on a marginal text soon moves to an analogy to a canonical text. He suggests that new historicism supplement its attention to the self-fashioning of high-cultural individuals with studies of popular collective self-fashioning and give up policing its borders with Marxism. For other recent discussions of new historicism, see Don E. Wayne, "Power, Politics, and the Shakespearean Text: Recent Criticism in England and the United States," *Shakespeare Reproduced: The Text in History and Ideology,* ed. Jean E. Howard and Marian F. O'Connor (New York: Methuen, 1987), pp. 47–67; Joseph Litvak, "Back to the Future: A Review-Article on the New Historicism, Deconstruction, and Nineteenth-Century Fiction," *Texas Studies in Literature and Language* 30 (1988), 120–49; and Carolyn Porter, "Are We Being Historical Yet?" *South Atlantic Quarterly* 87 (1988), 743–86.

64. Greenblatt, *Shakespearean Negotiations.* See F. C. Copleston, *Aquinas* (Harmondsworth: Penguin, 1955), p. 71.

65. For another view, see Edward Shils, *Center and Periphery: Essays in Macrosociology* (Chicago: University of Chicago Press, 1975).

66. Tillyard, *The Elizabethan World Picture.* The first significant oppositions to, and modifications of, Tillyard's position are Rossiter, *Angel with Horns* (the lecture "Ambivalence: The Dialectic of the Histories" was delivered in 1950); Traversi; and Knights, *Some Shakespearean Themes.*

67. White, *Metahistory,* esp. pp. 1–42; *Tropics of Discourse: Essays in Cultural Criticism* (Baltimore: Johns Hopkins University Press, 1978); and "The Question of Narrative."

68. M. I. Finley, Introduction to Thucydides, *History of the Peloponnesian War,* trans. Rex Warner (1956; Harmondsworth: Penguin, 1972), pp. 24–26; Michael Grant, Introduction to Tacitus, *The Annals of Imperial Rome,* trans.

M. Grant, rev. ed. (Harmondsworth: Penguin, 1977), pp. 10–12; Aristotle, *Poetics* 9, in *Introduction to Aristotle,* ed. Richard McKeon (New York: Modern Library, 1947), pp. 635–37; see A. R. Burn, Introduction to Herodotus, *The Histories,* trans. Aubrey de Selincourt, rev. ed. (Harmondsworth: Penguin, 1972), pp. 25–26.

69. C. S. Lewis, *English Literature in the Sixteenth Century* (Oxford: Oxford University Press, 1954), p. 61.

70. Irving M. Copi, *Introduction to Logic,* 4th ed. (New York: Macmillan, 1972), esp. pp. 351–53; see John Hospers, *An Introduction to Philosophical Analysis,* 2d ed. (Englewood Cliffs, N.J.: Prentice-Hall, 1967), pp. 476–86. The work on analogy is vast. Mark Turner makes an especially telling point on analogy that relates to Greenblatt's project: "A culture's common conceptual categories and their relations, which I will call its category structures, highlight certain connections between concepts, and mask possible alternative connections. Analogies exist to unmask, capture, or invent connections absent from or upstaged by one's category structures." Mark Turner, "Categories and Analogies," in *Analogical Reasoning: Perspectives of Artificial Intelligence, Cognitive Science, and Philosophy,* ed. David H. Helman (Dordrecht: Kluwer Academic, 1988), p. 3, see pp. 4–24. See, for instance, Harald Hoffding, *Le concept d'analogie,* trans. René Perrin (Paris: J. Vrin, 1931); David Burrell, *Analogy and Philosophical Language* (New Haven: Yale University Press, 1973); Humphrey Palmer, *Analogy* (London: Macmillan, 1973); W. H. Leatherdale, *The Role of Analogy, Model, and Metaphor in Science* (Amsterdam: North Holland, 1974); Raimo Anttila, *Analogy* (The Hague: Mouton, 1977); Sidney Homan, *When the Theatre Turns to Itself: The Aesthetic Metaphor in Shakespeare* (Lewisburg: Bucknell University Press, 1981); J. F. Ross, *Portraying Analogy* (London: Cambridge University Press, 1981); Herbert Hochberg, *Logic, Ontology, and Language* (Munich: Philosophia, 1984); Brian Vickers, "Analogy versus Identity: The Rejection of Occult Symbolism, 1580–1680," in *Occult and Scientific Mentalities in the Renaissance,* ed. B. Vickers (Cambridge: Cambridge University Press, 1984), pp. 95–163.

71. Jacques Derrida, *Speech and Phenomena, and Other Essays on Husserl's Theory of Signs,* trans. David Allison (Evanston: Northwestern University Press, 1973; French version 1967).

72. In "The Forms of Power" and in "Towards a Poetics of Culture" in *The New Historicism,* pp. 1–14, Greenblatt outlines his views of his practice and theory of new historicism. In one of his most recent defenses or explanations of new historicism, Greenblatt says that this movement, and he in particular, have resisted three aspects of a standard definition of "historicism": the view that "man" can do little to alter the processes at work in history; the theory that historians must avoid value judgments about

the past; and veneration of the past and tradition. Greenblatt, "Resonance and Wonder," in *Literary Theory Today,* ed. Peter Collier and Helga Geyer-Ryan (Ithaca: Cornell University Press, 1990), p. 74. Greenblatt's most recent book has just been released, but, unfortunately, I have not been able to obtain a copy before the completion of my study. For influences on new historicism, see Michel Foucault, "The Subject and Power," *Critical Inquiry* 8 (1982), pp. 777–95; Shils; Clifford Geertz, *The Interpretation of Cultures* (New York: Basic Books, 1973), and "Centers, Kings, and Charisma"; and Michel Leiris, *La Possession et ses aspects théâtraux chez les Ethiopiens de Gondar* (Paris: Plon, 1958). Bacon, Marx, Nietzsche, cultural anthropologist like Geertz and Victor Turner, feminist works like *Sisterhood Is Powerful,* the Warburg Institute, Michel Foucault, Stephen Orgel, Jacques Derrida, and other influences find their way into explanations of the origins of new historicism.

73. Dollimore, "Introduction," pp. 2–3; see pp. 4–15 for the following discussion. My comments on cultural materialism are scandalously brief and inadequate and are meant to be suggestive rather than representative. See Raymond Williams, *Problems in Materialism and Culture* (London: Verso, 1980). See also his *Culture* (Glasgow: Fontana, 1981). A debate between Catherine Belsey and Jonathan Dollimore and Alan Sinfield on the nature of cultural materialism occurs in *Textual Practice* 3 and 4.

74. See Stuart Hall, "Cultural Studies: Two Paradigms," in *Culture, Ideology, and Social Process: A Reader,* ed. Tony Bennett et al. (London: Batsford, 1981), pp. 19–37.

75. Heywood, *An Apology for Actors* (rpt. London: Shakespeare Society, 1841), p. 53, and Calvert, quoted in V. C. Gildersleeve, *Government Regulation of Elizabethan Drama* (New York: Columbia University Press, 1908), quoted in Dollimore, "Introduction," p. 8.

76. Kathleen McLuskie, "Feminist Deconstruction: The Example of Shakespeare's 'Taming of the Shrew,' " *Red Letters* 12, 33–40, cited in Dollimore, "Introduction," pp. 11, 17.

77. I share this view with Williams, Dollimore, and Lentricchia. See Frank Lentricchia, *Criticism and Social Change* (Chicago: University of Chicago Press, 1983). Howard, "New Historicism in Renaissance Studies," and Montrose, "Renaissance Literary Studies," discuss some British cultural materialists and Marxists. In *The Place of the Stage* Mullaney states his preference for the term "cultural materialism" over "new historicism" and says that these related movements on both sides of the Atlantic share assumptions about hegemonic culture that Raymond Williams most ably articulated. According to Mullaney, Williams developed Gramsci's concept, viewing hegemonic culture as neither static nor singular nor as synonymous

with cultural domination but as heterogeneous and plural social formations and as dynamic representations and interpretations (Mullaney, pp. x–xii). Unlike Mullaney, Howard Felperin prefers "new historicism." Although I am sympathetic to Felperin's theoretical position, which he outlines clearly and vigorously, he has certain reasons for theoretical reconciliation that stem in part from the relative decline of deconstruction, a decline that bears a complex relation to Ortwin de Graef's unearthing of Paul de Man's book and music reviews for *Le Soir* and his ten articles for *Het Vlaamsche Land* between December 1940 and November 1942 and the intricate reaction to this finding, especially of the anti-Semitic "Jews in Contemporary Literature." Felperin approaches new historicism from a deconstructive position, which itself has weakened institutionally while new historicism has strengthened, so that the skeptical olive branch may be extended as much for pragmatic institutional reasons as in the face of a common enemy. Where once new historicism needed deconstruction, now the opposite is true. The blurring of binary opposites has taken a new turn. But new historicism and cultural materialism do, as Felperin says, assume that suspicion of, and skepticism toward, power and the dominant ideology's desire to contain, just as deconstruction seeks to question idealism and certainty. See Felperin, *The Uses of the Canon: Elizabethan Literature and Contemporary Theory* (Oxford: Clarendon Press, 1990), pp. v–vii. On de Man, see Barbara Johnson, "The Surprise of Otherness: A Note on the Wartime Writings of Paul de Man," in *Literary Theory Today*, ed. Peter Collier and Helga Geyer-Ryan (Ithaca: Cornell University Press, 1990), pp. 13–22. See also Christopher Norris, *Paul de Man: Deconstruction and the Critique of Aesthetic Ideology* (London: Routledge, 1988).

78. Carolyn Porter, pp. 27–62. Williams, *Writing and Society* (London: Verso, 1983), p. 189, cited in Carolyn Porter, p. 58.

79. Judith Cook, p. 64

80. Natalie Zemon Davis, " 'Women's History' in Transition: The European Case," *Feminist Review* 3/4 (1975–76), 90.

81. See Howard, "Crossdressing," 419–20, see also 418–40.

82. Angela Pitt, "Women in the Histories," *Shakespeare's Women* (London: David and Charles, 1981), pp. 136–63, and Marilyn French, "Power: The First Tetralogy," *Shakespeare's Division of Experience* (New York: Ballantine, 1981), pp. 35–69. See also Carol Rutter (with others), *Clamorous Voices: Shakespeare's Women Today*, ed. Faith Evans (London: Women's Press, 1988), which discusses actresses' interpretations of Kate in *The Taming of the Shrew*, Isabella in *Measure for Measure*, Lady Macbeth, Helena in *All's Well That Ends Well*, Imogen, and Rosalind but does not discuss the roles of women in the histories. L. T. Fitz (Linda Woodbridge) questions the sexist attitudes of

male reviewers of *Antony and Cleopatra*. Fitz mentions the early feminist work of Rose Grindon (1909) and Lucie Simpson (1928) on the play. See Fitz (Woodbridge), "Egyptian Queens and Male Reviewers: Sexist Attitudes in *Antony and Cleopatra* Criticism," *Shakespeare Quarterly* 18 (1977), 298, see 297–316.

83. Phyllis Rackin, "Anti-Historians: Women's Roles in Shakespeare's Histories," *Theatre Journal* (October 1985), 329–44. Patricia Parker, *Literary Fat Ladies* (London: Methuen, 1987), pp. 17–23, 237. Jardine, esp. p. 131. Gayle Whittier, "Falstaff as a Welshwoman: Uncomic Androgyny," *Ball State University Forum* 20 (1979), 25–35.

84. See Ruth Kelso, *Doctrine for the Lady of the Renaissance* (Urbana: University of Illinois Press, 1956). Lawrence Stone supports this view that the new learning of the Renaissance and the Reformation reduced the learning, prestige, and power of women, though he does attribute some power to Elizabethan women, but most of the powers he lists are passive. See his *The Family, Sex, and Marriage in England, 1500–1800* (London: Weidenfeld and Nicolson, 1977), pp. 154–55, 199. Bonnie S. Anderson and Judith P. Zinsser contend that the early phase of the Reformation accepted women as spiritual equals to men, but as the reformed churches became more institutionalized men in those churches, like those in the Counter-Reformation, asserted their authority over women and viewed them as inferiors. See *A History of Their Own: Women in Europe from Prehistory to the Present*, 2 vols. (New York: Harper and Row, 1988), esp. 1:254, 259, and 2: 28–30. For discussions of the homosexual and homosocial, see Alan Bray, *Homosexuality in Renaissance England* (London: Gay Men's Press, 1982), and Eve Kosofsky Sedgwick, *Between Men: English Literature and Male Homosocial Desire* (New York: Columbia University Press, 1985).

85. Joan Kelly, *Women, History, and Theory: The Essays of Joan Kelly* (Chicago: University of Chicago Press, 1984), p. 22, see pp. 33, 39–47 for the discussion below; see Patricia Parker, p. 6.

86. For more on Aristotle's and the Neoplatonists' views on women, see Ian Maclean, *The Renaissance Notion of Woman: A Study in the Fortune of Scholasticism and Medical Science in European Intellectual Life* (Cambridge: Cambridge University Press, 1980), pp. 7–8, 24–26. Maclean asserts that "in spite of the influence of Neoplatonism, then, the scholastic infrastructure of the Renaissance notion of woman remains intact" (p. 25).

87. Coppélia Kahn, "Rewriting," pp. 35–36. Kahn aptly cites Nancy Chodorow's work on the Elizabethan family, where she argues that the fundamental masculine sense of self is established through a denial of the male's first link with the feminine. Chodorow asserts that this denial taints the man's attitudes toward women and inhibits his general ability to affiliate.

See Nancy Chodorow, *The Reproduction of Mothering: Psychoanalysis and the Sociology of Gender* (Berkeley: University of California Press, 1979), and Kahn's *Man's Estate: Masculine Identity in Shakespeare* (Berkeley: University of California Press, 1981). See Patricia Parker, p. 23, for the discussion below.

88. *Narrative and Dramatic Sources of Shakespeare,* 8 vols., ed Geoffrey Bullough (London: Routledge and Kegan Paul, 1957–75), 4:182.

89. Hawes's *Pastime of Pleasure* (Early English Text Society), vol. 173, II. 156–57, and Raphael Holinshed, *Chronicles of England, Scotland and Ireland,* 1808, ed., iii. 64, in *The Second Part of King Henry IV,* ed. A. R. Humphreys (London: Methuen, 1966, rpt. 1977), p. 4.

90. Nancy Vickers, " 'The Blazon of Sweet Beauty's Best': Shakespeare's *Lucrece,*" in *Shakespeare and the Question of Theory,* ed. P. Parker and G. Hartman (New York: Methuen, 1985), esp. pp. 95–97. Patricia Parker, esp. pp. 126–40.

91. See Harold Newcomb Hillebrand, *The Child Actors: A Chapter in Elizabethan Stage History* (Urbana: University of Illinois Press, 1926); W. Robertson Davies, *Shakespeare's Boy Actors* (New York: Macmillan, 1939); Juliet Dusinberre, *Shakespeare and the Nature of Women* (London: Macmillan, 1975), p. 10; and Phyllis Rackin, "Androgyny, Mimesis, and the Marriage of the Boy Heroine on the English Renaissance Stage," *PMLA* 102 (1987), 29–41.

92. Simon Shepherd, *Amazons and Warrior Women,* p. 29. Allison Heisch and Joan Kelly conclude that only viragos, women whose virile souls were caught in women's bodies—as Boccaccio explains it, exceptions to the female sex—could aspire to the Renaissance ideal of "man." See Joan Kelly, p. 71; Heisch, "Queen Elizabeth I and the Persistence of Patriarchy," *Feminist Review* 4 (1980), 45–56. For a similar view, see Belsey, *The Subject of Tragedy,* p. 180. I discuss gender in the Second Tetrology at length in an essay that constitutes part of my manuscript "Translating Shakespeare." A more general analysis occurs in Susan D. Amussen, "Gender, Family and the Social Order, 1560–1725," in *Order and Disorder in Early Modern England,* ed. Anthony Fletcher and John Stevenson (Cambridge: Cambridge University Press, 1985), pp. 196–205.

At the outset of the Afterword, I said that I would not attempt to digest every recent book and article that I discovered as *Theater and World* was going to press. Even though I have not had time to incorporate the following important studies (as they came into my hands at the proof stage), I want to call my readers' attention to them: Ralph Berry, *Shakespeare and Social Class* (Atlantic Highlands: Humanities Press International, 1988), esp. pp. 75–94; Larry S. Champion, *"The Noise of Threatening Drum": Dramatic Strategy and*

Political Ideology in Shakespeare and the English Chronicle Plays (Newark: University of Delaware Press, 1990), esp. pp. 99–128; Phyllis Rackin, *Stages of History* (see chapter 2, note 12, where I was able to make a brief reference to Rackin's study); Constance Jordan, *Renaissance Feminism: Literary Texts and Political Models* (Ithaca: Cornell University Press, 1990); and Timothy Hampton *Writing from History: The Rhetoric of Exemplarity in Renaissance Literature* (Ithaca: Cornell University Press, 1990).

SELECTED BIBLIOGRAPHY

Abel, Lionel. *Metatheatre: A New View of Dramatic Form*. New York: Hill and Wang, 1963.

Abrams, Richard. "Rumour's Reign in *2 Henry IV*: The Scope of Personification." *English Literary Renaissance* 16 (1986), 467–95.

Adelman, Janet. " 'Anger's My Meat': Feeding, Dependency, and Aggression in *Coriolanus*." In *Representing Shakespeare: New Psychoanalytic Essays*. Ed. Murray M. Schwartz and Coppélia Kahn. Baltimore: Johns Hopkins University Press, 1980, pp. 129–49.

Allen, Charles A., and G. D. Stephens, eds. *Satire: Theory and Practice*. Belmont, Calif.: Wadsworth, 1962.

Alternative Shakespeares. Ed. John Drakakis. London: Methuen, 1985.

Althusser, Louis. *For Marx*. Trans. Ben Brewster. London: Allen Lane, 1983.

Altick, Richard. "Symphonic Imagery in *Richard II*." *PMLA* 62 (1947), 339–65.

Altieri, Joanne. "Shakespeare and the Imperial Myth." In *The Theatre of Praise: The Panegyric Tradition in Seventeenth-Century Drama*. Newark: University of Delaware Press, 1986, pp. 39–73.

Alvis, John. "A Little Touch of the Night in Harry: The Career of Henry Monmouth." In *Shakespeare as Political Thinker*. Ed. John Alvis and Thomas G. West. Durham, N.C.: Carolina Academic Press, 1981, pp. 95–125.

Amussen, Susan D. "Gender, Family and Social Order, 1560–1725. In *Order and Disorder in Early Modern England*. Ed. Anthony Fletcher and John Stevenson. Cambridge: Cambridge University Press, 1985, pp. 196–205.

Anderson, Bonnie S., and Judith P. Zinsser. *A History of Their Own: Women in Europe from Prehistory to the Present.* 2 vols. New York: Harper and Row, 1988.

Ankersmit, F. R. "Historiography and Postmodernism." *History and Theory* 28 (1989), 137–53.

———. "Reply to Professor Zagorin." *History and Theory* 29 (1990), 275–96.

Anonymous. "The Famous Victories of Henry the Fifth." In *The History of Henry IV (Part One).* Ed. Maynard Mack (Signet Ed.). New York: New American Library, 1965.

———. *Here followeth a notable treatyse named the Ordynarye of Chrystyanyte or of crysten men.* London: Wynken de Worde, 1502.

———. "The Reign of King Edward the Third." In *Three Elizabethan Plays.* Ed. James Winny. London: Chatto and Windus, 1959.

———. "The Troublesome Raigne of King John." In *Narrative and Dramatic Sources of Shakespeare.* Ed. Geoffrey Bullough, vol. 4. London: Routledge & Kegan Paul, 1962.

———. *Woodstock: A Moral History.* Ed. A. P. Rossiter. London: Chatto and Windus, 1946.

Anttila, Raimo. *Analogy.* The Hague: Mouton, 1977.

Aristotle. *The "Art" of Rhetoric.* Trans. J. H. Freese. Loeb ed. London: Heinemann, 1926; rpt. 1959.

———. *The "Ethics" of Aristotle.* Trans. J. A. K. Thomson, 1953. Harmondsworth: Penguin, 1955; rpt. 1975.

———. *Introduction to Aristotle.* Ed. Richard McKeon. New York: Modern Library, 1947.

———. "On the Art of Poetry." In *Classical Literary Criticism.* Ed. T. S. Dorsch. Harmondsworth: Penguin, 1965; rpt. 1975, pp. 33–75.

Armstrong, John. *Plays: One.* New York: Grove Press, 1977.

Armstrong, Nancy. *Desire and Domestic Fiction: A Political History of the Novel.* New York: Oxford University Press, 1987.

Aspects of Shakespeare's "Problem Plays." Ed. Kenneth Muir and Stanley Wells. Cambridge: Cambridge University Press, 1982.

Augustine. *The City of God.* Trans. Marcus Dods et al. New York: Random House, 1950.

———. *Concerning the City of God against the Pagans.* Trans. Henry Bettenson. Harmondsworth: Penguin, 1972.

Axton, Marie. *The Queen's Two Bodies: Drama and the Elizabethan Succession.* London: Royal Historical Society, 1977.

Babula, William. "Whatever Happened to Prince Hal?: An Essay on 'Henry V.' " *Shakespeare Survey* 30 (1977), 47–59.

Bacon, Francis. *Works.* Ed. James Spedding, R. L. Ellis, and D. D. Heath. 15 vols. New York: Hurd and Houghton, 1864.

Bacquet, Paul. *Les pièces historiques de Shakespeare: La deuxième tetralogie et "Henri VIII."* Vol. 2. Paris: Presses universitaires de France, 1979.

———. *Les pièces historiques de Shakespeare: La première tetralogie et "le Roi Jean."* Vol. 1. Paris: Presses universitaires de France, 1978.

Baker, Herschel. *The Race of Time: Three Lectures on Renaissance Historiography*. Toronto: University of Toronto Press, 1967.

Bakhtin, Mikhail M. *Rabelais and His World*. Trans. Hélène Iswolsky. Cambridge, Mass.: MIT Press, 1968.

Baldwin, T. W. *William Shakspere's Small Latine and Lesse Greeke*. 2 vols. Urbana: University of Illinois Press, 1944.

Baldwin, William, et al. *A Mirror for Magistrates*. Ed. Lily B. Campbell. Cambridge: Cambridge University Press, 1938.

Bale, John. *The Dramatic Writings of John Bale*. Ed. John S. Farmer. London, 1907.

Balibar, Etienne, and Pierre Macherey. "On Literature as an Ideological Form." In *Untying the Text: A Post-Structuralist Reader*. Ed. Robert Young. London: Routledge, 1981, pp. 79–99.

Bamber, Linda. *Comic Women, Tragic Men: A Study of Gender and Genre in Shakespeare*. Stanford: Stanford University Press, 1982.

Barber, C. L. *Shakespeare's Festive Comedy: A Study of Dramatic Form and Its Relation to Social Custom*. Princeton: Princeton University Press, 1959.

Barish, Jonas. *The Antitheatrical Prejudice*. Berkeley: University of California Press, 1981.

Barkan, Leonard. "The Theatrical Consistency of *Richard II*." *Shakespeare Quarterly* 29 (1978), 5–19.

Barker, Francis. *The Tremulous Private Body: Essays on Subjection*. London: Methuen, 1984.

Barroll, J. Leeds. "A New History for Shakespeare and His Time." *Shakespeare Quarterly* 39 (1988), 441–64.

———. *Shakespearean Tragedy*. Washington: Folger Books, 1984.

———. "The Social and Literary Context." In *"Revels" History of the Drama in English: Vol. III, 1576–1613*. Gen. eds. Clifford Leech and T. W. Craik. London: Methuen, 1975, pp. i–94.

Barthes, Roland. "The Death of an Author." In *The Discontinuous Universe*. Trans. Richard Howard. New York: Basic Books, 1972, pp. 7–13.

———. "Inaugural Lecture." In *A Barthes Reader*. Ed. Susan Sontag. New York: Hill and Wang, 1982, pp. 457–78.

Barton, Anne. (See Anne Righter.) *Ben Jonson, Dramatist*. Cambridge: Cambridge University Press, 1984.

———. "He that Plays the King: Ford's *Perkin Warbeck* and the Stuart History Play." In *English Drama: Forms and Development: Essays in*

Honour of Muriel Clara Bradbrook. Ed. Marie Axton and Raymond Williams. Cambridge: Cambridge University Press, 1977, pp. 69–93.

———. "The King Disguised: Shakespeare's *Henry V* and the Comical History." In *The Triple Bond: Plays, Mainly Shakespearean, in Performance*. Ed. Joseph G. Price. University Park: Pennsylvania State University Press, 1975, pp. 92–117.

———. "Shakespeare: His Tragedies." In *English Drama to 1710*. Ed. Christopher Ricks. London: Sphere, 1971, pp. 215–52.

———. "*Troilus and Cressida*." *The Riverside Shakespeare*. Ed. G. Blakemore Evans. Boston: Houghton Mifflin, 1974.

Barton, John. *Playing Shakespeare*. London: Methuen, 1984.

Bate, Jonathan. *Shakespearean Constitutions: Politics, Theatre, Criticism, 1730–1830*. Oxford: Clarendon Press, 1989.

Battenhouse, Roy. "*Henry V* as Heroic Comedy." In *Essays on Shakespeare and Elizabethan Drama in Honor of Hardin Craig*. Ed. Richard Hosley. Columbia: University of Missouri Press, 1962, pp. 163–82.

———. "The Relation of Henry V to Tamburlaine." *Shakespeare Survey* 27 (1974), 71–79.

Baumlin, James S. "Generic Context of Elizabethan Satire: Rhetoric, Poetic Theory, and Imitation." In *Renaissance Genres*. Ed. B. K. Lewalski. Cambridge, Mass.: Harvard University Press, 1986, pp. 444–67.

Bavande, William. *A woork of Ioannes Ferrarius Montanus touchynge the goodorderynge of a commonweele. . . .* London, 1559.

Beckerman, Bernard. "The Use and Management of the Elizabethan Stage." In *The Third Globe: Symposium for the Reconstruction of the Globe Playhouse, Wayne State University, 1979*. Detroit: Wayne State University Press, 1981, pp. 151–63.

Belsey, Catherine. "Disrupting Sexual Difference: Meaning and Gender in the Comedies." In *Alternative Shakespeares*. Ed. John Drakakis. London: Methuen, 1985, pp. 166–90.

———. *The Subject of Tragedy: Identity and Difference in Renaissance Drama*. London: Methuen, 1985.

Bentley, Gerald Eades. *The Professions of Dramatist and Player in Shakespeare's Time, 1590–1642*. Princeton: Princeton University Press, 1986.

Berger, Harry, Jr. "Psychoanalyzing the Shakespeare Text: The First Three Scenes of the *Henriad*." In *Shakespeare and the Question of Theory*. Ed. Patricia Parker and Geoffrey Hartman. New York: Methuen, 1985, pp. 210–29.

Berry, Edward I. *Patterns of Decay: Shakespeare's Early Histories*. Charlottesville: University Press of Virginia, 1975.

———. *Shakespeare's Comic Rites*. Cambridge: Cambridge University Press, 1985.

Berry, Philippa. *Of Chastity and Power: Elizabethan Literature and the Unmarried Queen*. London: Routledge, 1989.

Berry, Ralph. *Shakespeare and Social Class*. Atlantic Highlands, N.J.: Humanities Press International, 1988; rpt 1989.

——. *Shakespeare's Comedies: Explorations in Form*. Princeton: Princeton University Press, 1972.

Bevington, David. *From Mankind to Marlowe: Growth in Structure in the Popular Drama of Tudor England*. Cambridge, Mass.: Harvard University Press, 1962.

——. *Medieval Drama*. Boston: Houghton Mifflin, 1975.

——. "Shakespeare vs. Jonson on Satire." In *Shakespeare 1971: Proceedings of the World Shakespeare Congress, Vancouver, August 1971*. Ed. Clifford Leech and J. M. R. Margeson. Toronto: University of Toronto Press, 1972, pp. 108–22.

——. *Tudor Drama and Politics: A Critical Approach to Topical Meaning*. Cambridge, Mass.: Harvard University Press, 1968.

Birney, Alice Lotvin. *Satiric Catharsis in Shakespeare: A Theory of Dramatic Structure*. Berkeley: University of California Press, 1973.

Black, J. D. *The Art of History: A Study of Four Great Historians of the Eighteenth Century*. London, 1936. Rpt. New York: Russell and Russell, 1965.

Black, James. "Counterfeits of Soldiership in *Henry IV*." *Shakespeare Quarterly* 24 (1973), 372–82.

Black, Max. *Models and Metaphors: Studies in Language and Philosophy*. Ithaca: Cornell University Press, 1962.

Blanpied, John. *Time and the Artist in Shakespeare's English Histories*. Newark: University of Delaware Press, 1983.

——. " 'Unfathered Heirs and Loathly Births of Nature': Bringing History to Crisis in *2 Henry IV*." *English Literary Renaissance* 5 (1975), 212–31.

Blissett, William. "Samuel Daniel's Sense of the Past." *English Studies* (Amsterdam) 38 (1957), 49–63.

Bloch, Marc. *The Historian's Craft*. Trans. Peter Putnam. New York: Alfred A. Knopf, 1953.

Bloom, Allan. "*Richard II*." In *Shakespeare as Political Thinker*. Ed. John Alvis and Thomas G. West. Durham, N.C.: Carolina Academic Press, 1981, pp. 51–61.

Bloom, Allan, with Harry V. Jaffa. *Shakespeare's Politics*. New York and London: Basic Books, 1964.

Blundeville, Thomas. *Of Wryting And Reading Hystories*. London, 1574; facsimile—Amsterdam: Theatrum Orbis Terrarum, 1979.

Boas, Frederick. *Shakspere and his Predecessors*. New York: Charles Scribner's Sons, 1896.

Bodin, John. *Method for the Easy Comprehension of History* (1565). Trans. Beatrice Reynolds. New York: Columbia University Press, 1945.

Bodini, Jo. *Methodus Ad Facilem Historiarum Cogitionem*, Lazari Zetzneri (1599). Toronto: Centre for Reformation and Renaissance Studies, rare book.

Bolen, Francis. *Irony and Self-Knowledge in the Creation of Tragedy*. Salzburg Studies in English Literature 19. Salzburg: Universität Salzburg, 1973.

Bond, Edward. *Bingo; Scenes of Money and Death (and, Passion)*. London: Methuen, 1974.

———. *Lear*. London: Methuen, 1971.

Bono, Barbara J. "Mixed Gender, Mixed Genre in Shakespeare's *As You Like It*." In *Renaissance Genres*. Ed. B. K. Lewalski. Cambridge, Mass.: Harvard University Press, 1986, pp. 189–212.

Boose, Linda. "The Family in Shakespeare Studies; or—Studies in the Family of Shakespeareans, or—The Politics of Politics." *Renaissance Quarterly* 40 (1987), 707–42.

Booth, Stephen. *"King Lear," "Macbeth," Indefinition, and Tragedy*. New Haven: Yale University Press, 1983.

Booth, Wayne C. *The Rhetoric of Fiction*. Chicago: University of Chicago Press, 1961; rpt. 1975.

———. *The Rhetoric of Irony*. Chicago and London: University of Chicago Press, 1974.

Borinski, Ludwig. "Shakespeare's Conception of History." *Bulletin de la Faculté des Lettres de Strasbourg* 63.8 (1965), 835–54.

Boris, Edna Z. *Shakespeare's English Kings, the People, and the Law: A Study in the Relationship between the Tudor Constitution and the English History Plays*. Cranbury, N.J.: Associated University Presses, 1974.

Bowers, Fredson. "Theme and Structure in *King Henry IV*, Part 1." In *The Drama of the Renaissance: Essays for Leicester Bradner*. Ed. E. M. Blistein. Providence: Brown University Press, 1970, pp. 42–68.

Bradford, Alan T. "Drama and Architecture under Elizabeth I: The 'Regular' Phase." *English Literary Renaissance* 14 (1984), 3–28.

Bradley, A. C. *Shakespearean Tragedy: Lectures on "Hamlet," "Othello," "King Lear," and "Macbeth."* 1st ed. 1904; 2d ed. 1905. London: Macmillan, 1957; rpt. 1966.

Bradshaw, Graham. *Shakespeare's Scepticism*. Brighton: Harvester Press, 1987.

Branmuller, A. R. *"King John* and Historiography." *English Literary History* 55 (1988), 309–32.

Braudy, Leo. *Narrative Form in History and Fiction: Hume, Fielding, and Gibbon.* Princeton: Princeton University Press, 1970.

Bray, Alan. *Homosexuality in Renaissance England.* London: Gay Men's Press, 1982.

Brecht, Bertolt. *Stücke.* 12 vols. Berlin: Suhrkamp, 1953–59.

Breisach, Ernst. *Historiography: Ancient, Medieval, and Modern.* Chicago: University of Chicago Press, 1983.

Brennan, Anthony S. "That Within Which Passes Show: The Function of the Chorus in *Henry V.*" *Philological Quarterly* 58 (1979), 40–52.

Briggs, Julia. *This Stage-Play World: English Literature and Its Background, 1580–1625.* Oxford: Oxford University Press, 1983.

Bristol, Michael. *Carnival and Theater: Plebian Culture and the Structure of Authority in Renaissance England.* New York: Routledge, 1985.

Brockbank, Philip. "Shakespeare: His Histories, English and Roman." In *English Drama to 1710.* Ed. Christopher Ricks. London: Sphere, 1971, pp. 166–200.

Brockett, Oscar Gross. "Satire in English Drama, 1590–1603." Dissertation. Stanford University, 1953. Rpt. Ann Arbor: University Microfilms, 1981.

Bromley, John C. *The Shakespearean Kings.* Boulder: Colorado Associated Press, 1971.

Brooks, Cleanth, and Robert B. Heilman, eds. "Shakespeare, *Henry IV, Part 1.*" In *Understanding Drama: Twelve Plays.* New York: Holt, 1945; rpt. 1948.

Bruner, Jerome. *Actual Minds/Possible Worlds.* Cambridge, Mass.: Harvard University Press, 1986.

Bryant, J. A., Jr. *Shakespeare and the Uses of Comedy.* Lexington: University Press of Kentucky, 1986.

Büchner, Georg. *Sämtliche Werke und Briefe.* Ed. Werner R. Lehmann. Hamburg: Wegner, 1977.

Bullough, Geoffrey. "The Uses of History." In *Shakespeare's World.* Ed. James Sutherland and Joel Hurstfield. London: Edward Arnold, 1964, pp. 96–115.

Burckhardt, Sigurd. *Shakespearean Meanings.* Princeton: Princeton University Press, 1968.

Burke, Kenneth. *A Grammar of Motives.* New York: Prentice-Hall, 1945.

Burke, Peter. *The Renaissance Sense of the Past.* London: Edward Arnold, 1969.

Burn, A. R. Introduction. In Herodotus, *The Histories.* Trans. Aubrey de Selincourt, rev. ed., Harmondsworth: Penguin, 1972, pp. 7–37.

Burrell, David. *Analogy and Philosophical Language.* New Haven: Yale University Press, 1973.

Burton, Robert. *The Anatomy of Melancholy: What it is, with all the kinds, causes, symptomes, prognostickes & severall cures of it.* Ed. Holbrook Jackson. London, 1932. Rpt. New York: Vintage, 1977. Origin. publ. Oxford, 1621.

Calderwood, James. *Metadrama in Shakespeare's Henriad: "Richard II" to "Henry V."* Berkeley: University of California Press, 1979.

———. *Shakespearean Metadrama.* Minneapolis: University of Minnesota Press, 1971.

Callaghan, Dympna. *Women and Gender in Renaissance Tragedy: A Study of "King Lear," "Othello," "The Duchess of Malfi" and "The White Devil."* Atlantic Highlands: Humanities Press International, 1989.

Calvin, John. *Institutes of the Christian Religion.* Ed. John T. McNeill. Trans. Ford L. Battles. Philadelphia: Westminster Press, 1960.

Camden, Carroll. *The Elizabethan Woman.* Houston: Elsevier, 1952.

Camden, William. *Annales rerum Anglicarum et Hibernicarum regnante Elizabetha.* 2 vols. London: S. Watersoni, 1615.

———. "The Author To the Reader." In *The History of the Most Renowned and Victorious Princess Elizabeth. . . .* Rev. with additions. London: M. Flesher for J. Tonson, 1688.

———. *Britannia siue florentissimorum regorum, Angliae, Scotiae, Hiberniae chorographica descriptio.* 2 vols. London: R. Newbury, 1586.

———. *Remains Concerning Britain.* Ed. R. D. Dunn. Toronto: University of Toronto Press, 1984.

Camp, W. A. "Echoes of History." *An Introduction to Virgil's "Aeneid."* Oxford: Oxford University Press, 1969, pp. 95–105.

Campbell, Lily B. *Shakespeare's "Histories": Mirrors of Elizabethan Policy.* San Marino: Huntington Library, 1947; rpt. 1968.

Campbell, Oscar James. *Comicall Satyre and Shakespeare's "Troilus and Cressida."* San Marino: Huntington Library, 1938.

———. *Shakespeare's Satire.* New York: Oxford University Press, 1943; rpt. 1945.

Candido, Joseph. "The Name of King: Hal's Titles in the *Henriad.*" *Texas Studies in Literature and Language* 26 (1984), 61–73.

Carlson, Marvin. *Theories of the Theatre: A Historical and Critical Survey, from the Greeks to the Present.* Ithaca: Cornell University Press, 1984.

Carlyle, Thomas. "History as Biography." In *The Varieties of History: From Voltaire to the Present.* Ed. Fritz Stern. New York: Meridian, 1956, pp. 90–107.

Carroll, W. C. *The Metamorphoses of Shakespearean Comedy.* Princeton: Princeton University Press, 1986.

Case, Sue-Ellen. *Feminism and Theatre.* London: Macmillan, 1988.

Cervantes, Miguel de. *The Adventures of Don Quixote*. Trans. Jim Cohen, 1950. Harmondsworth: Penguin, 1984.

Chambers, E. K. *The Elizabethan Stage*. Vol. 2. Oxford: Clarendon Press, 1923.

Champion, Larry. *"The Noise of Threatening Drum": Dramatic Strategy and Political Ideology in Shakespeare and the English Chronicle Plays*. Newark: University of Delaware Press, 1990.

———. *Perspective in Shakespeare's English Histories*. Athens: University of Georgia Press, 1980.

Chapman, George. *The Works of George Chapman: Plays*. Ed. R. H. Shepherd. London, 1874.

Chief Pre-Shakespearean Dramas: A Selection of Plays Illustrating the History of the English Drama from Its Origin Down to Shakespeare. Ed. Joseph Quincy Adams. Boston: Houghton Mifflin, 1924.

Chodorow, Nancy. *The Reproduction of Mothering: Psychoanalysis and the Sociology of Gender*. Berkeley: University of California Press, 1979.

Cicero. *De Officiis*. Trans. Walter Miller. Loeb ed. London: Heinemann, 1913.

———. *De Oratore*. Trans. E. W. Sutton (also C. Stuttaford and H. A. Rackham). Loeb ed. Vol. 1, 1942. London: Heinemann, 1979.

Clemen, Wolfgang. *The Development of Shakespeare's Imagery*. German ed. 1936. London: Methuen, 1951.

———. "Past and Future in Shakespeare's Drama." *Publications of the British Academy* 52 (1966), 231–52. Rpt. in Wolfgang Clemen. *Shakespeare's Dramatic Art: Collected Essays*. London: Methuen, 1973, pp. 124–46.

Cochrane, Eric. *Historians and Historiography in the Italian Renaissance*. Chicago: University of Chicago Press, 1981.

Cohen, Walter. *Drama of a Nation: Public Theater in Renaissance England and Spain*. Ithaca: Cornell University Press, 1985.

———. "Political Criticism in Shakespeare." In *Shakespeare Reproduced: The Text in History and Ideology*. Ed. Jean E. Howard and Marion F. O'Connor. New York: Methuen, 1987, pp. 18–46.

Coke, Edward. *The Reports of Sir Edward Coke*. 2d ed. London: H. Twford, etc., 1680.

———. *The Reports of Sir Edward Coke*. Vol. 4. Ed. John Farquhar Fraser. London: Joseph Butterworth and Son, 1826.

Coleridge, Samuel Taylor. *Lectures and Notes on Shakspere and Other English Poets*. London: Bell, 1883; rpt. 1895.

Colie, Rosalie. *Paradoxia Endemica: The Renaissance Tradition of Paradox*. Princeton: Princeton University Press, 1966.

———. *The Resources of Kind: Genre-Theory in the Renaissance*. Ed. Barbara K. Lewalski. Berkeley: University of California Press, 1973.

Collingwood, R. G. *The Idea of History*. Ed. T. M. Knox. Oxford: Clarendon Press, 1946; rpt. 1948.

Comic Drama: The European Heritage. Ed. H. D. Howarth. London: Methuen, 1978.

Connor, W. Robert. *Thucydides*. Princeton: Princeton University Press,
1984.

Cook, Albert. *The Dark Voyage and the Golden Mean: A Philosophy of Comedy*.
Cambridge, Mass.: Harvard University Press, 1949.

Cook, Ann Jennalie. *The Privileged Playgoers of Shakespeare's London, 1576–
1642*. Princeton: Princeton University Press, 1981.

Copi, Irving M. *Introduction to Logic,* 4th ed. New York: Macmillan, 1972.

Copleston, F. C. *Aquinas*. Harmondsworth: Penguin, 1955.

———. *A History of Medieval Philosophy*. London: Methuen, 1972.

Corbett, Edward P. J. *Classical Rhetoric for the Modern Student*. 2d ed. New
York: Oxford University Press, 1971.

Corneille, Pierre. *Théâtre*. Ed. Pierre Lièvre and Roger Callois. Paris:
Bibliothèque de la Pléiade, 1950.

Cornford, Francis M. *The Origin of Attic Comedy*. Cambridge University
Press, 1934.

Council, Norman. *When Honour's at the Stake: Ideas of Honour in Shakespeare's
Plays*. London: Allen and Unwin, 1973.

Coursen, H. R. *The Leasing Out of England: Shakespeare's Second Henriad*.
Washington: University Press of America, 1982.

Courtenay, Thomas. *Commentaries on the Historical Plays of Shakespeare*. 2
vols. London: Henry Colburn, 1840. Rpt. New York: AMS Press, 1972.

Cowan, Louise, "God Will Save the King: Shakespeare's *Richard II*." In
Shakespeare as Political Thinker. Ed. John Alvis and Thomas G. West.
Durham, N.C.: Carolina Academic Press, 1981, pp. 63–81.

Crewe, Jonathan V. "The Hegemonic Theater of George Puttenham."
English Literary Renaissance 16 (1986), 71–85.

Culler, Jonathan. "Apostrophe." In *The Pursuit of Signs: Semiotics, Literature,
Deconstruction*. Ithaca: Cornell University Press, 1981, pp. 135–55.

Curtius, Ernst. *European Literature and the Latin Middle Ages*. Trans. Willard
R. Trask. Bern, 1948; New York: Harper and Row, 1963.

Cutts, John. "Christian and Classical Imagery in *Richard II*." *Universitas* 2
(1974), 70–76.

Daniel, Samuel. *The Civil Wars*. Ed. Laurence Michel. New Haven: Yale
University Press, 1958.

———. *Works*. Ed. Alexander B. Grossart. 1885–86. New York: Russell and
Russell, 1963. (*The Collection of the History of England* appears in vols. 4
and 5.)

Danson, Lawrence. *"Henry V:* King, Chorus, and Critics." *Shakespeare Quarterly* 34 (1983), 27–43.

David, Richard. "Shakespeare's History Plays: Epic or Drama?" *Shakespeare Survey* 6 (1953), 129–39.

Davies, W. Robertson. *Shakespeare's Boy Actors.* New York: Macmillan, 1939.

Davis, Natalie Zemon. "Women on Top: Symbolic Sexual Inversion and Political Disorder in Early Modern Europe." In *The Reversible World: Symbolic Inversion in Art and Society.* Ed. Barbara Babcock. Ithaca: Cornell University Press, 1978, pp. 147–90.

———. " 'Women's History' in Transition: The European Case." *Feminist Review* 3/4 (1975/76).

Dawson, Anthony. "*Measure for Measure,* New Historicism, and Theatrical Power." *Shakespeare Quarterly* 39 (1988), 328–41.

Dean, Leonard F. "From *Richard II* to *Henry V:* A Closer View." In *Shakespeare: Modern Essays in Criticism.* Ed. Leonard F. Dean. New York: Oxford University Press, 1957; rev. 1967; rpt. 1975.

———. "*Richard II:* The State and the Image of the Theatre." *PMLA* 67 (1952), 211–18.

———. "Tudor Theories of Historical Writing." *University of Michigan Contributors to Modern Philology* 1 (1941), 1–24.

de Grazia, Margreta. *Shakespeare Verbatim.* Oxford: Clarendon Press, 1991.

de Man, Paul. *Blindness and Insight: Essays in the Rhetoric of Contemporary Criticism,* 1971. Minneapolis: University of Minnesota Press, 1983.

———. *The Rhetoric of Romanticism.* New York: Columbia University Press, 1984.

———. "Semiology and Rhetoric." In *Allegories of Reading.* New Haven: Yale University Press, 1979, pp. 3–5.

Demosthenes. *The Orations of Demosthenes.* Trans. J. H. Vince. Vol. 1. Loeb ed. London: Heinemann, 1930.

Dennis, John. "On the Genius and Writings of Shakespeare (1711)." In *Eighteenth-Century Essays on Shakespeare.* Ed. D. Nichol Smith. 1st ed. Glasgow: MacLehose. 2d ed. Oxford: Clarendon Press, 1963, pp. 23–43.

Derrida, Jacques. "The Law of Genre." In *On Narrative.* Ed. W. J. T. Mitchell. Chicago: University of Chicago Press, 1981, pp. 51–79.

———. *Of Grammatology.* Trans. Gayatri C. Spivak, 1967. Baltimore: Johns Hopkins University Press, 1976.

———. *Speech and Phenomena, and Other Essays on Husserl's Theory of Signs.* Trans. David Allison. Evanston: Northwestern University Press, 1973 (French original, 1967).

Dessen, Alan C. "The Intemperate Knight and the Politic Prince: Late Morality Structure in *1 Henry IV.*" *Shakespeare Studies* 7 (1974), 147–71.

Dilthey, Wilhelm. *Pattern and Meaning in History: Thoughts on History and Society*. Ed. and trans. H. P. Rickman. New York: Harper and Row, 1962.

Dollimore, Jonathan. "Introduction: Shakespeare, Cultural Materialism, and the New Historicism." In *Political Shakespeare: New Essays in Cultural Materialism*. Ed. Jonathan Dollimore and Alan Sinfield. Ithaca: Cornell University Press, 1985, pp. 2–17.

————. *Radical Tragedy: Religion, Ideology, and Power in the Drama of Shakespeare and His Contemporaries*. Chicago: University of Chicago Press, 1984.

Dollimore, Jonathan, and Allan Sinfield. "History and Ideology: The Instance of *Henry V*." In *Alternative Shakespeares*. Ed. John Drakakis. London: Methuen, 1985, pp. 206–27.

Donaldson, Ian. "Jonson and Anger." In *English Satire and the Satiric Tradition*. Ed. Claude Rawson. Oxford: Basil Blackwell, 1984, pp. 56–71.

Doran, Madeleine. *Endeavors of Art: A Study of Form in Elizabethan Drama*. Madison: University of Wisconsin Press, 1954; rpt. 1964.

————. "Imagery in *Richard II* and in *Henry IV*." *Modern Language Review* 37 (1942), 113–22. Rpt. as "Appendix: Imagery in *Richard II* and in *1 Henry IV*." In *Shakespeare's Dramatic Language: Essays by Madeleine Doran*. Madison: University of Wisconsin Press, 1976, pp. 221–34.

Dray, William H. "Narration, Reduction, and the Uses of History." In *La Philosophie de l'histoire et la pratique historienne d'aujourd'hui = Philosophy of History and Contemporary Historiography*. Ed. David Carr et al. Ottawa: University of Ottawa Press, 1982, pp. 192–214.

————. "Narrative and Historical Realism." In *On History and Philosophers of History*. Leiden: Brill, 1989, ch. 7.

Dray, William H., Richard G. Ely, and Rolf Gruner. "Mandelbaum on History as Narrative: A Discussion." *History and Theory* 8 (1969), 275–94.

Drayton, Michael. *The Works of Michael Drayton*. Ed. J. William Hebel. 5 vols. Oxford, 1931–41. Rpt. Oxford: Blackwell, 1961.

Driver, Tom F. *The Sense of History in Greek and Shakespearean Drama*. New York and London: Columbia University Press, 1960; rpt. 1967.

Dryden, John. *The Works of John Dryden*. Ed. Edward N. H. Hooker and H. T. Swedenberg, Jr. Berkeley: University of California Press, 1956.

Dubois, Claude-Gilbert. *La Conception de l'Histoire en France au XVIe Siècle (1560–1610)*. Paris: A. G. Nizet, 1977.

duBois, Page. *History, Rhetorical Description, and the Epic: From Homer to Spenser*. Cambridge: Cambridge University Press, 1982.

Dubrow, Heather. *Captive Victors: Shakespeare's Narrative Poems and Sonnets.* Ithaca: Cornell University Press, 1987.

———. *Genre.* London: Methuen, 1982.

Duff, J. Wright. *Roman Satire: Its Outlook on Social Life.* Berkeley: University of California Press, 1936.

Duncan, Douglas. *Ben Jonson and the Lucianic Tradition.* Cambridge: Cambridge University Press, 1979.

Dusinberre, Juliet. *Shakespeare and the Nature of Women.* London: Macmillan, 1975.

Eagleton, Terence. *Shakespeare and Society: Critical Studies in Shakespearean Drama.* New York: Schocken Books, 1967.

Early Treatises on the Stage: Viz. Northbrooke's Treatise Against Dicing, Dancing, Plays, and Interludes; Gosson's School of Abuse; and Heywood's Defence of Stage Plays. London: Shakespeare Society, 1843.

Eco, Umberto. "Language, Power, Force." In *Travels in Hyperreality.* Trans. William Weaver, 1986. London: Pan, 1987, pp. 239–55.

———. *The Role of the Reader.* Bloomington: Indiana University Press, 1979.

Egan, Kieran. "Thucydides, Tragedian." In *The Writing of History.* Ed. R. H. Canary and H. Kosicki. Madison: University of Wisconsin Press, 1978, pp. 63–92.

Elam, Keir. *The Semiotics of Theatre and Drama.* London: Methuen, 1980.

Eliot, T. S. *The Complete Poems and Plays of T. S. Eliot.* London: Faber and Faber, 1969; rpt. 1975.

———. "Shakespeare and the Stoicism of Seneca." In *Selected Essays of T. S. Eliot.* London: Faber and Faber, 1932, pp. 126–40.

Elliott, John R., Jr. "History and Tragedy in *Richard II.*" *Studies in English Literature, 1500–1900* 8 (1968), 253–71.

Elliott, Robert C. *The Power of Satire: Magic, Ritual, Art.* Princeton: Princeton University Press, 1960.

Ellis-Fermor, Una. *The Frontiers of Drama.* London: Methuen, 1945; rpt. 1948.

Elyot, Thomas. *The Boke Named the Gouernour.* Ed. Henry Herbert Stephen Croft. 2 vols. London: Kegan Paul, Trench, 1880.

The Empire Writes Back: Theory and Practice in Post-Colonial Literature. Ed. Bill Ashcroft, Gareth Griffiths, and Helen Tiffin. London: Routledge, 1989.

Empson, William. *Seven Types of Ambiguity.* 3d ed., rev. London: Chatto and Windus, 1953.

———. *Some Versions of Pastoral.* London: Chatto and Windus, 1935.

English Satire and the Satiric Tradition. Ed. Claude Rawson. Oxford: Basil Blackwell, 1984.

Evans, Bertrand. *Shakespeare's Tragic Practice*. Oxford: Oxford University Press, 1979.

Evans, Gareth Lloyd. "The Comical-Tragical Historical Method: *Henry IV.*" In *Early Shakespeare*. Gen. eds. John Russell Brown and Bernard Harris. Stratford-upon-Avon Studies 3. London: Arnold, 1961; rev. and rpt. 1967, pp. 145–63.

Faas, Ekbert. *Shakespeare's Poetics*. Cambridge: Cambridge University Press, 1986.

Farjeon, Herbert. *The Shakespearean Scene: Dramatic Criticisms*. London: Hutchinson, 1949.

Felperin, Howard. *Shakespearean Representation: Mimesis and Modernity in Elizabethan Tragedy*. Princeton: Princeton University Press, 1977.

———. *The Uses of the Canon: Elizabethan Literature and Contemporary Theory*. Oxford: Clarendon Press, 1990.

Ferguson, Arthur B. *The Chivalric Tradition in Renaissance England*. Washington: Folger Shakespeare Library, 1986.

———. *Clio Unbound: Perception of the Social and Cultural Past in Renaissance England*. Durham: Duke University Press, 1979.

Ferguson, Margaret W. *Trials of Desire: Renaissance Defences of Poetry*. New Haven: Yale University Press, 1983.

Ferguson, Margaret W., Maureen Quilligan, and Nancy J. Vickers. Introduction. In *Rewriting the Renaissance: The Discourses of Sexual Difference in Early Modern Europe*. Ed. M. W. Ferguson et al. Chicago: University of Chicago Press, 1986, xv–xxxi.

Fichter, Andrew. *Poets Historical: Dynastic Epic in the Renaissance*. New Haven: Yale University Press, 1982.

Fineburg, Leonard. *Introduction to Satire*. Ames: Iowa State University Press, 1967.

Finley, M. I. Introduction. In Thucydides, *History of the Peloponnesian War*. Trans. Rex Warner, 1956. Harmondsworth: Penguin, 1972, pp. 9–32.

The First Public Playhouse: The Theatre in Shoreditch, 1576–1598. Ed. Herbert Berry. Montreal: McGill-Queen's University Press, 1979.

Fish, Stanley. *Is There a Text in This Class? The Authority of Interpretive Communities*. Cambridge, Mass.: Harvard University Press, 1980.

Fitz, L. T. (See Linda Woodbridge.) "Egyptian Queens and Male Reviewers: Sexist Attitudes in *Antony and Cleopatra* Criticism." *Shakespeare Quarterly* 18 (1977), 297–316.

Fitzsimons, M. A. *The Past Recaptured: Great Historians and the History of History*. Notre Dame: University of Notre Dame Press, 1983.

Foakes, R. A. *Illustrations of the English Stage, 1580–1642*. London: Scholar Press, 1985.

———. *Shakespeare: The Dark Comedies to the Last Plays: From Satire to Celebration*. London: Routledge and Kegan Paul, 1971.

Forker, Charles. "Shakespeare's Chronicle Plays as Historical-Pastoral." *Shakespeare Studies* I (1965), 85–104.

Fornara, Charles W. *The Nature of History in Ancient Greece and Rome*. Berkeley: University of California Press, 1983.

Foster, Kenelm. *Petrarch: Poet and Humanist*. Edinburgh: Edinburgh University Press, 1984.

Foucault, Michel. *Discipline and Punish*. Trans. Alan Sheridan. New York: Random House, 1979.

———. *The History of Sexuality: An Introduction*. Trans. Robert Hurley. New York: Pantheon, 1978.

———. "The Subject and Power." *Critical Inquiry* 8 (1982), 777–95.

———. "What Is an Author?" In *Language, Counter-Memory, Practice: Selected Essays and Interviews*. Ed. Donald F. Bouchard. Ithaca: Cornell University Press, 1977, pp. 113–39.

Fowler, Alastair. *Kinds of Literature: An Introduction to the Theory of Genres and Modes*. Cambridge, Mass.: Harvard University Press, 1982.

French, Marilyn. "Power: The First Tetralogy." *Shakespeare's Division of Experience*. New York: Ballantine, 1981, pp. 35–69.

Fryde, E. B. *The Revival of a "Scientific" and Erudite Historiography in the Earlier Renaissance*. Cardiff: University of Wales Press, 1974.

Frye, Northrop. *Anatomy of Criticism: Four Essays*. Princeton: Princeton University Press, 1957; rpt. 1973.

———. "The Argument of Comedy" (1948). In *Theories of Comedy*. Ed. Paul Lauter. Garden City, N.Y.: Doubleday, 1964, pp. 450–60.

———. "The Great Code" (lecture). Senior Fellow Series. Massey College, University of Toronto, 1982.

———. *The Great Code: The Bible and Literature*. New York: Harcourt Brace Jovanovich, 1982.

———. *The Myth of Deliverance: Reflections on Shakespeare's Problem Comedies*. Toronto and Buffalo: University of Toronto Press, 1983.

———. "The Nature of Satire." In *Satura: Ein Kompendium moderner Studien zur Satire*. Ed. Bernard Fabian. Hildesheim: Georges Olms, 1975, pp. 108–22. Origin. pub. *University of Toronto Quarterly* 13 (1944), 75–89.

Furst, Lilian. *Fictions of Romantic Irony*. Cambridge, Mass.: Harvard University Press, 1984.

Fussner, F. Smith. *The Historical Revolution: English Historical Writing and Thought, 1580–1640*. London: Routledge and Kegan Paul, 1962.

———. *Tudor History and Historians*. New York: Basic Books, 1970.

Galbraith, V. H. "Historical Research in Medieval England." In *Kings and*

Chroniclers: Essays in English Medieval History. London: Hamelton Press, 1982, ch. 11, pp. 1–46.

Gallagher, Catherine. *The Industrial Reformation of English Fiction*. Chicago: University of Chicago Press, 1985.

Garber, Marjorie. "Shakespeare as Fetish." *Shakespeare Quarterly* 41 (1990), 242–50.

————. " 'What's Past Is Prologue': Temporality and Prophecy in Shakespeare's History Plays." In *Renaissance Genres: Essays on Theory, History, and Interpretation*. Ed. Barbara K. Lewalski. Cambridge, Mass.: Harvard University Press, 1986, pp. 301–31.

Gardiner, Judith Kegan. "Mind Mother: Psychoanalysis and Feminism." In *Making a Difference: Feminist Literary Criticism*. Ed. Gayle Greene and Coppélia Kahn. London: Methuen, 1985, pp. 113–45.

Gaudet, Paul. "The 'Parasitical' Counselors in Shakespeare's *Richard II*: A Problem in Dramatic Interpretation." *Shakespeare Quarterly* 33 (1982), 142–54.

Gay, Peter. *Freud for Historians*. New York: Oxford University Press, 1985.

————. *Style in History*. New York: Basic Books, 1974.

Gearhart, Suzanne. *The Open Boundary of History and Fiction: A Critical Approach to the French Enlightenment*. Princeton: Princeton University Press, 1984.

Geertz, Clifford. "Centers, Kings, and Charisma: Reflections on the Symbolics of Power." In *Culture and Its Creators: Essays in Honor of Edward Shils*. Ed. Joseph Ben-David and T. N. Clark. Chicago: University of Chicago Press, 1977.

————. *The Interpretation of Cultures*. New York: Basic Books, 1973.

————. *Local Knowledge*. New York: Basic Books. 1983.

The Geneva Bible, 1580.

Geoffrey of Monmouth. *History of the Kings of Britain*. Trans. Sebastian Evans (rev. Charles W. Dunn) 1903. New York: Dutton, 1958.

German Aesthetic and Criticism. Ed. Kathleen Wheeler. Cambridge: Cambridge University Press, 1984.

German Romantic Criticism. Ed. A. Leslie Willson. New York: Continuum, 1982.

Gestenburg, Heinrich Wilhelm. "Briefe über Merkwürdigkeiten der Literatur, 1766–67." In *Shakespeare in Germany, 1740–1815*. Ed. Roy Pascal. Cambridge: Cambridge University Press, 1937, pp. 55–71.

Geyl, Pieter. *Encounters in History*. Cleveland: World, 1961.

Giamatti, A. Bartlett. *The Earthly Paradise and the Renaissance Epic*. Princeton: Princeton University Press, 1966.

Gilbert, Allan. "Patriotism and Satire in *Henry V*." In *Studies in Shakespeare*.

Ed. Arthur D. Matthews and Clark M. Emery. Coral Gables, Fla.: University of Miami Press, 1953. Rpt. New York: AMS Press, 1971, pp. 40–64.

Gilbert, Felix. *Machiavelli and Guicciardini: Politics and History in Sixteenth-Century Florence.* Princeton: Princeton University Press, 1965.

Gildersleeve, V. C. *Government Regulation of Elizabethan Drama.* New York: Columbia University Press, 1908.

Goddard, Harold C. *The Meaning of Shakespeare.* Chicago: University of Chicago Press, 1951.

Godshalk, William Leigh. "Daniel's *History.*" *Journal of English and Germanic Philosophy* 63 (1964), 45–57.

Goethe, Johann Wolfgang. *Werke.* Ed. Eric Trunz et al. 14 vols. Hamburg: Wegner, 1948–60.

Goldberg, Jonathan. *James I and the Politics of Literature: Jonson, Shakespeare, Donne, and Their Contemporaries.* Baltimore: Johns Hopkins University Press, 1983.

———. "The Politics of Renaissance Literature: A Review Essay." *English Literary Renaissance* 16 (1982), 13–43.

———. *Writing Matter: From the Hands of the English Renaissance.* Stanford: Stanford University Press, 1990.

Goldman, Michael. *Acting and Action in Shakespearean Tragedy.* Princeton: Princeton University Press, 1985.

Gonzalez-Echevarriá, Roberto. *The Voices of the Masters: Writing and Authority in Modern Latin American Literature.* Austin: University of Texas Press, 1985.

Goodman, Godfrey. *The Fall of Man.* London: imprinted by F. Kyngston, 1616.

Gossman, Lionel. *Between History and Literature.* Cambridge, Mass.: Harvard University Press, 1990.

———. "History and Literature: Reproduction of Signification." In *The Writing of History: Literary Form and Historical Understanding.* Ed. R. H. Canary and H. Kozicki. Madison: University of Wisconsin Press, 1978, pp. 3–39.

———. "Literature and Education." *New Literary History* 13 (1982), 341–71.

Gosson, Stephen. "The Schoole of Abuse" (1579). In *Northbrooke's Treatise Against Dicing, Dancing, Plays, and Interludes: Gosson's School of Abuse; and Heywood's Defence of Stage Plays.* London: Shakespeare Society, 1843.

Gottfried, Rudolf B. "Samuel Daniel's Method of Writing History." *Studies in the Renaissance* 2 (1956), 157–74.

Gottschalk, Paul A. "Hal and the 'Play Extempore' in *1 Henry IV*." *Texas Studies in Literature and Language* 15 (1974), 605–14.

Gould, Gerald. "A New Reading of *Henry V*." *English Review* 29 (1919), 42–55. Rpt. as "Irony and Satire in *Henry V*." In *Shakespeare "Henry V": A Casebook*. Ed. Michael Quinn. London: Macmillan, 1969, pp. 81–94.

Grant, Michael. Introduction. In Tacitus, *The Annals of Imperial Rome*. Trans. M. Grant. Rev. ed. Harmondsworth: Penguin, 1977, pp. 7–28.

Granville-Barker, Harley. *Prefaces to Shakespeare*. Vol. 3. Princeton: Princeton University Press, 1946.

Greenblatt, Stephen J. "The Forms of Power and the Power of Forms in the Renaissance." *Genre* 15 (1982), 1–4.

———. "Invisible Bullets: Renaissance Authority and Its Subversion, *Henry IV* and *Henry V*." In *Political Shakespeare: New Essays in Cultural Materialism*. Ed. Jonathan Dollimore and Alan Sinfield. Ithaca: Cornell University Press, 1985, pp. 18–47.

——— Preface. *Allegory and Representation*. Ed. Stephen J. Greenblatt. Baltimore: Johns Hopkins University Press, 1981, pp. vii–xiii.

———. *Renaissance Self-Fashioning: From More to Shakespeare*. Chicago: University of Chicago Press, 1980.

———. "Resonance and Wonder." In *Literary Theory Today*. Ed. Peter Collier and Helga Geyer-Ryan. Ithaca: Cornell University Press, 1990, pp. 74–90.

———. *Shakespearean Negotiations: The Circulation of Social Energy in Renaissance England*. Berkeley: University of California Press, 1988.

———. *Sir Walter Ralegh: The Renaissance Man and His Roles*. New Haven: Yale University Press, 1973.

Greene, Thomas M. *The Light in Troy: Imitation and Discovery in Renaissance Poetry*. New Haven: Yale University Press, 1982.

———. *The Vulnerable Text: Essays on Renaissance Literature*. New York: Columbia University Press, 1986.

Grivelet, Michel. "Shakespeare's 'War with Time': The Sonnets and *Richard II*." *Shakespeare Survey* 23 (1970), 69–78.

Guicciardini, Francesco. *The History of Italy*. Trans. Sidney Alexander. New York: Macmillan, 1969.

———. *History of Italy and History of Florence*. Ed. John R. Hale. Trans. Cecil Grayson. New York: Twayne, 1964.

Gurr, Andrew. *Playgoing in Shakespeare's London, 1567–1642*. Cambridge: Cambridge University Press, 1987.

Gurr, Andrew, with John Orrell. *Rebuilding Shakespeare's Globe*. New York: Routledge, 1989.

Haigh, A. E. *The Tragic Drama of the Greeks*. 1896. Oxford: Clarendon Press, 1925.

Hall, Edward. *Hall's Chronicle* [etc.]. New York: AMS Press, 1965.

Hall, Stuart. "Cultural Studies: Two Paradigms." In *Culture, Ideology, and Social Process: A Reader.* Ed. Tony Bennett et al. London: Batsford, 1981, pp. 19–37.

Hampton, Timothy. *Writing from History: The Rhetoric of Exemplarity in Renaissance Literature.* Ithaca: Cornell University Press, 1990.

Handlin, Oscar. *Truth in History.* Cambridge, Mass.: Harvard University Press, 1979.

Hands, Terry. "Notes on the Working Text." In *The Royal Shakespeare Company's Production of "Henry V."* Ed. Sally Beauman. Oxford: Pergamon Press, 1976, pp. 14–27.

Harbage, Alfred. *Shakespeare's Audience.* New York: Columbia University Press, 1941.

Harris, Kathryn M. "Sun and Water Imagery in *Richard II*: It's Dramatic Function." *Shakespeare Quarterly* 21 (1970), 157–65.

Hart, Jonathan. "Alienation, Double Signs with a Difference: Conscious Knots in *Cymbeline* and *The Winter's Tale.*" *CIEFL Bulletin* (New Series) 1 (1989), 58–78.

———. "The Body Divided: Kingship in Shakespeare's Lancastrian Tetralogy." *CIEFL Bulletin* (New Series) 2 (1990), 24–52.

———. "Canadian Literature: In the Mouth of the Canon." *Journal of Canadian Studies* 23 (1988–89), 145–58.

———. "A Comparative Pluralism: The Heterogeneity of Methods and the Case of Possible Worlds." *Canadian Review of Comparative Literature* 15 (1988), 320–45.

———. "*Henry VIII*: The Play as History and Anti-History." *Aevum: Rassegna di Scienze Storiche-Linguistiche E Filologiche* (forthcoming, December 1991).

———. "*Henry V*: Towards the Problem Play." *Cahiers Elisabéthains* (forthcoming).

———. "Inside and Outside: Marlowe's Use of Address and Apostrophe." *Language and Style* (forthcoming).

———. Introduction. Special Issue. "Renaissance Narrative and Drama." *Canadian Review of Comparative Literature* 18, 2/3 (1991).

———. "Narratorial Strategies in *The Rape of Lucrece.*" *Studies in English Literature* (forthcoming, winter 1992).

———. "The New Historicism: Taking History into Account." *Ariel* 22 (1991), 93–107.

———. "Playboys, Killjoys, and a Career as Critic: The Accomplishment of Harry Levin." *Canadian Review of Comparative Literature* 16 (1989), 118–35.

——. "Stephen Greenblatt's *Shakespearean Negotiations.*" *Textual Practice* (forthcoming, fall 1991).

——. "Temporality and Theatricality in Shakespeare's Lancastrian Tetralogy." *Studia Neophilologica* 63 (1991), 69–88.

——. " 'Till Forging Nature Be Condemned of Treason': Representational Strife in *Venus and Adonis.*" *Cahiers Elisabéthains* 36 (1989), 37–47.

Hartman, Geoffrey. *Criticism in the Wilderness.* New Haven: Yale University Press, 1980.

Hattaway, Michael. *Elizabethan Popular Theatre: Plays in Performance.* London: Routledge and Kegan Paul, 1982.

Hawkes, Terence. *Shakespeare and the Reason: A Study of the Tragedies and Problem Plays.* London: Routledge and Kegan Paul, 1964.

——. "Swiser-Swatter: Making a Man of English Letters." In *Alternative Shakespeares.* Ed. John Drakakis. London: Methuen, 1985, pp. 26–46.

——. "Uses and Abuses of the Bard." *Times Literary Supplement*, 10 April 1987, 391–93.

Hay, Denys. *Annalists and Historians: Western Historiography from the Eighth to Eighteenth Centuries.* London: Methuen, 1977.

Hazlitt, W. C. *The Collected Works of William Hazlitt.* Ed. A. R. Walle and A. Glover. London: Dent, 1902–4.

Hegel, G. W. F. *The Philosophy of Fine Art.* 4 vols. Trans. F. P. B. Osmaston. London: G. Bell & Sons, 1920. Rpt. New York: Hacker, 1975.

Heilman, Robert. *Tragedy and Melodrama: Versions of Experience.* Seattle: University of Washington Press, 1968.

Heisch, Allison. "Queen Elizabeth I and the Persistence of Patriarchy." *Feminist Review* 4 (1980), 45–56.

Heller, Erich. *The Ironic German: A Study of Thomas Mann.* New York: Appel, 1973; corrected from 1958 original.

Helms, Lorraine. "Playing the Woman's Part." *Theatre Journal* 41 (1989), 190–200.

Hendrickson, G. L. "Satura Tota Nostra Est." In *Satire: Modern Essays in Criticism.* Ed. Ronald Paulson. Englewood Cliffs, N.J.: Prentice-Hall, 1971, pp. 37–65. Origin. pub. *Classical Philology* 22 (1927), 46–60.

Henniger, S. K., Jr. "The Sun-King Analogy in *Richard II.*" *Shakespeare Quarterly* 11 (1960), 319–27.

Hernadi, Paul. *Beyond Genre: New Directions in Literary Classification.* Ithaca: Cornell University Press, 1972.

Herodotus. *The Persian Wars*, book 2, ch. 5. Trans. George Rawlinson. In *Introduction to the Greek Historians.* Vol. 2. Ed. F. R. B. Goldolphin. New York: Random House, 1942.

Heywood, Thomas. "An Apology for Actors." In *Literary Criticism: Plato to*

Dryden. Ed. Allan H. Gilbert. Detroit: Wayne State University Press, 1962, pp. 553–64.

Hibbard, George. " 'The Forced Gait of a Shuffling Nag.' " In *Shakespeare 1971: Proceedings of the World Shakespeare Congress: Vancouver, August 1971.* Ed. Clifford Leech and J. M. R. Margeson. Toronto: University of Toronto Press, 1972, pp. 76–88.

———. *The Making of Shakespeare's Dramatic Poetry.* Toronto: University of Toronto Press, 1981.

Highet, Gilbert. *The Anatomy of Satire.* Princeton: Princeton University Press, 1962.

———. *The Speeches in Vergil's "Aeneid."* Princeton: Princeton University Press, 1971.

Hillebrand, Harold Newcomb. *The Child Actors: A Chapter in Elizabethan Stage History.* Urbana: University of Illinois Press, 1926.

History as Literature. Ed. Orville Prescott. New York: Harper and Row, 1970.

Hobday, C. H. "Imagery and Irony in *Henry V.*" *Shakespeare Survey* 21 (1968), 107–13.

———. "Why the Sweets Melted: A Study in Shakespeare's Imagery." *Shakespeare Quarterly* 16 (1965), 3–17.

Hochberg, Herbert. *Logic, Ontology, and Language.* Munich: Philosophia, 1984.

Hodgart, Matthew. *Satire.* London: Weidenfeld and Nicolson, 1969.

Hoffding, Harald. *Le concept d'analogie.* Trans. René Perrin. Paris: J. Vrin, 1931.

Hofstadter, Douglas. *Gödel, Escher, Bach: An Eternal Golden Braid.* New York: Basic Books, 1979.

———. *Metamagical Themas: Questing for the Essence of Mind and Pattern.* New York: Basic Books, 1985.

Holderness, Graham. *Shakespeare's History.* Dublin: Gill and Macmillan, 1985.

Holderness, Graham, Nick Potter, and John Turner. *Shakespeare: The Play of History.* Iowa City: University of Iowa Press, 1987.

Holinshed, Raphael. *Chronicles of England, Scotland and Ireland.* 6 vols. 1808; rpt. New York: AMS Press, 1978.

Holstun, James. "Ranting at the New Historicism." *English Literary Renaissance* 19 (1989), 189–225.

Homan, Sidney. *When the Theatre Turns to Itself: The Aesthetic Metaphor in Shakespeare.* Lewisburg, Pa.: Bucknell University Press, 1981.

Homer. *The "Iliad" of Homer.* Trans. Richard Lattimore. Chicago: University of Chicago Press, 1951.

————. The *"Odyssey" of Homer*. Trans. Richard Lattimore. Chicago: University of Chicago Press, 1967.

Hooker, John. "The Epistle Dedicatory." In *Holinshed's Chronicles of England, Scotland and Ireland: Volume 6: Ireland*. London: 1808; rpt. New York: AMS Press, 1965.

Hosley, Richard. "The Playhouses." In *The "Revels" History of the Drama in English: Volume III, 1576–1613*. Gen. eds. Clifford Leech and T. W. Craik. London: Methuen, 1975, pp. 119–235.

Hospers, John. *An Introduction to Philosophical Analysis*, 2d ed. Englewood Cliffs, N.J.: Prentice-Hall, 1967.

Howard, Jean. "Crossdressing, the Theatre, and Gender Struggle in Early Modern England." *Shakespeare Quarterly* 39 (1988), 418–40.

————. "The New Historicism in Renaissance Studies." *English Literary Renaissance* 16 (1986), 13–43.

————. "Old Wine, New Bottles." *Shakespeare Quarterly* 35 (1984), 236–37.

Hugo, Victor. *Oeuvres Complètes*. Ed. Jacques Seebacher and R. Laffont. Paris, 1988.

Huizinga, Johan. *Homo Ludens: A Study of the Play Element in Culture*. 1950; rpt. Boston: Beacon Press, 1955.

Hutchens, Eleanor. *Irony in "Tom Jones."* University: University of Alabama Press, 1965.

Iser, Wolfgang. *The Implied Reader*. Baltimore: Johns Hopkins University Press, 1974.

Ives, E. W. "Shakespeare and History: Divergencies and Agreements." *Shakespeare Survey* 38 (1985), 19–37.

Jackson, James L. "Shakespeare's Dog-and-Sugar Imagery and the Friendship Tradition." *Shakespeare Quarterly* 1 (1950), 260–63.

Jacobs, Henry E. "Prophecy and Ideology in Shakespeare's *Richard II*." *South Atlantic Review* 51 (1986), 3–18.

Jagendorf, Z. J. *The Happy End of Comedy: Shakespeare, Jonson, Molière*. Newark: University of Delaware Press, 1984.

Jameson, Fredric. *The Political Unconscious: Narrative as a Socially Symbolic Act*. Ithaca: Cornell University Press, 1981.

Jardine, Lisa. *Still Harping on Daughters: Women and Drama in the Age of Shakespeare*. Sussex: Harvester Press, 1983.

Javitch, David. *Poetry and Courtliness in Renaissance England*. Princeton: Princeton University Press, 1978.

Jenkins, Harold. *The Structural Problem in Shakespeare's "Henry the Fourth."* London: Methuen, 1956.

Johnson, Barbara. "Apostrophe, Animation, and Abortion." *Diacritics* 16 (1986), 29–49.

————. "The Surprise of Otherness: A Note on the Wartime Writings of Paul de Man." In *Literary Theory Today*. Ed. Peter Collier and Helga Geyer-Ryan. Ithaca: Cornell University Press, 1990, pp. 13–22.

Johnson, Samuel, "Preface to Shakespeare, 1765." In *Johnson on Shakespeare*. Ed. A. Sherbo. Yale ed. of the *Works*, vol. 7. New Haven and London: Yale University Press, 1968.

Jones, G. P. "*Henry V*: The Chorus and the Audience." *Shakespeare Survey* 31 (1978), 93–105.

Jonson, Ben. *Ben Jonson*. 11 vols. Ed. C. H. Herford and Percy Simpson. Oxford: Clarendon Press, 1925–52.

————. *Sejanus*. Ed. Jonas A. Barish. New Haven: Yale University Press, 1965.

Jordan, Constance. *Renaissance Feminism: Literary Texts and Political Models*. Ithaca: Cornell University Press, 1990.

Jorgensen, Paul A. " 'Redeeming Time' in Shakespeare's *Henry IV*." *Tennessee Studies in Literature* 5 (1960), 101–9.

————. *Shakespeare's Military World*. Berkeley and Los Angeles: University of California Press, 1956.

Jump, John. "Shakespeare and History." *Critical Quarterly* 17 (1953), 233–44.

Kahn, Coppélia. *Man's Estate: Masculine Identity in Shakespeare*. Berkeley: University of California Press, 1981.

Kantorowicz, Ernst H. *The King's Two Bodies: A Study in Mediaeval Political Theology*. Princeton: Princeton University Press, 1957.

Kastan, David Scott. *Shakespeare and the Shapes of Time*. Hanover, N.H.: University Press of New England, 1982.

————. "The Shape of Time: Form and Value in the Shakespearean History Play." *Comparative Drama* 7 (1973–74), 259–77.

————. " 'To Set a Form upon that Indigest': Shakespeare's Fictions of History." *Comparative Drama* 17 (1983–84), 1–16.

Kaula, David. " 'In War with Time': Temporal Perspectives in Shakespeare's Sonnets." *Studies in English Literature* 3 (1963), 45–57.

Kelley, Donald R. *Foundations of Modern Historical Scholarship: Language, Law, and History in the French Renaissance*. New York: Columbia University Press, 1970.

Kelly, Henry A. *Divine Providence in the England of Shakespeare's Histories*. Cambridge, Mass.: Harvard University Press, 1970.

Kelly, Joan. *Women, History, and Theory: The Essays of Joan Kelly*. Chicago: University of Chicago Press, 1984.

Kelly, Katherine E. "The Queen's Two Bodies: Shakespeare's Boy Actress in Breeches." *Theatre Journal* 42 (1990), 81–93.

Kelso, Ruth. *Doctrine for the Lady of the Renaissance*. Urbana: University of Illinois Press, 1956.

Kermode, Frank. *Romantic Image*. London: Routledge and Paul, 1957.

————. *The Sense of an Ending*. New York: Oxford University Press, 1967.

Kernan, Alvin. *The Cankered Muse: Satire of the English Renaissance*. New Haven: Yale University Press, 1959.

————. "The Henriad: Shakespeare's Major History Plays." In *Modern Shakespearean Criticism: Essays on Style, Dramaturgy, and the Major Plays*. Ed. Alvin Kernan. New York: Harcourt, 1970, pp. 245–75. Pub. in *Yale Review* 59 (1969), 3–32.

————. "The Plays and Playwrights." In *The "Revels" History of the Drama in English: Vol. III, 1576–1613*. Gen. eds. Clifford Leech and T. W. Craik. London: Methuen, 1975, pp. 237–474.

————. *The Playwright as Magician: Shakespeare's Image of the Poet in the English Public Theater*. New Haven: Yale University Press, 1979.

————. "Shakespeare and the Abstraction of History." In *Shakespeare: Pattern of Excelling Nature*. Ed. David Bevington and Jay L. Halio. Newark: University of Delaware Press, 1978, pp. 133–35.

Kierkegaard, Søren. *The Concept of Irony: With Constant Reference to Socrates*. Trans. Lee Capel. London: Collins, 1966.

————. *Either/Or: A Fragment of Life*. Trans. David and Lillian Swenson. 2 vols. Princeton: Princeton University Press, 1944.

King, John N. "Spenser's *Shepheardes Calender* and Protestant Pastoral Satire." In *Renaissance Genres*. Ed. B. K. Lewalski. Cambridge, Mass.: Harvard University Press, 1986, pp. 369–98.

————. *Tudor Royal Iconography: Literature and Art in an Age of Religious Crisis*. Princeton: Princeton University Press, 1989.

Kingsford, Charles Lethbridge. *English Historical Literature in the Fifteenth Century*. Oxford: Clarendon Press, 1913.

Kliger, Samuel. "The Sun Imagery in *Richard II*." *Studies in Philology* 45 (1948), 196–202.

Knight, G. Wilson. *The Olive and the Sword: A Study of England's Shakespeare*. London: Oxford University Press, 1944.

————. *This Sceptered Isle: A Study of Shakespeare's Kings*. Oxford: Blackwell, 1940.

Knights, L. C. "Notes on Comedy" (1933). In *Theories of Comedy*. Ed. Paul Lauter. Garden City, N.Y.: Doubleday, 1964, pp. 438–43.

————. *Some Shakespearean Themes*. London: Chatto and Windus, 1959.

————. *William Shakespeare: The Histories*. London: Longmans, 1962; rev. 1965.

Knowles, Richard. "Unquiet and the Double Plot *2 Henry IV*." *Shakespeare Studies* 2 (1966), 133–40.

Knox, Norman. *The Word "Irony" and Its Context, 1500–1755.* Durham: Duke University Press, 1961.

Kuhn, Thomas S. *The Copernican Revolution: Planetary Astronomy in the Development of Western Thought.* Cambridge, Mass.: Harvard University Press, 1957.

Kyd, Thomas. *The Spanish Tragedy.* In *Elizabethan and Stuart Plays.* Ed. Charles Read Baskervill et al. New York: Henry Holt, 1934, pp. 423–73.

La Branche, Anthony. " 'If Thou Wert Sensible of Courtesy': Private and Public Virtue in *Henry IV, Part One.*" *Shakespeare Quarterly* 17 (1966), 371–82.

LaGuardia, Eric. "Ceremony and History: The Problem of Symbol from *Richard II* to *Henry V.*" In *Pacific Coast Studies in Shakespeare.* Ed. Waldo McNeir and Thelma N. Greenfield. Eugene: University of Oregon Press, 1966, pp. 68–88.

Laister, M. L. W. *The Greater Roman Historians.* Berkeley: University of California Press, 1966.

Lamming, George. *The Pleasures of Exile.* London: Michael Joseph, 1960.

Lanham, Richard. *The Motives of Eloquence: Literary Rhetoric in the Renaissance.* New Haven: Yale University Press, 1976.

Lattimore, Richmond. Introduction. *The "Iliad" of Homer.* Trans. R. Lattimore. Chicago: University of Chicago Press, 1951, pp. 11–55.

———. Introduction. *The "Odyssey" of Homer.* Trans. R. Lattimore. Chicago: University of Chicago Press, 1967, pp. 1–24.

Law, Robert Adger. "The Composition of Shakespeare's Lancastrian Tetralogy." *Texas Studies in Literature and Language* 3 (1961), 321–27.

———. "Links between Shakespeare's History Plays." *Studies in Philology* 50 (1953), 168–87.

———. "Structural Unity in the Two Parts of *Henry the Fourth.*" *Studies in Philology* 24 (1927), 223–42.

Lawrence, William Witherle. *Shakespeare's Problem Comedies.* 1931. Rev. 1960. Harmondsworth: Penguin; rpt. 1969.

Leatherdale, W. H. *The Role of Analogy, Model, and Metaphor in Science.* Amsterdam: North Holland, 1974.

Leech, Clifford. *Christopher Marlowe: Poet for the Stage.* Ed. Anne Lancashire. New York: AMS Press, 1986.

———. "Shakespeare and the Idea of the Future." *University of Toronto Quarterly* 35 (1965–66), 213–28.

———. "The Unity of 2 *Henry IV.*" *Shakespeare Survey* 6 (1953), 16–24.

Lefranc, Pierre. *Sir Walter Ralegh: Écrivain: l'oeuvre et les idées.* Paris: Librairie Armand Colin, 1968.

Leggatt, Alexander. "*Henry VIII* and the Ideal England." *Shakespeare Survey* 38 (1985), 131–43.

———. *Shakespeare's Political Drama: The History Plays and the Roman Plays.* London: Routledge, 1988.

Leiris, Michel. *La Possession et ses aspects théâtraux chez les Ethiopiens de Gondar.* Paris: Plon, 1958.

Lentricchia, Frank. *Criticism and Social Change.* Chicago: University of Chicago Press, 1983.

Levin, Harry. "Falstaff's Encore." *Shakespeare Quarterly* 32 (1981), 5–17.

———. *The Gates of Horn: A Study of Five French Realists.* New York: Oxford University Press, 1963.

———. *The Myth of the Golden Age in the Renaissance* (1969). Oxford: Oxford University Press, 1971.

———. *Playboys and Killjoys: An Essay on the Theory and Practice of Comedy.* New York: Oxford University Press, 1987.

Levin, Richard. "Hazlitt on *Henry V,* and the Appropriation of Shakespeare." *Shakespeare Quarterly* 35 (1984), 134–41.

———. *Love and Society in Shakespearean Comedy: A Study of Dramatic Form and Content.* Newark: University of Delaware Press, 1985.

———. *The Multiple Plot in English Renaissance Drama.* Chicago: University of Chicago Press, 1971.

———. *New Readings vs. Old Plays: Recent Trends in the Reinterpretation of English Renaissance Drama.* Chicago: University of Chicago Press, 1979.

———. "Women in the Renaissance Theatre Audience." *Shakespeare Quarterly* 40 (1989), 165–74.

Levy, F. J. *Tudor Historical Thought.* San Marino, Calif.: Huntington Library, 1967.

Lewalski, Barbara K. "Introduction: Issues and Approaches." In *Renaissance Genres: Essays on Theory, History, and Interpretation.* Ed. Barbara K. Lewalski. Cambridge, Mass.: Harvard University Press, 1986, pp. 1–14.

Lewis, C. S. *English Literature in the Sixteenth Century.* Oxford: Oxford University Press, 1954.

Lewis, Wyndham. "The Greatest Satire Is Nonmoral." In *Satire: Modern Essays in Criticism.* Ed. Ronald Paulson. Englewood Cliffs, N.J.: Prentice-Hall, 1971, pp. 66–79.

Lindenberger, Herbert. *Historical Drama: The Relation of Literature to Drama.* Chicago: University of Chicago Press, 1975.

Litvak, Joseph. "Back to the Future: A Review-Article on the New Historicism, Deconstruction and Nineteenth-Century Fiction." *Texas Studies on Literature and Language* 30 (1988), 120–49.

Liu, Alan. "The Power of Formalism: The New Historicism." *English Literary History* 56 (1989), 721–71.

Livy. Trans. B. O. Foster. Loeb ed. London: Heinemann, 1952.

Lovejoy, Arthur. *The Great Chain of Being: A Study of the History of an Idea*. Cambridge, Mass.: Harvard University Press, 1936.

Lucas, F. L. *Seneca and Elizabethan Tragedy*. Cambridge: Cambridge University Press, 1922.

Lukács, Georg. *The Historical Novel*. Trans. Hannah and Stanley Mitchell. 1937. Boston: Beacon Press, 1963.

Lydgate, John. *Lydgate's "Fall of Princes."* Ed. Henry Bergen. Washington: Carnegie Institute, 1923.

Lyotard, Jean-François. "Judiciousness in Dispute; or, Kant after Marx." In *The Aims of Representation*. Ed. Murray Krieger. New York: Columbia University Press, 1987, pp. 23–67.

Macaulay, Thomas Babington. "History and Literature." In *The Varieties of History: From Voltaire to the Present*. Ed. Fritz Stern. New York: Meridian, 1956, pp. 71–89.

MacCary, T. W. *Friends and Lovers: The Phenomenology of Desire in Shakespeare's Comedy*. New York: Columbia University Press, 1985.

Macherey, Pierre. *A Theory of Literary Production*. Trans. Geoffrey Wall. London: Routledge, 1978. (French orig. 1970).

Machiavelli, Niccolò. *Machiavelli: The Chief Works and Others*. Trans. Allan Gilbert. Vol. 3. Durham: Duke University Press, 1965.

———. *The Letters of Machiavelli*. Trans. Allan Gilbert. New York: Capricorn, 1961.

Macia-Lees, Frances E., Patricia Sharpe, and Colleen Ballerino Cohen. "The Postmodernist Turn in Anthropology: Cautions from a Feminist Perspective." *Signs* 15 (1989), 7–33.

Mack, Maynard. "The Muse of Satire." In *Satura: Ein Kompendium moderner Studien zur Satire*. Ed. Bernard Fabian. Hildesheim; New York: Georges Olms, 1975, pp. 190–201. Orig. pub. *Yale Review* 41 (1951), 80–92.

Maclean, Hugh. "Time and Horsemanship in Shakespeare's Histories." *University of Toronto Quarterly* 35 (1966), 229–45.

Maclean, Ian. *The Renaissance Notion of Woman: A Study in the Fortunes of Scholasticism and Medical Science in European Intellectual Life*. Cambridge: Cambridge University Press, 1980.

Maguin, François. "The Breaking of Time: *Richard II, Hamlet, King Lear, Macbeth* (The Hero's Stand in and Against Time)." *Cahiers Elisabéthains* 7 (1975), 25–41.

Maguin, Jean-Marie. "Shakespeare's Structural Craft and Dramatic Technique in *Henry V*." *Cahiers Elisabéthains* 7 (1975), 51–67.

Maitland, Frederic William. *The Collected Papers of Frederic William Maitland*.

Ed. H. A. L. Fisher. Vol. 3. Cambridge: Cambridge University Press, 1911.

———. *Maitland: Selected Essays*. Ed. H. D. Hazeltine, G. Lapsley, and P. H. Winfield. Cambridge: Cambridge University Press, 1936.

Major, John M. *Sir Thomas Elyot and Renaissance Humanism*. Lincoln: University of Nebraska Press, 1964.

Mandelbaum, Maurice. "A Note on History as Narrative." *History and Theory* 6 (1967), 413–19.

Manheim, Michael. *The Weak King Dilemma in the Shakespearean History Play*. Syracuse: Syracuse University Press, 1973.

Marcus, Leah S. *The Politics of Mirth: Jonson, Herrick, Milton, Marvell, and the Defense of Old Holiday Pastimes*. Chicago: University of Chicago Press, 1986.

———. *Puzzling Shakespeare: Local Reading and Its Discontents*. Berkeley: University of California Press, 1988.

———. "Shakespeare's Comic Heroines, Elizabeth I, and the Political Uses of Androgny." In *Women in the Middle Ages and the Renaissance: Literary and Historical Perspectives*. Ed. Mary Beth Rose. Syracuse: Syracuse University Press, 1986, pp. 135–53.

Margeson, John M. R. "Dramatic Irony in Jacobean Tragedy." 2 vols. Dissertation. University of Toronto, 1952.

———. *The Origins of English Tragedy*. Oxford: Clarendon Press, 1967.

Marlowe, Christopher. *The Complete Works of Christopher Marlowe*. Ed. Irving Ribner. New York: Odyssey Press, 1963.

———. *Tamburlaine, Part 1*. In *English Drama: 1580–1642*. Ed. C. F. Tucker Brooke and Nathaniel Burton Paradise. Lexington, Mass.: D.C. Heath, 1933.

———. *Tamburlaine, Parts One and Two: Text and Major Criticism*. Ed. Irving Ribner. Indianapolis: Bobbs-Merrill, 1974.

Martin, Ronald. *Tacitus*. Berkeley: University of California Press, 1981.

Mauss, Marcel. *A General Theory of Magic*. Trans. Robert Brain. New York: Norton, 1975. (French orig. 1950.)

Maveety, Stanley R. "A Second Fall of Cursed Man: The Bold Metaphor in *Richard II*." *Journal of English and Germanic Philology* 72 (1973), 175–93.

Maxwell, J. C. "Simple or Complex? Some Problems in the Interpretation of Shakespeare." *Durham University Journal* 46, new series 15 (1954), 112–15.

McAlindon, Thomas. *English Renaissance Tragedy*. London: Macmillan, 1986.

McArthur, Herbert. "Tragic and Comic Modes." *Criticism* 3 (1961), 36–45.

McCanles, Michael. "The Authentic Discourse of the Renaissance." *Diacritics* 10 (1980), 77–87.

McCuskor, Honor. *John Bale, Dramatist and Antiquary.* Byrn Mawr, Pa., 1942.

McGuire, Richard. "The Play-within-the Play in *1 Henry IV.*" *Shakespeare Quarterly* 18 (1967), 47–52.

McKee, John. *Literary Irony and the Literary Audience: Studies in the Victimization of the Reader in Augustan Fiction.* Amsterdam: Rodopi, N.V., 1974.

McKisack, May. "Samuel Daniel As Historian." *Review of English Studies* 23 (1947), 226–43.

McLaverty, J. "No Abuse: The Prince and Falstaff in the Tavern Scenes of *Henry IV.*" *Shakespeare Survey* 34 (1981), 105–11.

McLuskie, Kathleen. "Feminist Deconstruction: The Example of Shakespeare's *Taming of the Shrew.*" *Red Letters* 12, 33–40.

McNeir, Waldo F. "The Comic Scenes in *Richard II.*" *Neuphilologische Mitteilungen* 73 (1972), 815–22.

———. "Structure and Theme in the First Tavern Scene (II.iv) of *1 Henry IV.*" In *Pacific Coast Studies in Shakespeare.* Ed. Waldo F. McNeir and Thelma N. Greenfield. Eugene: University of Oregon Press, 1966, pp. 89–105.

Medieval Historical Writing in the Christian and Islamic Worlds. Ed. D. O. Morgan. London: University of London Press, 1982.

Medvedev, P. N., and M. M. Bakhtin. *The Formal Method in Literary Scholarship: A Critical Introduction to Sociological Poetics.* Trans. Albert J. Wehrle. Baltimore: Johns Hopkins University Press, 1978.

Mellor, Anne K. *English Romantic Irony.* Cambridge, Mass.: Harvard University Press, 1980.

Men in Feminism. Ed. Alice Jardine and Paul Smith. London: Methuen, 1987.

Mercier, Joseph. "Shakespeare and the Function of Irony." Dissertation. University of Connecticut, 1969. Rpt. Ann Arbor: University Microfilms, 1981.

Merrix, Robert P. "The Alexandrian Allusion in Shakespeare's *Henry V.*" *English Literary Renaissance* 2 (1972), 321–33.

———. "The Phaeton Allusion in *Richard II*: The Search for Identity." *English Literary Renaissance* 17 (1987), 277–87.

———. "Structural Satire in Shakespeare's Henry Plays." Dissertation. University of Cincinnati, 1965. Rpt. Ann Arbor: University Microfilms, 1981.

Meyricke, Gelly. (The Examination of Meyricke 17th Feb. 1600 [*Domestic State Papers, Elizabeth,* vol. 278, no. 78]). Augustine Phillipps. (The Examination of Phillipps 18th Feb. 1600 [ibid., no. 85]); William Lambard. In John Nichols, *Progresses and Processions of Queen Elizabeth.* In *The Shakespeare Allusion-Book: A Collection of Allusions to Shakespeare from 1591 to 1700 . . .* , vol. 1, comp. C. Ingleby et al. Re-ed. and rev. J. Munro, 1909. Freeport, N.Y.: Books for Library Press, 1970.

Michel, Laurence, and Cecil C. Seronsy. "Shakespeare's History Plays and Daniel: An Assessment." *Studies in Philology* 52 (1955), 549–77.

Miller, Nancy K. "Arachnologies: The Woman, the Text, and the Critic." In *The Poetics of Gender.* Ed. Nancy K. Miller. New York: Columbia University Press, 1987.

———. *Subject to Change: Reading Feminist Writing.* New York: Columbia University Press, 1988.

Miner, Earl. "In Satire's Falling City." In *The Satirist's Art.* Ed. James Jensen and Marvin R. Zirker, Jr. Bloomington: Indiana University Press, 1972, pp. 3–27.

Montaigne, Michel de. *Essays.* Trans. J. M. Cohen. Harmondsworth: Penguin, 1958; rpt. 1971.

Montgomery, Robert L., Jr. "The Dimensions of Time in *Richard II.*" *Shakespeare Studies* 4 (1969), 73–85.

Montrose, Louis A. "*A Midsummer Night's Dream* and the Shaping Fantasies of Elizabethan Culture: Gender, Power, Form." In *Rewriting the Renaissance.* Ed. M. Quilligan, M. W. Ferguson, and N. Vickers. Chicago: University of Chicago Press, 1986, pp. 65–87.

———. "Renaissance Literary Studies and the Subject of History." *English Literary Renaissance* 16 (1986), 5–12.

More, Thomas. *The Complete Works of St. Thomas More.* Ed. Richard S. Sylvester. New Haven: Yale University Press, 1963.

Moretti, Franco. "A Huge Eclipse: Tragic Form and the Deconsecration of Sovereignty." *Genre* 15 (1982), 7–40.

———. "Representing Power: *Measure for Measure* in Its Time." In *The Power of Forms in the English Renaissance.* Ed. Stephen Greenblatt. Norman, Okla.: Pilgrim Books, 1982, pp. 139–56.

———. *Signs Taken for Wonders: Essays in the Sociology of Literary Forms.* London: Verso, 1983.

Morgann, Maurice. *An Essay on the Dramatic Character of Sr. John Falstaff.* Ed. William Arthur Gill. London: T. Davies, 1777. Rpt. London: Frowde, 1912.

Morison, Samuel Eliot. "History as a Literary Art." In *By Land and By Sea.* New York, 1953.

Morton, A. L. "Shakespeare's Historical Outlook." *Shakespeare-Jahrbuch* (Weimar), 100–101 (1964–65), 208–26; or *Zeitschrift für Anglistik und Amerikanistik* (East Berlin) 12 (1964), 299–43.

Moye, Richard H. "Thucydides' 'Great War': The Fiction in Scientific History." *Clio* 19 (1990), 161–80.

Muecke, D. C. *The Compass of Irony*. London: Methuen, 1969.

———. *Irony*. London: Methuen, 1970; rpt. 1976.

Muir, Kenneth. Introduction. *Shakespeare: The Comedies: A Collection of Critical Essays*. Ed. Kenneth Muir. Englewood Cliffs, N.J.: Prentice-Hall, 1965, pp. 1–10.

———. "Shakespeare and the Tragic Pattern." *Publications of the British Academy* 44 (1959), 145–62.

———. "Shakespeare's Imagery—Then and Now." *Shakespeare Survey* 18 (1965), 46–57.

Mullaney, Steven. *The Place of the Stage: License, Play, and Power in Renaissance England*. Chicago: University of Chicago Press, 1988.

Müller, Adam. "Fragmente über William Shakespeare." In *Ueber die dramatische Kunst* (1806). In *Shakespeare in Germany, 1740–1815*. Ed. Roy Pascal. Cambridge: Cambirdge University Press, 1937, pp. 153–63.

———. " 'Lecture VII' of Twelve Lectures on Rhetoric." Trans. Dennis R. Bormann and Elizabeth Leinfeller. In *German Romantic Criticism*. Ed. A. Leslie Willson. New York: Continuum, 1982, pp. 245–56.

Munz, Peter. *The Shapes of Time: A New Look at the Philosophy of History*. Middletown, Conn.: Wesleyan University Press, 1977.

Murray, Gilbert. *The Rise of the Greek Epic*. 2nd ed. Rev. and enlarged. Oxford: Clarendon Press, 1911.

Murry, John Middleton. *Shakespeare*. London: Cape, 1936.

Myers, Henry Alonzo. *Systematic Pluralism: A Study in Metaphysics*. Ithaca: Cornell University Press, 1961.

Nafla, Louis. *Law and Politics in Jacobean England: The Tracts of Lord Chancellor Ellesmere*. Cambridge: Cambridge University Press, 1977.

Narrative and Dramatic Sources of Shakespeare. 8 vols. Ed. Geoffrey Bullough. London: Routledge and Kegan Paul, 1957–75.

Neely, Carol Thomas. "Constructing the Subject: Feminist Practice and New Renaissance Discourses." *English Literary Renaissance* 18 (1988), 5–18.

Neff, Emery. *The Poetry of History: The Contribution of Literature and Literary Scholarship to the Writing of History since Voltaire*. New York: Columbia University Press, 1947.

The New Historicism. Ed. H. Aram Veeser. New York: Routledge, 1989.

New Testament. Trans. William Tyndale, 1526. London: David Paradine, 1976.

Newman, Karen. "Renaissance Family Politics and Shakespeare's *The Taming of the Shrew*." *English Literary Renaissance* 16 (1986), 86–100.

Nicholl, James. "The Development of Shakespeare's Artistry: Irony in the Comedies and Romances." Dissertation. University of Texas at Austin, 1970. Rpt. Ann Arbor: University Microfilms, 1981.

Noling, Kim H. "Grubbing Up the Stock: Dramatizing Queens in *Henry VIII.*" *Shakespeare Quarterly* 39 (1988), 291–306.

Norris, Christopher. *Deconstruction: Theory and Practice.* London: Methuen, 1982.

———. *Paul de Man: Deconstruction and the Critique of Aesthetic Ideology.* London: Routledge, 1988.

Northbrooke, John. "Treatise. . . ." In *Early Treatises on the Stage; Viz. Northbrooke's Treatise Against Dicing, Dancing, Plays, and Interludes; Gosson's School of Abuse; and Heywood's Defence of Stage Plays.* London: Shakespeare Society, 1843.

Norton, Thomas, and Thomas Sackville. *Gorboduc; or Ferrex and Porrex.* In *Chief Pre-Shakespearean Dramas: A Selection of Plays Illustrating the History of the English Drama from Its Origin Down to Shakespeare.* Ed. Joseph Quincy Adams. Boston: Houghton Mifflin, 1924.

———. *Gorboduc.* In *Elizabethan and Stuart Plays.* Ed. Charles Read Baskerville et al. New York: Henry Holt, 1934, 79–109.

Nouchaud, Michel. *L'utilization de l'histoire par les orateurs attiques.* Paris: Belles Lettres, 1982.

Novalis [Friedrich Hardenberg]. "Aphorisms and Fragments." In *German Romantic Criticism.* Ed. A. Leslie Willson. New York: Continuum, 1982, pp. 62–83.

Novy, Marianne. *Love's Argument: Gender Relations in Shakespeare.* Chapel Hill: University of North Carolina Press, 1984.

Nuttall, A. D. *A New Mimesis: Shakespeare and the Representation of Reality.* London: Methuen, 1983.

Nye, Russell, B. "History and Literature: Branches of the Same Tree." In *Essays on History and Literature.* Ed. Robert H. Brenner. [Columbus]: Ohio State University Press, 1966.

O'Connell, Michael. "The Idolatrous Eye: Iconoclasm, Anti-theatricalism, and the Image of the Elizabethan Theater." *English Literary History* 52 (1985), 279–310.

Ogden, Charles, I. A. Richards, and J. Wood. *Foundations of Aesthetics.* New York: Lear, 1925.

Olivier, Laurence. "Henry V." In *On Acting.* New York: Simon and Schuster, 1986, pp. 90–105.

On Puns: The Foundations of Letters. Ed. Jonathan Culler. Oxford: Blackwell, 1988.

Orgel, Stephen. *The Illusion of Power: Political Theater in the English Renaissance.* Berkeley: University of California Press, 1975.

Ornstein, Robert. *A Kingdom for a Stage: The Achievement of Shakespeare's History Plays.* Cambridge, Mass.: Harvard University Press, 1972.

————. *Shakespeare's Comedies: From Roman Farce to Romantic Mystery*. Newark: University of Delaware Press, 1986.

Orrell, John. *The Quest for Shakespeare's Globe*. Cambridge: Cambridge University Press, 1983.

The Oxford English Dictionary. The Compact Edition. 2 vols. New York: Oxford University Press, 1971; rpt. 1973.

Page, Denys L. *History and the Homeric "Iliad."* Berkeley: University of California Press, 1959.

Palmer, Barbara D. " 'Ciphers to This Great Accompt': Civic Pageantry in the Second Tetralogy." In *Pageantry in the Shakespearan Theater*. Ed. David M. Bergeron. Athens: University of Georgia Press, 1985, pp. 114–29.

Palmer, D. J. "Casting Off the Old Man: History and St. Paul in *Henry IV.*" *Critical Quarterly* 12 (1970), 267–83.

Palmer, Humphrey. *Analogy*. London: Macmillan, 1973.

Palmer, John. *Political Characters in Shakespeare*. London: Macmillan; 1945; rpt. 1957.

Parker, Patricia. *Literary Fat Ladies*. New York: Methuen, 1987.

Parker, Robert B. "The Prince and the King: Shakespeare's Machiavellian Cycle." *Revue des Langues Vivantes* 38 (1972), 241–53.

Pater, Walter. *Selected Essays*. Ed. H. G. Rawlinson. London: Macmillan, 1927. Origin. pub. 1889.

Patrides, C. A. *The Grand Design of God*. London: Routledge and Kegan Paul, 1971.

————. *The Phoenix and the Ladder: The Rise of the Christian View of History*. Berkeley: University of California Press, 1964.

Patterson, Annabel. *Shakespeare and the Popular Voice*. Oxford: Basil Blackwell, 1989.

Pavel, Thomas. *Fictional Worlds*. Cambridge, Mass.: Harvard University Press, 1986.

Payne, Michael. "Irony in Shakespeare's Roman Plays." Dissertation. University of Oregon, 1969. Rpt. Ann Arbor: University Microfilms, 1981.

Pearce, Josephine. "Constituent Elements in Shakespeare's English History Plays." In *Studies in Shakespeare*. Ed. Arthur D. Matthews and Clark M. Emery. Coral Gables, Fla.: University of Miami Press, 1953. Rpt. New York: AMS Press, 1971, pp. 145–52.

Pechter, Edward. "The New Historicism and Its Discontents: Politicizing Renaissance Drama." *PMLA* 102 (1987), 292–303.

Pepper, Stephen C. *World Hypotheses: A Study in Evidence*. Berkeley: University of California Press, 1942.

Percy, Thomas. *Reliques of English Poetry* (1765). In *Shakespeare: The Critical*

Heritage: Vol. 4, 1753–1765. Ed. Brian Vickers. London: Routledge and Kegan Paul, 1976, pp. 544–45.

Perkins, William. *Of the Symbol or Creede of the Apostles*. Printed by John Legate, University of Cambridge, 1597.

Philias, Peter G. "Shakespeare's *Henry V* and the Second Tetralogy." *Studies in Philology* 62 (1965), 155–75.

Pierce, Josephine. "Constituent Elements in Shakespeare's English History Plays." In *Studies in Shakespeare*. Ed. A. Matthews and C. Emery, 1953. New York: AMS Press, 1971.

Pierce, Robert. *Shakespeare's History Plays: The Family and the State*. Columbus: Ohio State University Press, 1971.

Pinciss, G. M. "The Old Honor and the New Courtesy: *1 Henry IV*." *Shakespeare Survey* 31 (1978), 93–105.

Pitt, Angela. "Women in the Histories." In *Shakespeare's Women*. London: David and Charles, 1981, pp. 136–63.

Plato. *Laws*. Trans. R. G. Bury. Loeb ed. 2 vols. London: Heinemann, 1926.

———. *The Republic*. Trans. Paul Shorey. Loeb ed. 2 vols. London: Heinemann, 1930; rpt. 1946.

———. *"The Republic" of Plato*. Trans. Allan Bloom. New York: Basic Books, 1968.

———. *"The Republic" of Plato*. Trans. Francis Macdonald Cornford, 1941. New York: Oxford University Press, 1945.

Plowden, Edmund. *Commentaries or Reports*. London, 1816.

Plutarch. *The Age of Alexander: Nine Greek Lives by Plutarch*. Trans. Ian S. Kilvert. Harmondsworth: Penguin, 1973.

Poisson, Rodney. "Ambivalence in Shakespeare's Histories: A Reconsideration of the Second Tetralogy." Dissertation. University of Washington, 1959. Rpt. Ann Arbor: University Microfilms, 1981.

Polybius of Megalopolis. "World History." In *Greek Historical Thought: From Homer to the Age of Heraclitus*. Trans. Arnold J. Toynbee. New York: New American Library, 1952, bk. 1.

Pompa, Leon. "Narrative Form, Significance, and Historical Knowledge." In *La Philosophie de l'histoire et la pratique historienne d'aujourd'hui = Philosophy of History and Contemporary Historiography*. Ed. David Carr et al. Ottawa: University of Ottawa Press, 1982, pp. 143–57.

Poovey, Mary. *Uneven Developments: The Ideological Work of Gender in Mid-Victorian England*. Chicago: University of Chicago Press, 1988.

Pope, Alexander. "Preface to Edition of Shakespeare (1725)." In *Eighteenth-Century Essays on Shakespeare*. Ed. D. Nichol Smith. 1st ed. Glasgow: MacLehose, 1903. 2d ed. Oxford: Clarendon Press, 1963, pp. 344–58.

Porter, Carolyn. "Are We Being Historical Yet?" In *The States of Theory:*

History, Art, and Critical Discourse. Ed. David Carroll. New York: Columbia University Press, 1990, pp. 26–62. Originally published in *South Atlantic Quarterly* 87 (1988), 743–86.

Porter, Joseph. *The Drama of Speech Acts: Shakespeare's Lancastrian Tetralogy.* Berkeley: University of California Press, 1979.

Press, Gerald A. *The Development of the Idea of History in Antiquity.* Montreal: McGill–Queen's University Press, 1982.

Preston, Thomas. "A Lamentable Tragedie Mixed Full of Pleasant Mirth, Containing the Life of Cambises, King of Percia . . ." In *Chief Pre-Shakespearean Dramas: A Selection of Plays Illustrating the History of the English Drama from Its Origin Down to Shakespeare.* Ed. Joseph Quincy Adams. Boston: Houghton Mifflin, 1924.

Prior, Moody. *The Drama of Power: Studies in Shakespeare's History Plays.* Evanston: Northwestern University Press, 1973.

Puttenham, George. *The Arte of Englishe Poesie* (1589). Ed. Gladys D. Willcock and Alice Walker. 1936. Cambridge University Press, 1970.

Pye, Christopher. *The Regal Phantasm: Shakespeare and the Politics of Spectacle.* London: Routledge, 1990.

Quinones, Ricardo J. *The Renaissance Discovery of Time.* Cambridge, Mass.: Harvard University Press, 1972.

Quintilian. *The "Institutio Oratoria" of Quintilian.* Trans. H. E. Butler. 4 vols., 1921–22. Loeb ed. London: Heinemann, 1933–36.

Rabkin, Norman. "Either/Or: Responding to *Henry V.*" In *Shakespeare and the Problem of Meaning.* Chicago: University of Chicago Press, 1981, pp. 33–62.

———. "Rabbits, Ducks, and *Henry V.*" *Shakespeare Quarterly* 28 (1977), 279–96.

———. *Shakespeare and the Problem of Meaning.* Chicago: University of Chicago Press, 1981.

Racine, Jean. *Oeuvres complète.* Ed. Raymond Picard. Paris: Bibliothèque de la Pléiade, 1950.

Rackin, Phyllis. "Androgyny, Mimesis, and the Marriage of the Boy Heroine on the English Renaissance Stage." *PMLA* 102 (1987), 29–41.

———. "Anti-Historians: Women's Roles in Shakespeare's Histories." *Theatre Journal* 37 (October 1985), 329–44.

———. "The Role of the Audience in Shakespeare's *Richard II.*" *Shakespeare Quarterly* 36 (1985), 262–81.

———. *Shakespeare's Tragedies.* New York: Ungar, 1978.

———. *Stages of History: Shakespeare's English Chronicles.* Ithaca: Cornell University Press, 1990.

Ralegh, Walter. *Selections: From His Writings and Letters.* Ed. G. E. Hadlow. Oxford: Clarendon Press, 1917.

Reed, Robert Rentoul, Jr. *Crime and God's Judgment in Shakespeare*. Lexington: University Press of Kentucky, 1984.

Reese, M. M. *The Cease of Majesty: A Study of Shakespeare's History Plays*. London: Arnold, 1961; rpt. 1968.

Rewriting the Renaissance: The Discourses of Sexual Difference in Early Modern Europe. Ed. Margaret W. Ferguson et al. Chicago: University of Chicago Press, 1986.

Ribner, Irving. *The English History Play in the Age of Shakespeare*. New York: Barnes and Noble, 1957; rev. 1965.

———. "The Idea of History in Marlowe's *Tamburlaine*." *English Literary History* 20 (1953), 251–66.

———. "The Political Problem in Shakespeare's Lancastrian Tetralogy." *Studies in Philology* 49 (1952), 171–84.

Richards, I. A. *Principles of Literary Criticism*. London: Routledge, 1925; rpt. 1949.

Richter, Jean Paul Friedrich. "School for Aesthetics." In *German Romantic Criticism*. Ed. A. Leslie Willson. New York: Continuum, 1982, pp. 31–61.

Ricks, Don. *Shakespeare's Emergent Form: A Study of the Structures of the "Henry VI" Plays*. Logan: Utah State University Press, 1968.

Ricoeur, Paul. *Reality of the Historical Past*. Milwaukee: Marquette University Press, 1984.

Riggs, David. *Shakespeare's Heroical Histories: "Henry VI" and Its Literary Tradition*. Cambridge, Mass.: Harvard University Press, 1971.

Righter, Anne. (See Anne Barton.) *Shakespeare and the Idea of the Play*. London: Chatto and Windus, 1962; rpt. 1964.

Roazen, Paul. *Freud: Political and Social Thought*. New York: Vintage, 1968.

Rorty, Richard. *Contingency, Irony, and Solidarity*. Cambridge: Cambridge University Press, 1989.

Rose, Mark. "Conjuring Caesar: Ceremony, History, and Authority in 1599." *English Literary Renaissance* 19 (1989), 291–304.

Rose, Mary Beth. *The Expense of Spirit: Love and Sexuality in English Renaissance Drama*. Ithaca: Cornell University Press, 1988.

Ross, J. F. *Portraying Analogy*. Cambridge: Cambridge University Press, 1981.

Rossiter, A. P. *Angel with Horns and Other Shakespeare Lectures*. Ed. Graham Storey. London: Longmans, 1961.

Roth, Michael S. *Knowing and History: Appropriations of Hegel in Twentieth-Century France*. Ithaca: Cornell University Press, 1988.

Rubenstein, E. "*1 Henry IV*: The Metaphor of Liability." *Studies in English Literature, 1500–1900* 10 (1970), 287–95.

Rüsen, Jörn. "Rhetoric and Aesthetics of History: Leopold von Ranke." *History and Theory* 29 (1990), 190–204.

Rutter, Carol (with others).*Clamorous Voices: Shakespeare's Women Today*. Ed. Faith Evans. London: Women's Press, 1988.

Sacchio, Peter. *Shakespeare's English Kings: History, Chronicle, and Drama*. New York: Oxford University Press, 1977.

Sahel, Pierre. "Les Ambiguités Politiques de *Richard II*." *Études Anglaises* 33 (1980), 20–31.

———. "Henry V, Roi Idéal?" *Études Anglaises* 28 (1975), 1–14.

Said, Edward. *Orientalism*. New York: Pantheon, 1978.

———. "The Problem of Textuality: Two Exemplary Positions." *Critical Inquiry* 4 (1978), 673–714.

Sallust. Trans. J. C. Rolfe. Loeb ed. 1921. London: Heinemann, 1965.

Salter, F. M. "The Play within the Play of *First Henry IV*." *Proceedings and Transactions of the Royal Society of Canada* 3d ser. 40.2 (1946), 209–23.

Sanders, Wilbur. *The Dramatist and the Received Idea: Studies in the Plays of Marlowe and Shakespeare*. Cambridge: Cambridge University Press, 1968.

Schanzer, Ernest. *The Problem Plays of Shakespeare: A Study of "Julius Caesar," "Measure for Measure," and "Antony and Cleopatra."* London: Routledge and Kegan Paul, 1963.

Schelling, Felix E. *The English Chronicle Play*. New York: Haskell House, 1902.

Schiller, Friedrich. *"Naive and Sentimental Poetry" and "On the Sublime": Two Essays*. Trans. Julius A. Elias. New York: F. Unger, 1966; rpt. 1975; origin. pub. 1793.

———. *Werke*. Ed. Julius Peterson et al. Weimar: Böhlau, 1943.

Schlegel, August Wilhelm. *Lectures on Dramatic Art and Literature*. Trans. John Black. 2d ed., rev. London: George Bell and Sons, 1900.

Schlegel, Friedrich. "Athenaeum Fragments" (1799). Trans. Peter Firchow. In *German Aesthetic and Criticism: The Romantic Ironists and Goethe*. Ed. Kathleen Wheeler. Cambridge: Cambridge University Press, 1984, pp. 44–54.

———. "Dialogue on Poetry." Trans. Ernst Behler and Roman Struc. In *German Romantic Criticism*. Ed. A. Leslie Willson. New York: Continuum, 1982, pp. 84–133.

———. *Lectures on the History of Literature Ancient and Modern*. German ed. pub. 1815. London: H. G. Bohn, 1859.

———. "Letter about the Novel" (1799). In *German Aesthetic and Criticism: The Romantic Ironists and Goethe*. Ed. Kathleen Wheeler. Cambridge: Cambridge University Press, 1984, pp. 73–80.

————. *Literary Notebooks, 1797–1801*. Ed. Hans Eichner. Toronto: University of Toronto Press, 1957.

Schlösser, Anselm. "Der Widerstreit von Patriotismus und Humanismus in *Heinrich V*." *Zeitschrift für Anglistik und Amerikanistik* (East Berlin) 12 (1964), 244–56.

————. *Shakespeare: Analysen und Interpretationen*. Berlin and Weimar: Aufbau-Verlag. 1977.

Scott, Joan Wallach. *Gender and the Politics of History*. New York: Columbia University Press, 1988.

Scoufos, Alice Lyle. "Gads Hill and the Structure of Comic Satire." *Shakespeare Studies* 5 (1970), 25–52.

Sedgewick, G. G. *Of Irony: Especially in Drama*. 1st ed. 1935; 2d ed. Toronto: University of Toronto Press, 1948.

Sedgwick, Eve Kosofsky. *Between Men: English Literature and Male Homosocial Desire*. New York: Columbia University Press, 1985.

Seidel, Michael. *Satiric Inheritance: Rabelais to Sterne*. Princeton: Princeton University Press, 1979.

Sen Gupta, S. C. *Shakespeare's Historical Plays*. London: Oxford University Press, 1964.

————. *The Whirligig of Time: The Problem of Duration in Shakespeare's Plays*. Bombay: Orient Longmans, 1961.

Seronsy, Cecil C. "The Doctrine of Cyclical Recurrence and Some Related Ideas in the Works of Samuel Daniel." *Studies in Philology* 54 (1957), 387-407.

Shaaber, M. A. "The Unity of *Henry IV*." In *Joseph Quincy Adams Memorial Studies*. Ed. J. G. McManaway et al. Washington: Folger Library, 1948, pp. 217–27.

Shakespeare, William. *The Complete Works*. Gen. ed. Alfred Harbage. New York: Viking, 1969; rpt. 1975.

————. *The First Part of Henry VI*. Ed. Andrew S. Cairncross. Arden ed. London: Methuen, 1962.

————. *The First Part of the History of Henry IV*. Ed. John Dover Wilson. Cambridge: Cambridge University Press, 1946.

————. *The First Part of King Henry IV*. Ed. A. R. Humphreys. Arden ed. London: Methuen, 1960, rpt. 1965.

————. *Hamlet*. Ed. Harold Jenkins. Arden ed. London: Methuen, 1982.

————. *Henry V*. Ed. Gary Taylor. Oxford: Clarendon Press, 1982.

————. *Henry V* (film). Director, Laurence Olivier. 1944.

————. *King Henry V*. Ed. John Dover Wilson. Cambridge: Cambridge University Press, 1947.

————. *King Henry V*. Ed. J. H. Walter. Arden ed. London: Methuen, 1954; rpt. 1977.

―――. *King Henry VIII.* Ed. R. A. Foakes. Arden ed. London: Methuen, 1957.

―――. *King John.* Ed. E. A. J. Honigmann. Arden ed. London: Methuen, 1954; rpt. 1959.

―――. *King Richard II.* Ed. Peter Ure. Arden ed. London: Methuen, 1961; rpt. 1978.

―――. *King Richard III.* Ed. Antony Hammond. Arden ed. London: Methuen, 1981.

―――. *A Midsummer Night's Dream.* Ed. Harold F. Brooks. Arden ed. London: Methuen, 1979.

―――. *The Riverside Shakespeare.* Ed. G. Blakemore Evans. Boston: Houghton Mifflin, 1974.

―――. *The Second Part of Henry the Fourth.* Ed. M. A. Shaaber. New variorum ed. Philadelphia and London: J. B. Lippincott, 1940.

―――. *The Second Part of the History of Henry IV.* Ed. John Dover Wilson. Cambridge: Cambridge University Press, 1961.

―――. *The Second Part of King Henry IV.* Ed. A. R. Humphreys. Arden ed. London: Methuen, 1966; rpt. 1977.

―――. *Shakespeare's Sonnets.* Ed. Stephen Booth. New Haven and London: Yale University Press, 1977.

―――. *William Shakespeare. The Complete Works.* Ed. Stanley Wells and Gary Taylor. Oxford: Clarendon Press, 1986.

―――. *The Winter's Tale.* Ed. J. H. P. Pafford. Arden ed. London: Methuen, 1963.

*The Shakespeare Allusion-Book: A Collection of Allusions to Shakespeare from 1591 to 1700. . . .*Vol. 1. Ed. John Munro. Comp. C. Ingleby et al. London: Chatto and Windus, 1909. Reissued by E. K. Chambers. London: Oxford University Press, 1932. Rpt. Freeport, N.Y.: Books for Libraries Press, 1970.

Shakespeare in Germany, 1740–1815. Ed. Roy Pascal. Cambridge: Cambridge University Press, 1937.

Shakespeare and the Question of Theory. Ed. Patricia Parker and Geoffrey Hartman. New York: Methuen, 1985.

Shakespeare Reproduced: The Text in History and Ideology. Ed. Jean E. Howard and Marion F. O'Connor. New York: Methuen, 1987.

Sharpe, Robert. *Irony in the Drama: An Essay on Impersonation, Shock, and Catharsis.* Chapel Hill: University of North Carolina Press, 1959.

Shaw, George Bernard. *The Collected Works of Bernard Shaw.* New York: William A. Wise, 1930.

―――. *Shaw on Shakespeare: An Anthology of Bernard Shaw's Writings on the Plays and Production of Shakespeare.* Ed. Edwin Wilson. New York: Dutton, 1961.

Shaw, John. "The Staging of Parody and Parallels in *1 Henry IV*." *Shakespeare Survey* 20 (1967), 61–73.

Shelley, Percy Bysshe. *Works*. Ed. R. Ingpen and W. E. Peck. London: E. Benn, 1965.

Shepherd, Simon. *Amazons and Warrior Women: Varieties of Feminism in Seventeenth Century Drama*. Brighton: Harvester Press, 1981.

———. "Women and Males." In *Marlowe and the Politics of Elizabethan Theatre*. Brighton: Harvester Press, 1986, pp. 178–207.

Shils, Edward. *Center and Periphery: Essays in Macrosociology*. Chicago: University of Chicago Press, 1975.

Shklar, Judith K. *Legalism*. Cambridge: Harvard University Press, 1962.

Showalter, Elaine. "Representing Ophelia: Women, Madness, and the Responsibilities of Feminist Criticism." In *Shakespeare and the Question of Theory*. Ed. P. Parker and G. Hartman. New York: Methuen, 1985, pp. 77–94.

Sidney, Philip. "An Apology for Poetry." In *English Critical Texts: 16th Century to 20th Century*. Ed. D. J. Enright and Ernst de Chickera. London: Oxford University Press, 1962; rpt. 1975, pp. 3–49.

Siegel, P. N. *Shakespearean Tragedy and the Elizabethan Compromise: A Marxist Study*. Washington: University Press of America, 1983.

Smalley, Beryl. *Historians in the Middle Ages*. London: Thames and Hudson, 1974.

Smidt, Kristian. *Unconformities in Shakespeare's History Plays*. London: Macmillan, 1982.

Smith, Barbara Herrnstein. "Narrative Versions, Narrative Theories." *Critical Inquiry* 7 (1980), 214–36.

———. *On the Margins of Discourse*. Chicago: University of Chicago Press, 1978.

———. *Poetic Closure*. Chicago: University of Chicago Press, 1968.

Smith, Gordon R. "Shakespeare's *Henry V*: Another Part of the Critical Forest." *Journal of the History of Ideas* 37 (1976), 3–26.

Solger, Karl. *Erwin; or, Four Dialogues on Beauty and Art* (1816). Trans. Joyce Crick. In *German Aesthetic and Criticism: The Romantic Ironists and Goethe*. Ed. Kathleen Wheeler. Cambridge: Cambridge University Press, 1984.

Solomon, Brownwell. "Thematic Contraries and the Dramaturgy of *Henry V*." *Shakespeare Quarterly* 31 (1980), 343–56.

Somerset, J. A. B. "Falstaff, the Prince, and the Pattern of *2 Henry IV*." *Shakespeare Survey* 30 (1977), 35–47.

Spencer, Benjamin T. "*2 Henry IV* and the Theme of Time." *University of Toronto Quarterly* 13 (1944), 394–99.

Spenser, Edmund. "A Letter of the Authors . . . to . . . Sir Walter Raleigh etc." In *The Faerie Queene: Book One*, in *Works* (variorum). Ed. Edwin Greenlaw et al. Vol. 1. Baltimore: Johns Hopkins University Press, 1932, pp. 167–70.

———. *The Works of Edmund Spenser*. Ed. Edwin Greenlaw et al. Variorum ed. 10 vols. Baltimore: Johns Hopkins University Press, 1932–49.

Sprat, Thomas. *The History of the Royal Society of London, for the improving of natural knowledge*. London: Printed by T. R. for J. Martyn and J. Allestry, 1667.

Sprinker, Michael. *Imaginary Relations: Aesthetics and Ideology in the Theory of Historical Materialism*. New York: Verso, 1987.

Spurgeon, Caroline F. E. *Shakespeare's Imagery and What It Tells Us*. Cambridge: Cambridge University Press, 1935.

States, Bert O. *Irony and Drama: A Poetics*. Ithaca: Cornell University Press, 1971.

Stern, Fritz. Introduction. *The Varieties of History: From Voltaire to the Present*. Ed. Fritz Stern. New York: Meridian, 1956, pp. 11–32.

Stewart, Susan. *On Longing: Narratives of the Miniature, the Gigantic, the Souvenir, the Collection*. Baltimore: Johns Hopkins University Press, 1984.

Stodder, John Henry. *Satire in Jacobean Tragedy*. Salzburg Studies in English Literature 35. Salzburg: Universität Salzburg, 1974.

Stone, Lawrence. *The Crisis of the Aristocracy, 1558–1641*. Oxford: Clarendon Press, 1965.

———. *The Family, Sex, and Marriage in England, 1500–1800*. London: Weidenfeld and Nicolson, 1977.

Stoppard, Tom. *Travesties*. London: Faber and Faber, 1975.

Stow, John. *The annales of England, from the first habitation untill 1592*. London: R. Newbery, 1592.

Stříbrný, Zdeněk. "Henry V and History." In *Shakespeare in a Changing World: Essays on His Times and His Plays*. Ed. Arnold Kettle. London: Lawrence and Wishart, 1964, pp. 84–101.

———. "The Idea and Image of Time in Shakespeare's Second Historical Tetralogy." *Shakespeare-Jahrbuch* (Weimar) 111 (1975), 51–66.

Strong, Roy. *The Cult of Elizabeth*. London: Thames and Hudson, 1977.

———. *Portraits of Queen Elizabeth I*. Oxford: Clarendon, 1963.

Struever, Nancy S. *The Language of History in the Renaissance: Rhetoric and Historical Consciousness in Florentine Humanism*. Princeton: Princeton University Press, 1970.

Styan, J. L. "The Delicate Balance: Audience Ambivalence in the Comedy of Shakespeare and Chekhov." *Costerus* 2 (1972), 159–84.

Sutherland, W. O. S., Jr. *The Art of the Satirist: Essays on the Satire in Augustan England*. Austin: University of Texas Press, 1965.

Suzman, Arthur. "Imagery and Symbolism in *Richard II.*" *Shakespeare Quarterly* 7 (1956), 355–70.

Swift, Jonathan. *"Gulliver's Travels" and Other Writings.* Ed. Ricardo Quintana. New York: Modern Library, 1958.

Swinburne, Algernon. *A Study of Shakespeare.* London: Chatto and Windus, 1880.

Tacitus. *The Annals of Imperial Rome.* Trans. Michael Grant, 1956. Harmondsworth: Penguin, 1977.

———. *The Histories.* Trans. Clifford H. Moore. Loeb ed. London: Heinemann, 1937.

Talbert, E. W. *The Problem of Order: Elizabethan Political Commonplaces and an Example of Shakespeare's Art.* Chapel Hill: University of North Carolina Press, 1962.

Tate, Nahum. *King Lear.* Ed. James Black. Lincoln: University of Nebraska Press, 1975.

———. Prefatory Epistle. "The History of King Richard the Second. Acted . . . Under the Name of the Sicilian Usurper" (etc.). In *Shakespeare: The Critical Heritage: Vol. 1, 1623–1692.* Ed. Brian Vickers. London and Boston: Routledge and Kegan Paul, 1974, pp. 321–41.

Tener, Robert. *The Phoenix Riddle: A Study of Irony in Comedy.* Salzburg Studies in English 44. Salzburg: Universität Salzburg, 1979.

Tennenhouse, Leonard. *Power on Display: The Politics of Shakespeare's Genres.* New York: Methuen, 1986.

———. "Strategies of State and Political Plays: *A Midsummer Night's Dream, Henry IV, Henry V, Henry VIII.*" In *Political Shakespeare: New Essays in Cultural Materialism.* Eds. Jonathan Dollimore and Alan Sinfield. Ithaca: Cornell University Press, 1985, pp. 109–29.

Tennyson, Alfred. *Works.* Ed. Hallam Tennyson. Rpt. 1907–8. ed. Westport, Conn.: Greenwood Press, 1970.

Teskey, Gordon. "Theatrical Self-Reference in Shakespeare." *College English Association Critic* 46 (1984), 27–37.

Thayer, C. G. *Shakespearean Politics: Government and Misgovernment in the Great Histories.* Athens: Ohio University Press, 1983.

Theophrastus. *The Characters of Theophrastus.* Trans. J. M. Edmonds. Loeb ed. London: Heinemann, 1929.

———. *The Characters of Theophrastus.* Trans. Walter Miller. Loeb ed. London: Heinemann, 1913.

Theories of Literary Genre. Ed. Joseph P. Strelka. University Park: Penn State University Press, 1978.

The Third Globe: Symposium for the Reconstruction of the Globe Playhouse, Wayne State University, 1979. Ed. C. Walter Hodges, S. Schoenbaum, and L. Leone. Detroit: Wayne State University Press, 1981.

Thirlwall, Connop. "On the Irony of Sophocles." *Philological Museum* 2 (1833), 483–537. Rpt. in *Remains Literary and Theological of Connop Thirlwall*. Ed. J. J. Stewart Perowne. Vol. 3. London: Daldy, Isbidster, 1878, pp. 1–57.

Thompson, Alan Reynolds. *The Dry Mock: A Study of Irony in Drama*. Berkeley: University of California Press, 1948.

Thomson, J. A. K. *Irony: An Historical Introduction*. London: Allen and Unwin, 1926.

Thomson, Peter. *Shakespeare's Theatre*. London: Routledge and Kegan Paul, 1983.

Thucydides. *Works*. Trans. Benjamin Jowett. Oxford: Clarendon Press, 1900.

Tieck, Ludwig. "Tony—A Drama in Three Acts by Th. Korner" (date uncertain). Trans. Mark Ogden. In *German Aesthetic and Criticism: The Romantic Ironists and Goethe*. Ed. Kathleen Wheeler. Cambridge: Cambridge University Press, 1984.

Tilley, Morris Palmer. *A Dictionary of the Proverbs in England in the Sixteenth and Seventeenth Centuries*. Ann Arbor: University of Michigan Press, 1950.

Tillyard, E. M. W. *The Elizabethan World Picture*. London: Chatto and Windus, 1943.

———. *Shakespeare's History Plays*. London: Chatto and Windus, 1944.

———. *Shakespeare's Problem Plays*. Toronto: University of Toronto Press, 1949; rpt. 1971.

Toliver, Harold E. "Falstaff, the Prince, and the History Play." *Shakespeare Quarterly* 16 (1965), 63–80.

———. "Shakespeare and the Abyss of Time." *Journal of English and Germanic Philology* 64 (1965), 234–54.

Trafton, Dan A. "Shakespeare's Henry IV: A New Prince in a New Principality." In *Shakespeare as Political Thinker*. Ed. John Alvis and Thomas G. West. Durham, N.C.: Carolina Academic Press, 1980, pp. 83–94.

Traversi, Derek. *Shakespeare from "Richard II" to "Henry V."* Stanford: Stanford University Press, 1957.

Trousdale, Marion. *Shakespeare and the Rhetoricians*. Chapel Hill: University of North Carolina Press, 1982.

Turner, Frederick. *Shakespeare and the Nature of Time: Moral and Philosophical Themes in Some Plays and Poems of William Shakespeare*. Oxford: Clarendon Press, 1971.

Turner, Mark. "Categories and Analogies." In *Analogical Reasoning: Perspectives of Artificial Intelligence, Cognitive Science, and Philosophy*. Ed. David H. Helman. Dordrecht: Kluwer Academic, 1988, pp. 3–24.

Ullmann, B. L. "History and Tragedy." *Transactions and Proceedings of the American Philological Association* 73 (1942), 25–53.

———. "The Present State of the Satura Question." *Studies in Philology* 17 (1920), 379–401.

Ure, Peter. *William Shakespeare: The Problem Plays*. London: Longmans and Green, 1961.

van den Berg, Kent T. *Playhouse and Cosmos: Shakespearean Theater as Metaphor*. Newark: University of Delaware Press, 1985.

Vega, Lope de. *Coleccion de piezas escogidas de Lope de Vega. Calderón de la Barca Tirso de Molina*. . . . Paris: Baudry, 1840, Microform.

Vellacott, Phillip. *Ironic Drama: A Study of Euripides' Method and Meaning*. Cambridge: Cambridge University Press, 1975.

The Venerable Bede. *The Ecclesiastical History of the English Nation*. Trans. John Stevens, 1910. London: Dent, 1951.

Vickers, Brian. "Analogy versus Identity: The Rejection of Occult Symbolism, 1580–1680." In *Occult and Scientific Mentalities in the Renaissance*. Ed. B. Vickers. Cambridge: Cambridge University Press, 1984, pp. 95–163.

Vickers. Nancy. " 'The Blazon of Sweet Beauty's Best': Shakespeare's *Lucrece*." In *Shakespeare and the Question of Theory*. Ed. P. Parker and G. Hartman. New York: Methuen, 1985, pp. 95–115.

Walch, Gunter. "*Henry V* as Working-House of Ideology." *Shakespeare Survey* 40 (1988), 63–68.

Waller, G. F. *The Strong Necessity of Time: The Philosophy of Time in Shakespeare and Elizabethan Literature*. The Hague: Mouton, 1976.

Walsh, P. G. *Livy: His Historical Aims and Method*. Cambridge: Cambridge University Press, 1961.

Waswo, Richard. *Language and Meaning in the Renaissance*. Princeton: Princeton University Press, 1987.

Watson, Robert N. "Horsemanship in Shakespeare's Second Tetralogy." *English Literary Renaissance* 13 (1983), 274–300.

Wayne, Don E. "Power, Politics, and the Shakespearean Text: Recent Criticism in England and the United States." In *Shakespeare Reproduced: The Text in History and Ideology*. Ed. Jean E. Howard and Marion F. O'Connor. New York: Methuen, 1987, pp. 47–67.

Webber, Joan. "The Renewal of the King's Symbolic Role: From *Richard II* to *Henry V*." *Texas Studies in Literature and Language* 4 (1963), 530–38.

Weimann, Robert. "Bifold Authority in Shakespeare's Theatre." *Shakespeare Quarterly* 39 (1988), 401–17.

———. *Shakespeare and the Popular Tradition of the Theater: Studies in the Social Dimension of Dramatic Form and Function*. Trans. Robert Schwartz. Baltimore: Johns Hopkins University Press, 1978. (Orig. German 1967.)

Wellek, René. *A History of Modern Criticism: The Romantic Age*. New Haven: Yale University Press, 1955.

Wells, Robin Headlam. *Shakespeare, Politics, and the State*. London: Macmillan, 1986.

Westlund, Joseph. *Shakespeare's Reparative Comedies: A Psychoanalytic View of the Middle Plays*. Chicago: University of Chicago Press, 1984.

Wheeler, Richard P. *Shakespeare's Development and the Problem Comedies: Turn and Counter-Turn*. Berkeley: University of California Press, 1981.

Whigham, Frank. *Ambition and Privilege: The Social Tropes of Elizabethan Courtesy Theory*. Berkeley: University of California Press, 1984.

White, Hayden. "The Historical Text as Literary Artifact." *Clio* 3 (1974), 277–304. Rpt. in his *Tropics of Discourse: Essays in Cultural Criticism*. Baltimore: Johns Hopkins University Press, 1978, pp. 81–100; in *The Writing of History: Literary Form and Historical Understanding*. Ed. R. H. Canary and H. Kosicki. Madison: University of Wisconsin Press, 1978, pp. 41–62; and in *Critical Theory since 1965*. Ed. Hazard Adams and Leroy Searle. Tallahassee: Florida State University Press, 1986, pp. 395–410.

———. *Metahistory: The Historical Imagination in Nineteenth-Century Europe*. Baltimore: Johns Hopkins University Press, 1973.

———. "The Politics of Historical Interpretation: Discipline and De-Sublimation." In *The Politics of Historical Interpretation:* Ed. W. J. T. Mitchell. Chicago: University of Chicago Press, 1983, pp. 119–45.

———. "The Question of Narrative in Contemporary Historical Theory." *History and Theory* 23 (1984), 1–33.

———. "The Structure of Historical Narrative." *Clio* 1 (1972), 5–20.

———. *Tropics of Discourse: Essays in Cultural Criticism*. Baltimore: Johns Hopkins University Press, 1978.

Whittier, Gayle. "Falstaff as a Welshwoman: Uncomic Androgny." *Ball State University Forum* 20 (1979), 25–35.

Wickham, Glynne. *Early English Stages, 1300–1660*. Vol. 2: 1576–1600, part 2. London: Routledge and Kegan Paul, 1972.

———. *The Medieval Theatre*. London: Weidenfeld and Nicolson, 1974.

———. "The Stage and Its Surroundings." In *The Third Globe: Symposium for the Reconstruction of the Globe Playhouse, Wayne State University, 1979*. Ed. C. Walter Hodges, S. Schoenbaum, and L. Leone. Detroit: Wayne State University Press, 1981. pp. 136–50.

Wikander, Matthew H. *The Play of Truth and State: Historical Drama from Shakespeare to Brecht*. Baltimore: Johns Hopkins University Press, 1986.

Wilcox, D. *The Development of Florentine Humanist Historiography in the Fifteenth Century*. Cambridge, Mass.: Harvard University Press, 1969.

Wilde, Oscar. *Essays by Oscar Wilde*. Ed. Hesketh Pearson. London: Methuen, 1950.

Wilders, John. *The Lost Garden: A View of Shakespeare's English and Roman History Plays*. London: Macmillan, 1978.

Willbern, David. "Shakespeare's Nothing." In *Representing Shakespeare: New Psychoanalytic Essays*. Ed. Murray Schwartz and Coppélia Kahn. Baltimore: Johns Hopkins University Press, 1980, pp. 244–63.

Williams, Raymond. *Culture*. Glasgow: Fontana, 1981.

———. *Marxism and Literature*. Oxford: Oxford University Press, 1977.

———. *Problems in Materialism and Culture*. London: Verso, 1980.

———. *Writing and Society*. London: Verso, 1983.

Williamson, George. *The Senecan Amble: Prose Form from Bacon to Collier*. Chicago: University of Chicago Press, 1951.

Williamson, Marilyn. "The Courtship of Katherine and the Second Tetralogy." *Criticism* 17 (1975), 326–34.

———. "The Episode with Williams in *Henry V.*" *Studies in English Literature, 1500–1900* 9 (1969), 275–82.

———. *The Patriarchy of Shakespeare's Comedies*. Detroit: Wayne State University Press, 1986.

Wilson, F. P. *Marlowe and the Early Shakespeare*. Oxford: Clarendon Press, 1953.

Wilson, John Dover. *The Fortunes of Falstaff*. Cambridge: Cambridge University Press, 1943.

Wilson, R. Rawdon. *In Palamedes' Shadow: Explorations in Play, Game, and Narrative Theory*. Boston: Northeastern University Press, 1990.

Winnicott, D. W. "Transitional Objects and Transitional Phenomena." In *Playing and Reality*. London: Tavistock, 1971, pp. 1–25. Originally published in the *International Journal of Psycho-Analysis* 34 (1953).

Winny, James. *The Player King: A Theme of Shakespeare's Histories*. London: Chatto and Windus, 1968.

Wiseman, Timothy. *Clio's Cosmetics: Three Studies in Greco-Roman Literature*. Leicester: Leicester University Press, 1979.

The Woman's Part: Feminist Criticism of Shakespeare. Ed. Carolyn Ruth Lenz, Gayle Greene, and Carol Thomas Neely. Urbana: University of Illinois Press, 1980.

Woodbridge, Linda. (See L. T. Fitz.) *Women and the English Renaissance: Literature, and the Nature of Womankind, 1540–1620*. Urbana: University of Illinois Press, 1984.

Worcester, David. *The Art of Satire*. New York: Russell and Russell, 1940; rpt. 1960.

Wordsworth, William. *Lyrical Ballads 1798*. Ed. W. J. B. Owen. 2d ed. Oxford: Oxford University Press, 1969; rpt. 1978.

Wright, Louis B. *Middle Class Culture in Elizabethan England.* Chapel Hill: University of North Carolina Press, 1935.

Wrightson, Keith. *English Society, 1580–1680.* New Brunswick: Rutgers University Press, 1982.

Yates, Francis. *Astraea: The Imperial Theme in the Sixteenth Century.* London: Routledge and Kegan Paul, 1975.

———. *Theatre of the World.* London: Routledge and Kegan Paul, 1969.

Zagorin, Perez. "Historiography and Postmodernism: Reconsiderations." *History and Theory* 29 (1990), 263–74.

Zitner, Sheldon P. "Aumerle's Conspiracy." *Studies in English Literature, 1500–1900* 14 (1974), 239–57.

INDEX